A COMPANION TO HEIDEGGER'S
INTRODUCTION TO METAPHYSICS

A COMPANION TO HEIDEGGER'S

INTRODUCTION TO METAPHYSICS

edited by RICHARD POLT AND GREGORY FRIED

Yale University Press / New Haven and London

Designed by Mary Valencia.
Set in Adobe Garamond and Syntax type by Keystone Typesetting, Inc., Orwigsburg, Pennsylvania.
Printed in the United States of America by Edwards Brothers, Ann Arbor, Michigan.

ISBN: 0-300-08523-0 (cloth : alk. paper)
   0-300-08524-9 (pbk. : alk. paper)
Library of Congress Catalog Number: 00–049990

A catalogue record for this book is available from the British Library.

The paper in this book meets the guidelines for permanence and durability of the Committee on Production Guidelines for Book Longevity of the Council on Library Resources.

10   9   8   7   6   5   4   3   2   1

CONTENTS

CONTENTS

EDITORS' INTRODUCTION

Martin Heidegger's *Introduction to Metaphysics,* delivered as a lecture course in 1935 and first published, with revisions, in 1953, has long stood as a familiar landmark for students of Heidegger's thought. It is known for its incisive analysis of the Western understanding of Being, its original interpretations of Greek philosophy and poetry, and its vehement political statements.

Our new translation of *Introduction to Metaphysics* (Yale University Press, 2000) provided an occasion to invite a group of scholars to reconsider this classic text. But aside from this occasion, the text itself invites renewed attention. Its perhaps familiar phrases contain unfamiliar possibilities—surprising, even disturbing thoughts. Furthermore, nearly a half-century after its publication, our own greater knowledge demands that we return to the *Introduction* with new eyes. First, the ongoing publication of the *Gesamtausgabe* or collected edition of Heidegger's writings (1975–) offers us the opportunity to locate the *Introduction to Metaphysics* in the context of his developing work. The *Gesamtausgabe* includes Heidegger's 1919–1945 lecture courses as well as private texts such as the *Contributions to Philosophy* (1936–1938) that contain his most serious and concentrated thoughts. Second, we now know a great deal about Heidegger's political acts and opinions during the Third Reich and can benefit from a large body of reflections on the meaning of his connections to fascism. Finally, the world's philosophical thinking has continued its slow course—a course that perhaps cannot be termed progress but does generate new perspectives. From these perspectives, Heidegger's lectures become relevant in unsuspected ways. It is by providing this ever-renewed relevance that the *Introduction to Metaphysics* proves to be a genuine classic.

The chapters in this volume are grouped into three areas: the question of

Being, Heidegger and the Greeks, and politics and ethics. These themes are all related, for in *Introduction to Metaphysics* Heidegger tries to provoke his audience into a confrontation with Being by way of an encounter with Greek thinking and poetry—and this project is charged with practical urgency. Because the themes of the *Introduction* are tightly interwoven, readers will find overlaps and echoes among these chapters. They will also find some disagreements, for we have not attempted to impose uniformity on our contributors' range of views and approaches.

The Question of Being

Our first group of chapters considers the overriding question of Heidegger's thought: the problem of how we understand what it means for any being, including ourselves, to be. This understanding of Being gives us the status of Dasein—the entity who constitutes a "there," a site where beings as a whole have meaning. For Heidegger, our understanding of Being is woven into the fabric of our actions, thoughts, and speech, and it is intimately involved in the great turning points of our history. The question of Being is also the question of appearing and nothing, and the question of logic and language.

In the chapter that opens this volume, "*Kehre* and *Ereignis:* A Prolegomenon to *Introduction to Metaphysics,*" Thomas Sheehan places the 1935 lectures within the context of Heidegger's thought as a whole. Scholars have traditionally interpreted the trajectory of Heidegger's thinking in terms of a *Kehre*, or "turn," that separates *Being and Time* from the works produced in the 1930s and thereafter with *Introduction to Metaphysics* understood to be a landmark in this alleged turn. Sheehan argues that this interpretation is momentously wrong. It misreads the *Kehre* as a change that took place in *Heidegger's thinking*, whereas in fact it names the movement intrinsic to *Ereignis* itself. *Ereignis*, the key term of Heidegger's later thought, is usually translated as "appropriation," and it refers to the central topic of his thought: the drawing of human being into what is "proper" to it, namely, to be the finite place where being is revealed. Sheehan provides highly detailed references to Heidegger's texts and to his predecessors in the metaphysical tradition, but the clarity of his thesis and argumentation make his chapter accessible even to readers who are new to Heidegger's work.

Charles E. Scott's "The Appearance of Metaphysics" emphasizes the disjunction between Heideggerian thinking and its metaphysical predecessors. Scott takes Heidegger's lecture course, particularly its opening moves, as an opportunity to explore how metaphysics can lead beyond itself. Metaphysics consists of "ways of thinking in which people expect to find a grounding way of being that gives an enduring presence to originate, sustain, and connect all ways of life." This metaphysical foundationalism tries to obviate the multi-relational, embodied, and mortal character of disclosure. By revealing the history of metaphysics in a nonmetaphysical way, Heidegger's lectures open the possibility that metaphysics might be "turned away from its own predisposition to find a deathless ground for truth and knowledge." We then might discover not only a new way of thinking—a thinking that attends to *phusis* as the event of appearance and emergence, for example—but also new ways of life.

Charles Guignon, in "Being as Appearing: Retrieving the Greek Experience of *Phusis*," also takes *phusis* as an indication of a new kind of thinking about Being—an "event ontology" as opposed to the traditional "substance ontology." Guignon examines the way in which Heidegger's interpretation of *phusis* unites Being with appearance, becoming, and strife. He then shows that an event ontology can prove fruitful in interpreting artworks, history, and human beings, allowing us to understand ourselves not as things but as disclosive happenings. He closes by considering Heidegger's account of truth as appearing, or "unconcealment," and tackles the difficult question of the sense in which an understanding of Being can be "true."

Taking up a theme announced in the first line of *Introduction to Metaphysics,* Richard Polt's "The Question of Nothing" explores Being by way of its constant companion and rival. Polt places Heidegger's references to "Nothing" (*das Nichts*) in the context of the history of metaphysics and the development of Heidegger's thought, showing that both Heidegger and his predecessors use the term in a variety of ways. In order to make sense of this complex issue, Polt distinguishes between "the Being of beings" (what it means for beings to be) and "Be-ing" (the happening in which the Being of beings becomes accessible to Dasein). He argues that at the heart of Heidegger's uses of Nothing is an insight into the "temporal finitude" of both Dasein and Be-ing. Thanks to our entanglement in "a past that we cannot change and a future that is subject to death," we are able to receive a fragile and contingent meaning of Being.

In "The Scattered *Logos:* Metaphysics and the Logical Prejudice," Daniel Dahlstrom considers the critique of logic that runs through many of Heidegger's works, including the *Introduction to Metaphysics.* In Heidegger's account, the Western tradition inverts the relation between thinking and Being. Thinking was once a *logos* that responded to the primal *logos* (or "gathering") of Being itself, but thinking has now become a logic (a theory of assertion) that presumes to dictate to Being. Dahlstrom not only explores this argument but goes beyond Heidegger in order to consider two possible responses to it: the position that logic is metaphysically neutral and the position that conformity to logic is a prerequisite for all truth.

Dieter Thomä's chapter turns to *logos* in the sense of language. Disagreeing with the unitarian interpretation of Heidegger's philosophical career that is presented by Thomas Sheehan and by Heidegger himself, Thomä reads Heidegger's thinking as punctuated by several shifts. On this reading, *Introduction to Metaphysics* represents a brief stage in Heidegger's path that, when it comes to the question of language, has advantages over both his earlier and his later positions. Before and after the *Introduction*, argues Thomä, Heidegger falls prey to a dichotomy between "context" (our entanglement in a world, a totality of significations) and "name" (the affirmation of the unique Being of ourselves or other entities). The conception of naming in the *Introduction to Metaphysics*, despite its obscurities, has the merit of letting naming make room for beings in their mystery and uniqueness within a larger context. Thomä discerns ethical dimensions to this thought that Heidegger does not pursue.

Heidegger and the Greeks

It is by way of a confrontation with the Greek beginnings of metaphysics that the *Introduction to Metaphysics* develops its distinctive approach to the question of Being. Such a confrontation, as *Auseinandersetzung,* is a respectful yet critical retrieval of the latent possibilities of the Greek inception. This inception can be discerned, according to Heidegger, not only in the fragmentary texts of the early Greek thinkers but in the work of Greek poets and in the vocabulary of the Greek language. The chapters in the second part of our anthology focus on Heidegger's confrontation with Greek language, thinking, and tragedy.

Gregory Fried's "What's in a Word? Heidegger's Grammar and Etymology of 'Being'" explains how Heidegger's exploration of language in the second chapter of the *Introduction* goes beyond conventional linguistics in order to evoke the Greek understanding of Being as constancy and presence. Fried then compares Heidegger's efforts to the philosophical-linguistic investigations of Charles Kahn, particularly in reference to the theory of linguistic relativism—that is, the position that "the very question of Being itself is an accident of the Indo-European family of languages." Despite their differences, both Kahn and Heidegger show that there is a way of linking Greek reflection on Being to the Greek language without *reducing* metaphysical problems to accidents of language and thus falling into linguistic relativism. Furthermore, argues Fried, we must learn to see the question of Being as a question that is relevant to *all* languages and that calls for detailed exploration of the ways in which various languages serve as the "house of Being."

In "Heidegger's Interpretation of *Phusis* in *Introduction to Metaphysics*," Susan Schoenbohm traces Heidegger's nuanced and shifting readings of this key Greek word. *Phusis* serves as the crux of his confrontation with the Greek understanding of Being and as the key to his interpretations of Heraclitus and Parmenides. Yet the notion of *phusis* seems deeply ambiguous. Does *phusis* name a particular sort of entity, or beings as such, or the meaning of "to be," or the event in which such a meaning emerges? Schoenbohm argues that the *Introduction to Metaphysics* succeeds in developing "a way of thinking of the meaning of *phusis* which points beyond the ambiguities of the meaning of the word (but not beyond the questioning) to an understanding of being without substance that transforms an interpretation of being as permanent nature." Such an understanding has "revolutionary consequences for our understanding both of 'nature' in the more restricted modern sense, and of beings as a whole, including ourselves." As Guignon's and Scott's chapters attest, the notion of *phusis* can provide a powerful impetus for our own meditations.

Clare Pearson Geiman, in "Heidegger's *Antigones*," provides an interpretation of *Introduction to Metaphysics'* striking reading of Sophocles, contrasting it with the reading that Heidegger was to give in 1942, in his lecture course on Hölderlin's "The Ister." The 1935 reading tends to glorify the violent, creative acts of great individuals, including the statesman, the thinker, and the poet. But Geiman argues that the 1942 reading reveals a decisive shift in Heidegger's thinking, in which Heidegger comes to interpret poetry in a way that is fundamentally opposed to *technē*. In this move, Heidegger finally breaks free of the lingering subjectivism of his earlier thinking—and thus moves beyond the tendencies that had once attracted him to totalitarian politics. His later reading of *Antigone* suggests "a radical departure from politics as we have understood it up to now, that is, as the human agent's personal or collective attempt to systematically order and control both physical and human nature."

Politics and Ethics

The political dimension of *Introduction to Metaphysics* is unmistakable—not only because of its brief, disturbing reference to the "inner truth and greatness" of National Socialism but because of its continuing insistence on linking the question of Being to "the spiritual fate of the West." The lecture course can be read as a concerted attempt to revolutionize the Nazi revolution—that is, to deepen it by purging it of its own metaphysical presuppositions and bringing it into a genuine relation to the Greek inception. Thus, Heidegger repeatedly praises recent developments in German life, only to brand them superficial in the next breath. This political rhetoric is accompanied by a critique of morality and "the ought" as they are traditionally conceived. The contributors to the third part of this anthology explore the details and contexts of Heidegger's conception of politics and ethics—not in order to reduce his thought to his behavior, but in order to do justice to the many aspects and implications of his thinking.

Michael E. Zimmerman's "The Ontological Decline of the West" explores the dynamic of inception, decline, and fall that is at work in Heidegger's understanding of history. This dynamic plays a crucial part not only in Heidegger's account of the history of metaphysics but in his interpretation of the political situation of Germany and of the technological age. Zimmerman compares Heidegger's vision of history to the thought of Oswald Spengler, author of *The Decline of the West*. Despite their differences, both Heidegger and Spengler were participants in a widespread reaction against the liberal-progressive interpretation of history propounded by the neo-Kantians, among others. Zimmerman argues that, for all its insights, Heidegger's understanding of history fails to do justice to the "nobility" of modernity—"its effort to foster individual personal development by emancipating humankind from material deprivation, political authoritarianism, and religious dogmatism."

In " 'Conflict Is the Father of All Things': Heidegger's Polemical Conception of Politics," Hans Sluga investigates the emphatic yet ambiguous political thinking of *Introduction to Metaphysics* as it relates to Heidegger's reading of early Greek thought. Heidegger embraces the Heraclitean concept of *polemos*, or confrontation, not only as a key to Being but also as a key to authentic political action. As Sluga puts it, "Everything given calls . . . for a creative transcendence through force. It calls also for men of force able to bring about such transcendence." Sluga compares such notions to the polemical political thought of Carl Schmitt, for whom politics is based on the distinction between friend and enemy. Sluga concludes with a sympathetic account of Heidegger's critique of absolute values. Despite the error of Heidegger's entanglement with National Socialism, his thought still offers the appealing possibility of "an 'ethics' that shuns authoritative oughts and goods, and sets out, instead, to find particular and historical paradigms to follow—an 'ethics,' we might say, that envisions possibilities of living rather than injunctions, constraints, fixed and unquestionable blueprints of life."

Theodore Kisiel, in "Heidegger's Philosophical Geopolitics in the Third Reich," analyzes not only the notorious geopolitical remarks in Heidegger's lecture course but their counterparts in other lecture courses and notes of the mid-thirties. Furthermore, Kisiel investigates the controversies that were generated by the publication of *Introduction to Metaphysics* in 1953 and touches on Heidegger's relation to companion thinkers such as Spengler, Max Scheler, Ernst Jünger, and Friedrich Naumann. Kisiel's "intertextual" approach provides a rich and multifaceted account of Heidegger's geopolitics—that is, his interpretation of his nation "in its geographical location, spiritual position, and poietic-ontological site" at the "heart of Europe."

In "At the Crossroads of Freedom: Ethics Without Values," Frank Schalow sheds light on a brief but crucial section of *Introduction to Metaphysics:* Heidegger's discussion of "the ought." Anyone who wishes to reflect on Heidegger's strengths or inadequacies as an ethical thinker must consider his critique of the concept of value and understand why his rejection of values is not necessarily tantamount to nihilism. Schalow provides the background necessary to understand this dimension of Heidegger's thought. He begins with Heidegger's criticisms of the value theories of Scheler and of Heinrich Rickert and proceeds to Heidegger's developed account of the history of Being and the place of values within this history. Schalow's conclusion points out the limitations of Heidegger's own views as well as the potential promise of his thinking for our future ethical reflection: "the presupposition of ethics, or freedom, must be rediscovered at the historical juncture where Being reveals itself to human existence."

In quoting *Introduction to Metaphysics,* all the contributors have used our translation as their first point of reference. They have, however, been at liberty to change the translation in accordance with their own reading of the text and their own rhetorical predilections. In particular, several contributors have chosen to translate *Sein* as "being" rather than "Being"; Theodore Kisiel prefers "be-ing," and Susan Schoenbohm and Charles E. Scott favor a lowercase "dasein" in addition to a lowercase "being." Such differences in translation are a necessary part of philosophical interpretation and conversation.

BIBLIOGRAPHICAL NOTE

The following conventions are observed throughout this anthology.

Unless otherwise indicated, parenthesized numbers refer to the pagination of Martin Heidegger, *Einführung in die Metaphysik* (Tübingen: Niemeyer, 1953). This pagination is provided in the margins of *Introduction to Metaphysics,* trans. Gregory Fried and Richard Polt (New Haven: Yale University Press, 2000). Contributors to this anthology have used the Fried and Polt translation as their first point of reference, but have been given free rein to modify the translation, and not all such modifications have been noted. All emphasis in quotations is in the original unless otherwise noted.

SZ = *Sein und Zeit* (Tübingen: Max Niemeyer Verlag), cited by the pagination of the later editions, beginning with the seventh edition (1953). Unless otherwise indicated, the translation used is that of John Macquarrie and Edward Robinson, *Being and Time* (New York: Harper & Row, 1962).

GA = Martin Heidegger, *Gesamtausgabe* (Frankfurt am Main: Vittorio Klostermann, 1975–), followed by the volume number and page number. The following volumes of Heidegger's *Gesamtausgabe,* or collected edition, are cited in this anthology.

GA 1 = *Frühe Schriften,* ed. Friedrich-Wilhelm von Herrmann (1978; written 1912–1916)

GA 2 = *Sein und Zeit,* ed. Friedrich-Wilhelm von Herrmann (1977; first published 1927). Translations: *Being and Time,* trans. John Macquarrie and Edward Robinson (New York: Harper & Row, 1962); *Being and Time,* trans. Joan Stambaugh (Albany: SUNY Press, 1996)

GA 3 = *Kant und das Problem der Metaphysik,* ed. Friedrich-Wilhelm von

Herrmann (1991; first published 1929). Translations: *Kant and the Problem of Metaphysics,* trans. James S. Churchill (Bloomington: Indiana University Press, 1962); *Kant and the Problem of Metaphysics,* trans. Richard Taft, 4th ed. (Bloomington: Indiana University Press, 1996)

GA 9 = *Wegmarken,* ed. Friedrich-Wilhelm von Herrmann (1st ed. 1976, 2nd ed. 1996; written 1919–1958). Translation: *Pathmarks,* ed. William McNeill (Cambridge: Cambridge University Press, 1998)

GA 15 = *Seminare,* ed. Curd Ochwadt (1986; seminars held 1951, 1966–1969, 1973)

GA 19 = *Platon: Sophistes,* ed. Ingeborg Schüßler (1992; lecture course, 1924–1925). Translation: *Plato's Sophist,* trans. Richard Rojcewiz and André Schuwer (Bloomington: Indiana University Press, 1997)

GA 20 = *Prolegomena zur Geschichte des Zeitbegriffs,* ed. Petra Jaeger (1st ed. 1979, 2nd ed. 1988, 3rd ed. 1994; lecture course, 1925). Translation: *History of the Concept of Time: Prolegomena,* trans. Theodore Kisiel (Bloomington: Indiana University Press, 1985)

GA 21 = *Logik: Die Frage nach der Wahrheit,* ed. Walter Biemel (1st ed. 1976, 2nd ed. 1995; lecture course, 1925–1926). Translation: *Logic: The Question of Truth,* trans. Thomas Sheehan and Reginald Lilly (Bloomington: Indiana University Press, forthcoming)

GA 24 = *Die Grundprobleme der Phänomenologie,* ed. Friedrich-Wilhelm von Herrmann (1975, 2nd ed. 1989, 3rd ed. 1997; lecture course, 1927). Translation: *The Basic Problems of Phenomenology,* trans. Albert Hofstadter (Bloomington: Indiana University Press, 1982)

GA 26 = *Metaphysische Anfangsgründe der Logik im Ausgang von Leibniz,* ed. Klaus Held (1st ed. 1978, 2nd ed. 1990; lecture course, 1928). Translation: *The Metaphysical Foundations of Logic,* trans. Michael Heim (Bloomington: Indiana University Press, 1984)

GA 29/30 = *Die Grundbegriffe der Metaphysik: Welt—Endlichkeit—Einsamkeit,* ed. Friedrich-Wilhelm von Herrmann (1st ed. 1983, 2nd ed. 1992; lecture course, 1929–1930). Translation: *The Fundamental Concepts of Metaphysics: World, Finitude, Solitude,* trans. William McNeill and Nicholas Walker (Bloomington: Indiana University Press, 1995)

GA 31 = *Vom Wesen der menschlichen Freiheit: Einleitung in die Philosophie,* ed. Hartmut Tietjen (1st ed. 1982, 2nd ed. 1984; lecture course, 1930). Translation: *On the Essence of Human Freedom,* trans. Ted Sadler (London: Athlone, forthcoming)

GA 34 = *Vom Wesen der Wahrheit: zu Platons Höhlengleichnis und Theätet,* ed. Hermann Mörchen (1st ed. 1988, 2nd ed. 1997; lecture course, 1931–

1932). Translation: *The Essence of Truth—The Nature of Death,* trans. Ted Sadler (London: Athlone, forthcoming)

GA 38 = *Logik als die Frage nach dem Wesen der Sprache,* ed. Günter Seubold (1998; lecture course, 1934)

GA 39 = *Hölderlins Hymnen "Germanien" und "Der Rhein,"* ed. Susanne Ziegler (1st ed. 1980, 2nd ed. 1989; lecture course, 1934–1935)

GA 40 = *Einführung in die Metaphysik,* ed. Petra Jaeger (1983; lecture course, 1935, first published 1953)

GA 41 = *Die Frage nach dem Ding: Zu Kants Lehre von den transzendentalen Grundsätzen,* ed. Petra Jaeger (1984; lecture course, 1935–1936, first published 1962). Translation: *What Is a Thing?,* trans. W. B. Barton Jr. and Vera Deutsch (Chicago: Henry Regnery Co., 1967)

GA 42 = *Schelling: Vom Wesen der menschlichen Freiheit (1809),* ed. Ingrid Schüßler (1988; lecture course, 1936, first published 1971). Translation: *Schelling's Treatise on the Essence of Human Freedom,* trans. Joan Stambaugh (Athens: Ohio University Press, 1985)

GA 43 = *Nietzsche: Der Wille zur Macht als Kunst,* ed. Bernd Heimbüchel (1985; lecture course, 1936–1937, first published with revisions in 1961). Translation: *Nietzsche,* vol. 1, *The Will to Power as Art,* trans. David Farrell Krell (San Francisco: Harper & Row, 1979)

GA 45 = *Grundfragen der Philosophie: Ausgewählte "Probleme" der "Logik,"* ed. Friedrich-Wilhelm von Herrmann (1st ed. 1984, 2nd ed. 1992; lecture course, 1937–1938). Translation: *Basic Questions of Philosophy: Selected "Problems" of "Logic,"* trans. Richard Rojcewicz and André Schuwer (Bloomington: Indiana University Press, 1994)

GA 51 = *Grundbegriffe,* ed. Petra Jaeger (1st ed. 1981, 2nd ed. 1991; lecture course, 1941). Translation: *Basic Concepts,* trans. Gary E. Aylesworth (Bloomington: Indiana University Press, 1993)

GA 52 = *Hölderlins Hymne "Andenken,"* ed. Curd Ochwadt (1st ed. 1982, 2nd ed. 1992; lecture course 1941–1942)

GA 53 = *Hölderlins Hymne "Der Ister,"* ed. Walter Biemel (1st ed. 1984, 2nd ed. 1993; lecture course, 1942). Translation: *Hölderlin's Hymn "The Ister,"* trans. William McNeill and Julia Davis (Bloomington: Indiana University Press, 1996)

GA 54 = *Parmenides,* ed. Manfred S. Frings (1st ed. 1982, 2nd ed. 1992; lecture course, 1942–1943). Translation: *Parmenides,* trans. André Schuwer and Richard Rojcewicz (Bloomington: Indiana University Press, 1992)

GA 55 = *Heraklit: Der Anfang des abendländischen Denkens. Logik: Heraklits*

Lehre vom Logos, ed. Manfred S. Frings (1st ed. 1979, 2nd ed. 1987, 3rd ed. 1994; lecture courses, 1943, 1944)

GA 56/57 = *Zur Bestimmung der Philosophie,* ed. Bernd Heimbüchel (1987; lecture courses, 1919). Translation: *The Idea of Philosophy: Towards a Definition of Philosophy,* trans. Ted Sadler (London: Athlone, forthcoming)

GA 59 = *Phänomenologie der Anschauung und des Ausdrucks,* ed. Claudius Strube (1993; lecture course, 1920)

GA 61 = *Phänomenologische Interpretationen zu Aristoteles: Einführung in die phänomenologische Forschung,* ed. Walter Bröcker and Käte Bröcker-Oltmanns (1st ed. 1985, 2nd ed. 1994; lecture course, 1921–1922)

GA 63 = *Ontologie (Hermeneutik der Faktizität),* ed. Käte Bröcker-Oltmanns (1st ed. 1988, 2nd ed. 1995; lecture course, 1923). Translation: *Ontology: The Hermeneutics of Facticity,* trans. John van Buren (Bloomington: Indiana University Press, 1999)

GA 65 = *Beiträge zur Philosophie (Vom Ereignis),* ed. Friedrich-Wilhelm von Herrmann (1st ed. 1989, 2nd ed. 1994; written 1936–1938). Translation: *Contributions to Philosophy (From Enowning),* trans. Parvis Emad and Kenneth Maly (Bloomington: Indiana University Press, 1999)

GA 66 = *Besinnung,* ed. Friedrich-Wilhelm von Herrmann (1997; written 1938–1939)

GA 68 = *Hegel,* ed. Ingrid Schüßler (1993; written 1938–1939, 1941, 1942)

GA 69 = *Die Geschichte des Seyns,* ed. Peter Trawny (1998; written 1938–1940)

GA 79 = *Bremer und Freiburger Vorträge,* ed. Petra Jaeger (1994; written 1949 and 1957)

Part I

THE QUESTION OF BEING

Chapter 1

KEHRE AND EREIGNIS: A PROLEGOMENON TO INTRODUCTION TO METAPHYSICS

THOMAS SHEEHAN

Interpretations of Heidegger often fail to distinguish between two very different matters—on one hand "the turn" *(die Kehre)* and on the other "the change in Heidegger's thinking" *(die Wendung im Denken)*, that is, the shift in the way Heidegger formulated and presented his philosophy beginning in the 1930s. Failure to make this distinction can be disastrous for understanding Heidegger, and the danger becomes more acute the closer one gets to texts like *Introduction to Metaphysics,* where both the "turn" and the "change" begin to come into their own.[1]

The first issue, the *Kehre,* is emphatically not an alteration in Heidegger's thinking, not an episode that could be dated to a period in his philosophical career. Rather, it is one name among many for the abiding topic of Heidegger's work: the radically inverted meaning of being, grounded in finitude, that stands over against the metaphysical ideal of being as full presence and intelligibility. The turn is indeed a kind of movement, but not the movement that Heidegger's thought underwent in the 1930s. Rather, Heidegger associates the turn with *Ereignis* (usually translated as "appropriation"), and specifically with the way *Ereignis* operates: *"Die im Ereignis wesende Kehre."*[2] The turn is the inner movement of *Ereignis* whereby (1) finitude opens a clearing in human being (2) in which entities can appear as this or that.

The second issue, the change in thinking, refers to a shift in how Heidegger formulated and expressed that inner movement of *Ereignis.* It is a change in *das Denken/Sagen der Kehre.*[3] If the turn refers to Heidegger's central topic—the giving of being in connection with the opening up of Dasein—then the "thinking and saying of the turn" refers to Heidegger's efforts to articulate that state of affairs. And as a subset of that, "the *change* in thinking" refers to Heidegger's shift in orientation from the transcendental-horizonal approach of 1926–1928 to the *seinsgeschichtlich* (dispensing-of-being) approach of the remainder of his career. But this shift in orientation is not the turn itself. The distinction here is between the *Kehre*—the inner movement of *Ereignis*—and a change in how Heidegger expressed that movement.[4]

In his famous letter to William J. Richardson (April 1962) Heidegger acknowledged "*eine Wendung in meinem Denken*," "a change in my thinking,"[5] and to this day the best analysis of that shift in orientation remains Richardson's *Heidegger: Through Phenomenology to Thought*. That book definitively proved that the breakthrough from the earlier to the later Heidegger took place in his lecture "Vom Wesen der Wahrheit," first delivered in December 1930, and that *Introduction to Metaphysics,* the lecture course of summer 1935, clearly indicates that "Heidegger II has taken full possession."[6]

Richardson takes pains to distinguish between (1) Heidegger's focal topic, *die Sache des Denkens* (which Heidegger explicitly identified with the *Kehre* operative in *Ereignis*) and (2) what Richardson calls the "shift of focus" or "'reversal' in manner and method"[7] that unfolded in Heidegger's work in the 1930s as he continued pursuing that single topic. If Heidegger characterized his professional career in the phrase *"auf einen Stern zugehen,"* then the *Kehre* operative in *Ereignis* was the "one and only star" that guided his journey, not any twist or turn along the way.[8]

But this crucial distinction is not always maintained in the scholarship. The shift of focus to which Richardson refers is what many Heideggerians erroneously call the *Kehre* in Heidegger's thinking, a confusion that flies in the face of Heidegger's insistence that "First and foremost the *Kehre* is not a process that took place in my thinking and questioning. It belongs, rather, to the very *issue* that is named by the titles 'Being and Time'/'Time and Being.' . . . The turn operates within the *issue itself*. It is not something that I did, nor does it pertain to my thinking only."[9]

The present chapter, which is intended as a prolegomenon to a fresh reading of *Introduction to Metaphysics,* attempts to sort out what Heidegger means by "the turn operative in *Ereignis.*" (I reserve for another occasion a discussion of the "change in thinking" that took place in Heidegger's work in the 1930s.) The chapter focuses on the meaning of *Ereignis* that Heidegger developed in *Beiträge zur Philosophie (Vom Ereignis)* (1936–1938) and from that vantage point looks back to Heidegger's interpretation of the pre-Socratics in *Introduction to Metaphysics* (1935).[10]

Although, as Richardson correctly argues, 1935 marks the official debut of the later Heidegger, nonetheless important details still had to be worked out. *Introduction to Metaphysics* certainly does give evidence of Heidegger's changed approach to the meaning of being, but nowhere in that lecture course does Heidegger thematically explain the "*Kehre* operative in *Ereignis*," nor do those terms, with their technical meanings, appear in the text. Instead, Heidegger elaborated the *Kehre* and *Ereignis* indirectly and unthematically via interpretations of Sophocles, Parmenides, and Heraclitus. It would take him at least another year to make *Kehre/Ereignis* the focus of explicit treatment, and that first happened in his *Beiträge zur Philosophie*. Only there did "the turn operative in *Ereignis*" move to center stage and the corresponding change in Heidegger's presentation of that topic get locked in.

In what follows I argue that Heidegger's focal topic was not "being" (the givenness or availability of entities for human engagement) but rather what *brings about* being, namely, *Ereignis*—the opening of a clearing in which entities can appear as this or that. This clearing occurs when *Dasein*—which I translate as "openness"—is opened up by its own finitude. But neither *Ereignis* nor the turn is an "event" in the usual sense (much less an event that occurred in Heidegger's thinking) but rather the presupposition of all human events. The chapter then argues that *Ereignis* was almost—but not quite—envisioned by the early Greek thinkers, and it concludes that in the 1930s Heidegger changed his orientation but not his central topic.

1. HEIDEGGER'S TOPIC WAS NOT "BEING," EITHER IN ITS TRADITIONAL ONTOLOGICAL SENSE OR IN A PHENOMENOLOGICALLY TRANSFORMED SENSE.

In order to sort out what "the turn operative in *Ereignis*" is, we must first be clear about what Heidegger's topic was and was not. We begin with two negatives: (1) Heidegger's fundamental topic was not "being" *tout court* (the is-ness of whatever is) and (2) it was not a phenomenologically reinterpreted being (being as the givenness or availability of entities for human engagement).

In the first place Heidegger's focal topic was not "being" *(das Sein)* in any of its traditional philosophical meanings. That is, it did not coincide with the three overlapping ways in which classical metaphysics had treated being, namely as

a. *ontological:* any entity's
  - thatness (existence: not-being-nothing)
  - whatness (essence: being this or that)
  - howness (mode: being in this way or that)

5

b. *transcendental:* any entity's transgeneric status as
  - something *(res)*
  - one *(unum)*
  - distinct from others *(aliquid)*
  - desirable *(bonum)*
  - knowable *(verum)*[11]
c. *theological:* the highest entity's state of perfect self-coincidence,
  - not only between its thinking and the object of its thought,[12]
  - but also and above all within itself.[13]

But likewise Heidegger's central topic was not "being" in a phenomenological sense. It is true that Heidegger's first step in retrieving the unsaid from the classical tradition was to see that, in all the above instances, the being of entities is implicitly some form of the presence of entities: not merely their presence-to-themselves or their presence-out-there apart from human beings, but their *presence to and availability for possible human engagement*—their humanly specific ("ad hominem") givenness and accessibility. In this implicit phenomenological sense, the being of entities is their ability to be of concern to human beings, that is, to be significant, understandable, usable. Thus in what follows, the term "givenness" always means "humanly specific givenness," and I use it interchangeably with "availability" and "accessibility"—that is, usability, understandability—to name the being of entities.[14]

One of Heidegger's major achievements was to have rendered that implicit state of affairs explicit, by phenomenologically shifting the meaning of τὸ εἶναι from an entity's "being-out-there" to its "appearing-as" (φαίνεσθαι, *Erscheinung*),[15] that is, its "intelligibility" in the broadest sense.[16] Throughout his work Heidegger insisted that, properly understood, τὸ ὄν (whatever-is) is τὸ ὄν ὡς ἀληθές (whatever-is as *accessible*) and that "being" means not the mere ontological thereness of entities but their givenness as the available.[17] This change is visible in Heidegger's reinterpretation of οὐσία/*Sein* (an entity's being) as παρουσία/*Anwesen* (an entity's givenness to possible human engagement), in keeping with the principle "Being as the givenness of entities *concerns* Dasein."[18] Thus *das Sein des Seienden* = *das Anwesen des Anwesenden* = ἡ παρουσία τοῦ παρόντος = the givenness or availability or accessibility (hence the usability and understandability) of whatever is. The *realm* of givenness-itself (that is, the field of possible concern) is what Heidegger called "world," and the a priori human engagement with that realm is what he called "being-in-the-world."[19]

Heidegger found this phenomenological notion of being to be the dominant, if implicit, view in ancient Greek philosophy. In *Introduction to Metaphysics,* for example, he argues that one of the earliest names for the appearance of entities was φύσις. The emergence (φύειν) that this Greek word indicates is not some prehuman appearance of entities, their coming-to-be prior to or apart from the receptive openness that is human being. Rather, φύσις refers to the givenness of entities *within* τὸ νοεῖν, and φύειν names the emergence of such givenness in correlation with that receptive openness.[20] Thus in *Introduction to Metaphysics* Heidegger equates φύσις and ἀλήθεια.[21] And from beginning to end, he argued that the givenness of entities requires a human site—a "dative"—in order to occur at all.[22]

Nonetheless, being as the givenness and availability of entities was not Heidegger's fundamental topic. In either form—whether as the mere-thereness (οὐσία) of entities or as their givenness (παρουσία)—being is still that which makes entities be as they are, either in the form of their ontological thatness, whatness, and howness, or in the form of their phenomenological emergence, stable appearance, and availability as this or that. Both of these issues lie within the confines of metaphysics and its ontological difference (entities-in-their-being).[23] Thus even when Heidegger phenomenologically reinterpreted the various instances of "is" as so many forms of "is-present-as," he still had broached only *die Leitfrage,* the guiding question of metaphysics. This serves, at best, as the antechamber to the *Grundfrage,* the fundamental question that reaches beyond metaphysics to the topic of Heidegger's own thought.[24]

2. HEIDEGGER'S OWN QUESTION WAS: WHAT BRINGS ABOUT BEING AS THE GIVENNESS OR AVAILABILITY OF ENTITIES?

Heidegger's fundamental question was: What produces (ποίει, *läßt sein*) givenness? What enables being as παρουσία or *Anwesen* to be given at all?[25] And insofar as this givenness requires a correlative human site in order to occur, the question becomes: What is responsible for the *correlation* between an entity's givenness and the dative of that givenness? Whatever the answer to that question may turn out to be, *it* is what Heidegger meant by *die Sache des Denkens,* the single topic of his thought. Provisionally and heuristically we may designate this focal issue as "the enabling power" that makes possible the correlation of givenness/being and its dative.

Heidegger calls this enabling power "*ein drittes,*"[26] a τρίτον τι (*Sophist* 250b) or *tertium quid* over and above both being as an entity's givenness and the dative of that givenness. Insofar as it makes παρουσία possible, this enabling power is ἐπέκεινα τῆς παρουσίας, "beyond" being-as-givenness, in a way that is analogous (but only analogously) to what Plato called τὸ ἀγαθόν. This enabling power as *tertium quid* is also beyond the ontological difference, insofar as it lets that unity-in-difference come forth.[27]

The fundamental question "What brings about givenness?" entails a *preparatory*-fundamental question: What is the dative of such givenness? Heidegger's answer was: intentional or "open" comportment.[28] And the essence of such comportment he called "*Dasein*."[29]

Heidegger insisted that *Dasein*, as the essence of human being and acting, means "being-the-*Da*."[30] Here "the *Da*" is understood as "the open" *(das Offene)*.[31] And for Heidegger "the open" is the same as *Lichtung*,[32] *Welt*,[33] Ἀλήθεια,[34] being-as-such,[35] the truth of being,[36] difference,[37] and *Ereignis*.[38] In other words the *Da*, taken in its fullness, is nothing less than *die Sache des Denkens*. It would be preferable, therefore, to avoid translating *Dasein* with variations on the word "there" (being-there, there-being, being-the-there). Rather, *Dasein* means "openness," that is, "being-open" and "being-the-open" in all the senses of "open" just listed.

For Heidegger the verbal emphasis in "Dasein" falls on the second syllable: Da-*sein*, "*being* the open."[39] The point is that the open is what we "have to be" (compare *zu-sein*).[40] But human beings do not "open up the open" by their own subjective powers. Rather, the open is "thrown or pulled" open *(geworfen/ereignet)*, "drawn out" in such a way that, within that open*ed* site, the availability of entities occurs. This "open*ed*ness" is what Jean Beaufret had in mind when he interpreted *Dasein* as *l'ouverture*,[41] and it is the meaning we intend when we render this key term as "openness."

The word "openness" captures important meanings that Heidegger retrieved from Aristotelian ψυχή for his own understanding of *Dasein*.[42] In *De Anima* Aristotle argues that ψυχή is the very essence of human being; that, qua receptive, it has its nature as possibility;[43] and that, as this possibility, it is essentially open to and revelatory of the being of entities other than itself.

For Aristotle, human ψυχή, whether in sense perception (τὸ αἰσθάνεσθαι) or intellectual knowledge (τὸ νοεῖν), is a πάσχειν τι, a transcendental openness-to-receive.[44] By its very nature, ψυχή is δεκτική (Latin, *susceptiva*), actively open to receive the forms (that is, the being) of other entities.[45] This is what medieval philosophers meant when they described the soul as *quod natum est convenire cum omni ente*.[46] Precisely as such receptive openness, ψυχή in its noetic form is ontologically structured to reveal the being of everything that appears: ἡ ψυχή τὰ ὄντα πώς ἐστι πάντα (Γ 8, 431 b 21). In short, for Heidegger:

1. ψυχή, properly retrieved, is the openness that the being of entities requires (*braucht*) in order to be revealed: ὁ τόπος εἰδῶν (Γ 4, 429 a 27–28).[47]
2. The very essence of ψυχή is to "belong to" (*zugehören:* to get its *raison d'être from*) being.
3. And that essence consists in letting-be-seen the being of all entities: ὁ νοῦς εἶδος εἰδῶν (Γ 7, 432 a 2).

The *tertium quid* that makes possible the correlation of (1) the givenness of entities and (2) intentional comportment as the dative of this givenness—the central topic of Heidegger's thought—goes by a host of titles, all of which, in spite of their distinct nuances, are fundamentally the same: *Da, Welt, Offene, Zeit, Lichtung, Ereignis, Kehre, Seyn,* ~~Sein~~, *Ermöglichung der Offenbarkeit des Seienden,* and the list goes on.[48] We emphasize again: None of these titles directly names being as the givenness or availability of entities (ἡ παρουσία τοῦ παρόντος, ἡ ἀλήθεια τοῦ ἀληθοῦς), much less as the mere ontological "thereness" of entities (τὸ εἶναι τοῦ ὄντος). What these titles designate is not the givenness of entities but *what brings that about.* They refer not to παρουσία but to its *origin.* What, then, is this enabling origin of givenness?

3. HEIDEGGER'S ANSWER TO HIS FUNDAMENTAL QUESTION WAS: *EREIGNIS*, THE OPENING OF A CLEARING IN HUMAN BEING.

These two moves—the phenomenological interpretation of being as the givenness of entities and the thematization of open comportment as its dative—were only preparatory to raising the fundamental question concerning the *tertium quid* that makes possible the correlation of the two. For that, Heidegger focused on the dynamics that bring together givenness and human being, and specifically on the reciprocity of "needing" and "belonging." This reciprocity (*Gegenschwung*)[49] between the fact that givenness needs its dative (*das Brauchen*) and the dative's *belonging* to givenness (*das Zugehören*) is what Heidegger means by *das Ereignis,* and it is the central topic of his thought.

Heideggerians usually describe this reciprocity as the relation between being and *Dasein*. Precisely here, in the way the story of being is generally told, lies the danger of a major misunderstanding. It is an easy error to let an entity's being-as-givenness slide back into its being-as-mere-presence, to reduce παρουσία to mere οὐσία. In turn this slippage fosters a quasi hypostasization of being, whereby *das Sein* is represented as something (however ethereal) that lies "out there beyond entities," something we can "pursue" and possibly "relate to," as if it were an ontological object standing over against us.[50]

In the literature this bifurcated view—*Dasein* on one side, being on the other—has generally taken two forms, with their apposite narratives: (1) the now passé "dominant *Dasein*" story, according to which human beings transcendentally "project" being, as if they themselves were the source of the availability of entities, and (2) the still popular "Big Being" story, according to which Being Itself, lying hidden somewhere beyond our ken, occasionally pulls back the veil and reveals Itself to properly disposed human beings—who in our days are, almost exclusively, paid-up Heideggerians.

Heidegger rejected both forms of this crude confabulation, whether *Dasein* "projecting" being[51] or being "projecting itself" to *Dasein*.[52] His own story—complex at first glance, but finally quite simple—was that of *Ereignis,* the opening of the clearing.

Again: the specific issue in *Ereignis* is the reciprocity between "need" *(das Brauchen)* and "belonging" *(das Zugehören):* entities need a human dative (the clearing) in order to be understood *as* this or that, and the *raison d'être* of human being is to belong and to be that clearing. This reciprocity is a matter of give-and-take: the clearing is "given" only when human being is "taken," drawn or thrown into its essential openness. *Ereignis* and *die Kehre* are the same, and they are this movement of give-and-take, of belonging and needing:

1. The reciprocity of needing and belonging is what constitutes *Ereignis:* "*Dieser Gegenschwung des Brauchens und Zugehörens macht das Seyn als Ereignis aus.*"[53]
2. And this reciprocity, which constitutes *Ereignis* (*das in sich gegenschwingende Ereignis*),[54] is what Heidegger means by the *Kehre,* the back-and-forthness between belonging and needing: (a) *Ereignis* is the opening of a clearing to which human being essentially belongs, (b) which clearing, in turn, is needed for the "appearance of being," that is, for entities to be understood *as* this or that. "*Die Er-eignung des Da-Seins durch das Seyn und die Gründung der Wahrheit des Seins im Da-sein—die Kehre im Ereignis.*"[55]

The single topic of Heidegger's philosophy is this "giving of the clearing" *(Geschick des Seyns)* by the opening up of *Dasein (Ereignis).* This grounding movement is inherently "reciprocal" ("*Gründen ist hier kehrig*");[56] it is the "reciprocal grounding of being and its dative" ("*die kehrige Gründung von Sein und Da-sein*"),[57] and as such it is the turn that operates at the heart of *Ereignis.*

In short, as openness is opened up *(ereignet),* there occurs givenness-as-such ("world" or "clearing") as the possibility of the givenness (or being) of this or that entity. But this is only a formal indication of where the turn is located and how it is structured. The sketch needs to be fleshed out. What exactly is *Ereignis,* and how does it work? What opens up openness?

4. THE CLEARING OCCURS WHEN OPENNESS IS OPENED UP BY ITS OWN FINITUDE.

What is it, finally, that opens up openness? Heidegger's most formal answer is: "the self-withdrawing" *(das Sichentziehende).*[58] The "self-withdrawing" is that which intrinsically withdraws and, in the process, draws us out into ἔκστασις. As Heidegger put it: "What withdraws from us draws us along with it by that very withdrawal."[59] This is what he means by *Ereignis,* the withdrawl that opens up openness: *"Entzug ist Ereignis."*[60]

But what is it exactly that "intrinsically withdraws," that "refuses to become present" because "its very essence" is to remain "hidden"?[61] What is it that draws us out with it and, in the process, gives givenness-as-such? It would be easy to fall back on the Big Being story and to hypostasize *das Sichentziehende* into "Being Itself" in its absential mode ("the Lethe") and to have "It" (whatever "It" is)[62] do the drawing-out and the giving. But that would be only metaphysics in another form, and thus the destruction of everything Heidegger stood for.

Heidegger's own story is quite different. Its backdrop, which often remains implicit, is very traditional and Aristotelian. Although in the final analysis Heidegger undid that tradition, he first took care to master it, and he recommended that Heideggerians do the same. "You would be well advised," he told his students in 1952, "to put off reading Nietzsche for the time being and first study Aristotle for ten to fifteen years"[63]—the way Heidegger himself did. It was out of that Aristotelian background, properly reinterpreted, that Heidegger elaborated his own story of *Dasein* and the movement of *Ereignis.*

In Aristotelian metaphysics, being ("reality") is analogical: it comes in degrees, ranging hierarchically from the most perfect to the least. The degree of an entity's being is the degree of its perfection, and perfection (τὸ τέλειον) is measured by how far an entity has "come full circle" (compare τέλος as circle)[64] and "returned to" or fulfilled its essence. The highest degree of having come full circle is God's perfect self-coincidence, which entails perfect presence-to-itself: νόησις νοήσεως. Short of God, everything else has being to the degree it approximates that ontological-cognitive closure.

Conversely, to the degree that an entity is still "open," it is ontologically imperfect. But human being is *essentially* open (ἐκστατικόν). Never all-at-once and complete, it is ever in a state of becoming, always on the way to itself, but never arriving at full self-presence. Human being is defined by its constitutive lack-in-being—what *Being and Time* called ontological "guilt" *(Schuldigsein)*. Unable to overcome this essential lack, we can never complete the circle and become fully self-coincident.[65]

Our inevitable lack-in-being *is* our finitude, which opens us up. It throws or pulls us into our ineluctable becoming—and thereby opens the open. *Ereignis* is not a matter of Big Being (the Lethe) heteronomously "appropriating" us from some Beyond.[66] Rather, it is our own intrinsic self-absence that draws us out into openness, into the movement of becoming, and thereby into the possibility of understanding both givenness itself ("world") and the givenness of this or that entity.

Fated to be always open, human being is likewise fated to be exposed and receptive. *Dasein* is thrown into the necessity of being-present-unto,[67] into needing the presence of other entities. But such other-presence, like *Dasein's* own self-presence, is never all-at-once and complete but always partial and imperfect. Condemned to σύνθεσις and διαίρεσις, we know only the *finite* intelligibility of entities. Our lack-in-being makes it impossible for us to know by way of intellectual intuition and makes it necessary for us to know only through *entwerfen auf,* "taking-as" (or "projecting"). We take things *as* this or that, thereby see them *to be* such and so, understand that they *are* one thing or another, and thus know their *being.*

On one hand this synthetic-differential knowing is a plus. Our very finitude—thrown and (only for that reason) able to "take-as"—guarantees that we do understand the being of things. We are condemned to ontology, which, before it is a thematic science, is a matter of relating to entities mediately through their being-as, rather than directly by intellectual intuition. On the other hand, such mediate knowledge of entities is a "defect," a mark of imperfection. "Ontology is an index of finitude. God does not have it."[68] In any case, the finitude registered in our openness is what guarantees that there is "being" as the finite availability and understandability of entities.

Whether in the earlier language of thrownness and projection or in the later language of *Ereignis* and *Geschick*, it is *Dasein's* own finitude or lack-in-being— always "withdrawing," ever "absent" and intrinsically "hidden"—that makes possible the emergence of being-as-such.[69] For Heidegger, therefore, this lack-in-being, as the source of the giving of being, was from beginning to end *die Sache des Denkens,* the issue most worthy of thought.

5. THE TURN IS NOT AN "EVENT" IN THE USUAL SENSE (MUCH LESS AN EVENT IN HEIDEGGER'S THINKING) BUT RATHER THE PRESUPPOSITION OF ALL HUMAN EVENTS.

Inasmuch as it is the same as *Ereignis,* the turn cannot be an event that took place in Heidegger's thought. In fact, it is not an event at all in the usual sense of that term.[70] One can certainly date when Heidegger's *insight* into the turn led to *die Wendung im Denken,* the reorientation of his thinking (namely, 1930–1938, and especially 1936–1938). But it is a very different matter with the turn itself. When Heidegger was asked how the turn took place *("ist geschehen")* within his thinking, he did two things. First he denied the premise: "There is no particular kind of happening connected with the turn."[71] And then he located the turn where it properly belongs: "The supposed 'happening' of the turn," he wrote, " 'is' *Seyn* as such,"[72] that is, *Ereignis,* the opening up of *Dasein.*[73]

It follows that the only way to understand how the turn functions (as contrasted with when it took place) is from within the turn itself, that is, from within *Ereignis. "Es läßt sich nur aus der Kehre denken."*[74] Insofar as *Ereignis* is the "most proper, exclusive, and ineluctable" fact of human being, it constitutes the ultimate *praesuppositum* of everything we are and do.[75] Whether we reflect on *Ereignis* or ignore it, whether we embrace it as the ground of our being or flee from it, it is always the presupposed. That is to say: *Ereignis* is that ultimate state of affairs which always-already (πρό) subtends (ὑπό) and grounds (κείμενον) human being: τὸ προϋποκείμενον πρῶτον.[76]

One's own grounding in this ultimate *praesuppositum* is what the early Heidegger called "thrownness" *(Geworfenheit)* and what the later Heidegger called "being-opened-up" *(Ereignet-sein).*[77] So too the act of resolutely embracing that groundless ground is what the early Heidegger called "taking over one's thrownness" *(Übernahme der Geworfenheit)*[78] and what the later Heidegger called "taking over the fact of being-opened-up" *(Über-nahme der Er-eignung).*[79] Thrownness and openedness are the same.[80]

One's always-already-opened-ness constitutes the ultimate circularity of human being and is the basis of all the other circularities that characterize thinking and acting—for example, the hermeneutical circle, the so-called relativism of *Dasein,* and so forth.[81] It is thus the basis of the circular protreptic in which Heidegger's thinking reaches its culmination: γένοι᾽ οἷος ἐσσί, "become what you essentially are."[82] This exhortation indicates the final goal of Heidegger's work: to "reappropriate one's openness" in the sense of embracing the *praesuppositum* that makes one be human. This is the force behind Heidegger's frequently repeated admonition to let oneself be caught up in *Ereignis-Kehre* rather than spending one's career talking about the reorientation that took place in his thinking.[83]

6. *EREIGNIS* WAS ALMOST—BUT NOT QUITE—
ENVISIONED BY THE EARLY GREEK THINKERS.

As Heidegger sees it, there were strong intimations of *Ereignis* in pre-Socratic philosophy, and in *Introduction to Metaphysics* he finds virtually all the elements of this topic in the texts of Heraclitus and Parmenides. Even these thinkers, however, failed to pose the fundamental question of *Ereignis* either explicitly or in its fullness. Let us consider the positive side first.

(1) In Heidegger's view, Heraclitus and Parmenides were aware of the process whereby entities become accessible, and they named this movement with such kinetic titles as ἀλήθεια, φύσις, λόγος: the unconcealing, emerging, or gathering of entities into givenness.

(2) They further understood that being-as-givenness does not occur "out there," independent of human beings. They saw that it requires an open site in order to happen, and they understood this openness as belonging to (getting its *raison d'être* from) givenness.[84]

(3) They also were aware of the correlativity between the fact that givenness needs a dative *(das Brauchen)* and the dative's belonging to givenness *(das Zugehören)*.[85] Parmenides expressed that very state of affairs when he said that εἶναι and νοεῖν are τὸ αὐτό (fragment 5).

(4) Most important, beyond merely understanding the movement of entities into givenness, Heraclitus also had a sense of the emergence of givenness itself *(die Bewegung des Erscheinens)* and even intimated that the source of that movement-into-presence was a withdrawal-into-absence *(das Sichverbergen)*. The text Heidegger principally has in mind here is Heraclitus' fragment 123: φύσις κρύπτεσθαι φιλεῖ, which Heidegger interprets to mean "The source of the emergence of givenness itself is, by its very nature, concealed."[86]

It would seem, then, that all the elements of *Ereignis* are present in these early texts. But not quite. What Heraclitus and Parmenides lacked was insight into the fit of these constituent elements. Beyond naming the correlation of givenness itself and receptive openness, and apart from hinting that an intrinsically concealed absence is the source of being as givenness, these early Greek thinkers failed to say exactly *how* that correlation happens or *what* brings about the emergence of givenness. In other words, they lacked a developed and thematic grasp of how absence (finitude) opens up human being in such a way that, within that clearing, entities can be understood. As far as Heidegger was concerned, the Greeks simply did not think *Ereignis.*[87]

7. CONCLUSION: IN THE 1930S HEIDEGGER CHANGED HIS ORIENTATION BUT NOT HIS CENTRAL TOPIC.

The reorientation of Heidegger's thinking that became visible in *Introduction to Metaphysics* was far less dramatic—and the difference between the earlier and the later Heidegger much less pronounced—than is usually suggested in the literature. In that regard Richardson's assessment of the later Heidegger's relation to the earlier is as correct as it is succinct: "The difference: only one of focus."[88]

Moreover, the reorientation was not due to Heidegger's altering, much less surrendering, the topic he originally settled on in *Being and Time.* As he told Richardson, the "change in thinking" was not an "about-face" *(eine "Umkehr"),*[89] nor was it "a consequence of altering the standpoint of *Being and Time,* much less of abandoning its fundamental issue."[90] Rather, it was merely a filling out *(Ergänzung)*[91] of the question posed in *Being and Time.* The reorientation took place, he said, as a result of his "sticking with the issue-for-thought of *Being and Time,* i.e., inquiring into the perspective that *Being and Time,* at p. 39, had already designated by the title 'Time and Being.' "[92] Specifically, the reorientation was the result of Heidegger's enhanced appreciation of how human being is opened up, and in particular of how thrownness—which he came to read as "being-opened-up"—always has priority over projection.[93]

In other words, what *did* change (but more slightly than scholars usually allege) was only, as Richardson says, the "manner and method" of Heidegger's approach,[94] whereas what stayed the same were both the *question* and the *answer* that Heidegger had in place by 1927.

The question was never focally about being or about human being, that is, about either side of a supposed noetic-noematic divide between the understanding of being *(Seinsverstehen)* and the understandability of being *(Seinsverständlichkeit).* The question was always about the fit of the two, the *tertium quid* that brings together and thus makes possible both givenness and its dative. Inasmuch as this fit is *das transcendens schlechthin,*[95] it is beyond or otherwise than what it brings together. In 1943 Heidegger listed some names for what his question was always about: the "meaning," "truth" or "openness" that makes it possible for us to understand entities in their being.[96] "*Das*

Ereignis" and *"die Kehre im Ereignis"* were only two in a long line of titles for *what must always already be the case* if givenness and its dative are to come together at all. But the various titles aside, the question remained the same.

And so did the answer. In both the earlier and the later Heidegger, the "giving" of being as presence requires the "taking" of *Dasein* by absence, that is, the opening up of human being by finitude. Before the 1930s Heidegger described this movement of give-and-take as the interface of *Geworfenheit* and *Entwurf:* being "thrown open" as grounding the possibility of "taking as." During the 1930s Heidegger began describing the same issue as the interplay of *Ereignet-sein* and *Es-gibt-Sein:* being-opened-up as the ground for understanding the being of entities, *Ereignis* as making possible *Seinsgeschick.* But at no stage in his thinking did Heidegger conceive of the "opening up of the open" as an achievement of subjectivity.[97] Rather, he always saw the open as grounded in *Dasein's* being opened up by its own finitude.

Introduction to Metaphysics stands on the brink of the full-blown reorientation that Heidegger's thought would undergo between 1936 and 1938. Delivered as a lecture course one year before the term *"Ereignis"* moved to center stage, the *Introduction* does not thematically explain the *Kehre* or *Ereignis.* Nonetheless, those issues are there without the titles—for example, in Heidegger's discussion of the bivalent reciprocity between *das Brauchen* (being's need of its dative) and *das Zugehören* (the dative's belonging to being). Likewise, *Dasein's* nature as thrown-openness is present in Heidegger's allusions to homelessness and neediness (compare *Not, Nötigung*).[98] In this 1935 lecture course Heidegger was beginning to find the language that had repeatedly failed him in 1926–1928, when he first attempted the transition to "Time and Being."[99]

Therefore, yes, *Introduction to Metaphysics* does represent a step forward in thinking and saying the turn; however, such thinking and saying is not the turn itself. And yes, it does represent a shift in Heidegger's *presentation* of his abiding central topic. But in the end, *Introduction to Metaphysics* simply allowed Heidegger's thinking to catch up a bit with the single issue he spent his life pursuing.

Chapter 2

THE APPEARANCE OF METAPHYSICS

CHARLES E. SCOTT

Heidegger gives his students and us a considerable challenge as he leads them and us into metaphysical thought. One problem that we must face arises out of a tradition that has not shown clearly the differences among representational knowledge, evaluative considerations, and thinking. He says in the early pages of his introductory lectures that thinking must not be confused with knowledge, that the priority of knowledge over thought has, in fact, turned what is often recognized as professional philosophy into a miscontrual of philosophy (6–7). More specifically, he directs us to think of metaphysics without the misconstruals that have formed most of what we can say about metaphysics as well as other ways of knowing that are based on a metaphysical turn of mind. It seems that academic knowledge about metaphysics and metaphysical thinking itself are allied and require a new approach—a genuine introduction—to show what happens in metaphysical orientations. He states that we are facing a crisis, one that leads us toward the necessity of a decision (28–30, 34, 38, 84). This movement is motivated by a grounding question in our lineage that is found in metaphysical thought and that leads to another way of thinking. *The* issue of this course for him is found in this grounding question and in the context of a Western, lost sense for being, one that comes to expression in a cheapening of beings, in a lack of resonance for the being of what occurs, and in a decadent sense that "being" counts for nothing. (Although many people capitalize "being" when they write about Heidegger, I have elected to put it in the lower case. I make this decision because using a capital letter for being inevitably suggests in English either a highest being or something with transcendental status, and those meanings make impossible an understanding of Heidegger's use of the word.) The decisiveness of this issue in this context means that something definitive, something with intrinsic and ultimate worth in our Western world, is at stake when metaphysical thought appears, that a dying of "spirit" must be reversed, or we shall destroy ourselves by ways of life that give primary meaning to what we can use, control, and change to suit our momentary purposes. For Heidegger "destruction" means living with no sense for life's sheer, uncontrollable eventfulness and its dimension of disclosure, which has no use and is not any kind of being. Heidegger invests his introductory course with this sense of crisis and finds in this introductory thinking, in this investment in the appearance of metaphysics, the possibility of making metaphysics appear in such a way as to transform it and to bestow upon thinking a new life. This possibility for a new life has its origins in a question of being that begins and sustains Western thought and that Western thought also hides and misconstrues.

The question of being, the "first" in rank of all questions and the one that he wants to make explicit for thought and in thought, is not found only in formulations (1). It occurs in despair (that is, depression) "when . . . the sense of things grows dark, . . . in heartfelt joy. . . [when] all things are transformed and surround us as if for the first time, . . . in a spell of boredom, when we are equally distant from despair and joy . . . when the stubborn ordinariness of beings lays open a wasteland in which it makes no difference to us whether beings are or are not" (1). In such psycho-physiological situations we undergo a sense not only that beings come and go but that being—the very event of life—also is fragile—fragile not only because being might not be a being that continues infinitely but fragile also because everything that is might not be founded on something definite, law-abiding, and constant in itself. Our experiences of despair, joy, and boredom suggest that things might be supported finally by nothing at all, nothing so negatively empowered in our circumference of life that things can cease forever or arise as though originated again in a moment of repetition. Our lives—our bodies—seem to carry an apprehension that the eventuation of everything occurs without dependence on something outside of the reach of disastrous eradication. And such a sensibility can be composed of prereflective moods and does not necessarily rely on disciplined observation. The question of being, in other words, seems to be closer to a physical sense (one belonging to occurrences of *phusis*) than to a philosophical formulation.

I want to emphasize that Heidegger is leading us into a question that is not primarily theoretical and that when he proposes to lead us into metaphysics—to introduce us to it—by means of a way of thinking that is not traditionally metaphysical, he is proposing a considerable transformation in the ways we connect in our prereflective alertness to the lives that we confront, as well as proposing a transformation of the ways we think philosophically. The direction in which he is taking us is one in which we will find that thinking is not primarily like what we call theorizing or intellection, but rather is an alert occurrence in which things appear without the benefit of human, creative, subjective, a priori faculties. Such occurrences, in which beings come to light, that is, come to appear, are ones that people undergo but do not do, and Heidegger will give much attention to descriptions of language and thinking that are not grounded by the images and values of subjective formation. In this effort he would like for metaphysical thinking to appear in its own movements and words but also to appear as much as possible in an eventful alertness that does not happen the way metaphysical thought happens. He wants to introduce us to metaphysics by way of its self-showing in thought that is not quite metaphysical. And hence he wants to introduce us to an attempt at nontraditional thinking.

I consequently take with emphasis his beginning by connecting the question of being to affective occurrences that are not theoretically or intellectually structured. That connection suggests (although Heidegger does not use the word "body") that in some circumstances we can be more alert in our bodies to the question of being than we are in our disciplined intelligence. And "bodies" here names living, physical (that is, of *phusis*) happenings that are bred through and through by culture-forming events, by people-forming experiences and interpretations, and by a dimension in life for which we have no good name and that seems (and feels) like it is always coming to die. The *question* of being, in other words, seems like it is bred in us, it seems that we find ourselves in its sway and defined in part by its anomalous trajectory, a trajectory that appears to have less to do with a determined presence than with possibility and groundless eventuation. In this context I would like to suggest the phrase "bodies of thought" and to mean by it living and alert events that are both physical and extensive beyond the intentions and abilities that compose one of their aspects, subjectivity. Bodies of thought are marked by occurrences of appearance that have the dimension of world-reach, of a vast expanse of history and cultural memory invested (above all for Heidegger) in language and art, and invested also in values, ways of doing practical things, and institutions. Thus when thinking happens, much more than a shared subjectivity or the limitations of personal experience takes place (physically happens). Add to this the dimension of eventuation, which is neither a group of determinations nor the totality of determinations, but rather is the disclosive happening of whatever happens, and we have a figuration of thinking bodies as regions of vast indetermination and determination at once.

"Thus," he says early in his first lecture, "if we properly pursue the question, 'Why are there beings at all instead of nothing?'" in its sense as a question,

> we must avoid emphasizing any particular, individual being, not even focusing on the human being. For what is this being, after all! Let us consider the Earth within the dark immensity of space in the universe. We can compare it to a tiny grain of sand; more than a kilometer of emptiness extends between it and the next grain of its size; on the surface of this tiny grain of sand lives a stupefied swarm of supposedly clever animals, crawling all over each other, who for a brief moment have invented knowledge. And what is a human lifespan amid millions of years? Barely a move of the second hand, a breath. Within beings as a whole there is no justification to be found for emphasizing precisely *this* being that is called the human being and among which we ourselves happen to belong. (3)

But, he says, when beings as a whole occur in the question of why, human beings have quite a distinct and significant relation to beings as a whole, in contrast to human beings' seeming insignificance in the universe when they and the universe are considered in objective and theoretical terms. For by means of the singularly human question "Why are there beings instead of nothing at all?" people are opened up to themselves and to beings as a whole (3–4). Indeed this question, lived, as I suggest, in a thinking body, holds open a region in which things present themselves without finality, present themselves as a whole, without "any particular preference" for one being over another; for in this opening "every being counts as much as any other" (3). The reason Heidegger calls this question the *Grund*frage, the *grounding* question, is that the sense of questioning both holds in question a possible ground of being *and* functions as the grounding for *all* appearing things: appearing things happen in question. To appear means to happen with the question of why implanted in their existence. There is nothing to insure the survival of anything. All beings appear to come to pass (4). When *the* question holds, no being has the privilege of escaping this pervasive sense of questioning and becoming the ground of everything else. This questionableness, when it is pervasive of everything, grounds human openness to beings at the same time that it ungrounds any candidate for a grounding explanation of the whole. "What is asked in this question rebounds upon the questioning itself, for the questioning challenges beings as a whole but does not after all wrest itself free from them" (4). Beings as a whole happen in question, and the question too happens in question. In that double rebound we find the possibility for thinking to which Heidegger introduces us in these lectures. In such thinking a prereflective sensibility that is definitive for Western culture comes to disciplined enactment, and in *that* enactment everything that is thought appears in the self-presentation of its ungrounded ways of being. It presents the ungrounding ground of the question of being in the passing quality of its self-disclosures. When such a sensibility pervades the appearances of metaphysical occurrences, such as the appearance in these lectures of the thought of canonized Western philosophers, no particular being prevails. And when no particular being prevails among the phenomena, traditional metaphysics is basically disturbed, since it composes ways of thinking in which people expect to find a grounding way of being that gives an enduring presence to originate, sustain, and connect all ways of life. Traditional candidates for this kind of grounding include God, gods, nature, reason, universal order, and transcendental subjectivity. Indeed, metaphysics is loosened from its own sense of grounding, and Heidegger's aim in these lectures is to show traditional metaphysical thought in such a way that in its presentation no one being or group of beings prevails. In that appearance metaphysics might well appear nonmetaphysically and be turned away from its own predisposition to find a deathless ground for truth and knowledge. Were that to happen we might find that the question "Why are there beings at all instead of nothing?" is not subject to an explanatory or sufficient answer. We might rather find that it, as an unanswerable question, connects us to the uncontrollable, unceasable openness of human mortality.

In reference to Heidegger's lyrical account of human insignificance in the universe, I can now say that for him, the meanings of our lives can be found outside of the range of the theoretical observations that illustrate our "objective" meaninglessness. Our experiences of meaning and significance arise out of the ungrounding work of the *question* of being, not out of answers to or resolutions of that question. It does not make any difference that we are hardly noticeable on a map of the universe. What defines our difference is found in the ways we live in and out of the *question* of being. That means also that our difference and our best hope for discovering the meaning of our difference are for Heidegger found most appropriately in the ways whereby we take our departure from traditional metaphysical thought, which always grounds the whole of beings in some privileged being. Such privileging seems always to lead to some kind of mapping and measuring in which meaning depends on correctness of evaluative judgment, or on an objective claim that something or other defines and regulates the whole in an ordered way, or on some body of beliefs that have their power primarily by virtue of a willed affirmation. In such ways of thinking, meaning depends on the objective truth of the claims or on the subjectivity of their affirmation, and in the consequent processes of authorization, validation, and proof, Heidegger finds a life-denying nihilism that persistently leads to the recognition and validation of beings on the basis of some being that they are not. To lose the question of being is to lose the possibility of affirming and thinking *in* the events, the coming to pass, of beings themselves—and *that* loss comes to mean for Heidegger the triumph of hierarchical usage and manipulation of beings, a pervasive cultural accomplishment that he will name technology. So in this introduction he is leading us away from the power of technology by which we use up our world for the sake of some dominant being or way of being that insidiously undercuts the disclosures of beings in the questionableness of their own events—and by that undercutting, destroys the origination of meaning in the singularity of our lives on this tiny planet. His most persistent and remarkable claim, I believe, is found in his thought that by ungrounding metaphysically generated grounds for life, we are released to what is most meaningful—and what is most unprovable and least illustratable—in our lives.

One of the goals that Heidegger has for us as he introduces us to metaphysics is to learn how to ask the question "Why are there beings at all instead of nothing?" If we learn how to ask it—and this learning is a definitive aspect of learning how to think outside the circumference of traditional metaphysics—we will turn what we experience as thinking from an activity of external and internal observation to "a distinctive occurrence that we call a *happening*" (4). He calls the happening of the question "provocative" and contrasts it to a mere repetition of the word "why" that takes appearances at a measurable face value. In its provocative happening the why-question recoils back upon itself—it cannot eliminate itself by answering itself—and *in* the occurrence of the recoil something happens. He calls this happening a leap away from "all the previous safety" that people (he says "dasein") have enjoyed because of the ground for existence that they have found in metaphysical ways of life (4). The question occurs in the event of the leap, not in observations about a leap that detaches lives from metaphysical securities. This means that if Heidegger is successful in his introduction the leap happens in his introductory thought, and if we are successful in following his course we will undergo the leap that composes his thought. "The asking of this question happens only in the leap and as the leap, and otherwise not at all" (4).

He notes that at this early stage of the introduction he is only talking about the leap and that he must position himself and us to be ready for a transformation of thinking. At this point the question has not come to thought; it stands before us as a possibility. But he wants to make clear that the leap is not external to the occurrence of ground as question (as distinct from ground as a particular being)—"the leap [*Sprung*] of this questioning attains its own ground by leaping, performs it in leaping . . . an attaining-the-ground-by-leaping" (5). The leap is *ur-sprünglich* in the sense that it is the occurrence of ground-in-question.

We can see in this notation the importance that theoretical intellection has for Heidegger. It is preparatory for thinking just as our metaphysical tradition is preparatory for the thought that constitutes a departure from it. A key element in this departure happens when the question recoils on itself and does not occasion a definitive answer by reference to something that resolves it. To resolve the question of being by reference to a definitive being obscures the leap that inheres in the question, makes it virtually indiscernible, and defers the possibility of thinking. But now Heidegger marks his own deferral, recognizes that these observations do not compose thinking, and suggests, in a promissory note, that we must go beyond preliminary observations about thinking if we are to engage in thinking. The leap is yet to come.

There is, however, an uncertainty in posing this difference between highly disciplined observations and thinking. Heidegger suggests this uncertainty when he says that "we want to be clear about this from the start: it can never be determined objectively whether anyone is asking—whether we are actually asking this question, that is, whether we are leaping, or whether we are just mouthing the words" (5). It seems to me that his observations require some experience of the difference that he articulates. Whereas I might merely repeat the difference that he points out, show the history and prospect of this difference, and develop a learned scholarship of the growth of his conception of the leap without ever engaging in the leap, his work in this book has a different resonance when compared to that of such scholarship. On one hand, he is warning us that accuracy regarding his statements and a high passing grade on a test of the course's contents would not necessarily mean that we had learned a thing about thinking. On the other, he seems to be speaking from an encounter with the leap. That's not something, he tells us, that we can know for sure. But he does seem to know that we cannot know that for sure. And it must be the case that he cannot know it for sure either, because we are not talking about something that can occur objectively or with the certainty of a private, subjective experience. We are dealing with a kind of event in which the whole of beings shifts, in which, for example, following the explication that he gives of faith and questioning (5–6), the traditional force of religious and theological teachings fades to irrelevance and the world appears without need of or interest in holistic answers or worshipful responses to the question of being. The world's presentation shifts to such a degree that metaphysical stabilities appear as obstructions, irritations, and oppressions. This means that the ways we feel most at home in the world and most estranged from it change, that our feelings regarding a creator God change, that what gives us to hope and despair changes—that our entire body of thought undergoes a major qualitative shift. The validity of such a shift is not something that Heidegger can prove or illustrate. But it composes a shift in which he can write and think.

He seems to me to pose the issue of the question in the processes of such a shift, and these processes seem to be a part of this introduction's movement and content. "Actually asking this [question of why there are beings at all instead of nothing]," he says, "means venturing to exhaust, to question thoroughly, what is inexhaustible and belongs to this question by unveiling that which it demands us to question. Whenever such a venture occurs, there is philosophy" (6, tr. altered). On those terms, Heidegger is carrying out "philosophy" in the immediacy of the question's power as he brings us toward its world-transformative enactment. Or, as he puts it, "philosophy, then, is not a kind of knowledge which one could acquire directly" (7). It comes to expression with the indirection of a transforming body of feelings, senses, and concepts, with an "unfolding resonance" that comes to the fore out of a history that has figured such resonance by inattention or suppression. Philosophy arises as an alertness to the questionableness that seems to live in our definitive assertions and beliefs, to motivate them, and to be carried in a troubled way by them. Philosophy does not compose a specific task or agenda. It unfolds without a general law in stages of incompletion, turns of sensibility, and crises of identity (7).

Heidegger's posing the question thus seems to involve considerably more than a theoretical position or a series of "objective" observations, and if we stand outside of the question in posing it—if we do not experience it recoiling on itself—we have not followed Heidegger in his preliminary philosophical step. In order to make that step we must undergo the power of the question's enactment and find our deepest senses of grounding shaken to the extent of jeopardizing what we hold to be true of beings as a whole. "There is no gradual transition from the customary by which the question could slowly become more familiar. . . . [In] this proposal of and talk about the question, we must not defer, or even forget, the questioning" (7). We must, rather, begin by allowing a leap that composes a dimension of Heidegger's first lecture, a beginning leap in his thought out of unquestioned convictions and clarity in the powers of a metaphysically grounded world. And such a leap, which shakes metaphysical certainties, composes the first move in our introduction to metaphysics and the first step toward thinking.

In the disorientation of the leap a change takes place not only in the appearances of beings but also in the appearing of the whole of beings. With the assumption that his account of dasein—of human being—as being-in-the-world holds for this introduction, we can say that Heidegger is not proposing only that we make a personal decision to attempt to suspend our metaphysical ideas and feelings. He is saying that we need to become attentive to a forceful, if largely unattended, historical dimension in the world's appearing. "Historical dimension" in this context is elaborated by his phrase "the authentic happening in the history of a people" (7). And he uses the words "resonance" and "innermost harmony" to speak of people's connections with "the authentic happening" (7). Later he will use the word "attuned" in a similar context (37), and he will say that being has "demands" that require certain distinctions when we are attuned to it (104). We can be misattuned to the grounding question by resonances that accompany the prioritization of beings in our everyday metaphysical lives. And we also, often in seemingly useless aspects of daily life, can find accord *(Einklang)* with a different kind of priority that dwells inchoately in our history and thus in our being-in-the-world—and thus in the way things come to appear. When we keep in mind that being-in-the-world does not name a state of subjectivity but rather names the occurrence of disclosure—the extensive, multirelational, worldly, and historical happenings of disclosure and hence of appearing—we can see that the disorientation of the leap inheres in being-in-the-world, that it has to do with the way the world—beings as a whole—appears. It is not a matter only of our deciding to let ourselves be disoriented, but rather is a matter of finding in the appearing of things resonance with a sharp divergence between the demands of beings and the requirements of the question that happens resolutely and unresolvably in being-in-the-world. The leap precedes any action or resolution that we might have regarding it. This disorientation, then, is in a people's history, in the very events that constitute the disclosures and appearances of whatever happens. And the issue is one of our becoming alert to this questionableness that accompanies the way things are and thinking with this alertness in a dimension of occurrences that is obscured by a metaphysical orientation to things and their being.

The alertness that pervades Heidegger's language and thought is one that he would like us to share. We might discover that things do not appear only metaphysically, that there is available to us in our history an attunement that is different from the attunement of experiences of groundedness in a dominant being or way of being, that this other dimension requires a transformation in the ways we philosophize, structure our curricula, believe and trust, connect with people and things, and interpret what is most important for our lives. Our history composes a body of attunement that is characterized by a disorienting leap that puts traditional ways of thought radically in question and that ungrounds the whole of beings in a grounding question. "That knowing which ignites and threatens and compels all questioning and appraising" arises in its demands and possibilities out of the appearing of things (8).

In the context of the "burdening" of the grounding question, the dangers of "familiar judgments" and "supposedly genuine experiences," and the "extraordinary" and untimely manner of genuine questioning, Heidegger turns to the Greeks, and by this turning he opens our access to the site of the leap in our history and thus in our lives (9–10). This move tells us what he means, in part, by "historical." It means that being-in-the-world for him names a constitutive connection with Greek culture in the appearances of everything, that our body of thought—our most basic conceptions, feelings, predispositions, and preferences—is invested by a Greek lineage, and that the appearance of metaphysics and the nonmetaphysical grounding question occurs in that lineage. The word that he chooses to elaborate the leap is *phusis*. By that word we find not only a site of the leap. We find as well something about language, thinking, and appearing.

"The naming force" of the word *phusis* is found in its naming, among other things, "the naming force of language and words" (11). That force of language and words, and, as he will later say, of thought, happens as the coming to be and presence of things: "things first come to be and are" in word, in language (11). As *phusis* enacts its own naming power it brings to appearance the arising and persistence, the being, of whatever is. It is a word first said in a prereflective sensibility, one that we need to learn how to give to appear in thought if we are to think in the power of the grounding question. And if we can learn how to think *phusis,* in its enactment we will be in touch with one of the most important resonances in our history: we will be thinking both of and in the coming to be and persistence of beings, for thought as Heidegger finds it is a primordial power of appearing. The words "*phusis*" and "being," and the grounding question, are enacted—"said"—in thought. By leaping back to this Greek word we thus find ourselves in an original dimension of our history, one that is characterized by a leap to the grounding question that we must uncover if we are to encounter traditional metaphysics in its nontraditional aspect. By this leap to the Greek word and thought of *phusis* Heidegger is thus giving attention to a contemporary dimension of world-occurrences and bringing our concentration toward a leap in our history to the grounding question that happens now in the appearing of things. Heidegger is inviting us to leap to a dimension in our history where a leap from grounding to the question of grounding occurs.

Phusis does not appropriately name a specific quality or a kind of thing, and when Heidegger says that *phusis,* for the Greeks, names beings as a whole and the being of beings, he means that it names the power of arising and finite persistence (11–12). In this context, Heidegger's word *Walten* is translated as "sway." *Phusis* happens as "emerging-abiding sway" (11, 13). *Walten* is closely related to the English word "wield." Both words suggest governance, rule, determining power. This meaning can be expressed by such phrases as "he wielded his sword expertly" or "she wielded her power wisely." One can also express the idea of *Walten* by saying that a festive atmosphere held sway over the entire community, or that a person's dream swayed all of her actions. In Heidegger's thought, however, *phusis* as many of the Greeks found it names the sway, rule, or power of emerging and abiding that is without an initiating subject or an original and continuing Source. It suggests finite enactment of arising and coming to appear that is different from the beings that come to appear and from the specific words or thoughts by virtue of which the enactment occurs. This idea makes it awkward to refer to *phusis* "itself," because *phusis* does not name a presence or being of any kind. In its lack of presence *phusis* occurs in question—it occurs in passing. Nothing other than its finite events supports it or backs it up. Coming-to-presence—beginning and persisting—is not a presence. So when he speaks of *phusis* as emerging-abiding sway, he suggests an anomalous power, anomalous in the context of our dominant perceptions of pervasive rules of causation and definitive connections (see 13). His additional claims are that *phusis* happens in linguistic and thinking events and that when we are attuned to this arising, appearing dimension of language and thought we are in touch with an unresolvable questionableness that has moved and formed Western philosophy. The "naming force" of *phusis* happens as naming force comes to appear in the Greek alertness: in it emerging-abiding sway becomes a phenomenon in their language and hence becomes available for philosophical problematization. As he says later in the lectures, *phuein* occurs as "the emerging that reposes in itself, [as] *phainesthai,* lighting-up, self-showing, appearing" (77). "Being means appearing," and "the emerging sway is an appearing" that is not the same as what appears (77). The questionableness of the appearing event, as we have seen, is found in the absence of a being by which we could explain the arising of the referent of the word "itself" in the phrase "reposes in itself."

Phusis thus appears in Greek language and thought not primarily as something observed in "nature" but as the power of language and thought to give things to appear. In gaining access to a dimension of history in our lives, Heidegger leaps to a dimension of appearing that is beyond what appears; he leaps "over beyond" *(meta)* the things that appear now *(ta phusika)* and takes our full attention to a region in our history where the leap to questions beyond beings arise (13). The appearing of *phusis* in Greek language and thought is reenacted by its reappearing in Heidegger's move to the word that figures a grounding question for what we know as the history of metaphysics. Heidegger's turn to *phusis* early in these lectures gives appearance to a naming force *(phusis)* that gives to appear the naming force of language and thought. And this move composes an instance of *phainesthai* that is definitive in his introducing us to metaphysics: "the discussion of *phusis*, 'physics' in the ancient sense, is in itself already beyond *ta phusika*, on beyond beings, and is concerned with being. 'Physics' determines the essence and the history of metaphysics from the inception onward" (14). He intends to "open" up our questioning and knowing to the appearing of *phusis*. This introductory opening happens to the extent that we undergo a resurgence of the coming to pass—not of Greek knowledge, not of something that we can comprehend exhaustively by means of scholarship—but of appearing in the appearances of things. Heidegger reinvokes the inadequacy of an objective understanding of what he says or what certain Greeks said: "This is a leadership [that is, an introduction] that essentially has no following. Whenever one finds pretensions to a following, in a school of philosophy for example, questioning is misunderstood" (15). Studies of Heidegger's connections to other philosophers, of Greek "theories" and culture, of the development of arguments and ideas in Western philosophy might well provide interesting information. But when we turn to thinking, something else is required. To introduce us to metaphysics Heidegger must lead us to participatory engagements, not with propositions, insights, and interrogative sentences and their histories, but with the uncertain coming to life of things in the appearances of language and thought; and it is in early Greek language and thought that Heidegger finds a lively arena for this encounter. As I have emphasized, for Heidegger this arena, far from being one in an abstract and distant past, is one that happens nonvoluntarily and contemporaneously in the lives of beings.

With the emphasis he places on *phusis* Heidegger has brought us to "the appearing that holds sway" largely subliminally in Western thought and to the appearing that now holds sway with alertness in his thought. In his language we are engaged in a retrieval of—a return to—the appearance of being—

phusis—in language that makes *phusis* available for thinking and that shows thinking in its *phusis*. Being, appearing, and thinking cannot be appropriately separated in the language and thought of *phusis,* and that means in this context that to reveal metaphysics in thought means to allow it to appear in the appearing of being, an appearing with which traditional metaphysical thought has lost touch. *Phusis* now appears in the language and conceptuality of these lectures as the unresolvable questionableness of being that is apparent in traditional thinking but that traditional thinking usually has attempted to resolve. Metaphysics appears to disclose the grounding question of thought by re-presenting it as an object—as a *Gegen-stand* of thought. Heidegger's intention is to show that this way of seeming to think of being at once lets it appear while setting it against *(gegen)* thought and losing its question: he intends to think metaphysical thinking in such a way that its quality of appearing stands out, and by this account to let us see the insubstantiality in being's appearing. Thinking in this case lets appear the conjunction of appearing and being in the thought that denies that conjunction. Toward the end of this discussion I will note in more detail the ways in which a separation of being, thought, and appearing leads to a division between thought and life, a division that figures objectification and one that is definitive for traditional philosophy. Now the question turns to the process by which thought, being, and appearing move from a sense of sameness to a sense of distinct differences.

How have being and thinking come to be separated? Primarily by a spirit-forming interest in showing that being is something determinant and constant. We are invested in our "flesh and blood" by a "prior line of sight" that holds being at a distance from thought, that expects thought to re-present something that is already essentially present (89). In this manner thought occurs as it sets something apart, considers it, deliberates about it, defines it by set rules for reasonable coherence: as we re-present things we use them, control them, set them in structures that define them by reproduction and imposition. When being is considered in this way it is set apart from thought and, as it were, it stands there in itself and available for a correct account.

This seemingly minor, merely philosophical development defines for Heidegger "the spiritual decline of the earth" in our tradition and culture. It is characterized by "the darkening of the world, the flight of the gods, the destruction of the earth, the reduction of human beings to a mass, the hatred and mistrust of everything creative and free" (29). He understands himself to be addressing consequences of this prior line of sight in our bodies and our world—in our flesh and blood, according to the statement I noted above—consequences that come with a sense of life that divides life from thought and appearance and makes all that appears to stand as though it consisted of things to be grasped and employed by the full range of our mentation and intention. This drift of human accomplishment turns us into employers of realities that stand ready for our putting them to work, whether we put them to work as material for imaginative constructions or as grounding beings for support of our lives.

How have we come to such a way of life? In a significant measure by a misappropriation in Greek philosophy of *phusis* and other related words, a misappropriation that composes a decisive moment in the history of our lives. This misappropriation had as its objective "controlling the urgency of being in seeming, in distinguishing being from seeming" (83). This moment happens, for example, with the appearance in metaphysical thinking of being and seeming. People took seeming with its dissembling, obscuring, and transient aspects as separate from being, and attached seeming to appearing. As this separation arose and persisted, being seemed to be quite other to seeming and appearing, and *this* appearing made being seem like something in itself. Being does not in this view dissemble or conceal. It is more like a stable, active Truth that is subject to discovery and re-presentation by means of ideas and structures of apprehension that are more or less correct in their regard of it. Being and thinking (and language) are then held in an opposition that requires thinking people to distinguish being from appearing events and thereby to obscure thoroughly thought's kinship with being in the emerging-abiding sway of appearing. Being, on the other hand, as Heidegger speaks of it in the context of many "ancient" poets and thinkers whose texts predate the division of thought and being that begins Western philosophy, happens with seeming, but never as what it seems to be. "It" is not an it. Being seems. "It" happens in question, indeterminately with determinations, fleeting, never as a presence.

The separation of being and thinking happened early in our tradition together with the separation of being from something that is inconstant or that passes away. Such separation constitutes "the decisive inception" of our traditional thought (94), one that Heidegger will refer to in his *Contributions to Philosophy* a few years after these lectures were given as the first beginning of Western thought. This beginning of philosophical reflection is based on the pervasive early Greek sense that being means appearing, and in this sense we also find the awareness that in appearing, things are gathered together. In language one thing is brought to another thing—things belong together in their appearances, but this early sense is severely interrupted as *phusis*, becoming, appearance, and thought are separated from being so that the very life of things is set apart from them. If being belonged to appearing and appearing to being, it would seem that being were beyond the control of all stabilizing presence, that the urgency of life itself were without reliable guidance, that the gathering and transforming of presences amidst passage and death composed the ground of life. And whereas the early Greek sense was that the emerging sway happens as appearing, that being happens as manifestation, and that manifestation, not something manifest, composes truth, later thinkers turned this sense into the thought that being and truth stand behind manifestation as something that is obscured by becoming and appearing. Being did not appear to them as intrinsically obscure. It is obscured by something that is not fully being. This reflective turn composes the decisive moment in Western thought, a division that takes being and appearing, and hence being and thinking, away from each other.

And yet this division nonetheless also holds being and appearing together in what could seem like a death grip if a person looks for a being that is free of mortality and transformation. Heidegger finds that philosophy gathers being and appearing together in the separation that would hold them apart, and this description marks a decisive moment for his introduction to metaphysics. For by showing their mutual belonging in an early inception of Western sensibility he wants to show that in thinking as we now find it, being appears without constancy of presence, and appearing brings being with it, even when they are held apart by philosophical doctrines that assert their separateness. This other, earlier beginning, before the separation of being and appearing (when compared to the later inception of philosophy in the separation of being and appearing), composes a prephilosophical sense of being in union with appearing. He finds that the word *phusis* persists in its prephilosophical meaning in the divisive inception and continuation of Western philosophy. Philosophy as a force of appearing lets being seem to be constant in the appearance of rules and meanings that deny their own origin in gathering appearances. The only constancy that seems to lie beyond these appearances is found in the appearance of being that belies the constancy that its metaphysical conception suggests: we find ourselves led to the ungrounding ground of the question "Why are there beings instead of nothing at all?" and to the recoil of the why back upon itself in the appearing of being, as a figuration of metaphysical constancy.

We can see the emphasis that he places on the life of thinking and the definitive force of that life in our cultures in Heidegger's claims that the thought of being without substance is forecast by Parmenides and Heraclitus and by the Greek language itself as it is found in the texts of Homer, Sophocles, and Pindar, and that this sense of being without substance is lost in the formation of Western metaphysics. He introduces us to an early incision and division in the manifest togetherness of appearing, being, and thought—a "decision," he calls it, *in* the way things come to appear (84). And by virtue of this powerful division, appearing, thought, and being are held together as divided on the basis of the earlier experience of their belonging together, a togetherness that figures both a primordial uncertainty of being and a disposition toward affirmation of what is by virtue of its disclosure and not by virtue of something certain and outside of its disclosiveness. As we become alert to this intrinsic yet divided connection of appearing, being, and thought in our tradition, we find that our thinking occurs in the lineage of the question of being as well as in a lineage of effort to resolve the question. We also may find in our thinking an anxious predisposition to discover a constancy of being and to locate it outside of the inconstancy of appearing. But as we draw closer and more alertly to the life of Western thinking in the struggle with the question, we find ourselves not just before but in the life of *phusis,* the emerging-abiding sway of appearing. Thinking happens as the inception and fragile continuation of what appears as thought. Being occurs as this inception and continuation within a troubled history of the question of being.

I return to Heidegger's account of the insignificance of human life when it is viewed from the perspective of the universe's magnitude. There is, he suggests, no objective basis for the assumption of human value in the universe. When we look with the theoretical discipline of modern astrophysics, for example, we find vast distance and the silence of human expression. When *phusis* is converted into disciplines of objective gaze, human being fades to a minuscule moment of passing struggle on a chancy, tiny sphere of minerals and motion. Thought appears to be alone in its singularity, and being seems to be a trivial abstraction. Even the question "why?" is exhausted by the silence that surrounds it. People long for a confirming contact with something "out there" that will let them know factually and objectively that humans are not alone, and this longing arises in response to a sense of aloneness that objectification generates. Beliefs and ideas that attempt to resolve the sense of insignificance that is produced by human objectivity, conviction, or rational proof reenact the urgency of being in the fragility of its appearances. And the meaning of such beliefs and ideas is found in the question that they expose in their efforts to resolve it. By being alert to the appearance of metaphysical thought, Heidegger has introduced us both to its origination of objectivity and to its meaning in what it attempts to escape—its life's own "appearancial" quality. By its effort to escape, metaphysical thought has set in motion a kind of spirit, a body of thought, that leads to the sense of isolation and seems resolvable only by acts of willed belief or by authoritative rules of systematic thought—beliefs and thoughts that exemplify the isolation of human insistence. But when *phusis* is affirmed in its union with appearing and when thought is affirmed as *phusis,* Heidegger finds that objective aloneness is not the problem. Living in the question of being is the issue. Living in this question provides ways of thinking that are preoccupied with meanings that occur with them, with their histories and futures, their dangers and fulfillments, and with bodies that appear to pass in the freedom of endeavors to find how to be well as we encounter ourselves in appearances of being.

Chapter 3

BEING AS APPEARING: RETRIEVING THE GREEK EXPERIENCE OF *PHUSIS*

CHARLES GUIGNON

1. THE AIMS OF *INTRODUCTION TO METAPHYSICS*

Heidegger begins the lecture course *Introduction to Metaphysics* with what he calls the fundamental and guiding question of metaphysics: Why is there something rather than nothing? The course, it seems, will introduce students to the subject of metaphysics—the study of the Being of beings—and it will begin with the famous question posed by Leibniz. But Heidegger quickly seems to shift ground when he says that before we can ask this fundamental question of metaphysics, we should first ask a "prior question," the question of how it stands with Being (25). With this prior question, the lecture course seems to run off the rails of the standard introductory philosophy course. The question has a colloquial, almost slangy ring to it—just as one might ask "How's he doing?" *(Wie steht es um ihn?)*, Heidegger asks, "How's it going with Being?"

What motivates this shift in the questioning at the outset of *Introduction to Metaphysics?* A few hints in the book show that the prior-question of metaphysics is actually a question central to Heidegger's thought. In the course of the lectures we learn that the question "How does it stand with Being?" is interchangeable with the question "What is the meaning of Being?" (32). Moreover, since *meaning* is what opens itself up to us in understanding (63–64), to ask about the meaning of Being is to ask about how we understand Being. So the claim is that before we can address the fundamental question of metaphysics, we first need to clarify our understanding of Being. Heidegger points out that the need to get clear about our understanding of Being is especially pressing today because our modern world tends to assume that the Being of beings is so self-evident and transparent that the word "Being" is actually empty and meaningless. This is why Nietzsche described "Being" as one of "the most universal and emptiest concepts, the final wisp of evaporating reality."[1] For most of us, as for Nietzsche, there are only the ordinary things we perceive around us—to talk of their "Being" is meaningless.

Responding to Nietzsche's dismissal of the very idea of Being, Heidegger poses the question of the meaning of Being as an either-or: "Is Being a mere word and its meaning a vapor, or does what is named with the word 'Being' hold within it the spiritual fate of the West?" (32). As its ominous tone indicates, this question has profound importance. In Heidegger's view, many of the most pressing problems in the contemporary world arise because of the tacit understanding of Being that pervades and guides our thought and practices. We tend to see the world as a collection of objects on hand for our knowing and manipulation, and we even begin to see ourselves as "human resources" to be mobilized in the project of mastering the earth. This narrowed down and unreflective stance toward things governs our relations to all aspects of the earth, but it itself remains unnoticed. Our understanding of Being, Heidegger says, is "dark, confused, covered over and concealed"; as a result, "for us Being is only an empty word with an evanescent meaning" (63). The "spiritual decline of the earth" we see everywhere today (29)—the "darkening of the world" and "disempowering of mind or spirit" (34, translation modified)—results from the fact that "human beings . . . peoples in their greatest machinations and exploits, have a relation to beings but have long since fallen out of Being" (28). The result is *nihilism,* the pervasive tendency to get lost in dealings with beings while remaining oblivious to Being (155).

Heidegger's claims about modern nihilism make sense against the backdrop of his understanding of the history of Western metaphysics. On this historical account, early Greek thinkers and poets—in particular, the pre-Socratics and the tragedians—inaugurated a particular understanding of Being at the dawn of history. On the basis of a "fundamental orientation to Being" (86), the Greeks were able to name and so think of beings as such and as a whole as *phusis.* Through this act of naming and thinking, Western philosophy—and, indeed, in Heidegger's view, Western history itself—was first set on its course. As the lectures of *Introduction to Metaphysics* make clear, this inceptive understanding of the Being of beings was full-bodied and fertile, carrying with it a rich array of productive tensions and insights into fundamental connections that shaped all of Greek experience.

According to this story, somewhat later in the development of Greek thought, especially in the thought of Plato and Aristotle, the initial burst of illumination was deformed into the rather constricted understanding of Being as "beingness," *ousia* (24). The understanding of Being as *ousia,* which appears with the "ending" of Greek philosophy's inception, was itself transformed in Roman thought and language into the understanding of Being as "substance"—that which "lies under"—and this conception of Being has been passed down, with minor variations on the theme, through the centuries to our own time. Thus, the history of metaphysics has been a story about "the slow ending of this history, in whose midst we have long been standing" (136), a story of deformation, degeneration, decline, and stagnation in which Western civilization has fallen away from the initial explosion of insight and energy at its source to today's complacent assurance that in knowing about objects, we know all there is to know about Being.

In terms of this story, we can understand how Heidegger sees his task in this lecture course and in philosophy generally. Since the Greek world contains the "basic traits, though distorted and repressed, displaced and covered up, [that] still sustain our own world" (96), we need to "return to the Greek conception of Being," a conception that, even as "entirely flattened out and rendered unrecognizable, is the conception that still rules even today in the West" (45). The project of *retrieving* the Greek sources of our understanding of Being is unavoidably historical: it calls for "tearing down a world that has grown old and . . . building it truly anew, that is, historically" (96). As Heidegger says, "the Greek conception of the essence of Being . . . has long ruled our historical Dasein," and so we have the task of reflecting on "the provenance of our *concealed history*" by working out the "history of Being" (70).

The *Introduction to Metaphysics* therefore undertakes the task of recovering the earliest ways of understanding Being for the purpose of revitalizing our contemporary understanding. What this retrieval is supposed to provide is a way of replacing the substance ontology that dominates Western thought with an alternative understanding of Being, an understanding that emphasizes the way beings show up in (and as) an unfolding *happening* or *event.* We might call this alternative outlook an "event ontology." In terms of this understanding, Heidegger can reconceptualize various domains of beings in terms he gets from his readings of such Greek concepts as *kinēsis, genesis, energeia, polemos* and, of course, *phusis.*[2] This way of thinking about things is *truer* and more in touch with things than our current substance ontology, Heidegger seems to hold, because it is more "originary" or "inceptive": as an "inceptive truth" (89) it expresses the oldest and most basic understanding of the Being of beings in Western civilization. As such an originary truth, it also holds the promise of a more fertile understanding of Being for our future.

Why should we think that inceptive understandings are truer than current views? So far as I can see, Heidegger in the *Introduction to Metaphysics* makes no attempt to argue in favor of this thesis. Perhaps he would say that the event ontology is truer in the sense that it is "more primordial" (to use the vocabulary of *Being and Time*) than the substance ontology, that is, it is more basic because the understanding of Being as constant presence *(beständige Anwesenheit)* can be shown to be derived from and parasitic on the deeper understanding of Being as an event of arising and abiding. Or he might hold that the event ontology should be given serious consideration because it gives us an illuminating way of thinking about particular sorts of beings—especially artworks, historical events, and human existence itself. This latter point, at any rate, is what I hope to show in this chapter. As to the question whether the event ontology is correct in some absolute sense (a question which, given Heidegger's view of truth, seems ill-formed), I take no position.

As we saw, the story in the foreground of *Introduction to Metaphysics* is about the dawn of metaphysics in ancient Greece, its decline and calcification up to the present, and the prospects for rejuvenation today. But there is also, I believe, another story in the background of this work, a story that will become increasingly prominent in Heidegger's writings in the years after these lectures. This background story, which is hinted at in a long addendum to the text added in 1953 (14–15), starts from the assumption that the first inception in early Greek thought did not just begin metaphysics, where this is understood as revealing the beingness *(Seiendheit)* of beings, but was also to some extent "premetaphysical" insofar as it embodied a tacit awareness not just of beings but also of Being as such (later called *Seyn*), where "Being" is understood as pointing to the ground and source of any possible understanding of beingness—something Heidegger will soon call the "event of appropriation" *(Ereignis)*. On this view, the Greeks understood, however dimly, that every revealing is always necessarily at the same time a concealing. But they never fully thematized this insight—as Heidegger says, they "experienced [*ousia*] without question as the meaning of Being" (46). Because they "never returned to this ground of Being" but instead always remained at the "foreground" level of characterizing what shows up—namely, beings—the experience of the meaning of Being had slipped into oblivion by the time of Plato and Aristotle and it has remained forgotten to this day.[3] In the light of this background story, the foreground story of what leads into metaphysics (what *führt in die Metaphysik ein*), by telling a story about how metaphysics gets started, is at least implicitly a story both about what it was like before there was metaphysics and also about how metaphysics can be overcome by an "other inception" that retrieves what was only implicit in the first inception: the question of Being as such (29).

Given this background story, it seems that any account of the role of *phusis* in *Introduction to Metaphysics* should (a) show the limitations of this concept insofar as it is a name for the beingness of beings, and (b) make clear how this concept points to what is beyond metaphysics, namely, Being itself.

Since Heidegger's discussion of *phusis* is explicated in detail elsewhere in this volume,[4] I shall limit myself to giving a rough, intuitive account of the concept and then concentrate on showing how such a notion is illuminating in trying to make sense of things that the substance ontology fails to make intelligible. After making a case for understanding artworks, human beings, and history in terms of the event ontology, I address the question of whether Heidegger's views open the door to a vicious relativism or an untenable antirealism.

2. BEING, APPEARING, BECOMING, SEEMING

Heidegger's foreground story begins with the "true inception" of Western thought (10), the "fundamental experience of Being" (11) that led the early Greeks to give the name *phusis* to beings as such and as a whole. *Phusis* refers to what arises from itself, what unfolds, what comes-into-appearance and endures in appearance. These traits are summed up by Heidegger in saying that *phusis* is the name for the "emerging-abiding sway," where the word translated "sway" *(Walten)* suggests the movement of a surging force that relentlessly unfolds in the form of beings of distinctive sorts. At one point in *Introduction to Metaphysics* Heidegger seems to say that the sway is identical to "beings as a whole" (115), but generally he holds that the sway is Being as experienced by the Greeks. It should be obvious that this distinction is quite important, for if the sway were seen as consisting of beings with determinate characteristics that come to be manifest as *phusis,* then Heidegger would be committed to the Kantian idea of "things-in-themselves" existing prior to and independent of their ways of becoming manifest, and such a view would open him up to questions about the precise Being of these *Dinge an sich* independent of any interpretations or ways of becoming manifest—questions that proved devastating to Kantian theories. For this reason, it is best to think of the emerging-abiding sway as referring primarily to Being itself as it presented itself to the Greeks, and as referring only derivatively to the beings experienced in this way.

The conceptual links *phusis* has to other key concepts underlying Greek experience are spelled out over the course of *Introduction to Metaphysics*. First, *phusis* is found to contain within itself the idea of *appearing* as this was understood by the Greeks. Heidegger tells us that a being whose way of Being is *phusis* "puts itself forth" (the verb *sich dar-stellen* is often translated as "presents itself," 46): it appears in the open, is lit up, and so is accessible to observers.

Phusis is "that which arises into the light," *phainesthai,* and is essentially connected to "*phuein,* to illuminate, to shine forth and therefore to appear" (54). It therefore expresses the idea of a "phenomenon" as defined in *Being and Time* (section 7A): that which manifests itself or appears in the light, that which emerges out of concealment in order to show forth as such and such. On Heidegger's interpretation of Greek thought, then, there is at a basic level no real difference between Being and appearing. On the contrary, "Being means appearing. Appearing does not mean something derivative. . . . Being essentially is [*west als*] appearing" (77, translation modified). This is why the Greeks could see truth as residing primarily in beings rather than in propositions or thoughts: "Insofar as a being as such *is,* it places itself into and stands in *unconcealment, alētheia.* . . . On the grounds of the unique essential relation between *phusis* and *alētheia,* the Greeks could say: beings as beings are true" (77–78).

Second, Heidegger claims that, for the Greeks, *becoming* is not something different from Being. Instead, "becoming is a shining forth [*Schein*] of Being" (87, translation modified) in which beings emerge into presence as what they are. For this reason, seeming *(Schein)* is not necessarily deceptive or misleading. In its original sense, Heidegger says, "seeming as appearing is the becoming of Being" (88). At the level of the originary appearing of things, there is no way to drive in a wedge between the view *(Anblick)* things present and what they truly are.

The third and most important characteristic of *phusis* is the way it happens initially as *polemos* (strife). Heidegger bases his reading of the concept of *polemos* on Heraclitus' well-known fragment 53, which is conventionally translated as: "War is the father of all and the king of all, and it has shown some as gods and others as men, made some slaves and others free." Heidegger takes this to mean that, for Greek thought, there is a primal strife or struggle that first draws beings out of concealment and lets them stand forth *as* such and such, that is, as having determinate characteristics in relation to each other in a field of contrasts or differences. The context of meaningful relations that emerges in this way is called a *world.* Seen from this standpoint, a world initially comes into being through an "originary struggle" (47), a primordial unfolding of oppositions and distinctions on the basis of which beings come to *be* at all. This shining-forth of beings in their "*as*-structure" (to use the vocabulary of *Being and Time*)—their ways of showing up *as* this or that—is described as "the originarily emergent self-upraising of the violent forces of what holds sway, the *phainesthai* as appearing in the broad sense of the epiphany of a world" (48).

Following the lead of Heraclitus' fragment, then, Heidegger maintains that the originary struggle is prior to the appearance of humans and gods, and so cannot be thought of as the work of humans (or gods). The "disjunction of gods and humans happens only in *polemos,* in the confrontational setting-apart-from-each-other [*Aus-einander-setzung*] (of Being). Only such struggle . . . lets gods and human beings step forth in their Being" (110). But to say that originary struggle first lets humans appear on the scene is not to say that it is something that happens prior to or independent of the human altogether. Throughout his writings Heidegger always insisted that *Being* is possible only where there are humans, or Dasein.[5] In *Introduction to Metaphysics,* for example, he says that "insofar as [Being] holds sway and appears, apprehension *also* necessarily occurs *along with* appearance," and, since "human beings have a part in the happening of this appearance and apprehension, . . . they must themselves be" (106). The inextricable bond between Being and humans is evident even in Heidegger's later writings. In 1955 he wrote: "Presence ('Being') as presence is always and in each case presence to the human essence"; and again: "We always say too little about 'Being itself' when, in saying 'Being,' we leave out presence *to* the human *essence* and thereby fail to recognize that this [human] essence goes to make up [*mitausmacht*] 'Being.' "[6] If the Being of any being is inseparable from its becoming accessible *as* such and such to those beings that can be *open* to anything, namely, human beings, then *phusis* can never be thought of as something that occurs totally independent of Dasein.

Nevertheless, the *Introduction to Metaphysics* seems to imply that there is a primal articulation of Being that occurs prior to the appearance of a fully formed people with an explicit sense of who they are. Heidegger claims, for example, that original *polemos* happens in language, understanding, building and poetry, but these cannot be thought of as products of human agency: "The violence-doing of poetic saying, of thoughtful projection, of constructive building, of state-creating action, is not an application of faculties that the human being has, but is a disciplining and disposing of the violent forces by virtue of which beings disclose themselves as such, insofar as the human being enters into them" (120). This suggests that the original linguistic articulation of the Being of beings that occurs in *naming* is not carried out in a language invented by humans, for, as Heidegger asks, "How is humanity ever supposed to have invented that which pervades it in its sway [for example, language], due to which humanity itself can *be* as humanity in the first place?" (120). In other words, since language is a condition for the possibility of there being humans at all, we cannot assume that humans first appeared on the scene and then later, like the biblical Adam, invented language ex nihilo. And from this one might be tempted to conclude that there must have been a primal language that existed *before* humans appeared, and that the creative naming and preserving that occurs through the saying and works of human "creators" is something secondary and derivative.

There is an important insight here that Heidegger shares with such thinkers as Ferdinand de Saussure and Ludwig Wittgenstein,[7] namely, the awareness that, because the meaning of a word is determined by its web of relations to other words as embedded in a set of linguistic practices, and because humans are, as the Greeks saw, the "language animal" *(zōon logon echōn)*, there is no way to suppose that humans first existed and then later invented first one word, then another, and so on. To see how language emerged, then, we need to make use of something like Wittgenstein's metaphor, "Light dawns gradually over the whole."[8] This image of a dawning light seems to be what is implied by Heidegger's descriptions of the originary struggle that is prior to the appearance of humans and their explicit acts of naming. Any attempt to unpack the concept of *phusis* will have to make sense of this notion of an originary struggle that occurs before there are humans with a full-fledged sense of who they are.

3. ARTWORKS, HUMANS, AND HISTORY AS EXAMPLES OF *PHUSIS*

In this section I want to do two things. First, I want to clarify Heidegger's conception of *phusis* by examining examples he gives and by devising some examples of my own. These examples will also clarify how original struggle can be thought of as in some sense prior to the appearance of humans. Second, I want to make Heidegger's event ontology plausible by showing how it can help us make sense of important phenomena that are not easily comprehended by the traditional substance ontology.

In three public lectures delivered the same year as the *Introduction to Metaphysics* course, published as "The Origin of the Work of Art," Heidegger gives an account of works of art as exemplary forms of *phusis*. According to "The Origin of the Work of Art," a great work of art is best thought of not as an object with properties but rather as an event or happening: an emergence-into-Being that shapes and transforms a world. The event-character of the artwork is evident in the central example of this essay, the Greek temple. According to Heidegger's compelling description, the Greek temple plays the role of organizing and giving structure to the world of the people who live in its shadow. In the way it stands firmly in the ground, it makes manifest the Being of those beings surrounding it *as* the kinds of being they are: "Standing there, the building holds its ground against the storm raging above it and so first makes the storm manifest in its violence. . . . The steadfastness of the work contrasts with the surge of the surf, and its own repose brings out the raging of the sea."[9] The temple, by appearing on the scene, imparts a determinate meaning to everything around it and allows a world to shine forth in a determinate way.

The world brought about by the temple defines and illuminates the Being of beings as *phusis*, the "emerging and arising in itself and in all things" (OWA, 42). The description of the temple in the art lectures reveals that the artwork itself has the characteristics attributed to *phusis* in *Introduction to Metaphysics*. The Being of the temple consists in its emerging in an opening or clearing, its self-manifesting *(phainesthai)*. The work of art is described as an ongoing event of *appearing* that originates in a world-defining creative act and as a *becoming* that is carried forward into the future by the "preservers" who continue to define the meaning of the temple for the community.

The work also displays the characteristics of *phusis* in the way it brings about a *polemos,* or strife: it inaugurates and sustains a struggle between, on one hand, what now, thanks to the work, has measure and limits and so is determinate and focused and, on the other, what yet remains indeterminate, "not mastered, . . . concealed, confusing" (OWA, 55). Because the artwork maintains and manifests this fundamental "conflict of measure and unmeasure" (OWA, 70), it demands a *decision* from those whose Being it helps define. As Heidegger says, the temple "first gathers around itself the unity of those paths and relations in which birth and death, disaster and blessing, victory and disgrace, endurance and decline acquire the shape of destiny for [historical] human being" (OWA, 42). Yet insofar as the ultimate meaning those "paths and relations" have for a people depends on how they, as preservers, decide to interpret them, the struggle is open-ended. "As a world opens itself, it submits to the decision of an historical humanity the question of victory and defeat, blessing and curse, mastery and slavery. The dawning world brings out what is yet undecided and measureless, and thus discloses the hidden necessity of measure and decisiveness" (OWA, 63).

In his description of how the Greek temple inaugurates a struggle, Heidegger says we should not suppose that, on his account, there first were people living together, and these people one day decided to build a temple. This would be wrong because, on this view, it is the work of art that first enables humans to stand forth as having an identity of a particular sort, and so to *be* human in the full sense of that word: "Men and animals, plants and things, are never present and familiar as unchangeable objects, only to represent incidentally also a fitting environment for the temple, which one fine day is added to what is already there." Instead, "the temple, in its standing there, first gives to things their look and to men their outlook on themselves" (OWA, 42–43).

Heidegger's point is that it is only within the opening made possible by a work of art that humans can begin to experience themselves *as* such and such and so can *become* human in a determinate way. On this account, then, it would be wrong to say that humans created the temple for the same reason it is wrong to say that humans created language: if humans can come into existence and *be* humans only within the clearing opened by the work, they could not exist prior to the work. The Greeks, for example, became the Greeks they were only through the world shaped by the temple and other world-defining works of art, just as we today have the sensibilities we have in part through, for example, our encounter with Shakespeare's plays, as Harold Bloom argues in *Shakespeare: The Invention of the Human.*[10]

Heidegger's description of the dawning world that emerges into presence with the artwork helps us understand the description of originary struggle in *Introduction to Metaphysics.* In the metaphysics lectures, Heidegger describes the way a work of art "puts Being to work in a being" in such a way that, through the artwork, "everything else that appears and that we can find around us [including, Heidegger could add, our own determinate identity as humans of a particular sort] first becomes confirmed and accessible, interpretable and understandable, *as a being*" (122). Given Heidegger's story, the original, founding determination of the Being of beings in Western civilization was accomplished by the creative works of artists, thinkers, and statesmen in ancient Greece. This foundational act was the beginning of history in the Western world, and all subsequent attempts to understand the Being of beings are answerable to the "inceptive truth" of this first beginning. If we then go on to look for what was there before this founding act, we will find only inchoate, partial, and yet-unformulated interpretations embodied in the confusing array of practices of people who still lack a fully formed sense of human identity.

For example, it seems reasonable to suppose that the Greeks received their earliest sense of who they were from the epic poems of Homer. If we ask about the forms of life of the Mycenean warrior-chiefs as they actually were prior to the formulations of the relations of honor, status, bravery, duty, and fame in Homer's works, we will find that we have little basis for our speculations, since our main source of information about the period is the Homeric tradition itself. In fact, even for the Greeks, the understanding of earlier times was something they learned primarily from the Homeric sagas. So although we know that there was an articulation of beings prior to Homer's works, the nature of that original articulation is, to a great extent, shrouded in "mystery." That is why Heidegger says that the attempt to understand primal history, "if it is anything at all, . . . [is] *mythology*" (119, emphasis added)—that is, it is a matter of retrospectively reading our later, fully formed understanding of the world back into the traces of an earlier time whose actual nature is lost to us. According to Heidegger's story, then, the world-defining "creators" who appeared at the dawn of our civilization drew on the yet-indeterminate "saying" of the prehistorical world as they undertook the project of naming the beings that would henceforth *count* or *matter* for Western culture. But the originary struggle that gathered and differentiated beings before these creators appeared on the scene itself lies in darkness.

To return to the account in "The Origin of the Work of Art," Heidegger tells us that the work of art inaugurates strife or struggle in the way it takes over what has come before and gives it a form *(Gestalt)* that "transport[s] us out of the realm of the ordinary" and brings forth "a being such as never was before and never will come to be again" (OWA, 66, 62). As an exemplary instance of *phusis,* the artwork is portrayed as an event in which the very Being of the work is something that is constantly transmitted and defined anew through future generations of *preservers* who take the work up and retrieve its possibilities of meaning for new contexts. To take a contemporary example, we can see how such Alfred Hitchcock films as *Psycho* and *The Birds* led us to experience the world and ourselves differently, shaping us as people with the peculiar anxieties of modernity. We can also see how the Being of these films is preserved in the works of preservers who quote and commemorate Hitchcock's work in their own films (though not, as a rule, in remakes aimed at capitalizing on a famous name).

But even such "static" works as paintings and sculptures can be understood as events in which the Being of the work depends on those who come after and preserve the work. We can see this in the evolution of paintings of Madonna and Child scenes from the Middle Ages to today's images of motherly love, or in the regular reappearance of neoclassical styles of architecture. Here, retrieving the "inceptive truth" of the original is not a matter of revivalism, unthinking mimicry, but rather of transforming and reinterpreting the original in the light of one's current context. This conception of the artwork as *phusis,* as an unfolding, becoming, and appearing in which the Being of the work is realized and defined by future generations, has received an extended and compelling formulation in the aesthetic theories of Heidegger's student Hans-Georg Gadamer.[11]

Artworks therefore provide one powerful example of a kind of being whose Being is best thought of in terms of *phusis.* A second example of beings that exemplify the event ontology are human beings themselves. In *Introduction to Metaphysics* there is an implicit story about how humans emerge into presence in the distinction Heidegger draws between humans in general and humans who have achieved "selfhood." "Humanity first comes to itself and is a self only as questioning-historical," he writes. "The selfhood of humanity means this: it has to transform the Being that opens itself to it into history, and thus bring itself to a stand" (110). According to this account, humans in some sense existed many millennia ago, and in those prehistorical times they opened up a clearing in which beings could show up in determinate ways. But these humans only became *selves,* that is, humans in the full sense of the word, when they were able to gather together their practices and give them a coherent focus and direction—that is, a history. Heidegger pictured the focusing that makes selfhood possible in different ways in different stages of his development. In the 1920s, this self-focusing was seen as something achieved by individuals who confronted their death in such a way that they existed as a unified "running forward" toward their ownmost mortal existence ("Being-a-whole"). By the 1930s, however, this focusing and direction was seen as something to be accomplished by an entire people *(Volk):* in the *Beiträge zur Philosophie,* for example, he writes, "The question concerning the truth of Being prepares the domain of selfhood in which, historically working and acting, the human being—We—formed as a people, first come to the self."[12]

Whether humans are seen as an "I" or a "We," however, what is important is that, in Heidegger's view, humans realize their Being and become human in the fullest sense only when they transform themselves from being dispersed and unfocused to being "in each case mine" *(je meines),* where this means gathered together and oriented in a unified, coherent way. Only when they have become "selves" in this sense can they become the kind of meaningful opening in which beings can show up *as* such and such. This drawing together and focusing, according to Heidegger, is necessitated by Being: "Being, the overwhelming appearing, necessitates the gathering that pervades and grounds Being-human" (134). And, as we just saw, the bringing into focus of a coherent, unified "clearing" or "opening" occurs when the initially inchoate background of interpretations and practices handed down from earliest times is transformed into *history.*

Humans, understood in terms of their relation to Being, therefore have a dual nature. On one hand, they are agents whose modes of being make possible the clearing or context in which beings can first show up as accessible or intelligible in some way or other. On the other, they are respondents who receive an understanding of Being and have to make something of it in the questioning stand they take. "Being" here refers to what lets anything show up at all, and there can be Being in this sense only because human practices and modes of apprehending "receive the appearing of beings" (128) and in doing so let beings (including human beings, encountered *as* individuals, peoples, rational animals, or whatever) show up in determinate ways.[13]

Humans can play the role they play in disclosing beings only because their own Being is characterized by a distinctive sort of *movement*, the movement characteristic of *phusis*. In *Being and Time*, Heidegger described this movement, which is definitive of Dasein's Being, as a *Zeitigung* (from *sich zeitigen*), literally, a "coming to fruition" in which a being, emerging-into-presence, becomes what (as potentiality) it has always already been. This conception of *Zeitigung*, or "temporalizing," is, as Thomas Sheehan has pointed out, grounded in Heidegger's reading of such Greek concepts as *genesis* and *kinēsis*.[14] In *Introduction to Metaphysics* Heidegger considers how beings whose way of Being is *phusis* are thought of as having a *telos*, or end, where "end" is understood neither as the final state of a process nor as a goal external to the being but as a "completion in the sense of coming to fulfillment [*Vollendung*]," the realization of the potentiality built into that being from the outset. Because the limit *(peras)* or end for a being's unfolding is part of the Being of the entity, "limit and end are that whereby beings first begin to *be*." That which reaches its proper limit, gathering itself together and achieving a unity of shape and thereby "fulfilling" its limit, is said to have *form (morphē)* (46). Viewed as *phusis*, then, all things move toward the achievement of their proper form— they are characterized, in Aristotle's terminology, by *entelecheia*.[15]

Although Heidegger does not think that humans have either a pregiven *telos* or a final actualization, his description of a human being as an ongoing *happening* that is "*stretched along* between birth and death" (SZ, 374) draws on the conception of "moving-toward-fruition" he finds in Greek thought. The characterization of human existence as an unfolding, future-directed life story or life course is contained in Heidegger's description of Dasein as a "thrown projection." To say that a human exists as a thrown projection is to say that our lives display two basic aspects. On one hand, we find ourselves already thrown into a specific worldly context and situation, with a range of choices behind us and undertakings already begun. This aspect of "beenness" *(Gewesenheit)* is what we must take up and carry forward in our actions. On the other, to be human is to be "already ahead of oneself," under way in realizing tasks that gain their meaning from one's self-understanding as an agent in the world. Seen from this standpoint, each of our actions expresses and sketches out some overarching interpretation of what our lives are all about. To be human, on this view, is to be "futural" *(zukünftig)* in the sense that one is always "coming toward" *(zu-kommend)* some anticipated fulfillment of one's possibilities—for example, realizing one's identity as a home craftsman, as good-natured, or as gay—by taking up the resources opened up in the past in acting in the present.

For Heidegger, then, human existence is to be understood in terms of the dynamic temporal structure of "coming-to-fruition" or "temporalizing." A student, for example, is constituting her identity as a student of a particular sort in her ways of acting in the academic context that defines her thrownness. If she engages in her studies in a low-key and laid-back way, then that is the kind of identity as a student she is creating for herself, and this is so regardless of whatever intentions or plans may be in her mind. In this respect, according to Heidegger's conception of humans, you *are* what you *do*. Your identity or *Being* is defined entirely by your actions as they contribute to realizing the "end" that organizes and gives sense to your life—in the case of the student, mastering one's field and getting a degree. As Heidegger puts it, "we are [what] we were, and we will be what we receive and appropriate from what we were, and here the most important factor will be *how* we do so."[16] Note that, on this account of human existence, there is simply no role to be played by the traditional distinctions between mind and body, inner self and outer show, or intentions and physical behavior. There is no way to drive in a wedge between my ways of presenting myself in the public world and a "real me" underlying my ways of appearing in the world. Here, my *Being* just *is* my appearing.

Seen in this way, human beings clearly have the characteristics of *phusis* as described in *Introduction to Metaphysics*. The Being of *Dasein* consists in its appearing—its concrete ways of coming-into-presence—and its becoming—its ongoing movement toward the realization of its ownmost possibility of being complete. Human existence also embodies a *polemos,* or tension: so long as we are alive, we live in the tension between what is factical and therefore constraining—what we have been and now are—and what we are "not yet" insofar as we exist as a futural projection out into an open realm of possibilities. And like the beings conceived as *phusis* by the Greeks, our lives are characterized as "being-toward-the-end" or being toward (one's) completion, a conception of life's directedness Heidegger calls "Being-toward-death." As Heidegger points out, "death" here does not refer to the fact that we will all die at some future point but instead to the fact that our lives are moving toward the realization of a form, and that each of us is responsible for the form his or her life ultimately has. Where Heidegger's view of human existence differs from the Greek conception of *entelecheia* is that his notion of being-toward-the-end does not assume that there is some fixed end (for example, rational animal, citizen in the *polis*) we all have in advance solely by virtue of the fact that we are human.

Instead, on Heidegger's view, it is up to each of us to determine what our lives will amount to by taking over possibilities made accessible in the public world.

The conception of life as a movement toward wholeness provides the basis for Heidegger's conception of authentic existence. In living out our lives, Heidegger suggests, we can choose to make our lives our own *(eigen)* by seizing on what we do with resoluteness, intensity, and steadfastness, thereby imparting focus, continuity, and coherence to our life stories, or we can live in such a way that our lives are disjointed, adrift, unfocused, and anonymous. The former, "owned" mode of existence is authentic *(eigentlich)*, whereas the latter, "disowned" mode is inauthentic. An authentic existence is one that fulfills Pindar's admonition to "Become what you are."[17] This dictum, according to Heidegger, says that one should shine forth or appear as "what one originally and authentically already is: that which essentially unfolds as having been [*das Ge-Wesende*]" (77). To become what you are is to gather together and give focus to the meaningful context into which you are thrown by resolutely and clear-sightedly making something of it in all your actions, "right up to the end." On Heidegger's reading of this dictum, then, the ideal of becoming what you are is closer to Nietzsche's conception of imparting "style" to one's life than it is to the Greek ideal of realizing a specific potential with which one is born.[18]

Thinking of a human as an event or happening rather than as a substance or combination of substances has a number of advantages for making sense of familiar features of our lives. For one thing, the conception of human Being as the temporal unfolding of a life story enables us to think of our lives as narratives, with all that that implies.[19] In addition, Heidegger's characterization of human existence as an event in which "you *are* what you *do*" gives us a way of understanding human agency without relying on the traditional assumption (built into the subject-object model of our existence) that each and every action must be explained by some correlative mental event that caused it. On the view of human existence that Heidegger's event ontology provides, familiar human actions (giving someone a pat on the back) can be seen as flowing from character traits embodied in a person's entire way of life (being a kind and thoughtful person) without assuming the existence of any special mental activities or contents that caused this physical motion. This "expressivist" view of human agency (as I have called it elsewhere)[20] undercuts the confusing picture of humans as mind-matter conglomerates with peculiar causal characteristics and is more faithful to our actual, everyday phenomenological experience of human agency.

A third phenomenon that is comprehended especially well by the event ontology is history. We can appreciate the power of Heidegger's conception of history as a form of *phusis* if we contrast it with the standard view of history. According to the standard view, events have occurred in the past and they have left traces in documents and records. What we call "history" is, properly understood, a product of the work of historians. The historian sifts through the historical record and tries to devise a story about the past that is plausible and interesting. The task of selecting data and giving narrative form to the past is guided by the needs and concerns of the present. In the standard view, the historical record itself is always underdetermined as to its correct interpretation, so history is necessarily *fictive* to the extent that it involves emplotting or configuring events in a way that goes beyond anything actually given in the historical record.

Heidegger, in contrast, rejects the idea that history consists *either* of events in the past *or* of narratives constructed by historians in the present. "History is not equivalent to what is past," he says, nor is it "what is merely contemporary" (33–34). In place of the standard view, he offers a picture of history as an ongoing "happening" that embodies the same temporal structure as is found in human existence. Just as a person's life is a future-directed unfolding that draws on what has come before in making action possible in the present, history is a future-directed happening that constantly draws on what has come before in empowering the present. In Heidegger's words, "History as happening is determined from the future, takes over what has been, and acts and endures its way through the *present*" (34).

Described in this way, history is seen as having the kind of organic, self-emerging quality characteristic of *phusis*. Like human existence (and like all things the Greeks thought of as *phusis*), history is a movement toward realizing a form *(morphē)* that has been implicit in it since its inception. But to say that future-directedness determines the Being of history is not to assume that there is some sort of predestination or determinism controlling history. What it means is that history, in taking shape at its very beginnings, projects some vision of where things are going and what this history will amount to. It is then up to succeeding generations to take over the vision embodied in that sending and strive to achieve it. But such striving always involves reinterpretation and reenvisioning, so that every attempt to follow through on the historical sending not only transmits what came before but also transmutes it, redefining the historical sending for the ages yet to come while binding those future generations to what has come before.

Thus, Heidegger says that the questioning undertaken in *Introduction to Metaphysics* is historical in the sense that "it opens up the happening of human Dasein . . . to possibilities not yet asked about, to futures to come

[*Zu-künften*], and thereby also binds it back into its inception that has been, and thus sharpens and hardens it in its present" (34, translation modified). By speaking of "futures" in the plural, Heidegger makes it clear that the future-directedness of history is overdetermined in the sense that it embodies a range of possible outcomes and is therefore open to differing interpretations by those who carry it forward.

To see how history can embody a number of different meanings, consider the example of Christianity. Primitive Christianity in the first centuries pointed in a number of possible directions, and it has in fact been taken up and realized in different ways over the centuries. In our own time, the Christian message is carried forward in part in the belief in the equality of all souls before God, a belief that was preserved and made manifest in the speeches of Martin Luther King Jr. This example shows how history, by projecting commitments and ideals into the future, binds a people back into the heart of their sending or destiny as a community, and so provides a basis for meaningful choices in the present. The decisions we make in taking up the history that is handed down to us are not secondary, optional "applications" of what we receive but are instead the events that realize and define what our history is all about: "In this questioning, our Dasein is summoned to its history in the full sense of the word and is called to make a decision in it" (34). And the decisions we make determine who and what we are as participants in that history—as the responses of Americans to the civil rights movement determined their understanding of what it is to be part of a Judeo-Christian tradition.

This conception of history as a happening that embraces past, present, and future is filled out in *Introduction to Metaphysics* in terms of an account of "creators" and "preservers." As we have seen, Heidegger assumes that there is an understanding of Being that is opened up prehistorically as practices and forms of life begin to emerge and bring forth some sense of what things are all about. But the crucial event in the history of the West occurs when creators—artists, poets, thinkers, statesmen—first seize on this emerging understanding of Being and give it a coherent, focused form. It is through this creative act that "beings as such now first come into being" (47) and humans can first become "selves." In other words, it is through a crucial, world-defining creative act that things become defined *as* what they are: "the poets [at first] are *only* poets, but then are actually poets, the thinkers are *only* thinkers, but then are actually thinkers, the priests are *only* priests, but then are actually priests," and so on (117). What happens through the creative work is that *world* in the full sense of that word appears. "This becoming-a-world is authentic history, . . . the *phainesthai* as appearing in the broad sense of the epiphany of the world" (48).

Heidegger defines "world" as "the clearing of the paths of the essential guiding directions with which all decision complies" (OWA, 55). If world consists of paths and projections rather than facts and criteria, then we can see why the world can be sustained only through the decisions that are made by future generations of preservers. Only if those who follow in the footsteps of the creators maintain the original creative act through reinterpretation and revaluation can the world endure as a vital arena for human agency. This act of preserving calls for *struggle:* it is something that can be given shape only through the decisions made by future generations concerning how things are to count and what criteria are to be applicable in taking a stand with respect to the world. When such struggle fades away, the world comes to be leveled down to what is simply given: "Where struggle ceases, beings indeed do not disappear, but world turns away. . . . Beings now become just something one comes across; they are something found" (48, translation modified).

It should be obvious, then, that history provides a prime example of an entity whose Being is that of *phusis,* the emerging into Being or presencing through which something (in this case, the context in which anything can be) comes into Being. Through history, a meaningful, future-directed world arises, and on the basis of that happening humanity "first appears, that is (in the literal sense) itself comes to Being" (108). According to this account, history is an *appearing,* a *phainesthai,* in which the significance of a civilization's existence shines forth and becomes manifest *as* such and such. History is also a *becoming* in which a people can set out to "become what they are" because history itself, as a "pressing forth into its limits *(peras)*" and "striving to realize its form *(morphē)*" (see 46), provides the context in which people can find goals and directions. And, finally, it is a *polemos* or struggle to the extent that future generations have to make decisions about how this unfolding is to be carried on and brought to realization. Given this vision of history, Heidegger can say that his own aim in asking the "prior question" of metaphysics in his lectures is "to restore the historical Dasein of human beings—and this also always means our ownmost future Dasein, in the whole of the history that is allotted to us—back to the power of Being that is to be opened up originally" (32). In other words, his aim is to recover, preserve, and pass on the understanding of Being as *phusis* that "opened up originally" at the dawn of Western history.

4. THE EVENT ONTOLOGY AND THE POSSIBILITY OF TRUTH

At the start of this chapter I suggested that a full interpretation of the concept of *phusis* in *Introduction to Metaphysics* would have to explain why an account of *phusis* as the "beingness" of beings must be incomplete and potentially misleading unless it also considers "Being as such," where this is understood as the complex event of disclosing and concealing discussed in Heidegger's other works. The point is that there is a question more basic than the question about how we understand the Being of beings at any time, and that is the question of how any understanding of Being whatsoever is possible. Heidegger often calls this the question of the *truth* of Being. His view, worked out in many different ways over the years, is that an understanding of Being is possible only given an event *(Ereignis)*[21] involving the interplay of human *Dasein* and what *Introduction to Metaphysics* calls the overwhelming sway. Through this event, beings come to be disclosed in a certain light—they come forth *as* such and such within the context of a meaningful world—while at the same time other possibilities of appearing, along with the source of this disclosedness, are concealed. Given Heidegger's reading of the Greek word for truth, *alētheia,* as "unconcealment," it is possible to say that it is this event of "lighting" or "disclosing" that is *truth*. Thus, on Heidegger's view, truth at its most basic level is not a feature of propositions or judgments, that is, it is not a matter of correctness or of correspondence, as we normally suppose. Instead, truth is first and foremost the enabling condition that lets things show up at all: *that* they can become manifest or appear within a world.

This is why Heidegger can say, as we saw earlier, that "beings as beings are true" (78). If truth is understood as the disclosing that lets beings shine forth *as* such and such, then truth must reside at a basic level in the beings that show up in that disclosure. And, as a matter of fact, this way of thinking and talking is deeply ingrained in our historical language. We speak of "true gold" or a "true friend" and mean by such expressions that these things really *are* what they present themselves as being. A true friend, for example, is someone whose avowals and actions at any time turn out to be consistent with his or her ways of being over the course of a lifetime. Similarly, when we admire people for "being true to their principles," we mean that their ways of manifesting themselves at any time accord with their life-long commitments. Here, of course, Being is not something other than presentation or appearing; rather, it *is* appearing in a certain way. As a result, Heidegger says that Being is appearing and that seeming (as a shining forth, *Schein*) is a mode of manifestation of Being. To say that seeming is deceptive when it "disguises itself . . . inasmuch as it shows itself as Being" (83, translation modified), then, is to say that one way seeming leads us astray is when what shows up in some context fobs itself off as the only way things can appear—for example, the way beings in the modern world show up as objects.

On Heidegger's view, then, truth at its most basic level just is the way beings show up in the world. The prevailing conception of truth as a relation between beliefs and facts—truth as "correctness," the *adaequatio intellectus et rei*—is regarded as derivative from the more primordial truth expressed in the idea of a "true *X*." Since there are different ways things can show up in different contexts, truth can take different forms at different times and relative to different interests and concerns. "Being is strewn into the manifold of beings," Heidegger writes, and these beings, "as what appears, . . . give themselves an aspect" (78, translation modified). Because they can presumably give themselves different aspects under different conditions, Heidegger can say that things "stand in different truths."[22] We can see what this means by considering a humdrum example. You might see a field of flowers one moment as a scene of great romantic beauty, the next moment as a balanced ecological system, and a moment later as a potential source of money if you can sell the flowers. Each of these aspects the flowers present in our world is true in a straightforward sense, and there is no a priori reason to say that any one of these aspects is "truer" than the others. Until recently, most people would have seen the same field of flowers as a wonderful display of God's creation, or perhaps as an omen or as a source of magic potions. On Heidegger's account, as I understand it, these ways of taking the flowers were also true, though they are no longer true for many of us today.

The upshot of Heidegger's account of truth seems to be as follows: Truth at the most basic level is a disclosing, the result of a pas de deux between human Dasein and Being (where, in this context, "Being" is thought of as a previous manifestation of *polemos* that is circulating in the world at a particular time). Beings that show up in this disclosure are true in a secondary but related sense: they manifest the Being disclosed in the event of unconcealment. Since there are innumerable ways Being can be disclosed throughout the course of history and in different cultures, and since there are no restrictions on the ways a disclosure of Being at any given time might present different aspects (that is, no features of some brute, uninterpreted "thing-in-itself" that compel us to interpret things one way rather than another), it follows that there can be many truths, with no master truths or criteria that are better or "truer" than others.

The problem with this account of truth (as Ernst Tugendhat pointed out years ago) is that it has trouble accounting for the fact that the concept "true" gains its meaning from its contrast with the concept "false," so that the application of both concepts must be clear for either to be meaningful.[23] Throughout his writings Heidegger tried to explicate the contrasting term to "true" through his discussions of "being in untruth," "erring," and "concealedness."[24] But these discussions still seem to suggest that, for Heidegger, a number of logically incompatible ways of taking beings can all count as "true," whereas no particular way of taking things can be thought of as "truer" or more in touch with reality-as-it-is-in-itself than the others. As a consequence, Heidegger has been accused of being an antirealist and a pernicious relativist.

I believe that Heidegger was never an antirealist and that the "relativism" he embraces is the fairly harmless sort that anyone who is not in the thrall of some dogma would accept. Heidegger's position becomes clearer if we consider his example of the way a city appears from different lines of sight. "A city offers a grand vista. The view that a being has in itself, and so first can offer from itself, then lets it be apprehended at this or that time, from this or that viewpoint" (79). The city, like anything else, can show up for us only from some "perspective" or point of view (89). And, "the vista that offers itself alters with each new viewpoint" (79). To make this example precise, think of the different ways we can apprehend New York City. From a distance, from a scenic overlook on the Palisades perhaps, we can see the skyline of the city and experience its grandeur and beauty. Coming into the city, we begin to experience a messy array of neighborhoods and scenes, some of them frightening and ugly. We may watch the evening news and hear about the crime rates, homelessness, porno shops, drug abuse, racial tension, and so on. Suddenly the city looks unpleasant and repelling. We buy some city maps and discover the grid of streets and avenues, get a sense of the variety of parks, get a handle on the subway routes. Perhaps we take a helicopter ride and see the city's rooftops and breathtaking canyons. We spend some time with friends in a neighborhood and begin to feel the human warmth and vitality there.

These various views of the city all reveal different aspects of New York. Are the aspects commensurable in the sense that they can be added together to get one comprehensive, consistent overview? Perhaps not. How can the pervasive horrors of homelessness and ghetto living be made commensurate with neighborly warmth and the majesty of skyscrapers? And what system of calibration would enable us to undertake the task of commensurating street grids, historical records, crack houses, and the experience of a night on the town into a comprehensive, unified picture?

The fact that we can only get at incommensurable aspects or perspectives of the city might suggest that we can never really see the city itself. It is as if we are seeing slides of the city on a screen rather than the city. But surely this suggestion is absurd. When we see different aspects of New York, we are not seeing something *other* than New York, and we are certainly not seeing something that exists only in our heads. We are seeing *the city*. Aspects are not in any sense subjective: as Heidegger points out, "we must guard ourselves against cavalierly taking seeming as something just 'imaginary,' 'subjective,' and thereby falsifying it. Instead, just as appearing belongs to beings themselves, so does seeming" (80). It is New York City that shines forth and manifests itself as crime city and the city of romance and the heart attack capital of the world and . . .

It still seems that one might ask, What are these different aspects aspects *of?* Isn't there an ultimate level of reality that these different seemings display from different angles? Perhaps the ultimate molecular or atomic makeup of the city? Heidegger points out that there is no reason to assume such a thing, for even presumed facts are ultimately just aspects among others. Thus, he claims that there is no reason to think that the way the sun appears as it rises and sets is just an epiphenomenon of some true, ultimate state of reality underlying and distinct from those appearances: "The seeming in which sun and Earth stand— for example, the early morning of a landscape, the sea in the evening, the night—is an appearing. This seeming is not nothing. Neither is it untrue. Neither is it a mere appearance of relationships that *in nature* are really otherwise" (80, emphasis added). The distinction made in science (and rooted in the history of metaphysics) between surface appearance and underlying structure, between super- and base-structures, is, on Heidegger's view, valid only relative to a particular point of view and set of interests and has no privileged status in showing us how to understand "reality as it is in itself." The "facts" discovered by science are, in the end, aspects, perspectives, modes of seeming, and "this seeming is historical, and it is history, . . . and thus an essential domain of our world" (80). According to this view, history opens up "essential domains" for us, with the result that we gain access to different dimensions of beings, but there is no point to trying to ground these different modes of manifestation in some ultimate, perspective-free reality.

Heidegger's discussions of the city and the sun show how he is able to embrace a full-blooded realism about the world while holding to a plausible view of the relativity of what shows up in that world. Such a standpoint most likely will not satisfy those who think that if we want to grasp reality as it is "in itself" we must understand what it would be like if there were no humans in the universe. Those who seek such an "absolute conception of the world"[25] assume that insofar as such things as colors and sounds are "merely appearances," things that exist only in the minds of perceivers, we can get an idea of what is *really* out there in the world only if we can conceive of the world as it would be if there were no perceivers, in other words, without humans. In reply, Heidegger might ask what reason we have to suppose that a conception of the way the world would be without humans is in any way more in touch with "reality" than a conception of the world in which there are humans. After all, humans *are* in the universe, and what we call "reality" just is the reality in which humans play their distinctive role. The desire to know what the world would be like without humans starts to look as academic as the desire to know what the world would be like without Planck's constant—or, indeed, without rubber bands.

If Heideggerian realism and relativism are to be worked out in detail, we will need to give an account of the distinction between truth and falsity in the ordinary sense of those words. I suspect that such an account will be done in terms of an account of the practices of testing and validating truth-claims that have emerged in our history. What remains unclear in this way of understanding Heidegger's views is how he would respond to the standard reflexive objection against relativism: If everything is relative, what about this claim itself? Is it also relative? And critical questions can also be directed at the event ontology that underlies this view. One might ask: How are we to justify the understanding of Being that is drawn from *phusis?* Are there any reasons (other than pragmatic reasons) for saying that the event ontology is superior to the substance ontology it is supposed to supplant? These are, I believe, the most pressing questions that need to be answered by anyone who believes that there is something fundamentally right about the metaphysical views that emerge from *Introduction to Metaphysics.*

Chapter 4

THE QUESTION OF NOTHING

RICHARD POLT

> The *Being that is Himself* created Nothing,
> and rested, as He well deserved;
> then day had night, and company
> had man in the absence of the loved.
> *Fiat umbra!* Human thought began.
> And it raised the empty, universal egg,
> now insubstantial, colorless and cold,
> full of weightless vapor, in its hand.
> Take the zero whole, the hollow sphere,
> which you must view upright if you are to see it.
> Today that your beast's back can stand erect,
> and the miracle of nonbeing is complete,
> dedicate, poet, a song of the frontier
> to silence, to oblivion and to death.
>
> —Antonio Machado, "Al Gran Cero"

Why are there beings at all instead of nothing?

This striking question opens *Introduction to Metaphysics* as it had closed "What is Metaphysics?" in 1929.[1] It expresses the wonder that generates the Western metaphysical tradition. But instead of accounting for beings in the traditional way by categorizing them and identifying their first cause, Heidegger uses this "why-question" to indicate what he calls the "prior question": "How does it stand with Being?" (25).

What is this vague prior question inquiring into? First, it is an attempt to understand *what it means for beings to be;* it is a search for what distinguishes that which is from that which is not. Being, in this sense, is what characterizes beings as such. The *Introduction to Metaphysics* refers to this as "beingness," *Seiendheit* (23–24), but in other texts Heidegger dismisses beingness as an inadequate traditional concept.[2] So we need a broader term that will refer clearly to Being as what it means for beings to be, without restricting this meaning to traditional beingness; for this purpose I will use the expression "the Being of beings."

A second inquiry is also included in the question "How does it stand with Being?": Heidegger wants to think about the "fundamental happening" (153) that first *enables us to have access* to the Being of beings and thus makes it possible for beings to display themselves as such. This happening is what Heidegger's *Contributions to Philosophy* (1936–1938) would soon call the event of appropriation or "enowning" *(Ereignis)* and would also designate with the old-fashioned spelling *Seyn,* as opposed to mere *Sein* in the sense of the Being of beings.[3] I will render *Seyn* as "Be-ing."[4] Although the distinction between Be-ing and the Being of beings is not clearly drawn in *Introduction to Metaphysics,* we need to introduce this distinction in order to follow the text, for many parts of it are clearly designed to spur us into confronting the question of Be-ing. For instance, Heidegger wants us to be puzzled about how we have access to the Being of beings (23–27), and he suggests that logic cannot provide this access (92–93).

For Heidegger, our access to the Being of beings is what makes us properly human: that is, it enables us to be Dasein, or the entity for whom beings as such have significance. There can thus be no Dasein without Be-ing—and likewise, Be-ing cannot happen without Dasein (that is, the Being of beings cannot become accessible unless there is someone *to whom* it becomes accessible).[5] This means that the inquiry into Be-ing is not just a disinterested contemplation of beings in general but an inquiry into *ourselves.* "How does it stand with Being?"—taken as an inquiry into Be-ing—asks how *we* stand as Dasein. How do we have access to the Being of beings? Do we even have such access anymore? Are we standing properly at all? According to Heidegger, "*we are staggering*" (154). We are absorbed in beings but no longer engage with the Being of beings responsively and creatively (28). *Introduction to Metaphysics* thus attempts a diagnosis of the ontological palsy that has stricken us.

Throughout this ambitious project, "nothing" plays a crucial role. The "why-question" asks why there are beings instead of *nothing.* The "prior question," as we have interpreted it, inquires into our ability to distinguish beings from *nothing.* In fact, Heidegger's lectures take every opportunity to interweave the question of Being with the question of Nothing *(das Nichts).*[6]

Heidegger's talk of Nothing has provoked a wide variety of reactions.[7] But what *is* Nothing? Our answer will fall short if we take the word "nothing" out of context and let our reactions be determined by the connotations it has for us personally or by a preestablished logical system. Heidegger's discussions of Nothing must be understood not only within their immediate contexts but in relation to the entire history of metaphysics.

This chapter, then, tries to lay the foundation for an adequate interpretation of Heidegger's "Nothing." First, I review some other thinkers' treatments of Nothing and of the question, "Why is there something instead of nothing?" (sections 1 and 2). Heidegger himself refers to many of these views, and others provide illuminating parallels or contrasts to his approach. This brief survey will raise our major questions. Does Nothing actually play a role either in the Being of beings or in Be-ing? How are we to understand it? Should we accept or even embrace Nothing? Or would this be nihilistic, absurd, or evil?

Section 3 turns to Heidegger's own writings and shows that although he uses the term "Nothing" in various ways, these usages cohere around what we can call the *temporal finitude* of Dasein and Be-ing. We must remember from the start that Dasein and Be-ing are always interdependent for Heidegger: Dasein is the being who has access to the Being of beings, and Be-ing is the happening that enables Dasein to have such access. The finitude we are discussing, then, will always characterize both Dasein and Be-ing, even though Heidegger focuses primarily on Dasein's finitude in his earlier work and primarily on the finitude of Be-ing in his later work.[8]

The finitude of Be-ing and Dasein could be described in *negative* terms as the absence of a final ground. No entity is manifest to us as a supreme, fundamental entity. No absolute certainty is available to us. Thus, we have no unshakable ontological or epistemological ground for our understanding of the Being of beings—including the significance of our own existence. Thus Heidegger often describes our condition in terms of a groundless abyss *(Abgrund)*. This lack of ground implies a lack of perfect insight and self-sufficiency on our part, as well as a lack of stability and necessity in Be-ing.

These "lacks," however, are actually *positive* phenomena—indispensable and enabling features of the human condition. As Antonio Machado suggests in his poem, properly human existence and thought *require* the absence of complete perfection and fullness. For Heidegger, this is the case because we are radically *temporal,* enmeshed in a past that we cannot change and a future that is subject to death. Temporality is finite: that is, it excludes final grounds. But temporal finitude does allow us to exist and does give us access to beings, albeit in a finite way. Without temporal finitude, we could not be Dasein—and in turn, Be-ing could not happen. Respecting Nothing, then, does not mean falling prey to nihilism, but allowing Dasein and Be-ing to come into their own.

Section 4 reads the passages on Nothing in *Introduction to Metaphysics* in these terms. Throughout the text, Heidegger hints at the position I have just summed up and implies various criticisms of traditional interpretations of Nothing.

Section 5 assesses *Introduction to Metaphysics* as a whole and closes by considering Heidegger's own critiques of his lecture course.

1. THE HISTORY OF NOTHING

As Heidegger says, "The question about what is not and about Nothing has gone side by side with the question of what is, since its inception" (18). A thorough history of the topic would require a thorough history of philosophy itself.[9] What we can do here is provide a few pointers to the major discussions of Nothing in Western thought, as well as in some domains of Eastern thought that may have inspired Heidegger.

Western metaphysics can be read as the story of the gradual and partial vindication of Nothing in the face of Parmenides' rejection of it. Leaving behind his stark dichotomy between being and nonbeing, Plato and Aristotle reached an understanding of their interpenetration. In medieval thought, the question of Nothing is applied to the relation between creation and God. With Hegel, Kierkegaard, and Nietzsche, negativity and nihilism become defining possibilities for human life and consciousness, which must be acknowledged before they can be overcome. Within this story, we can discern several competing interpretations of Nothing, including Nothing as insubstantiality, negation, otherness, and meaninglessness.

"The first way [says] *is*, and *not-Being is not;* this is the way of persuasion."[10] Parmenides' poem, which inaugurates Western thinking about Nothing, immediately presents us with difficulties. First, is Parmenides speaking on behalf of that which is, or of Being? His favored expression, *to eon*, can have either meaning.[11] I will thus use the similarly ambiguous word "being" to translate *to eon*, as well as its ambiguous counterparts in later thought. The same puzzle affects the opposite of being.[12] This unclarity about the difference between *that which is not* and *not-Being* persists in later philosophy. Despite these ambiguities, clearly Parmenides affirms that being is, and nonbeing is not. This ultimate tautology constitutes a command to *think* the same as being, and even to *be* the same as being in one's own thinking.[13] In turn, thought must repel nonbeing, precisely because nonbeing repels thought: its darkness and untruth can be named only in a gesture of rejection. Since there is only being, there is no becoming, no emergence from or return to nonbeing. There is no multiplicity, no otherness by which one thing would *not be* something else. There is only the "well-rounded sphere" (fr. 8). Parmenides' rejection of nonbeing is thus a way of establishing the meaning of the Being of beings: to be is to be fully present and whole, self-sufficient, untouched by temporality and multiplicity.

Parmenides' pre-Socratic successors widely accept his principle that *what is* can neither come from nor become *what is not.*[14] Some try to reconcile this principle with change by conceiving of motion as a rearrangement of indestructible elements. The atomists save motion by affirming that nonbeing *is:* there are both indestructible atoms and *void.* (Here, "nonbeing" means the absence of solid, stable matter.)

The sophists did not neglect Nothing either: Gorgias makes the outrageous argument that there is neither being nor nonbeing—and even if there were something, it could be neither known nor expressed (fr. 3). A speech that tempts the audience to entertain this supreme paradox is truly a supreme rhetorical achievement.

It was sophistry that provoked Plato's extended meditation on nonbeing. Sophistical or false statements refer to *what is not,* but referring to nothing means not referring at all—so falsehood seems impossible (*Sophist* 237a). In order to get around this paradox, Plato's Eleatic Stranger must contradict Parmenides: nonbeing *is,* in the sense that each being *is other than* what it is not (258b). We must invite nonbeing, the ultimate stranger, into being, so that being may allow for truth and falsehood, connection and differentiation.[15]

Aristotle rejects Plato's reduction of nonbeing to otherness and falsehood (*Met.* N 2, 1089a 20–26) but takes up Plato's insight into the complexity of being. Aristotelian being is an interrelated multiplicity.[16] First, being divides into the predications, or categories: to be is to be a substance (an independent individual), to be something "said of" a substance (a species), or to be something "present in" a substance (a quality, quantity, and so on) (*Cat.* 2, 5). Furthermore, being can mean truth or actuality (*Met.* Δ 7). Just as being is "said in many ways," so is nonbeing: it can be applied in all the categories, and it also means falsehood or potentiality.[17] Aristotle does not *reject* potentiality, however: although it is not fully present, it has some being. Without potentiality, there could be no change, and thus there could be no nature at all.[18] Aristotle's concept of substance preserves some basic characteristics of Parmenides' being: actuality, endurance, unity, and self-sufficiency. For Heidegger, this substance ontology will prove inadequate for understanding our own existence, which is characterized by temporal finitude. Still, Aristotle's respect for the phenomena led him to an inclusive and nuanced account of what it means to be and not to be.

Hellenistic and medieval developments of Platonic and Aristotelian metaphysics generate new controversies that we cannot examine in detail. Typically, medieval thinkers interpret Nothing as nonsubstantiality—a lack of perfect self-sufficiency. This can be either a total absence of substances *(nihil negativum)* or a flaw or defect by which a substance falls short of fulfilling its essence *(nihil privativum).*[19] God, the most substantial substance, creates the world *ex nihilo (negativo)* and establishes the great chain of being, stretching from his full presence to complete absence. Finite creation thus stands between infinite perfection and Nothing.[20] Evil, then, is simply a *nihil privativum*—the absence of perfection that characterizes creatures as such—so we cannot even properly say that evil *is.*[21]

A dissident strain of medieval thought, beginning with Pseudo-Dionysius, *identifies* God with Nothing, for God incomprehensibly exceeds all created beings, and even (like the good and the One, in neo-Platonism) lies beyond being.[22] For negative theology, God is a Nothing "by excess," not "by default." Mystics such as Meister Eckhart seek to join God by aiming at "a pure Nothing."[23]

Most early modern philosophers avoid original speculation on Nothing, perhaps because of their distaste for both Scholasticism and mysticism. When Descartes writes, "I am . . . between supreme being and nonbeing,"[24] he merely borrows, perhaps insincerely, from the standard medieval scheme. (Pascal, however, invests a similar thought with genuine pathos when he describes man as suspended between "these two abysses of infinity and Nothing.")[25] Spinoza echoes Plato in his principle that "determination is negation": to be *thus* is not to be *otherwise.*[26]

Kant uses his categories in combination with Scholastic terminology to distinguish four meanings of "nothing."[27] In general, if an object is not or cannot be perceived, it is nothing. Since noumena (things in themselves) by definition cannot enter experience, Kant includes them as an example of nothing (A290/B347). He does not intend to deny, however, that noumena *exist* (Bxxvi). The question of Nothing is thus bound up with the problematic status of the noumenon in Kant.

Kant's successors give Nothing a much more prominent place. Romanticism introduces a new fascination with the idea that life is pervaded by Nothing.[28] At the same time, the renewal of metaphysical speculation in German idealism revives the problem of nonbeing. The closest antecedents of Heidegger's Nothing are to be found in nineteenth-century thought.

Hegel adopts Plato's concept of nonbeing as negativity and Spinoza's principle that all determination is negation: for Hegel, negativity develops consciousness and reality by introducing differentiation. Negativity drives the dialectical process of self-knowledge and self-fulfillment.[29] This negativity is not an indeterminate, empty Nothing but a determinate negation that moves us beyond both abstract Nothing and abstract Being.[30] Actuality begins only when Being and Nothing are overcome and absorbed in becoming and in the further concepts that develop dialectically from there.

For Hegel, dialectic is not a debater's technique but the mode in which the whole unfolds itself. Negativity thus includes not only theoretical disagreements but also war, pain, desire, labor, and love. In Hegel's thought, the question of Nothing takes on flesh and blood. Consider his description of the slave's fear of death: "this consciousness has been fearful, not of this or that particular thing or just at odd moments, but its whole being has been seized with dread [Angst] . . . [E]verything solid and stable has been shaken to its foundations. But this pure universal movement, the melting-away of everything stable, is the simple, essential nature of self-consciousness, absolute negativity."[31] This radical negation is an abyss that must be crossed on the way to self-knowledge.

Kierkegaard's *The Concept of Dread* is an extension of this Hegelian thought. Kierkegaard finds dread lurking not only in terror but in innocence: "In this state there is peace and repose; but at the same time there is something different . . . . What is it then? Nothing? But what effect does Nothing produce? It begets dread. . . . [L]anguage in this instance is also pregnant: it speaks of being in dread of Nothing."[32]

As an experience of meaninglessness, the phenomenon of *Angst* is closely related to nihilism. The word "nihilism" as a term of abuse goes back at least to the late eighteenth century,[33] and as a political position it goes back to mid-nineteenth-century Russian radicalism. With Nietzsche, nihilism takes center stage in philosophy. Nietzsche defines nihilism as a condition in which the highest values devalue themselves: life loses meaning.[34] Like the slave's *Angst* as conceived by Hegel, for Nietzsche nihilism is a crisis that can be a turning point. It marks the end of a history of self-deception and of a metaphysics that confuses what is with what is not. "The distinguishing marks which have been given to the 'true Being' of things are the distinguishing marks of not-Being, of Nothing—the 'true world' has been constructed by contradicting the actual world."[35] Nietzsche thus rejects the traditional ontology of substance in favor of the play of power and appearance. The very concept of Being is merely "the final wisp of evaporating reality."[36] In short, Nietzsche wants to overcome nihilism by reversing the Parmenidean scheme: change, plurality, and appearance are not nothing but rather reality; permanence, self-sufficiency, and unity are pious illusions.

We cannot review all twentieth-century thought about Nothing, but we must mention the view, widespread in analytic philosophy, that the "problems of nonbeing" are unfortunate confusions due to the peculiarities of Indo-European languages. Under the scrutiny of symbolic logic, the pseudo-problems disappear.[37] The flaw in this position is that our linguistics and logic, as Heidegger suggests, may merely be calcified remnants of the very tradition we are trying to criticize.[38]

Now we turn briefly to Eastern thought. Some have proposed that Heidegger borrowed extensively from Asian sources in his use of "Nothing."[39] In my opinion, the evidence does not support this strong conclusion. Heidegger did know some Taoist and Buddhist texts, however, and clearly he found them provocative. He himself suggests that the Buddhist notion of emptiness explains the warm reception that his thought found in Japan.[40] These are good reasons to look toward the East.

In crude terms, whereas Western metaphysics is periodically drawn to a Parmenidean concept of the Being of beings as permanence and self-sufficiency, Eastern thought is more open to transience and interdependence—phenomena often relegated to the realm of Nothing. A closer look, however, reveals that Nothing has been a topic of controversy in both traditions. In the West, as we have seen, many thinkers resist Parmenides. In the East, Hinduism has tended to promote a somewhat Parmenidean position through the concepts of *atman* (absolute self) and *brahman* (absolute being).[41] Buddhist "emptiness" is a direct rejection of these Hindu concepts and is thus indebted to them to a certain extent. Similarly, Taoist "nonaction" rejects the supposed rigidity of Confucianism.

The notion of *shunyata* (emptiness) is important to all sects of Buddhism.[42] Generally, it indicates an absence of "self-nature" or "self-Being" *(svabhava)*—that is, permanence and substantiality. The Mahayana schools apply this notion not only to the human ego but to all *dharmas*, or constituents of things. In Nagarjuna's influential interpretation, emptiness implies that we cannot claim either that things are or that they are not. The Mahamudra and Dzogchen schools give a more "positive" interpretation to emptiness, understanding it as an "openness" or luminosity—a suggestive notion for Heideggerians.

Taoism, too, is imbued with an appreciation for emptiness. In the *Tao Te Ching*, "Nothing" *(wu)* is associated with "nonaction" *(wu wei)*.[43] A jug cannot function without a void (chap. 11), and in general, presence needs absence: "The ten thousand things are born of being [*yu*]; being is born of Nothing" (chap. 40). Nonaction is the highest form of action, because it lets things follow their own way. To comply with the way of things, including the absence that enables them to be present, is the most effective relation to the world (chap. 48).[44]

We have seen that in both East and West, the question of Nothing forms part of the question of Being. But this question has at least two dimensions. First, it can be taken as a search for the Being of beings—what it means for beings to be. What *is* is often understood in terms of unity, permanence, self-sufficiency, and actuality. What *is not* is devoid of these features. For Parmenides, this makes nonbeing unspeakable and unthinkable. But most thinkers recognize that the reality we know—including the reality of our own existence—involves at least *some* multiplicity, change, interdependence, and potentiality. Metaphysics seeks the key to this interlaced structure of what is and what is not. For much of Western thought, the key is the concept of substance; however, if (as Nietzsche and the Buddhists suggest) the ontology of substance is merely a construct, a result of wishful thinking, then perhaps we need a radically insubstantial concept of beings as such.

The second dimension of the question of Being concerns us human beings more directly: how is it that we have access in the first place to what it means to be and not to be? This, in Heidegger's terms, is the problem of Be-ing. Although few thinkers raise this question explicitly, all assume some kind of answer to it. Some take propositional thought and logic as the key to the Being of beings and to Nothing; others, particularly when it comes to Nothing, prefer a nonintellectual relation, such as *Gelassenheit, Angst, wu wei,* or Buddhist meditation. These fundamental moods and practices seem to display Nothing—as a blissful illumination for some, a dreadful abyss for others.

The history of Nothing, then, leaves Heidegger with a rich tradition on which to draw, as well as two major questions: What are the basic traits of beings and nonbeings, and how do we gain access to the Being of beings?

2. THE ULTIMATE "WHY?"

The tradition also offers a third question: Why is there something instead of nothing? This question occupies an ambiguous position that cannot be reduced to the first two.

It may seem that the "nothing" in the why-question is reducible to "not anything" and that the question could be shortened to "Why is there something?" As Heidegger points out, however, the addition "instead of nothing" urges us to consider an alternative to beings as a whole (21–23). When we try to conceive of this alternative, we are led into the questions we listed at the end of section 1. All the problems of Nothing, then, lurk in the background of the why-question. The question has usually been developed in a different direction, however, involving questions of grounding and reason.

The why-question was formulated remarkably late. Creation myths describe a primordial act or event but do not ask why there are any acts or events in the first place. The Greek philosophers' search for the "first principles and causes" of beings, as Aristotle puts it (*Met.* A 2), generally remains *within* the realm of beings as a whole, taking their presence for granted. The medievals implicitly answer the why-question by reflecting on God as the creator whose existence is necessary. But it seems that the question was not raised *explicitly* until Leibniz.

For Leibniz, the question flows directly from the principle of sufficient reason, which he was also the first to articulate. *Nihil est sine ratione:* there is a sufficient reason why everything is rather than is not, and is as it is rather than otherwise.[45] Since the principle applies to all beings, we must ask why there is anything at all. In response, Leibniz establishes the necessary, eternal existence of God and then explains the existence of our universe in terms of God's goodness: as the best being, God creates the best of all possible worlds.[46]

From Kant's perspective, such arguments are quintessential misuses of pure reason. The search for grounds builds useful scientific systems as long as it is kept within the bounds of possible experience; however, when we search for an *unconditioned* ground, an explanation for the totality, we exceed possible experience and fall into dialectical illusion (*Critique of Pure Reason,* A308–309/ B365–366).

It is a mark of Schelling's deliberate rejection of Kant's critical philosophy that he resuscitates Leibniz's question and struggles with it perhaps more intensely than any other thinker has. In the various drafts of the unfinished *Ages of the World* (1811–1815), Schelling's goal is to grasp the origin of finite beings without simply explaining away the mystery of their givenness or "Being"—"this incomprehensibility, this active resistance to all thinking, this effectual darkness, this positive inclination to obscurity. [Previous philosophy] would have preferred to get rid of the uncomfortable altogether, to dissolve the unintelligible completely into understanding or (like Leibniz) into representation."[47] Schelling tries to grasp Nothing as "neither what is nor what is not, but only the eternal freedom to be" or as "the will that wills nothing."[48]

The why-question also surfaces in a surprisingly wide range of twentieth-century philosophy. One might expect that pragmatism would have no use for this conundrum, that analytic philosophy would dissolve it, and that traditional phenomenology would rigorously avoid it. (The why-question is an egregious violation of the Husserlian *epoché:* instead of bracketing existence and describing phenomena, it demands an ultimate explanation for all that exists.) But the question has in fact been taken seriously by pragmatists,[49] phenomenologists,[50] and analytic philosophers.[51] Interesting discussions of the theme can be found in Bergson,[52] Wittgenstein,[53] and Scheler—whom Heidegger admired. Scheler argues that the first of all insights is the recognition "that *there is not nothing.*"[54]

Finally, there are recurrent attempts to treat this metaphysical question as a physical one by confusing it with the empirical (though very difficult) question of how the observable universe began. This confusion leads to the so-called problem of initial conditions: "The laws of physics generally describe how a physical system develops from some initial state. But any theory that explains how the universe began must involve a radically different kind of law, one that explains the initial state itself."[55] Even if we established such a law, we would then be faced with the question of why *this* law is at work—for we can readily conceive that there could be a different law, or none at all. A formula cannot explain why there is something instead of nothing any better than a creation myth can; formulas merely describe patterns of behavior in beings.

Where does the why-question leave us? Traditionally, it either inaugurates a bold search for a first cause or is rejected because it tries to find causes where none can be found. But perhaps, if we set aside the problem of whether the question can be answered and listen to the question *itself,* it can open up a space in which we appreciate the gift of beings. After we stop taking beings for granted, and before we subordinate them to a supreme entity, act, or law that grants them, the why-question insists that we pay heed to the granting as such. The why-question can then become an act of gratitude, as well as a fresh opportunity to ask both the questions we listed at the end of section 1: what distinguishes what is from what is not, and how do we have access to the Being of beings?

3. HEIDEGGER'S NOTHINGS

By now we can see that when he speaks of Nothing, Heidegger is hardly inventing a new mode of speaking. He is drawing on a sometimes neglected aspect of a rich tradition in order to provoke us into questioning. What, then, does he mean by "Nothing"?

The question cannot be answered so simply, for Heidegger uses the expression tactically rather than strategically: it serves various functions for him in various contexts throughout his philosophical career.[56] A selective review of these contexts will allow us to weave together the various meanings of "Nothing." We will find that the central phenomenon is the *temporal finitude* of Dasein and Be-ing: our own subjection to mortality and contingency enables beings to acquire a fragile meaning for us in a contingent way, in the absence of final grounds.

As early as 1921–1922, Heidegger uses "Nothing" and "nihilation" *(Nichtung)* to indicate several aspects of ruination (*Ruinanz,* a term later replaced by "falling"). These include "the Nothing of historical eventlessness [*Ereignislosigkeit*], the Nothing of the lack of success, the Nothing of the lack of prospects, the Nothing of hopelessness" (GA 61, 146). The fundamental phenomenon can be defined formally as a "*not-coming-forth*" of Dasein (GA 61, 148). An insidious self-concealment inhabits everyday existence and must be combated by philosophy (GA 61, 153).

Being and Time interprets this self-concealment as inauthenticity *(Uneigentlichkeit)*. In contrast to 1921–1922, "Nothing" and "nullity" *(Nichtigkeit)* are now invoked to describe *revelatory* experiences (anxiety and the call of conscience) and the basic traits of Dasein that they display (death and guilt). These phenomena can still be seen as *lacks,* as signs of finitude; but it is clear that the proper response to this finitude is not to overcome it but to recognize it as such.

Following Hegel and Kierkegaard, Heidegger holds that *Angst* is not about any particular beings within the world—it is about nothing, or rather, Nothing. "Nothing" here means the world itself and Dasein's own existence as Being-in-the-world (SZ, 187).[57] Anxiety reveals Being-in-the-world as uncanny, or not-at-home (SZ, 188–189). At this moment the world is disclosed as meaningless, "and this insignificance manifests the nullity of that with which one can concern oneself—or, in other words, the impossibility of projecting oneself upon a potentiality-for-Being . . . which is founded primarily upon one's objects of concern" (SZ, 343). In anxiety we recognize that we cannot base our identities on any of the familiar things and acts on which we normally rely. All beings fade into irrelevance when one is faced with a genuine need to decide who one is.

Anxiety also manifests "the Nothing of the possible impossibility of [Dasein's] existence" (SZ, 266). This is the definition of "death" (SZ, 262) in the Heideggerian sense, which would more accurately be called "mortality." Death is a possibility that casts a shadow on our every choice, reminding us that it may be our last and investing our decisions with gravity. Dasein's wholeness does not consist in *eliminating* this possibility of death but in facing up to it clear-sightedly. This finitude is not a *nihil privativum* that holds Dasein back from full actuality, as an ontology of substance might suggest; instead, for Dasein, possibility is *higher* than actuality. Dasein authentically becomes itself only when it accepts and holds open the finitude of its potentiality (SZ, 262).

Conscience, according to Heidegger, speaks by remaining silent: it says nothing (SZ, 273). This is appropriate, because the caller of conscience is "Dasein in its uncanniness . . . the bare 'that-it-is' in the Nothing of the world" (SZ, 276–277). Conscience reveals guilt, which consists in the fact that Dasein has *not* laid the foundation for its own existence, has *not* devoted itself to itself, and is *not* possibilities other than the one it has chosen (SZ, 284–285). This indicates that care (Dasein's Being) is "*permeated with nullity*" (SZ, 285). Here, nullity is the finitude that accompanies our indebtedness to our past and our responsibility for our future.

To sum up, according to *Being and Time*, each of the three dimensions (or "ecstases," SZ, §65) of temporality is finite in a way that Heidegger describes in terms of Nothing or nullity. The past is finite in that it has thrown us into a particular configuration of facticity that cannot be unmade: we are *situated*. The present is finite in that none of the beings that present themselves to us in our world can serve as a final foundation for the meaning of the world itself; in the face of anxiety, the significance of beings melts away. We are always subject to anxiety, always fundamentally *uncanny*. The future is finite in that it forces us to follow one possibility at the expense of others, under the constant threat of death: we are *mortal*. None of these "Nothings," or conditions of finitude, is a flaw that could ideally be overcome if we were raised to a more blessed state; to eliminate any of these conditions would be to eliminate Dasein itself. Instead, we must resolutely accept the fact that we are situated, uncanny, and mortal. Nowhere in time and nowhere in the world can we find a necessary, absolute ground that would legitimate a final interpretation of our existence.

So far, one might think that Heidegger has invoked "Nothing" only for anthropological purposes. But since he is describing us not just as *homo sapiens* but as Dasein—the being who understands what it is to be—his descriptions should have further implications. The significance of beings as such, the Being of beings, can become accessible only to *us*, as finite Dasein. This suggests that the event in which the Being of beings becomes accessible (Be-ing) must itself be characterized by temporal finitude. It too must be, in some sense, situated, uncanny, and mortal.

This view is confirmed by one of Heidegger's most notorious discussions of Nothing: "What Is Metaphysics?" (1929). He begins by emphasizing science's devotion to "beings only, and besides that—nothing." He then asks: "What about this Nothing?"[58] This is a play on words, but behind the pun lies a serious claim: the meaning of "nothing" as negation, which can be analyzed successfully by logic, is subordinate to a "nihilation" that is at work more primordially than logic and science.[59]

Nihilation is displayed in anxiety, the experience of uncanniness. Nihilation tends to eliminate the difference between what is and what is not, so that "all things and we ourselves sink into indifference." But from this indifference, a fresh appreciation of the difference can emerge: "Nihilation . . . manifests . . . beings in their full but heretofore concealed strangeness as what is radically other—with respect to Nothing. In the clear night of the Nothing of anxiety the original openness of beings as such arises: that they are beings—and not nothing." Nihilation thus proves to be a crucial aspect of Be-ing itself: it allows us to have an understanding of the Being of beings, to be Dasein. "Da-sein means: being held out into Nothing."[60]

Heidegger is not making the nihilistic claim that beings have no meaning at all; he is claiming that their meaning must come to pass in a contingent way. It is precisely through our vulnerability to the threat of nihilation that we are able to recognize that beings *do* have meaning. Their meaning is fragile and subject to reinterpretation—but this very fragility is essential to meaning. Be-ing is finite in that it cannot be founded on the presence of some particular entity that serves as a ground for it; this means that it is constantly limited by the possibility of dissolution. Be-ing is mortal, we might say.

Our openness to the significance of beings as such, including their susceptibility to insignificance, is a precondition for asserting particular facts about beings; thus, nihilation is prior to all factual propositions, including scientific ones. In the very act of affirming its devotion to what really exists, science implicitly acknowledges the human ability to make sense of beings as such— and this implies a limit to sense, an edge where sense can fail us in an event of nihilation. This non-sense that constantly threatens the sense of the world is what Heidegger in "What Is Metaphysics?" calls Nothing. Whereas *Being and Time* used "Nothing" to characterize the finitude of Dasein, "What Is Metaphysics?" uses "Nothing" to characterize the finitude of Be-ing.

"What Is Metaphysics?" provoked Carnap's influential attack on Heidegger. Carnap argues that any use of the expression "Nothing" either is reducible to a negation or is an absurd attempt to turn nothing into something.[61] Unfortunately, Carnap completely disregards Heidegger's overall argument, which questions the basic presuppositions of Carnap's critique. Logical positivism affirms that beings are given (posited) in a way that conforms to the rules of assertion (logic). But logical positivism fails to ask how we have access to the

Being of beings, which is the precondition for this givenness of beings. Heidegger claims that we can understand the Being of beings only if there is a boundary where it verges on meaninglessness—for "Being itself is essentially finite and reveals itself only in the transcendence of Dasein which is held out into Nothing."[62] Our Being-in-the-world always brings with it a configuration of sense and non-sense, a happening of Be-ing and nihilation, that sustains our relations to particular entities. This Being-in-the-world is not primarily *logical*, because it cannot be founded on assertions: propositional truths presuppose a more primordial unconcealment.[63]

Aside from *Introduction to Metaphysics*, Heidegger addresses Nothing in several private writings of the late thirties, including *Contributions to Philosophy* and its successors, *Besinnung* and *Die Geschichte des Seyns*.[64] In these texts, Heidegger's thoughts on Nothing crystallize in a way that conditions all his later writings on the theme.[65] Here he indicates enowning, or the event of appropriation *(Ereignis)*, as the happening in which Be-ing and Dasein come into their own. We consider a few passages from these writings that add new usages of "Nothing" to those we have cited.

Heidegger now associates Being and Nothing ever more closely—a trend that is summed up in his late dictum "Being: Nothing: same."[66] Being itself (either as the Being of beings or as Be-ing) is "Nothing" in the sense that it is not an entity. (This usage recalls the negative theologians' references to God, who transcends all finite beings, as "Nothing.") But, says Heidegger, the point that Being is a nonentity is relatively superficial (GA 65, 246). In a deeper sense, Nothing is "the essential trembling [*Erzitterung*] of Be-ing itself" (GA 65, 266). Be-ing is now conceived as intrinsically mysterious or self-withdrawing. This "refusal" of Be-ing is its notness (*das Nichthafte*, GA 65, 8; compare GA 66, 58). Such a refusal is not simply a lack or absence but a "highest donation" (GA 65, 246; compare GA 65, 267 and GA 66, 295). By *giving way*, as it were, Be-ing gives *us* a way to be ourselves and to find a proper relation to beings. Heidegger struggles to find the language to express this combination of giving and withdrawing: "The ripeness is pregnant with the originary 'not.' . . . Here is the essentially unfolding notness of Be-ing as appropriation" (GA 65, 268).

But what does it mean to speak of the withdrawal of Being? We must not picture this as an occurrence in which some entity eludes us, so that we can see it only through a glass darkly. Being is not an entity at all and cannot hide or display itself in the way entities do. If we take Being as the Being of beings, then we can say that it "withdraws" in the sense that the significance of beings as such recedes into the background as we become absorbed in our dealings with particular beings.

If we take Being as Be-ing—the event that grants us access to the Being of beings in the first place—then we can say that it withdraws in still deeper senses. Not only are we normally unaware of the Being of beings, but we are unaware that the Being of beings is a *gift* that is granted only at rare and unique moments. Furthermore, even if we come to appreciate the unique event of appropriation, this event will still withdraw in the sense that it cannot be guaranteed, mastered, or founded metaphysically on some absolute entity or certainty. "Be-ing can never be said conclusively [*endgültig*]." This is not a flaw; instead, "inconclusive knowing holds fast the *abyss* and thus the essence of Be-ing" (GA 65, 460). As essentially inconclusive, Be-ing is contingent and finite. As finite, it must be distinguished from God, who (even, and especially, for negative theology) is infinite and absolute.

Since Be-ing takes place only in relation to Dasein, the finitude of Be-ing corresponds to a finitude in Dasein. We can remain open to Be-ing only if we are exposed to death and alienation—the "gone" or "away" *(Weg-sein)* at the heart of Dasein. We can then recognize "Nothing as the abyss at the edge of the ground" (GA 65, 325). This is very close to Heidegger's earlier accounts of anxiety: there is no unshakable foundation of meaning to which we can cling. In fact, in order for there to be meaning at all, it must be fragile. In anxiety, we recognize that Being is essentially unfamiliar, terrifyingly dis-placing (*ent-setzend:* GA 65, 483). The significance of beings cannot ultimately be domesticated, settled, and fixed. To put it otherwise, appropriation requires expropriation (GA 66, 312).[67]

In order for us to experience the finitude or withdrawal of Being as a gift, we have to respect it rather than simply ignore it. Heidegger thus proposes that we are faced with a decision: "Being or not-Being" (GA 65, 101; compare 264). This is not Hamlet's choice but a decision between letting the mystery of Being prevail and allowing beings to drift free of Be-ing and become "unbeings," empty things with no apparent meaning or depth. (Heidegger surely has in mind the objectified, technicized modern world.) We cannot say that indifference to the decision represents a third alternative, for "indifference would just be *the Being of unbeings,* only the *higher Nothing*" (GA 65, 101). "Nothing" in this sentence refers to a condition in which it makes no difference to us that beings are, rather than are not. In this condition, Be-ing is not merely elusive but lies in oblivion, obscured by beings—which are obvious and plentiful but seem to have no meaning.

We have found that Heidegger uses "Nothing" to refer to a wide variety of phenomena, including inauthenticity, uncanniness, death, guilt, meaninglessness, and the withdrawal of Be-ing. But in both his earlier and his later texts—

with obvious differences in emphasis and vocabulary—Heidegger is using these various senses of "Nothing" to awaken us to the temporal finitude that binds Dasein and Be-ing. A passage from *Die Geschichte des Seyns* sums up his position (GA 69, 168):

> Be-ing is Nothing.
> The Nothing nihilates.
> Nihilation refuses every explanation of beings on the basis of beings.
> But refusal provides the clearing within which beings can go in and out, can be revealed and concealed as beings.
> The Nothing dis-places. And this dis-placement out of beings and away from every appeal to them is the inceptive attunement through which human beings (and the gods) are *determined.*

In other words, the manifestation of beings as such is ungrounded and ungroundable. It is finite, in the sense that it cannot be guaranteed or finalized. Be-ing dis-places: it cannot be located or founded within the realm of beings, precisely because it is the happening that first opens up this realm. But this means that we, too, as the cultivators and receivers of Be-ing, are dis-placed: we can never define or control ourselves by appealing to any being that we encounter. In order to come into our own as Dasein, we must accept our own finitude.

Now we are ready to consider how *Introduction to Metaphysics* develops these thoughts and deploys them in an interpretation of the tradition.

4. INTRODUCTION TO METAPHYSICS: REDISCOVERING THE POWER OF BEING AND NOTHING

By placing the why-question at the opening of his lectures, Heidegger invokes the speculative heights of the metaphysical tradition—but he immediately introduces some distinctly Heideggerian concerns. The why-question embraces all beings, pushes beyond them, and at the same time puts us, the questioners, into question (3–4). It is an "originary leap" (5) by which we translate ourselves into the metaphysical domain.[68] For Heidegger, unlike Leibniz, the question is not raised primarily by reason but by fundamental moods, such as boredom, despair, and joy, which establish a relation to beings as a whole (1).[69] Here we can recognize the pattern set by *Being and Time*'s analysis of anxiety: profoundly revelatory moods do not allow us to rely on particular beings but instead force us into a domain where we must learn to grapple with the significance of beings as such. Here the why-question is not a demand for a highest entity but the relentless abolishment of all foundations within the realm of entities in general.

Heidegger quickly brings us face to face with the problem of Nothing. Even Nothing comes under the sway of the why-question, "not, as it were, because it is something, a being, since after all we are talking about it, but because it 'is' Nothing" (2). The "as it were" clause alludes to the ancient paradox of speaking of Nothing, only to dismiss it as superficial (compare 30). The Nothing is not an entity at all. However, it "is" some "thing" (in the broadest sense), and it does have its own way of unfolding and being given to us. (The other such "thing" will, of course, prove to be Being itself.)

Heidegger explores this mysterious status of Nothing in greater depth as he investigates the clause "instead of nothing" in the why-question (18–22). At first the clause looks redundant and even absurd. "Nothing" seems to tell us nothing—it is a dead end (18). We are back at the problem of speaking of Nothing, and here Heidegger considers the Parmenidean option: speaking of Nothing is a futile, self-canceling act. In the twentieth century, this ancient line of thought takes the form of logical positivism. Heidegger seems to be paraphrasing Carnap when he writes, "Talking about Nothing is illogical . . . [such talk] consists in utterly senseless propositions" (18).

We learn from a note (18) that Heidegger also has in mind his onetime teacher Heinrich Rickert's *Die Logik des Prädikats und das Problem der Ontologie*. This work is an instructive example of how traditional assumptions block the way to asking Heidegger's questions. As its title indicates, it is a resolutely *logical* approach to Being and Nothing: for Rickert, the problem of ontology is entirely a problem about predication, that is, assertion and negation. On the particular page to which Heidegger refers, Rickert interprets "Nothing" as "not-the-world" (where "the world" means beings as a whole). At the end of his book, Rickert glosses "Nothing" in Heidegger's "What Is Metaphysics?" as "the something about which nothing positive at all can be *asserted*," that is, "the something *for which we have no predicates*." Although Rickert does his best to find points of agreement with his former student, he cannot appreciate the radicalness of Heidegger's position. Rickert's interpretations of Nothing remain on the level of beings and simply assume that predication provides our main access to them. He is correct to suggest that Heidegger's "nihilation" has something to do with unintelligibility; what he fails to grasp is that this unintelligibility is not just a failure to form propositions about some particular mysterious thing but an insidious insignificance that constantly threatens our *entire* capacity to make sense of things—not only our assertions and negations but our whole existence. This constant threat stems from the radical finitude that pervades Dasein and Be-ing.

The very question of Nothing, then, lies outside the realm of logic—and perhaps outside the realm of civilization, progress, and positive thinking. "Talking about Nothing . . . undermines all culture and all faith. Whatever both disregards the fundamental law of thinking and also destroys faith and the will to construct is pure nihilism" (18).

To all these objections Heidegger responds, first, that the question of Nothing is as ancient as the question of beings as such. Whether the question is asked legitimately depends on the "manner" of asking it (18). The dismissal of talk of Nothing as illogical, unscientific, and nihilistic rests on a "misunderstanding" (19). Presumably, what has been misunderstood is the manner in which Heidegger is talking of Nothing. He is not trying to reify Nothing (it is not a thing), and he agrees that it cannot be understood scientifically (19–20). There are, however, nonscientific modes of understanding. Here he points to poetry (citing a passage from Hamsun) and cautions us that "we cannot begin to speak about Nothing immediately" (20).

But despite his discussions of "poetic thinking" and "thinking poetry" (110), Heidegger never *identifies* philosophy and poetry. What is philosophy, then? How is it different from science, and what gives it the right to evade the strictures of science and logic? Philosophy is "a thoughtful opening of the avenues and vistas of a knowing that establishes measure and rank, a knowing in which and from which a people conceives its Dasein in the historical-spiritual world and brings it to fulfillment—that knowing which ignites and threatens and compels all questioning and appraising" (8). What is *known* through philosophy is not a set of facts about beings, couched in established concepts, but a lay of the land, as it were—a fundamental orientation to our surroundings. This orientation opens up the *space* in which things become accessible and interpretable (139–140). Such an event of opening can also involve poetry, politics, and religion (47, 117); what distinguishes philosophy from these other originary activities is that philosophy involves knowing—that is, the ability "to stand in the openness of beings" (16), "*to be able to learn*" (17). Heidegger is trying to establish a sense of knowing that essentially involves questioning, ranking, historical self-awareness, and a relation to the whole, rather than the decontextualized ascertaining of particular facts. Science is the more superficial successor of philosophical knowing—the institutionalized establishment and systematic interrelation of assertions about the beings that have already been revealed (20, 33). Logic, in turn, is just a science of the formal aspects of assertions; it cannot deal with primordial unconcealment (91–92). Thus, "true talk of Nothing" in philosophy or poetry "always remains unfamiliar" (20), because philosophy and poetry are concerned with the originary opening of a world, the event that *establishes* and thus *precedes* familiar dwelling.

If we accept philosophical language as part of the opening of a world, then the "instead of nothing" clause of the why-question is not only meaningful but crucial in that it spurs us to move beyond the level of beings. We no longer look for an entity to serve as a final ground; we call entities as such into question. Now the givenness of beings starts to "waver" (21). This is not to say that we are unsure about the facts, or that we doubt that beings are present. As certain as all the facts about beings may be, beings *as such* are mysterious. Their givenness *as beings* has lost its self-evidence and become surprising, because we recognize an alternative to them: Nothing, that is, the possible lack of anything that would count as an entity. As Scheler puts it, we are now capable of experiencing the Being of every being as "an eternally astonishing *roofing of the abyss* of absolute nothing."[70] In Heidegger's terms, Be-ing is now happening: the Being of beings is displayed to us.

Heidegger now takes several bold steps: "The ground in question [that is, the reason or foundation sought by the why-question] is now questioned as the ground of the decision for beings over against Nothing—more precisely, as the ground for the wavering of the beings that sustain us and unbind us, half in being, half not in being, which is also why we cannot wholly belong to any thing, not even to ourselves; yet Dasein is in each case mine" (22). The why-question brings not only other beings but us ourselves into "suspense" (22). Here Heidegger sketches the interplay between appropriation and expropriation that is fundamental to his thought. As Dasein, we *belong* to our "Here" (117, 156) and to the beings manifest in it, and we *belong* to ourselves: that is, we are thrown into a concrete situation in which we are forced to take over the task of being who we are. As long as we remain Dasein, however, this belonging can never become an utter absorption. The boundaries of the Here are subject to reinterpretation, the meaning of beings is open to question, and our own selfhood is never simply given. The finitude of Dasein and Be-ing—the contingency of identity and meaning—is evoked by the phrase "instead of nothing."

Heidegger is now ready to transmute the why-question into the "prior question." The possibility of not-Being hovers over all beings (21, 23) and urges us to ask: "How does it stand with Being?" (25). We saw at the start of this chapter that this question has two dimensions as an inquiry into both the Being of beings and Be-ing: what is the Being of beings (what does it mean to acknowledge something *as a being:* 24), and how is it that we gain access to the Being of beings in the first place? At this point, the why-question cannot function as a rationalist search for a total explanation. Instead, it is an act of wondering at the difference it makes that there is something rather than nothing, a way of celebrating this difference and inquiring into it.[71] The Being of beings is precisely what distinguishes them from nonbeings. It turns out, however, that we cannot articulate what it is to be. The Being of beings is elusive—"almost like Nothing, or in the end *entirely* so" (27). The mood of celebration and wonder becomes a mood of longing and distress;[72] the lectures have been set on their course as a quest for the lost meaning of the Being of beings.

As this quest takes Heidegger into linguistics and the history of the restriction of Being, the question of Nothing falls into the background for a while, with the exception of two suggestive remarks in chapter 3. First, he claims that the "only other" of Being is Nothing; since "here there is nothing to be compared," Being is the most incomparable of all, and thus "what is most unique and most determinate" (60). This rather obscure thought is dramatically un-Hegelian.[73] For Hegel, all determination is negation: thus, the isolation of Being and Nothing from the wealth of interrelated beings, their lack of others from which they can be distinguished, makes Being and Nothing the most *in*determinate and emptiest of concepts. Heidegger, however, asserts the paradox that "Being, that which pertains to every being whatsoever and thus disperses itself into what is most commonplace, is the most unique of all" (60).[74] We may speculate that he is contrasting the seeming generality of the Being of beings (as beingness, or the universal characteristics of beings) with the uniqueness of Be-ing as a historical happening—a dispensation of the Being of beings allotted to a unique people at a unique moment.[75] As we will see in his discussion of the restriction of Being, this unique dispensation generates "others" to Being that, in the end, are not others at all.

In the second passage of interest to us in chapter 3, Heidegger remarks that he uses the word "Being" so broadly "that it finds its limit only at Nothing. Everything that is not simply nothing, *is*—and for us, even Nothing 'belongs' to 'Being' "(64). If we take this passage in conjunction with the previous one, it means that precisely because Nothing is Being's other, the question of Nothing is included in the question of Being. The happening of Be-ing as the event in which beings become unconcealed brings with it a region of concealment, a realm of what is refused the privilege of acknowledgment as a being. In fact, unconcealment is an ongoing *battle* against this region of concealment, a battle that can never be won, only neglected. If we neglect the battle, we fall into the illusion of taking our own understanding of beings and our own region of unconcealment as absolute.[76] Again, what is crucial is recognizing the intrinsic finitude of Be-ing—that is, its contingency and its susceptibility to an event of nihilation, an event that would collapse the boundary between what is and what is not.

This polemical interpretation of the relation between Being and Nothing, with the addition of *seeming* as an ambiguous third, orients Heidegger's interpretation of Parmenides in chapter 4. For Heidegger, Parmenides is not the one-sided thinker whom Plato and Hegel accused of neglecting Nothing. Parmenides *does* do justice to Nothing, precisely by rejecting it. By warning us against not-Being, Parmenides *recognizes* this path as "unviable": he "shows that, together with the path of Being, the path of Nothing must expressly be *considered*" (85). For the genuine thinker, "the terror of the second way to the abyss of Nothing has not remained foreign" (86). Although Nothing can never be made familiar (20), and in this sense it is always foreign, we can face it instead of ignoring it.

When Heidegger distinguishes seeming as a third path in Parmenides' poem, he claims, "The self-showing of the seeming belongs directly to Being and yet (at bottom) does not belong to it" (86). In other words, the emergence of beings brings manifestation (seeming) along with it—but the Being of beings cannot be *exhausted* by seeming, because manifestation is necessarily accompanied by darkness. "Being means: to appear in emerging, to step forth out of concealment—and for this very reason, concealment and the provenance from concealment essentially belong to Being" (87). Conversely, "Not-Being . . . means to step away from appearance, from presence" (78). If we identify concealment with one aspect of Nothing, then we can say that, in Heidegger's reading of pre-Socratic thought, it is Being's link to Nothing that allows seeming to have a character that is distinct from Being itself. In order for a being to be, it must appear (it must present itself in a look).But if we focus only on the appearance and forget the concealment from which the being emerged, then seeming degenerates into semblance: the thing's look can serve as a barrier that prevents the thing from manifesting itself in fuller, deeper ways (79). If, in contrast, we maintain our awareness of concealment, then we can take the seeming of a thing as a taste of its Being, as an incentive to go farther in wresting what is from what is not. This is, of course, a much more positive account of seeming than the usual interpretation of Parmenides, which interprets seeming as mere illusion, tantamount to nonbeing.

Heidegger's terse analysis of becoming in relation to seeming also makes use of Nothing. Since what becomes is "no longer Nothing, but . . . not yet what it is destined to be . . . becoming remains shot through with not-Being. However, it is not a pure Nothing, but no longer this and not yet that, and as such, is constantly something else" (87). From the Greek point of view, becoming is infected with negativity, with absence and otherness.[77]

In Heidegger's reading of Parmenides, then, thinking (or "apprehension") "is fundamentally a *de-cision for* Being *against* Nothing, and thus a confrontation *with* seeming" (128). The situation of the thinker is a crisis that plays out the basic drama of Dasein itself. Heidegger finds this crisis echoed in the poetry of Sophocles. We will forego a full account of Heidegger's interpretation of the ode from *Antigone*.[78] Instead, we will focus on his explicit introduction of Nothing in his translation of lines 360–361. A standard rendition of the sentence would be, "Resourceful in all, he meets nothing that is to come resourceless"—in other words, humanity is ready to deal with everything that may come. But Heidegger reads *ouden* as *das Nichts*, turning the line into a statement about the *limits* of resourcefulness: "Everywhere trying out, underway; untried, with no way out he comes to Nothing" (113). Even if this construal is implausible, it does fit well with the next line of the ode, which names death as the sole irresistible force.[79] In Heidegger's interpretation, then, our very ability to deal with beings implies an exposure to Nothing, which itself *cannot* be dealt with. We encounter beings thanks to the happening of Be-ing, but this happening also involves a relation to Nothing, in the sense of "ruin, calamity" (116). (Here we can hear echoes not only of *Being and Time* but of young Heidegger's descriptions of "ruination.") Because we are "the uncanniest," we cannot be familiar with the significance of beings, and handle them comfortably and effectively, without also being exposed to homelessness, strangeness, and death—the edges where significance breaks down and the contingency of meaning is revealed.[80] This uncanniness includes the possibility of not-Being-here, of rejecting Dasein itself (135). Heidegger is not recommending suicide, of course, but he views it as a genuine possibility for any authentic life.

The question of Nothing plays an important role at one more point in the text—its dramatic conclusion. Returning to the theme of nihilism, Heidegger defines it as "merely to chase after beings in the midst of the oblivion of Being" (155). This is "[to treat] Being as a nothing" in the sense of a triviality. To *include* Nothing in the question of Being, however, is to begin to overcome nihilism (155). When we take the question of Being seriously, we find that the Being of beings does have a particular meaning for us: it is "constant presence" (157), as opposed to inconstant *becoming*, superficial *seeming, thinking* about what is present and what *ought* to be present. Heidegger, however, points out quite simply that becoming, seeming, thinking and the ought are "*not* nothing": "*thus, the concept of Being that has been accepted up to now does not suffice to name everything that 'is'*" (155). This means that we need a fresh experience of the Being of beings. We should look for such an experience, he proposes, in the connection between Being and time (157). (If our interpretation of Heidegger's thought in section 3 is correct, it is precisely the temporality and historicity of Be-ing—the entanglement of Be-ing in mortality and contingency—that makes Be-ing finite, that is, essentially ungroundable and questionable.)

This conclusion brings us back to the question of the indeterminacy of Being. It turns out that the Being of beings does have a determinate meaning, because, contrary to what Heidegger had suggested earlier (60), Nothing is *not* its only other, at least not for us: within the determination or destiny *(Bestimmung)* of the West (154), the Being of beings is determined *(bestimmt)* in a fourfold way. This restriction turns out to be an overrestriction, however, because it implies that the four others of the Being of beings should be relegated to the realm of Nothing (that which is not), whereas in fact they deserve to be acknowledged as forming part of the Being of beings in some fuller, more adequate sense. However, if the Being of beings is now to be understood in such a broad sense that it *includes* becoming, seeming, thinking and the ought, does it once again become something so universal as to be empty? Heidegger would surely deny this. Be-ing—the *granting* of the Being of beings—is richly unique, thanks to its determination by time, that is, its historical finitude. Be-ing is a historically unfolding happening that allows a particular group of people to encounter themselves and their surroundings with a particular kind of sensitivity or insensitivity. This unique, contingent historical dispensation also brings with it a unique relation to Nothing—Being's constant companion and ownmost other.

5. ASSESSMENTS

We should not go too far in extracting a "doctrine" of Nothing from *Introduction to Metaphysics,* which is a voyage and a provocation, not a treatise. One might even say the same of Heidegger's thought as a whole. Still, we can sum up the course of the lectures as follows: Heidegger finds the mystery of Nothing within the why-question and uses it to point to the prescientific event of truth as the opening of a space that polemically distinguishes what is from what is not. We can then ask "how it stands with Being": what *is* the difference between beings and nonbeings, and how do we become open to what it means to be and not to be in the first place? In response to this question, Heidegger uncovers a forgotten genealogy of Being, a history in which Being has acquired a determinate sense that guides Western culture. When we return to the roots of this history, we become capable once again of facing Being and Nothing creatively and thoughtfully.

As his story unfolds, Heidegger points repeatedly to the temporal finitude of both Dasein and Be-ing. "Uncanniness," as presented in Heidegger's reading of Sophocles, becomes a dominant word for the temporal finitude of Dasein. Thanks to our uncanniness—the fact that "we cannot wholly belong to any thing, not even to ourselves" (22) as we struggle to establish a position within the whole of things—we are exposed to the Being of beings. The why-question can alert us to this uncanniness, awaken us from inauthenticity and indifference, and thus bring us beyond beings to the question of Being. Heidegger also suggests that Being not only is concealed and lost for us but is *intrinsically* "inclined toward concealment" (87). To take a few steps beyond his explicit statements, we can say that illumination always has a limit where it breaks down, because it can never be founded on some master entity. This breakdown of illumination (or "nihilation"), which is usually quivering at the threshold of our awareness, is crucial to the temporal finitude of the human condition.

Introduction to Metaphysics insists that Nothing, in its various senses, is a legitimate topic of thinking; far from leading to nihilism, such thinking is necessary in order to revive the question of Being. Surely Heidegger's claim is correct, for at least three reasons. First, any sense of the Being of beings involves a sense of what it means *not* to be; for instance, the Being of beings as presence implies not-Being as absence. Second, we may find that, within a certain sense of the Being of beings, what "is" requires *what "is not"*: for instance, what is present may depend on what is absent.[81] Finally, such discoveries, as well as other experiences, can reveal the limits of this sense of the Being of beings. We find that our understanding of the Being of beings is questionable: it is exposed to the threat of *nihilation,* because the event of Be-ing is finite—it has no unshakable ground.

Since this happening is not an entity, it cannot be addressed by science. It is not reducible to negation, falsehood, or otherness as they are understood in any logic, for logic is subordinate to the interplay of concealment and unconcealment, meaning and meaninglessness. Thinking about this interplay begins with acknowledging our own uncanniness. This acknowledgment brings us beyond the familiar realm of what is and what is not, leads us to question why there is something instead of nothing, and introduces us to the mysteries of Being and not-Being. To dismiss such a project as absurd or nihilistic would be to confuse it with an affirmation of meaninglessness. Instead, it affirms the *finitude* of meaning and thus opens meaning to an appreciative questioning.

Although *Introduction to Metaphysics* provides a coherent approach to the problem of Nothing and suggests a powerful critique of the tradition,

Heidegger himself did not always view the text as a success. A long later insertion (14–15) shows that he was apprehensive about the lectures' capacity to distinguish the question of the Being of beings from the question of "Being as such" (Be-ing). In two texts from the late 1930s, these doubts focus on the transition from the why-question to the prior question.

In a brief self-critique, Heidegger calls this transition "too thin and too artificial." *Introduction to Metaphysics* has failed to introduce the question of Be-ing; in fact, he goes so far as to suggest that no such introduction is possible on the basis of the metaphysical tradition. Instead, we must begin directly with an experience of "the essential unfolding [of Be-ing] itself" (GA 40, 217). The lecture course remained on the level of our *interpretations* of Being—our words, our concepts, and the historical limitations of both—without attaining "*the happening of Being*" (GA 40, 218–219).

In *Besinnung* (1938–1939), Heidegger stresses that the "why" of the why-question is too superficial. He asks (as he did already in *Introduction to Metaphysics,* 4): "Why the Why?" His answer: "for the sake of Be-ing, so that its truth, what belongs to it, may take place and find its ground: in Da-sein" (GA 66, 267). This ground—the fundamental Be-ing-Dasein nexus—is beyond all grounding. It "repels every Why" (GA 66, 270). Furthermore, metaphysics really begins not with the why-question but with the more basic *what*-question: "What are beings *as* beings?" (GA 66, 271). Neither the why-question nor the what-question adequately addresses the problem of Be-ing itself, however.

What is this problem? It is the problem of how beings as such become available to us in the first place. This primal event precedes and enables all explanation and all definition. Through this happening of Be-ing—as *Introduction to Metaphysics* says of the work of art—"everything . . . that appears and that we can find around us first becomes confirmed and accessible, interpretable and understandable, *as a being,* or else as an unbeing" (122). Or else as an unbeing: the happening of Be-ing brings with it the happening of Nothing, the tracing of a fragile frontier beyond which things can belong no more to the realm of the accessible and acceptable. Through its questions and interpretations, *Introduction to Metaphysics* challenges us to confront this boundary. Heidegger's assessment of his lecture course may have been too modest. Whether or not it transposes us into the essential unfolding of Be-ing, it succeeds in evoking the shadows and enigmas of the frontier.

Chapter 5

THE SCATTERED *LOGOS:*
METAPHYSICS AND THE LOGICAL PREJUDICE

DANIEL DAHLSTROM

What kind of introduction is the *Introduction to Metaphysics?* How is the term "introduction" being used in the title? Should it be conceived as an orientation into a well-defined but limited domain (such as an entry-level study of Newtonian mechanics)? Or is it more like a beginner's guide to a disease, therapy, or inevitable stage of development (think of "introductions" to cancer, psychoanalysis, or adolescence)? Or is it best construed as a preliminary sketch of some epoch-making historical event (like "An Introduction to the Cold War")? An element of each of these (and still other) kinds of introduction can be found in Heidegger's *Introduction to Metaphysics.* But there is an obvious reason to hesitate in superimposing the model of any of them onto an introduction to metaphysics. For the aforesaid introductions are introductions to studies or practices of particular beings, whereas the traditional scope of metaphysics, even when it is understood as entailing theology, is not so restricted; in Aristotle's epochal declaration, it is a study of "being as being."[1]

Yet appeal to the alleged distinctiveness of metaphysics is of little help in clarifying the nature of Heidegger's introduction since the term "metaphysics," as he himself notes in the 1953 edition, is "ambiguous" and, indeed, "*deliberately* ambiguous."[2] Heidegger's introduction to metaphysics is an introduction to an ambiguity. The ambiguity reflects what Heidegger calls the confusion about the question of being, namely, whether it is the question of "why there are entities at all and not rather nothing" or the question of "what the sense of being is."[3] The former is the basic question *(Grundfrage)* of metaphysics, namely, what is questionable for metaphysics, whereas the latter is the "prior question" *(Vorfrage),* the question that deserves to be asked first even if, in the process, metaphysics itself—precisely because of the aforesaid ambiguity—becomes questionable.[4]

Yet why write an introduction to an ambiguity—if not to expose and exploit it? The *Introduction to Metaphysics* is an attempt to demonstrate the questionableness of metaphysics. Of course, the term "questionableness" understates matters; the *Introduction to Metaphysics* is in fact meant to be an introduction to the end of metaphysics and the beginning of a way of thinking that is putatively more responsible and responsive to being. Nevertheless, in contrast to the strategy or accent of other cognate pieces (for example, the *Contributions to Philosophy,* composed over the next two years, or "Overcoming of Metaphysics," composed over the following decade), Heidegger attempts to show that there is a way of posing the metaphysically basic question—as it were, from within—such that it forces one to ask, not what entity accounts for any other entity (Scheler's query, the ontotheological query into the Supreme Being), but rather what it means to say that something is at all.[5] Since there would be no metaphysics without the seemingly obvious assumption *(Selbstverständlichkeit)* of this sense of being, the *Introduction to Metaphysics* attempts to reverse metaphysics by retrieving or, better, commemorating what metaphysics forgets or what has abandoned metaphysics—and thus what metaphysics ultimately presupposes.[6] That presupposition is twofold, inasmuch as metaphysics endemically forgets to probe the sense of being and inasmuch as what and how it probes presuppose that very sense.

Such an introduction to metaphysics must accordingly demonstrate how the question of the sense of being comes to be opaque. Heidegger traces this opacity to a certain inversion of the relation between thinking and being, an inversion that is tantamount to a kind of humanism. Though there are several variations to this inversion, it is generally in place when thinking—and, synecdochically, being human—is construed in some fashion not only as distinct from being but even as self-sufficient and capable by itself of setting the terms for an engagement with being, for thinking about being. Thinking in this case is meant, not in the sense of subjective musings but in the sense of objective judgment and inference, that is to say, genuine or legitimate thinking or use of language, deemed "legitimate" because regulated by its conformity to a "*logos*" determined by logic ("the science of thinking, the doctrine of the rules of thinking and the forms of what is thought").[7] This construal of thinking, together with its implications for thinking what it means "to be," is, Heidegger maintains, neither necessary nor complete. Nor does it matter whether this "logical *logos*" is understood merely as grammatically and historically codified rules for communication or as a system of techniques for making and showing inferences ("valid conditionals," as Quine puts it) that are ultimately explained along conventional, naturalistic, or transcendental lines.[8] In the following chapter this broadly conceived manner of construing the relation of thinking to being is dubbed "the logical prejudice," though with a different accent it might just as well be called the "metaphysical" (or even "humanistic") prejudice. By virtue of the prejudice, it bears emphasizing, metaphysics and logic are construed by Heidegger as two sides of the same coin. If an inability to ask what it means to be defines Western metaphysics, it is because metaphysical thinking is logical, all-too-logical—or so Heidegger would have us believe. As he puts it a decade later, "Metaphysics is in its essential core 'logic' " and "logic is the metaphysics of the *logos*."[9]

This thesis obviously requires considerable elaboration. Yet even at the general level at which it is presented here for purposes of introduction, there are some ready responses to it. In the first place, it may be argued, the reason logic enjoys its privileged status is precisely because, thanks to its formal character, it is metaphysically neutral—or at least as neutral as possible. From this vantage point, the supposed symbiosis of metaphysics and logic simply does not exist.[10] In the second place, the argument may be made that to suspend the logical prejudice is to forfeit any claim to truth or justification for thinking, including thinking about being. A distinction between correct and incorrect thinking is a staple of "traditional" or "classical" logic (as evidenced by, for example, the bivalent truth-functions of propositions and rules of inference based upon determinations of those functions). Accordingly, for classical logic, every meaningful, unambiguous proposition (statement, assertion, judgment, declarative sentence) is either true or false (which is also why some logicians regard tautologies as meaningless).[11] Any effort or pretension to think about being and to do so in a way that is alogical cannot be defended from charges of hopeless vagueness or arbitrariness. Thus, if metaphysics is prejudiced in some sense in favor of logic, it would seem to be a logical prejudice, that is to say, one that can scarcely be called into question.[12]

Nevertheless, in the *Introduction to Metaphysics* Heidegger endeavors to do just that by recapitulating the history of the prejudice and thereby demonstrating why it is understandable but not inevitable. The aim of this chapter is to clarify the nature of this endeavor and examine its efficacy. Section 1 begins with an attempt to determine what Heidegger understands by "logic" and why he regards it, so understood, as prejudicially foreclosing any questioning of what it means to be. Heidegger's strategy is to demonstrate a meaning of "*logos*," named and even experienced if not itself thought by early Greek thinkers, that becomes "scattered" in a subsequent devolution into logical thinking and—allegedly—can only be retrieved or commemorated by making a new beginning in thinking about what it means to be or, at least, preparing the way for beginning to think being historically *(seynsgeschichtliches Denken).*[13] In this connection Heidegger contrasts the pre-Socratic meaning of *logos* (a synonym for being itself) with a particular sort of *logos*, namely, the aspects of human language that subsequently preoccupy Western philosophers. Section 2 reviews Heidegger's account of the transformations of the use of the term *"logos"* at the inception of Western thinking, culminating in the logical prejudice. The account is motivated, Heidegger insists, not by antiquarian interests but by the very possibilities of another sort of thinking, one that is not paradigmatically logical. In section 3 the challenges to Heidegger's effort, mentioned above, are revisited in view of this historical turn.

1. THE LOGICAL PREJUDICE AND THE HISTORICAL STRATEGY OF ITS UNDOING

More than one-third of *Introduction to Metaphysics* is devoted to the theme "Being and Thinking," not least because the severing of thinking from being enjoys, in Heidegger's words, "a definitive dominance in Western Dasein"; this "fundamental orientation [*Grundstellung*] of the spirit of the West" is what his "attack," as he puts it, is actually meant for.[14] What defines this particular take on the relation between being and thinking is not just any thinking but, as noted above, thinking determined by logic, a theoretical science allegedly secure and reliable and independent of any particular worldview. Despite the tremendous diversity and discrepancy in regard to its constitution, "on the whole, a gratifying agreement prevails. Logic relieves us of the trouble of asking elaborate questions about the essence of thinking."[15]

Given the intense debate over the nature of thinking and logic in the half-century before 1935, it is tempting to conclude from this sarcastic remark that Heidegger had his head in the sand.[16] But there is also reason to resist such a temptation, at least until his account of logic has been given a hearing. After all, if he was oblivious to or dismissive of contemporaries' debates about the nature or status of logic (construed in some sense as the ultimate possible legitimation or criterion of genuine thinking), it may well be because he regarded such debates as (logically) prejudiced.[17] If logic's hold on what counts as legitimate thinking proves in fact to be a prejudice in some sense, then the prejudice in question can only be overcome by placing logic itself in question. The "logic" that Heidegger puts in question is "apophantic" and "formal," a science of inference based on quasi-theoretical assertions and their structure or, more particularly, their invariant forms (for example, truth-functional or quantificational "schemata").[18] The qualification "quasi-theoretical" is necessary since the assertions need not explicitly figure in a theory, including the theory of inference itself. For the purposes of logic, however, they have to conform to or be translatable into the sorts of well-formed theoretical sentences that are capable of figuring in an inference.

The determination of legitimate or genuine thinking—and thereby "being," insofar as it can be thought—in terms of a formal account of the *logos* as an assertion in the sense described enjoys, Heidegger suggests, only a relative (historical) validity. On one hand, it is not obvious why the doctrine of thinking is to be equated with such a science of assertions. It is not that there is no other way to determine thinking, indeed, truthful thinking (herein lies one of the reasons why Heidegger initially unpacks ordinary uses of "thinking" without "reference to assertion and discourse").[19] On the other hand, while thus contesting the necessity of delimiting study of thinking to a study of assertions, Heidegger is unwilling to regard this development as a matter of chance. Instead he suggests that the putatively self-evident validity of logic, seemingly secured by its consideration of the formal structures of assertions exclusively, is in fact dependent on a particular conception of what it means for any entity (or thing or object or theme) to be.[20]

Heidegger's charge is, accordingly, that the construal of formal logic as a necessary condition of meaningful thinking or discourse can prejudice our understanding of the relation between being and thinking. Logic, as Heidegger understands it in this connection, is tantamount to what Dummett has in mind when he observes that "there is just one logic, the familiar classical logic, which accords with the principle of bivalence."[21] The principle of bivalence states that "every meaningful sentence is determined as true or false" or, in other words, that we can entertain a sentence only if we understand its truth conditions, that is, what it would be for the sentence to be true and what it would be for the sentence to be false.[22] Bivalence thus becomes a mark of meaningfulness for thinking that restricts itself to this classical logical constant. For this sort of semantic theory (that is, theory of what can be meant or thought), Davidson's remark is typical: "to give truth conditions is a way of giving the meaning of a sentence."[23]

Inasmuch as classical formal logic, by virtue of its adherence to the principles of noncontradiction and excluded middle, maintains a distinction between what is and is not assertible (meaningful, thinkable), it would seem to presuppose some conception of being (what it means to be). The point is not that countenancing criteria for such a distinction is the same as identifying being with assertibility but rather that canons of what is and is not assertible, as tantamount to canons of what can and cannot be the case, necessarily invoke some sense of being (or, equivalently, truth). Thinking that toes the line of classical formal logic is, Heidegger insists, incapable of thinking what it invokes, however. (Though Heidegger makes the charge, a cognate idea is not foreign to some prominent studies of "classical logic." Thus, according to Wittgenstein in the *Tractatus,* the logical form of reality is, as it were, "shown," but cannot literally be "said.")[24] Heidegger's complaint, then, is that thinking that restricts itself to the structure of assertions and axiomatic principles of noncontradiction and excluded middle is left impotent to consider the meanings of "being" and "truth" that it presupposes.[25] Herein lies the source of the implausibility, from the point of view of classical formal logic, of making assertions about being (or "logical form") as though the latter were just another particular being.[26] If genuine (legitimate, pure) thinking is in some sense bound to its formal and apophantic character, then its very distinctiveness consists allegedly in its distinction from any content (reference, referentiality, being).

The fact that classical logic, by virtue of its formal (or symbolic) character, presupposes but does not itself articulate what it means "to be," is, it might be countered, precisely its virtue.[27] Classical logic puts constraints on science but does not overdetermine the reality of things that, in the end, it is the business of science (or some other practice) to establish. Rules or techniques of inference solely in terms of the connectives among propositions presuppose the truth or falsity of each noncompound proposition, but a so-called truth-functional logic can establish these rules without any pretensions to being able to elucidate what it means to determine propositions accordingly. In the case of so-called predicational or quantificational logic, a similar sort of ontological neutrality can be claimed.[28] The establishment of techniques for making inferences with quantifiers itself establishes neither what exists nor what it means to say of anything that it exists. A cognate point is made by Quine in his rebuttal of Carnap's injunction against metaphysical questions, that is, questions using "category words" (for example, do numbers exist?). There are, Quine notes, "no external constraints on styles of variables" and thus on categories, though there is every reason to look for the quantified variables of a theory in order to determine its "existential force."[29]

Heidegger, however, does not express any misgivings with logic insofar as it goes about the business of working out valid forms and techniques of inference. Nor is he engaged in a campaign against the interests of formal consistency, correctness, and propriety relative to science (that is, logic's independence from and its utility to science). His quarrel is with the sort of thinking—on the part of philosophers, scientists, and others—that ultimately follows logic's lead in bracketing questions of being and existence, even as it supposes a particular answer to them.[30] By virtue of its insistence on a uniform symbolism, classical logical thinking supposes either the constant presence of whatever it entertains (for example, meanings, references, entities, truth values) or, if the symbolism is meant to be disinterpreted, the potential presence of a range of objects in terms of which it may be interpreted or applied. In this supposition lies formal logic's normative but unreflected understanding of being.[31]

This quarrel with logical thinking supposes, of course, that there is some other and, indeed, more compelling way to think about what it means to be, something that it is incumbent on Heidegger to elucidate. Nevertheless, there is a tendency to construe logic (or an equivalent, for example, computer language), precisely in its collusion with a determination of meaning, as the main arbiter for ordinary thinking and discourse, for the translation from everyday uses of natural languages into the formal languages of specific sciences, as well as across scientific discourses. To the extent that there are senses of being other than that presupposed by logic, this totalizing tendency has the effect of foreclosing or, better, preempting inquiry into what it means to be. This sort of logical thinking, Heidegger wants to suggest, is the source of metaphysics, construed as a way of thinking that, with a kind of insular correctness, sets itself off from, even over against, being.[32] Heidegger accordingly has his sights not so much on logic as a science of inference based on the structure of assertions. His target is rather the impropriety of a certain extension of logic, often making common cause with logically constructed sciences, for which questioning what it means to be is, in more than one sense of the word, an empty gesture.[33] There is probably no better exemplification of this attitude than Quine's observation that "explication . . . of the existential quantifier itself, 'there is,' 'there are,' explication of general existence, is a forlorn cause."[34]

Heidegger proposes to combat the logical prejudice—not simply its construal of thinking, but above all the alleged severing of thinking from being, implicit in that construal—by demonstrating both that thinking is a way of being and that the logical prejudice, far from a "gift from heaven," has in fact a history.[35] His strategy is to begin with the inception of the relation between being and thinking, as a means of demonstrating their original—and originary—unity. His next move is to explain how thinking, initially construed as *logos,* first sets itself off from being and how this thinking subsequently came to be construed in terms of logic, as both the essence of thinking and the criterion of being (the logical prejudice of Western philosophy). Indeed, there is every reason to think that logic could emerge only after the distinction between being and thinking had been drawn and, indeed, drawn in a definite way and for a particular purpose. It seems hardly accidental, Heidegger observes, that logic as a discipline is an invention of school teachers, not philosophers, coinciding with the end of Greek philosophy, an era in which philosophy becomes "an affair of the school, of organization and technique" and being appears as an "idea," becoming the object of "science."[36]

Heidegger's refusal to attempt to understand the distinction between being and thinking by assuming that formal logic sets the outermost parameters or constitutes the end of the analysis of thinking does not mean either that he intends to outflank formal logic somehow by merely charting its history or that he intends to make common cause with contemporary opponents of intellectualism.[37] He has no pretensions of opposing concepts, judgments, and inferences (elements of traditional logic since Aristotle) with "mere feelings" or with an account of the history of logic, that is to say, the history of competing theories of forms of judgment and inference.[38] Nevertheless, his examination of the relation between being and thinking is profoundly historical *(seynsgeschichtlich)* in another sense and, indeed, in the sense of the history of thinking that precedes theoretical judgments, that is to say, judgments already circumscribed by a theoretical enterprise and its ontological commitments. Heidegger's strategy is to persuade his students of the necessity of moving from thinking about thinking in terms of logic as the science of forms of judgments to thinking about (commemorating: *Andenken*) a sort of thinking that not only is more rigorous and original than judgmental or propositional thinking within a theoretical framework but also is, in some as yet unspecified sense, equivalent to "unfolding the question of being as such."[39] The move is both critical and foundational, aimed at countering the logical prejudice by turning to the prejudicial, that is to say, pretheoretical thinking that presumably is essentially related to being and thus—in the unfolding of that relation—tantamount to the history of being, including its metaphysical oblivion.[40]

2. THE ORIGIN OF THE LOGICAL PREJUDICE: FROM THE GATHERING TO CORRECTNESS

The fact that the Greek doctrine of thinking is a doctrine of the *logos,* later understood as "logic," provides Heidegger with the essential clues to the origin of the logical prejudice. He reasons that, if there is a key to its origin, it is likely to be found by unpacking the pre-Socratic uses of the term and their appropriation by Plato and Aristotle. Heidegger undertakes to explain how thinking, though itself obviously a manner of being and thus (a) in some sense unified with being, came to be (b) differentiated from being, (c) identified with this differentiation, and (d) ultimately construed as determinant of being.[41]

a. The *Logos* as Being: Heraclitus and the Polemical Harmony

Heidegger begins his turn or, better, the return to thinking about thinking as belonging to being, by way of consideration of a pre-Socratic understanding of the unity of what the early Greeks construe as thinking and being, namely, *logos* and *phusis*. Heidegger adds, however, an important proviso, namely, that "*logos*" and "*legein*" initially did not mean anything like "thinking," "intellect," "reason," or even "language." Instead, they stood for something like "reading-off" *(Ablese)*, selecting and gathering wood, wine, and the like; in assembling or gathering these items (and, indeed, rather than others), differences become manifest.[42] Heidegger accordingly suggests that "gathering" is the "original meaning," indeed, the "basic meaning" of *logos*. Although Heidegger apparently overstates matters in this connection, it is true that, as early as "*legein*"and its cognates are used for something akin to "discourse" or "thinking," they are also used as cognates for "gathering" or "bringing together."[43]

More important, there is ample reason to suppose, Heidegger claims, that this original sense of "*logos*" as "gathering" is meant to elucidate the initial Greek understanding of being as *phusis*. Thus, in his first fragment Heraclitus sets up a parallel of sorts between the expressions "according to the *logos*" and "according to *phusis*." Moreover, in this and the second fragment, "*logos*" does not designate anything that could in any straightforward sense be considered a function of intentionality or language (for example, a sense, a word, or a doctrine).[44] Interpreting these fragments in terms of the root meaning of "*legein*,"Heidegger construes the Heraclitean *logos* as an original gathering or gatheredness of things and as equivalent, in that sense, to the surging and prevailing presence designated by "*phusis*."

What is meant by this "gathering"? One thing that is meant is the way in which particular beings are brought to the fore, passing from absence to presence, and related to one another or together. This gathering of beings is not itself a being or in any sense a product or function of beings, not even human beings. Moreover, Heraclitus emphasizes repeatedly (see fragments 1, 2, 34, 72) that, for all its constancy, a constancy on which human beings are themselves dependent, the *logos* is not understood by most people. They focus on beings instead of the *logos*, "the gatheredness of beings that stands in itself, that is, being" (100). As evidence of that all-too-human focus, Heidegger cites the commonplace observation that life is life and death, death, the one not to be confused with the other. By contrast, Heraclitus' insight into the being of life is the fact that it is at the same time death. The superior strength of the *logos* lies in a deep harmony that gathers and holds together disharmonies and is stronger than any surface harmony. This harmonic gathering, however, is not a predetermined order but a gathering storm *(Niederlage)*, a battle in terms of which beings as such first emerge. The *logos* is a gathering in the sense of a *polemos*, a creative (better: creating) conflict of countervailing forces.[45] Only through this struggle do particular beings, as it were, "come into their own," and in that sense this originating *polemos* is the very securing and transpiring of things, the way in which they are gathered up, that is to say, their being *(Logos)*. In the subsequent demise of this inceptive insight, the world turns away from *this* conflict, no longer affirming entities in this way and allowing them to maintain themselves (to be); instead they become objects, already found, finished and available, as a veritable fund (48). The nihilism of metaphysics, the technological conquest of all that is, lies in waiting.

b. The *Logos* as the Violence of Being:
Parmenides and the Essence of the Human

Heidegger's interpretation of the Parmenidean *Logos*, like that of the Heraclitean, is an argument for reinverting the traditional (post-Socratic, semantic) conception of the relation between being and thinking.[46] Heidegger's interpretation initially takes its bearings from two fragments in which the term "*logos*" does not appear, namely, fragment 5: "Being and thinking (more precisely, apprehending) are the same ('*in* their belonging together')" and fragment 8: "Apprehension and that for the sake of which apprehension happens are the same." After interpreting apprehension, precisely in its dependence on being, as definitive of being human, he turns to Parmenides' affirmation (in fragment 6) of apprehension's essential affinity with *logos*.

A reading of the *Antigone* choral ode, however, provides Heidegger with the key to his interpretation of the Parmenidean *Logos*. The chorus's declaration and subsequent elaboration of the utter uncanniness of being human—"Manifold is the uncanny, yet nothing is uncannier than man"—elucidate Parmenides' own statements about the relation between "being" and "apprehension" *(noein)*.[47] On Heidegger's reading of the *Antigone* choral ode, to be human is to belong to the overwhelming yet fitting violence of nature *(dikē)* and at the same time to do violence to it *(technē)*. In the light of this reading, the apprehending that, according to fragments 5 and 8, belongs to being and indeed exists for its sake, is a form of violence, a necessary struggle with, among other things, the familiar and immediate results of understanding and language, a struggle to take things up and thus disclose them for what they are. Relying on the basic similarity between *legein* and *noein* declared in fragment 6, Heidegger then extends to the *logos* itself this conception of apprehension as the human-defining act of doing violence. He thereby introduces a second sense of "*logos*"; in addition to *Logos* as the "gatheredness" of being, there is also the *logos* as the sort of gathering that is proper to being human.[48] Hearkening back to the parallel with the two senses of the "uncanny" *(deinon)* in the *Antigone* choral, Heidegger characterizes the human *logos* as the happening of what is most uncanny *(to deinotaton)* "in which, through doing violence, the overwhelming comes to appearance and is brought to stand" (131).

This human *logos,* Heidegger emphasizes, must be understood above all in relation to the primary *Logos* ("*Logos*" as a name for being), but this very relation demands of the human *logos* that it assume a certain posture (and thus a specific *technē,* a kind of violence) towards itself and its world. By gathering or bringing into the open the original gatheredness of being (as coming-into-concealment) and thereby bringing beings, including itself, into their own, the human *logos* is involved in an uncanny struggle with itself.[49] It has to gather itself together in the midst of the booming and buzzing confusion of things. This human *logos* or "gathering" is thus a turning away in one sense, but only by virtue of turning toward in another sense, "pulling beings together into the gatheredness *(Gesammeltheit)* of their being."[50] Bringing together the *logos* and the uncanniness of being human, the historical inception of determinations of humanity by the thinker (Parmenides) and the poet (Sophocles) respectively, Heidegger concludes: "*Logos* as gathering, as human self-gathering to fitting-ness [as a human being's way of gathering himself together for—or on the plane of—being as fittingness], first transposes being-human into its essence and thus sets it into the uncanny, inasmuch as at-homeness is ruled by the seeming of the customary, the usual and the trite."[51]

Heidegger's account of the human *logos,* the *logos* as definitive of being human, is as broadly conceived as his account of Dasein in *Sein und Zeit.* That is to say, his thesis is not the anthropological claim that primitive humans were gatherers; nor is his account of the relation between the two senses of "*logos*" as "gathering" (based on his readings of the pre-Socratics) merely a replay of the realist claim that any act of gathering requires a gathering or, better, gathered-ness of things in advance. Rather, his point is that the human *logos,* precisely as an act of violence, is the way in which "being is gathered in its gatheredness" (129). In other words, the human *logos* is marked by taking up (apprehending: *noein*) and gathering *(legein),* not just any gathering of beings, but rather the gathering by virtue of which they are; in other words, "being . . . in its gatheredness." Accordingly, Heidegger advises, the *technē* or violence done by the human *logos* does not turn away from things but instead "pulls them together into the gatheredness of being" (129).

Heidegger is rehearsing and deepening his earlier treatment of being and Dasein. Although being is ontologically different from every entity (and thus inaccessible to any ontic science), being is neither the general characteristics of beings as such (*Seiendheit, entitas,* beingness) nor something separate from them but precisely the very way that entities or beings *are.* In other words, being is distinct but not separate from entities. This basic insight of Heidegger's early writings is echoed in the EiM interpretation of "being" as the "originary gatheredness" of beings in the sense of their "coming-into-unconcealment" (130). At the same time, in *Sein und Zeit,* Dasein is construed as precisely the "being-here" or "world" in which beings are uncovered and their being disclosed. Similarly, in EiM Heidegger argues that *legein* of the human *logos* has the specific character it does, namely, to set forth entities in their unconcealment, precisely because the human *logos* (Dasein) is essentially related or referred to the *Logos (Sein)* as the original gatheredness of beings, their coming-into-unconcealment. What it means to be human is precisely to be the relation or "place" (in the language of *Sein und Zeit:* the *In-der-Welt-sein,* the *Da-sein*) for this coming-into-concealment. "The human *essence* shows itself here as the relation that first opens up being to humanity."[52]

According to Heidegger, the Greek inception of human history begins precisely with this determination of being human in terms of the human *logos* as the "revealing gathering" of being. This same conception of the human *logos* explains why language should itself be construed in terms of *logos,* something that, if Heidegger's etymologies are correct, is by no means self-evident.[53] In this way Heidegger briefly introduces an account of the *essence* of language— the way in which language *unfolds (west)*—that rests on a consideration of a distinctive sort of naming and saying.[54]

What does naming do? It is customary to think of naming as a way of designating some entity that is already at hand or has otherwise made itself apparent. So construed, the name or word can serve as a placeholder for the object named, typically in the latter's absence. Whatever merit and propriety this way of construing naming may have, it is not the sort of naming that Heidegger has in mind. Instead, an "act of violence" is Heidegger's favored description for the naming that accounts for the (genuine, paradigmatic) human *logos* of language (131). This act of violence is the sort of *originary* poetic or productive naming and saying that opens up an entity in its being. "In originary saying, the being of beings is opened up in the structure of its gatheredness. This opening-up is gathered in the second sense, according to which the word preserves what is originally gathered, and thus the word governs what holds sway, *phusis.* Human beings, as those who stand and act in logos, in gathering, are the gatherers."[55]

Only where the *Logos* (being) opens itself does the sound of a word become a word, and only where it is apprehended does merely "keeping one's ears open become hearing" (101). Here Heidegger shows his phenomenological pedigree. For the phenomenologist the first condition of all cognition is the fact that what is known *makes itself present* to the knower (the *Logos* as "coming-into-unconcealment"); the second condition is the way in which the knower attends to how what is known makes itself present. Since most people do not attend to being but rather to beings, it is left to only a few—thinkers and poets—to address being, provided, of course, that it opens itself to them.[56]

Language supposes the unconcealment of things—the *Logos* of their being— but not (or at least not primarily) in the sense of a semiotic system of signs and things signified, both already at hand. Instead, language supposes the unconcealment of things in the sense that it is itself part of the process of bringing entities into the open, gathering them together, uncovering them, and rescuing them from oblivion. In other words, language, so construed, is part of the *Logos* as the overwhelming gathering of entities into unconcealment. The human *logos* is itself fundamentally and thoroughly "linguistic" in this sense, gathering things up in their being (their *logos* as unconcealment).

Of course, the human *logos* as language in this paradigmatic sense is precisely poetic, inceptive language—but it also defines itself by the contrast with language that is not poetic. The uncanniness of language is such that, precisely in opening up being, it also makes possible a descent into palaver *(Gerede)* and a subordination of beings to the words that designate them. Instructive in this connection is Heidegger's observation that "the word, naming, puts the entity that opens itself . . . back into its being and preserves it in this openness, delimitation, and constancy"; the entity needs to be "put back" from some "immediately overwhelming assault."[57] As this observation suggests, the "originary" character of naming suggests that the entity has not come into its own or, in other words, that it requires the violence of the human *logos,* specifically, as language, in order to be gathered into the *logos* of being.[58] "Because the essence of language is found in the gathering *(Sammlung)* of the gatheredness *(Gesammeltheit)* of being, language in the sense of everyday talk comes to its truth only if the saying and hearing are related to *logos* as gatheredness, in the sense of being."[59]

Heidegger claims, as already noted, that in Parmenides' saying "the decisive determination of the essence of the human being is first fulfilled" (133). At this inception of Western thinking, the human *logos* is distinguished from—but not yet set over—the *logos* (being as *phusis*). Human being is defined as the very way of gathering and apprehending beings in their being, taking over in some measure the task of setting to work the way things appear and thereby "*governing* unconcealment, *preserving* it against concealment and covering-up" (133). Whereas here being and thinking are clearly distinguished and thus related, the essence of being human that results is not that of an animal possessing the *Logos* (or even the human *logos* or language), as the traditional definition would have it, but rather the *Logos* possessing the human being.[60] By opening up the being *(Logos)* of entities, the human *logos,* indeed, primarily as language, grounds being human.

c. The Beginning of the End

According to Heidegger, Greek philosophy was not up to the task of sustaining this conception of *Logos*. Plato and Aristotle mark the beginning of "the decline of the determination of *logos*" and, with that decline, the loss of the basic insight that thinking belongs to being—rather than vice versa (111, 130, 144). The first step in this decline is the transformation of the sense of being *(phusis)* into something that is by way of its relation to the human mind: the Platonic *idea.*[61] From its original meaning as the ongoing presence of what has emerged of itself and thus can be seen by human beings, being is construed as *idea* and *eidos* (the latter taken in an expanded sense, that is to say, not merely for what is visible with the naked eye but everything that can be apprehended). In other words, the primordial Greek conception of being as *phusis,* the entire event and way in which things emerge and manifest themselves to one another, is reduced to a particular mode of this self-presentation. "The visage offered by the thing, and no longer the thing itself, now becomes what is decisive."[62]

Given the ways in which "*phusis*" and "*logos*" each designate being for the pre-Socratics, it is not surprising that, hand in hand with this reduction of *phusis* to *idea,* the senses of "*logos*" are transformed.[63] Originary language *(logos),* it may be recalled, has a hand in the very event in which beings come to be and, in that sense, gather (the *legein* of *logos*). But language's capacity to preserve, iterate, and communicate what it has articulated also makes way for its downfall. For that capacity makes it possible to spread the word about something but "in such a way that the entity that was originally opened up in gathering is not itself properly experienced in each particular case."[64] The very iteration "disengages" itself, so to speak, from the entity, and this process can go so far that it becomes "mere hearsay" (141–142). At this point, saying and asserting become the place in which obscurity and distortion are contested and decisions made about what is true. The struggle for the truth becomes a struggle against distortion and—since, as in any struggle, one becomes dependent on the opponent—the struggle for truth becomes a struggle for the undistorted. The human *logos* thus comes to define itself by this struggle instead of defining itself by the *Logos* as the original gathering (or the truth as the unfolding) of things. Here the transition from the gathering *Logos*—"the happening of unconcealment, grounded in it and beholden to it"—to the *logos* of the assertion as "the locus of truth in the sense of correctness" is complete.[65] As an assertion, a *logos* says something about something else *(legein ti kata tinos)* as something that "already" underlies the former (the *hupokeimenon* or *subjectum*). Whereas the *Logos* at the inception of Greek thinking, as intimated by Heraclitus, is a name for being as an entity's historical struggle to come to unconcealment, so *logos* at the beginning of the end of Greek thinking is equivalent to "*logos apophantikos*," an assertion or judgment as something at hand standing over against the presence of what is asserted or judged. The Platonic *idea* and the Aristotelian *ousia,* for all their alleged differences, conspire in forging the logical prejudice by construing the being of beings as their constant presence.[66] The *logos* no longer merely diverges from—albeit within and for—being (as it does for Parmenides) but emerges over against it—think of Aristotelian or Kantian "categories"—as "the standard-setting domain that becomes the place of origin for the determinations of being."[67]

The history of the logical prejudice according to Heidegger can be summed up in three stages (including the present as the "slow end" of the third stage), each corresponding to a conception of *logos*. As indicated chiefly by the Heraclitean fragments, *Logos* as the "gathering of beings" and being in the sense of *phusis* are construed at the inception of Greek thinking as one. Parmenidean and Sophoclean texts then point to the disjoining of the *Logos,* so conceived, and the human *logos* as the uncanniest way of gathering, including the violence of naming and saying (the human *logos* as language). Finally, *logos* is identified with *logos apophantikos,* the assertion as the place of truth, now understood in the sense of correctness, a transformation elaborated by Aristotle and made possible by the Platonic reduction of *phusis* to *idea.* The stage is presumably set for the subsequent translation of *logos* into the *ratio* of a logic, not merely standing over against *phusis* but taking over and regulating the determination of the being of beings.[68]

3. ANOTHER BEGINNING: THINKING BEING-HISTORICALLY

Several pre-Socratic fragments afford Heidegger the opportunity of reformulating basic phenomenological insights in a premetaphysical light that suggests a way to a different, postmetaphysical beginning for thinking about being. That is to say, he recasts the unity of the difference between beings (including subject and object) and even between being and beings into the unfolding of the difference, the very "coming-into-unconcealment" that demands being be thought historically.[69] In certain respects this move deepens phenomenology's deepest insight: givenness (being as *Logos*) is presupposed by the apprehension *(logos),* but not in the sense of something already at hand. Rather, being is an event, unfolding *(wesen)* and historically appropriating *(ereignen)* both what is given and that to which it is given. Language itself is accordingly understood not primarily in terms of what is said or the one saying it, but rather in terms of the way that the saying itself historically answers to being (that is to say, is appropriated to and by the historical unfolding of being—more on this in a moment).[70] Hence, with good reason Heidegger understands his interpretation of the *logos* and its transformation into the logical prejudice not as a deepening of phenomenology's basic insights but as an attempt to disclose the original but obscured or forgotten experiences or events of being and their meaning. As he puts his efforts to interpret Parmenides' fifth fragment: "We are attempting to win back the originary truth of the saying."[71]

At the outset of this chapter certain challenges from a logical point of view were presented to Heidegger's views regarding the alleged symbiosis of metaphysics and logic. According to Heidegger, the logical prejudice that whatever can be thought or said must conform to the formal structure of bivalent assertions disables thinking about being (or, equivalently, inverts the relation between being and thinking). By contrast, from a logical point of view it seems that, in addition to reviving the discredited notion that logic, despite its formality, is wedded to metaphysics or at least a particular conception of being, Heidegger must forfeit any claim to nonarbitrariness since bivalence—or, as he would put it, "truth as correctness"—is essential to the logical prejudice.

A serious and useful critical engagement with these challenges can only be carried out in terms of a specific logical doctrine.[72] In certain respects Heidegger makes things easy for himself by speaking in broad historical terms about logic and by paying little attention to debates about such matters among his contemporaries.[73] Nevertheless, his account of the history of the logical prejudice provides some means of meeting those challenges. For, in the first place, neither the formality and thus the alleged metaphysical neutrality of formal or symbolic logic nor the universality of claims for bivalence, both of which are insisted on from some logical points of view, are self-evident. In the absence of self-evidence or argument, the claim that logic can, let alone should, be neutral on the question of being and the claim that every "saying" must be true or false are in need of justification. Indeed, by some accounts, these dimensions of formal logic can only be "shown" and not "said."[74]

Precisely at this juncture, Heidegger's history of the uses of *"logos"* recounts a way of thinking and saying what logic cannot. Both Heraclitus and Parmenides, on his reading, name being as the *Logos* in a way that reflects an experience of being as the "gathering of things," their coming-to-light, to presence. What they say is not incidental or after the fact but part of the gathering itself (even if not expressly so "thought" by them). The very possibility of thinking and saying (the human *logos*) answers first to the unfolding passage from absence to presence *(das Wesen der Wahrheit)*. As an original manner of gathering and unveiling, this saying is hardly neutral on what it means to be. Nor is it true or false in the sense of a bivalent assertion about something that may or may not be present. What Heraclitus and Parmenides say is, rather, the inception of thinking as a way of being, in which the emergence into presence is disclosed.

Could they have been wrong? Could Heidegger's interpretation be false? The answer, it seems to me, has to be an unequivocal "Yes!" but with the understanding that it will not do to argue for the impropriety of his interpretation by simply insisting on the prerogatives of formal apophantics. For then the pre-Socratic sayings and Heidegger's commemoration of them are construed as at-hand assertions or judgments about something present (in the sense of being on hand), and it is by no means obvious how *that* construal is to be not only meaningfully asserted but justified. If the pre-Socratic fragments and Heidegger's interpretation are true, it is not as theoretical or quasi-theoretical assertions about something other than themselves. Instead, like the existentials of Heidegger's earlier thought, their truth would consist precisely in disclosing what it means "to be" as modes of self-disclosiveness.

Still, Heidegger's criticism of the logical prejudice does not mean that his own account is not supposed to be subject to bivalence in some respect. His commitment to bivalence is evident in at least two respects. In the first place, it is no accident that one is hard pressed to find in Heidegger's writings and lectures, even as he rails against the pitfalls of thinking overdetermined by logical considerations, anything that amounts, formally, to an inconsistency or contradiction. He takes care to avoid the sort of affirmation of contradiction that Hegel and other dialectical thinkers explicitly—and seemingly quite confusedly—countenance.[75] Similarly, when Heidegger interprets the Parmenidean saying that thinking and being are the same, he immediately makes it clear that something other than strict logical identity is meant (on his reading, they are said to be the same in the sense of belonging to the same).

In the second place, Heidegger plainly faults certain ontological interpretations for their inadequacy. In Heidegger's entire corpus, but especially in the *Introduction to Metaphysics* and other works after 1930, the recurring theme is the insufficiency of certain conceptions of being, the common note of which is a constant presence (*idea, ousia, substantia, res cogitans et res extensa, Geist, Wille zur Macht,* force, energy). This theme, however, is part of an argument for an allegedly more adequate way of thinking about being, namely, "thinking-being-historically" *(seynsgeschichtliches Denken),* as he eventually dubs it. In other words, Heidegger makes tacit but unmistakable use of disjunctive dilemmas, the force of which depends on the law of excluded middle.

Heidegger takes pains, to be sure, to acknowledge the historical necessity of the purportedly inadequate conceptions of being or at least to demonstrate why they emerged. At least insofar as they are conceptions of being, he seems to be working with a principle of degrees of disclosedness (truth) and thus something weaker than bivalence (or even what Dummett dubs "valence," that is, true or not true). Nevertheless, Heidegger is also claiming that his conception of being as an appropriating event *(Ereignis)* underlies those inadequate conceptions and not vice versa. In other words, the contrasting ontological conceptions are not equivalent.

The fact that Heidegger presents his views about the origins and limitations of logic in apparent compliance with logical principles raises three important questions. (1) If Heidegger does, indeed, adhere to the principles of non-contradiction and bivalence in the ways suggested, does not that adherence undermine his argument against the logical prejudice? In other words, does it not countermand his own strictures against the sort of thinking that allows itself to be overdetermined by the formality of traditional logic? (2) Does not the very claim that one conception of being is adequate (true), the other inadequate (false), illustrate that bivalence runs through all discourse from top to bottom or, in other words, that every *logos* is true or false (or at least true or not true)? (3) Finally, is Heidegger not compelled, by the simple demands of logical consistency, to posit the constant presence of the "appropriating event" (in terms of which he interprets what it means to be)?

Despite being closely related to one another, these three questions are not equivalent. Heidegger's response to the first question would presumably be a plea for a distinction between different perspectives, one comparable, the other incomparable or originative. The claim that one ontological interpretation is true and another false supposes their comparability. Insofar as the interpretations are to be compared, each must be regarded from a purely formal (logical) point of view as in principle true or false. It is also possible, however, to inquire into the ontological presuppositions of the principles of noncontradiction and bivalence underlying this comparative perspective. The object of this sort of inquiry comprises, more precisely, the senses of "being" and "truth" presupposed by those principles. The perspective of this sort of inquiry, "external" in a sense to formal logic, aims to determine the originality of the presupposed senses. Heidegger's claim is that conceptions of being (or truth) as a constant presence are not original but in fact derivative of a more primordial appropriating event. Being is neither a thing nor its presence but rather an interplay of presence and absence. Nevertheless, as exemplified by Heidegger's own practice, this prelogical understanding of being can and must be presented in a logically coherent manner in order to be intelligible at all.

This sort of answer to the first question immediately raises the second question noted above, namely, whether there is a *logos* that is not subject to bivalence and yet eminently—indeed, preeminently—true. Heidegger's affirmative answer to this question can be regarded as a distinct kind of nominalistic verificationism. There is a *logos* that cannot be false since its very sense is its truth, the disclosure of and by it (hence, verificationist); this *logos* is named (hence, nominalistic), but not in such a way that the naming, the work of poets and philosophers, excludes any resources of language (including judgments and assertions). Being discloses itself historically and is accordingly named in a manner that is presupposed by any talk (including theoretical statements), not only about particular entities (or parts of being) but about being itself. Though not inaccurate at a certain level, this way of putting the matter is problematic inasmuch as the term "about" might convey a misleading distinction between the talk and being. The reflexive and verificationist character of being's disclosure (truth) consists precisely in the fact that the philosophical and poetic talk in question is among the very ways in which being appropriates human beings to itself; hence, its reflexiveness and truthfulness unfold prior to deliberate reflections or acts of judgment. (So, too, in *Being and Time*, Heidegger insists that talk *(Rede)* be construed as an existential, a way of being-here *(da-sein)* that is self-disclosive.) At the same time, far from being a theoretical assertion that may be true or false, this very disclosure (not unlike the more ordinary senses of "naming" or "sensing") is presupposed by such assertions.

Still, it may be countered, the demands of intelligibility (guaranteed by logical consistency) compel Heidegger to suppose the constant presence of being, however he otherwise purports to conceive it. On this score (the gist of the third question raised earlier), Heidegger would, indeed, seem to have painted himself into a corner. Although it is true that what is named need not be fully present, that is to say, that it is yet to come, the very assertion cannot help but petrify this happening (appropriating event) in a certain regard *(eidos)*. Logic, it would seem, is a ladder that cannot be kicked away.

Yet there is also no reason to kick it away, despite Heidegger's suggestions to the contrary. In order for us to entertain and deliberate, to compare and contrast, to infer and communicate, and the like, we require some measure of presence, stability, or invariance of meaning. This requirement remains even if what we are entertaining is itself absent, unstable, or varying. For purposes of thinking (in such cases), we suppose or imagine a sort of presence of absencing, the stability of an instability, the invariance of a variation. But there is nothing in the nature of such thoughtful (logical or linguistic) operations that requires the transfer of *that* imaginary or stipulative presence to the absence, that is, to what is entertained. To the extent that Heidegger is claiming otherwise, he fails to appreciate the imaginativeness of logic, an imaginativeness that secures a (semantic or ontological) neutrality.

Heidegger is in fact compelled to rely on the neutrality of logic, but this reliance need not undermine the force of his argument against the logical prejudice in Western thinking. Indeed, under a certain interpretation, that reliance can be said to underscore the legitimate object of his criticism. As stated above, Heidegger's problem is not with logic as the study of techniques of inference but with a kind of thinking about being that allows itself to be overdetermined by certain prerogatives of logic. Those prerogatives include an insistence on formality and the universality of formal criteria, together with a supposition of the constancy of the references of terms and assertions, in abstraction from their actual interpretation or instantiation. If being is, indeed, not a constant presence but precisely a more or less unsteady interplay of presence and absence, then to think being (that is to say, to think-being-historically) is to countenance the very limits and foundation of logic but to do so logically, namely, as *its* limits and foundation.

Nor can the metaphysical force of the logical prejudice in the subsequent history of Western thinking be underestimated. Insistence on thinking in formally invariant terms of what does or does not obtain can freeze the historicity of being in an ideal presence, that is to say, a presence that—in contrast to being—is at our disposal. Not surprisingly, metaphysicians are driven to some ever-present principle or constantly obtaining presence by the logic or, better, the logical prejudices of their thinking. Metaphysics depends on being, the coming-to-presence of things, but falls for the logical and anthropological pretense that only their presence can be *thought* or *said*. The *Logos* is, as it were, "scattered," and it can only be gathered again by a new beginning. It is no wonder that Heidegger's *Introduction to Metaphysics* is an introduction to logic.

Chapter 6

THE NAME ON THE EDGE OF LANGUAGE: A COMPLICATION IN HEIDEGGER'S THEORY OF LANGUAGE AND ITS CONSEQUENCES

DIETER THOMÄ

"I am not a leader of men, Willy, and neither are you. . . . I'm one dollar an hour, Willy! . . . I'm not bringing home any prizes any more, and you're going to stop waiting for me to bring them home! . . . I'm nothing! I'm nothing, Pop. Can't you understand that? . . . I'm what I am, that's all."

—Biff Loman in *Death of a Salesman*

1. THE *INTRODUCTION TO METAPHYSICS* AND HEIDEGGER'S TURNING

The question of how to read the *Introduction to Metaphysics* is intertwined with the question of the so-called turning *(Kehre)*. Time and again, Heidegger depicted his philosophical development as a slowly proceeding unfolding of "one question": the question of Being that is unfolded *as* a turning. Following this reading, the *Introduction to Metaphysics* is to be taken as an intermediary work that is to be located in a well-established framework, and only one problem must still be settled: in a turning executed in a well-rounded movement, the *Introduction to Metaphysics* has to be identified as a certain signpost offering links to *Being and Time* and to the first programmatic texts from the postwar period, and it is from these references that it shall obtain its own meaning and definition.

Heidegger himself, as the most authoritative (albeit inadvertent) witness, calls the general account of the *Kehre* into question. In a letter to Gadamer he stated that around 1928 "everything" in his thinking "was starting to slip."[1] That this slipping motion does not fit into a perfectly drawn turning can be learned from the original semantic context of the *Kehre,* which is basically a topographic one. Though you may keep your pace by *turning* on your way down from a pass, you have to face adventurous situations while *slipping* on a steep path down to the bottom of a mountain; your rate of acceleration is higher, and control is limited.

Thus it is anything but a surprise that the texts from the thirties show symptoms of his uncertainty, including the emancipation of the "moment" in the lecture course of 1929–1930, the reference to the "forces of earth and blood" *(erd- und bluthafte Kräfte)* in the Rectoral Address, the triad of "assignment, mission, and work" *(Auftrag, Sendung und Arbeit)* in the course on logic from 1934, the novel conflict between "world" and "earth" unfolded in "The Origin of the Work of Art" (1935–1936), the affirmative notion of the will in the first Nietzsche lectures, and the odd coinage of a "will to the event/ appropriation" *(Wille zum Ereignis)* in the posthumously edited *Contributions to Philosophy* of 1936–1938.[2] These phenomena hardly are to be reconciled with the ideal of the "*one* path" *(die eine Bahn)* Heidegger wants to follow faithfully.[3]

Even the so-called turning itself turns out to be ambiguous. Originally, it had been conceptualized as the movement that should lead to the completion of *Being and Time.* This, at least, was Heidegger's own programmatic self-interpretation in 1928.[4] The foundering of the turning that was to be executed within the framework of *Being and Time* hints at a flaw in its systematic core. As it was intended, yet could not be realized, the preconditions for the next steps, the movement that takes place in the thirties and forties, become complicated, too. Obviously, a newly designed turning would have to get a shape different from the turning implied in *Being and Time,* since otherwise the whole atmosphere of crisis, the doubts about the feasibility of the original project, would have been groundless. Therefore the new movement taking place has been labeled as a *second* turning. But the parameters for its actual starting point, the premises for its realization, remain unclear: after the foundering of *Being and Time* the landscape in which this next turning has to be inscribed is still uncharted. The new context is startling to Heidegger himself, who, while slipping, experiences staggering, changing perspectives and presents himself as a thinker in transition.[5]

Therefore I plead for a reading of Heidegger's texts that disputes the explanatory value of the turning and pays attention to the often surprising revisions and deviations that are found in Heidegger's texts after *Being and Time.* I cannot expand upon the more general aspects of Heidegger's philosophical development in the thirties here; the function of these introductory remarks merely consists in justifying a reading of the *Introduction to Metaphysics* that lies beyond Heidegger's forcefully, fiercely maintained claim of lifelong, only marginally damaged consistency. Breaking with this ideal will eventually have a liberating effect on the reading of the *Introduction*. It gains independence from its towering predecessor *Being and Time,* as well as from its progeny, for example, from the "Letter on Humanism," and it does not get totally lost in Heidegger's philosophical and political involvement in National Socialism, either.

In this chapter I will turn the tables and claim that shortcomings in both the early and the late thinking of Heidegger can be pointed out by means of the *Introduction to Metaphysics:* problems, to be precise, in the respective conceptions of language. This work gains an internal critical function that is helpful in the context of an independent account of Heidegger's philosophy that I wish to advocate. Moreover, it unfolds a soundly defensible argument concerning the plausibility and relevance of a particular use of language, namely, naming.

The naming that I take as the salient point of Heidegger's theory of language in the *Introduction* is elucidated as a particular stance toward things and persons, as a game belonging, as it were, to our repertory, as an act(ivity) that is part of human functioning. (I am not afraid of using terms that sound so odd to Heideggerians; they may blame me for naively ignoring his criticisms of ethics, subjective activities, or quasi-technological functionalism, but, alas, I cannot meet their objections in this short essay, except indirectly by making my argument as plausible as possible.)

I begin with brief sketches of Heidegger's early and late conceptions of language, pointing out a recurrent dilemma that could be called the strife between naming and context (sections 2 and 3). These sketches provide an indispensable background and contrast for my reading of the *Introduction to Metaphysics.* After those preludes, I focus on a keystone of the theory of language as presented in the *Introduction to Metaphysics:* a revised notion of naming that hints at a way out of the dilemma between naming and context with which the earlier and later conceptions are charged and provides Being with an unexpected role: the role of a servant of the name. By implying a certain conception of human behavior and interaction, "naming" in that particular sense turns out to have some ethical relevance, too. Heidegger does not follow this path any further—a reluctance affecting his own account that deserves attention nonetheless (section 4). Generally speaking, my chapter is part of an approach that takes Heideggerian arguments as incentives for a way of thinking that leads beyond him.

2. THE "WHOLE OF MEANINGS" AND THE DASEIN ON THE EDGE:
BEING AND TIME

The world in which Dasein exists is to be understood as "totality of significations," "referential context," "total relevance."[6] In *Being and Time,* language is presented in the context of "care": the disclosure of a world belongs to an ultimately practical context; the meaning of something that Dasein has to do with depends on the forms of "serviceability" and "usability"[7] attributed to it and thereby on the relations to other things. This is the pragmatic dimension of Heidegger's analysis of the worldliness of Dasein (stressed mainly, but not only, by scholars from the United States).[8] In 1925, Heidegger says: "Thus all taking, using, and instituting of signs are only a particular development of the specific concern in the environing world, insofar as it is to be made available."[9] By using something, Dasein presents itself in a specific mode of Being: as a "user" it is naturally involved in a certain practice, so that it cannot absolve itself from the world it is dealing with. Since this context belongs to its self-understanding, there is no longer a need for a desperate search launched by the subject to get in touch with a noumenal "outer world" or "reality": "Da-sein is initially and for the most part *together with* [or: *at home in*] the 'world' that it takes care of."[10]

There is a certain indecision, so far, concerning Dasein's pragmatic attitude, and one may consider two alternatives that present themselves as more conclusive conceptions of this attitude. *Either* one may take the practices the human being is engaged in as forms of coping with factual circumstances and constraints, as a strategy of assimilation and adaptation that follows the guidelines hidden in the qualities of the things one has to do with, *or* one may follow a stronger reading of Dasein's power of "disposing" or "mastering" and regard it as a person's being able to strive for deliberately pursued goals. Neither version really fits Heidegger's account, since both tend to isolate one side of Heidegger's contextualism: either the presupposition of a "real" world is made, or Dasein assumes a quasi-imperialist stance as a master of purposes and, thereby, of the universe.

Seemingly, the second version paves the way to a conception of the person that is determined to overcome the entanglement with a context, that is, with its "Being-in-the-world." Yet even in this case the problem remains that the person has to rely on something beyond herself—be it only in order to demonstrate her seizure of the world. Without this proof, her power would be vain. Hence even in this case the person remains dependent on the world, which leads us back to Heidegger's contextualized human being: "Da-sein has always already got itself into definite possibilities. As a potentiality for being which it *is*, it has let some go by; it constantly adopts the possibilities of its being, grasps them, and goes astray."[11] The Dasein is entangled with a context that is not simply itself but vanishes in the midst of its occupations. The surplus, the being-more than current concerns (compare SZ, 145), gets lost. This "falling prey" *(Verfallen)* becomes most evident in the subordination to the concern of others, the "Others," or "They": "As everyday being-with-one-another, Da-sein stands in *subservience* to the others. It itself *is* not; the others have taken its being away from it."[12]

Even though Dasein is interwoven with the world as a "whole of meanings" in everyday life, it is far from identifying itself with a selection of "meanings." Yet it has to figure out how to play the privileged role to which it seems to be entitled in the contextualized world. This quest leads Dasein beyond its various occupations and may be labeled as a quest for identity or for an appropriate self-understanding. It is this turn that leads beyond the merely pragmatic dimension of "Being-in-the-world."

Heidegger's contextualist approach has its own problems when it comes to the question of denomination and reference—problems that can be discerned in some contemporary advocates of this type of hermeneutics.[13] Instead of focusing on this epistemological and linguistic quarrel between contextualism and realism, I am more interested in the inner perspective of the idea of language outlined in *Being and Time,* namely, the question of how Dasein may talk about itself and express itself in an authentic way. In addition to covering or even seizing the world, language is supposed to stand for Dasein as it is, underpinning all further involvements, and to grasp its paramount status. Dasein approaches the threshold of what may be called a "language of itself" in the course of a contextual crisis that makes it aware of its own preeminent status: "The total relevance itself . . . ultimately leads back to a what-for which *no longer* has relevance, which itself is not a being of the kind of being of things at hand within a world, but is a being whose being is defined as being-in-the-world, to whose constitution of being worldliness itself belongs."[14] Dasein belongs to the world *and* is its very condition. The world is constituted by its projecting or disclosing faculty; hence Dasein cannot be a mere part of it. The question, then, is how the Dasein that is lost in everydayness can become aware of its own peculiar status; how it may be, as it were, awakened; how it becomes "accessible"[15] to itself; how it can take a stand as nothing but itself, absolved from the "worldly" meanings among which it is usually entangled and confounded.

It is "Being-towards-death" as "anticipation" (*Vorlaufen,* SZ, 262) that is hailed as the step by which all meanings can be left behind. By this procedure, culminating in a true encounter with oneself, everyday life as an incessant degradation of Dasein's singularity is suspended. Heidegger himself describes this process, leading to authenticity, as a purifying procedure: authentic Dasein is supposed to be unstained.[16] Beyond the pragmatic language evolving in the context of "care," another language seems to be desirable or even necessary as a way to corroborate the break with the familiar context. This specific form of language has to meet the conditions of authenticity, that is to say, it has to prevent any confusion between a single task and the person undertaking it, between one specific quality and the person to whom it is attributed. The requirements for what may be said then are simple: it has to refer to Dasein itself unmistakably, and any substantial attributions are to be avoided—except the fact that there *is* a world in which it is dwelling. Heidegger gives an accurate description of what can be said then: "In dying, in this way of Being-in-the-world, the world is that upon which Dasein is no longer dependent, the world remains only the pure Wherein of simply-still-Being. . . . Only in dying can I to some extent say absolutely, 'I am.' "[17]

"I am": this is left to be said. On this level, the language of authenticity consists in one telling expression (which is not precisely the "silence" Heidegger recommends in *Being and Time*). Its two elements serve complementary functions. The indexical term "I" makes sure that the fading of the "Me" in the intercourse with others or with the "Everyone" is halted, and stating that I "am" implies a turn against all the predicates that could be attributed to me (German, blond, blue-eyed, narrow-minded), and leaves nothing but a "Me" that could be more than that—or less, however its particular "dressing," fashions, or any further qualifications may be assessed. Emmanuel Martineau goes so far as to claim that, according to Heidegger, the "proper name" of Dasein should resound.[18] I would stick with the indexical "Me" that can be found in Heidegger himself, but Martineau's keen observation reveals Heidegger's bias in favor of words that preserve the exclusivity of an authentic Dasein, an exclusivity that literally consists in an exclusion of all "wrong naming," all inappropriate associations—the linguistic proxy of that exclusivity being the "I am." Given the tenacity of this indexical refuge, Dasein would be enabled to engage in the world without getting lost again.

It is not coincidental, though, that the "proper name" alluded to by Martineau is lacking in Heidegger's account. As long as the reference to an individual is a matter of self-reference, a proper name is useless: there is no doubt about which person is being referred to and no opportunity or necessity to baptize a person, to provide her with a name that may work beyond the situation to which this indexical expression ("me") belongs. One could go so far as to think of the word "Dasein" as nothing but Martineau's "proper name." Since in the moment of highest self-awareness all affiliations are interrupted, since nobody else is involved, the Dasein that I truly am cannot be someone other than myself. And I "am" nothing but the very world-disclosing faculty itself, also known as Dasein.

Yet there is a basic flaw in Heidegger's account of indexical being, of the "I am." In *Being and Time,* it is presented as an enclave in a world dominated by intentions, functions, relations, attributes, qualities that are teleologically oriented toward the "What-for" *(Worum-willen)* of Dasein. It is the "domination by others"[19] that it seeks to rebut by its self-affirmation. Accordingly, human beings shall become "masters of the power that we ourselves are."[20] The polemical stance of the "I am" is directed against the temptations and threats of the world. And this is where the problems with Heidegger's approach to indexicality become obvious.

Although Heidegger claims that everydayness should be maintained as a constituent of authentic existence, his linkage of the "I am" to pure facticity interferes with the attribution of individual properties. For the sake of Dasein's exclusivity, Heidegger has to restrain its exchange with beings, with the *Nichtdaseinsmäßige* as well as with other persons. With this, he is damaging the Dasein he wants to salvage; its room for self-realization is limited. To put it briefly: *name* and *context* struggle against each other; their relation, as unfolded in *Being and Time,* ends up in an aporia.

This is partly due to the fact that Heidegger's account of the "I am" remains incomplete. He needs the indexicality of the "I am"—or, following Martineau's suggestion, the "proper name"—in order to break with the "totality of significations" and its intriguing options. Accordingly, the "I am" seems to belong to a kind of a self-awarded achievement made possible by Dasein's singular effort. Yet there are some far-reaching implications of this would-be linguistic homestead for authenticity that Heidegger does not take into account. The "I am" cannot help being an act of interlocution directed to others; it is part of a complex language game. The comprehension of that *utterance* has to include this context. The "I am" may be a device for turning away from that very context, but, as an utterance, it does so by addressing a linguistic and communicative realm. Consequently, it can be assumed that the faculty of stating "I am" (or "you are") depends on complex conditions. Not merely formal linguistic conditions are to be fulfilled; the utterance "I am" may be felicitous only in a situation where a person is welcome to make her claim, where her insistence on being is not derided as meaningless. It is not necessary to enter the general debate on the relation between Heidegger's theory of Dasein and a philosophy of intersubjectivity or dialogicity here; my only point is that the concomitant circumstances of the language of authenticity are to be taken into account and that, in this regard, Heidegger's own account of authenticity is incomplete and misleading. I will get back to the still strange-sounding contention "I am" at the end of my chapter, but, for the time being, it suffices to hint at Heidegger's completely ignoring the communicative aspect of the language-game "I am." Strangely enough, this basic flaw in his conception of language is limited to his philosophy. In private letters, he acknowledges and even praises the all-but-trivial circumstances of the claim that "I am": he is fond of saying *amo—volo ut sis—*"I love—I want you to be."[21]

The isolation of Dasein as manifest in Heidegger's reading of the "I am" certainly belongs to the aspects he will attack as remainders of "subjectivism" in his later writings. This does not mean, though, that a critique of his early notion of indexicality and (implicitly) of the "name" must follow the guidelines of the late Heidegger. It is, rather, a critique of his later considerations that eventually points back at the *Introduction to Metaphysics*.

3. "SAYING" AS "SHOWING": "ON THE WAY TO LANGUAGE"

Most of the late texts that pay particular attention to naming are to be found in Heidegger's collection *On the Way to Language*. Stefan George's poem *Das Wort* serves Heidegger as a guideline here, with its allusion to the "name" and the line "Where word breaks off no thing may be" *(Kein ding sei wo das wort gebricht).*[22] The question is raised: "Is the name, is the word a sign?" and Heidegger replies: "Everything depends on how we think of what the words 'sign' and 'name' say." He does not follow the traditional definition of " 'name' in the sense of a mere designation": "Accordingly, we must stress as follows: no thing *is* where the word, that is, the name is lacking. The word alone gives being to the thing."[23]

Being does not mean factual existence here (whatever this might be). The Being of a thing is, rather, aroused or established by the word. Only with a little help from its name can a thing "be"; its Being is, as Heidegger puts it, "given" by the word. This relation is not the kind of "grasping" that is implied in the German *Begriff* as well as in the English (and Latin) "concept" *(conceptus).* Words are not "grasps" *(Griffe)*, Heidegger says,[24] and it is not far-fetched to take this remark as a critical comment on the governing attitude of Dasein in *Being and Time*, its pragmatic background and its bias toward domination.

Since the Being of a thing depends on the naming word, this word must have a certain gift: it seems to make a thing accessible in a way hitherto unperceived, unknown. Heidegger rejects the idea of a language that consists in logically combined assertions as a misconception of the "saga" that—as a "house of Being"[25]—harbors the things. This language as "saga," "saying," or "naming" has a demonstrative function: it is to be understood as "showing" (*Zeige*)[26] and may be interpreted as an attitude of respect; the unobtrusive gesture of "Here it is . . ." is implied in showing or hinting at something, as opposed to amassing information. Insisting on the name, or at least keeping sheer naming in mind, represents a veto against predication and its assertive form.

So far, Heidegger's late theory of language could be described as an *externalization* of his earlier conception: whereas in *Being and Time* linguistic indexicality endorsed the privilege of a Dasein surrounded by things caught, for their part, in a net of meanings and references, now the things themselves come into Being by their "names" and are "shown" by language. It is quite evident (although as yet unnoticed by commentators) that the demonstrative, indexical language, whose liberating effects were used for the benefit of Dasein in *Being and Time,* is now being transferred to the "things": instead of being captivated in a "whole" of correlations, they are singled out by their names.

Yet Heidegger is not content with a particularistic naming of "things." It should be noted that he does not confine the "showing" to a single word but takes it as a quality of language itself, of saying as showing. Not only a thing is named, but ultimately the world itself. The question remains, though, how a language that would be able to fulfill this task of showing a whole world should look. What kinds of linguistic operations are legitimate, and what others are to be banned since they conceal the world and lead astray? It is precisely this question that lacks a cohesive answer in Heidegger's later writings.

By applying naming not only to single things but to the world itself, Heidegger's late turn can be characterized as an *exaggeration* of naming. It is the world in general that, according to Heidegger, deserves to be named. Therefore, he can no longer adequately address the question of how names are to be linked, how the internal structure of an authentic language that would be more than an alignment of names could look. It is noteworthy, in this regard, that Heidegger reads "saying" as "showing." He alludes to visual experience as an immediate, simultaneous presentation of a complex matter, but the transference of this gift to language is doomed to failure.

Heidegger's most suggestive attempt to overcome the limitation of naming that is the price he pays for turning away from pragmatic domination is to be found in his late concept of the "fourfold" *(Geviert):* the gathering of "mortals," "gods," "earth," and "sky," or the "play" among them.[27] The "fourfold" may be regarded as a step beyond naming, as a structure that encourages internal relations and "reflections"—among playmates, so to speak. Accordingly, the appropriate understanding of a "thing" depends on a careful explication of its intrinsic references to those four players that are involved in the fourfold.

Yet the outcome of explanations guided by the idea of the fourfold is remarkably poor. By comparing, for instance, more and less authentic modes of using a pitcher, Heidegger makes claims that lack any plausible justification. (What is improper about using a pitcher for serving wine to your friends?)[28] Following his appeal to an original "ethics," Heidegger recommends certain attitudes and practices without ever raising or settling the question of how his preferences might be substantiated. But as unfortunate as the concept of fourfold is, it stems from an understandable intention: Heidegger's dissatisfaction with a language that is unable to convey the complexity of internal relations among the things or the players it is to deal with. But it is his own turn against the formerly well-established whole of meanings and references that urges him to neglect those relations and to stick with pure naming.

As a counterpart to the indexical "I am" that was introduced as an exclusive warrant for the Being of Dasein, the naming applied to a whole world suffers from inverted problems: the world that used to be disclosed and shaped in multifarious ways now appears as a bluntly applauded whole. After having overcome the opposition between Dasein and its context, Heidegger is entangled anew in the dilemma of name and context, yet in a different way: he distorts naming by applying it to a whole world.

4. "BEING" AS SERVANT OF THE NAME: THE *INTRODUCTION TO METAPHYSICS*

According to *Being and Time*, the beings Dasein is concerned with belong to a complex linguistic structure, a "whole of meanings." Dasein has to make sure that its understanding of the world does not lose ground; it has to meet the danger of chatter. Chatter, or "idle talk," is analyzed as a mode of language that does not go back to the "foundation of what is being talked about."[29] Obviously, the pragmatic ideal of a "whole" encompassing the beings is borrowed from the world of the craftsman, where every tool, every crooked timber has or could have a well-defined function and thereby a meaning. In *Being and Time*, Heidegger remains ambivalent in his strategies for avoiding chatter. One strategy is oriented toward pragmatic goals, projects, contexts; a second relies on a firm ground that is given, on things that can be seized upon. This ambivalence is reflected in the double meaning of the German word *Sache*, which, like the Greek *pragma*, means "matter" in the sense of topic as well as "matter" in the sense of thing or material. Yet it is fair to say that the matters that actually "matter" for Heidegger are nothing but things or, at least, involve things. Hence, finally, the two strategies are fused, and a project that does not conform to them may be regarded as superficial or phony.

A telling example for the double meaning of *Sache* is Heidegger's reading of *doxa* in the *Introduction to Metaphysics* (see 79). According to this reading, *doxa* is to be understood in terms of the "respect" and "aspect" of something; "viewpoints," then, are developed by individuals and depend on their respective perspectives. Far from favoring a constructivist argument, however, Heidegger seeks to save a connection between the vista offered by a thing and allegedly subjective considerations. (In German, *Ansicht,* translated as "view" here, can mean "aspect" and "sight" as well as "opinion.") According to Heidegger, *doxa* is more than an individual presupposition. The appearance, the vista of something belongs to the way it is, and *doxa* in the narrow, pejorative sense is to be understood as a distorted form of that original appearance that belongs to the thing itself *and* is properly articulated by authentic language: "In experiencing and busying ourselves with beings, we constantly construct views for ourselves from their look. This often happens without our looking closely at the thing itself. . . . Thus it can happen that the view that we adopt has no support in the thing itself" (79).

The striking preponderance, ontically but also ontologically, of things over, for instance, processes[30] and events is even more evident in the *Introduction to Metaphysics* than it is in *Being and Time.* This is due to Heidegger's growing reservations about Dasein's pragmatic stance, which is now under suspicion for resembling a dubious subjectivity. The new focus on things is corroborated by Heidegger's revision of what interests him in Being: whereas in the early essay on Jaspers's "Psychology of World Views" he favored the "I am" as a paramount expression of Being,[31] now he claims: "The definite and particular verb form 'is,' the *third person singular of the present indicative,* has a priority here" (70).

Beyond the pragmatic framework, *things* are still available, and what is overdue now is a new understanding of the human being in relation to them. These two aspects determine, in one way or the other, the *Introduction to Metaphysics.* Heidegger is still struggling with the second aspect here: his description of the human being, its "spirit" and "violence," is still haunted by problems urged on both by *Being and Time* and by his political involvement in 1933–1934. But with regard to the first aspect, the things and how they are conceived, Heidegger is about to break new ground. The *Introduction to Metaphysics* can be understood as a stage for these hesitant yet persistent new efforts. In what follows, I seek to present a reading of the theory of language set forth in this book, which is intended as a selective and cautious reconstruction: I seek to present a certain aspect of this theory as convincingly as possible, and this attempt will encourage or force me to take leave of some features of Heidegger's conception that may be regarded as crucial by himself or by some of his disciples.

As I have pointed out, Heidegger's starting point is the things, the allegedly undamaged remainders of the world as it was conceived in *Being and Time.* These beings that are opposed to Being itself are basically conceived as spatial entities; in a list of different kinds of "beings" (58), the least graphic or concrete entries are a "swarm of people" and "Hölderlin's hymns." It is far from clear whether, for example, "war," "election," "marriage," and "kiss" are accepted as members in that club of beings and whether they have a legitimate place in the world. Sometimes, Heidegger is indeed prone to a rather simplistic definition of beings: distinguishing between Being itself and the plenitude of, as it were, "regular" beings, he states: "Being cannot be touched and tasted, can neither be heard with the ears nor smelled" (101). Yet the converse—that regular beings *can*—would limit this group to what is to be grasped by the senses and would bar every complex phenomenon: a perverse conclusion. (Still, for the sake of his argument, one could say that, in the passage I quoted, Heidegger is aiming at the concealment of Being rather than at a definition of beings, and that he should not be blamed for a rather incidental remark; but given that this latter definition of beings does not work, the opposition supposedly pointing out a distinctive property of "Being itself" becomes senseless.)

The preponderance of things in Heidegger's world is a precondition for the conception of language unfolded in the *Introduction.* The language appropriate for a world that is basically a collection of things has to be a language of nouns, of names. Heidegger is fond of identifying "words" or even the singular "word" with language itself; repeatedly, he speaks of "the naming force of language and words" (11; compare 77), "one's way into the word, language" (131; compare 66), or "the word" as "naming" (131). The naming of things seems to be inherent in the idea of the word in general; according to Heidegger, the word implies a demonstrating or "indicat[ing]" act, which "get[s] beyond the level of meanings and get[s] at the thing" (66). This "demonstrative power" of "naming" is also stressed in other texts from the same period, mainly *What Is a Thing?* and "The Origin of the Work of Art."[32]

Heidegger seeks to confirm this indicative function of the word or name by further findings: by linguistic features as well as by an interpretation of "appearance." He says: "The article is originally a demonstrative pronoun. It means that what is indicated stands and is for itself, as it were. This naming that demonstrates and indicates always has a preeminent function in language" (52). And: "The essence of appearance involves this stepping-forth and stepping-away, this hither and hence in the genuinely demonstrative, indicative sense" (78).

Of course, Heidegger's conception is not a mere rehash of the simplistic idea of language as a concatenation of names ridiculed by Plato (on his way from *Cratylus* to the *Sophist*), Wittgenstein, and many others. The distinctiveness of the idea of language in the *Introduction to Metaphysics* is not, however, due to insights into the complex structural aspects of grammar and semantics (as is the case with Plato and Wittgenstein) but to an unusual understanding of naming itself.

What does it mean, then, "to win back intact the naming force of language and words" (11)? Apparently, it does not suffice to know the names of plenty of things; this knowledge, still available and easy to acquire, cannot be regarded as endangered or even lost by Heidegger. The dramatic tone of his lecture hints at something else; he seems to miss a *paramount mode* of naming. This as-yet-unattained naming has to be extremely delicate and vulnerable; it cannot be taken for granted. One has to explore favorable circumstances that endorse the particular naming at which Heidegger is aiming.

He says, "The question about *Being* will be most intimately intertwined with the question about *language* for us" (39). Since the salient point of his theory of language is nothing but naming, the specific relevance of Being for naming is to be elucidated. Being, then, does not belong among the things that are to be named. Even though there is a word such as "Being," the "thing, so to speak, is lacking" in this case (67): "Being" is not a name in the regular sense, and since Heidegger seems to believe that words (as names) are regularly linked to things, he takes the lack of a thing in the case of Being as something exceptional. I already alluded to the fact that Heidegger's simplistic opposition between all the normal words that hint at things and the one and only word, "Being," that hints at no-thing, cannot be sustained. The mere lack of reference to a thing cannot serve as a criterion for providing Being with a linguistic privilege and confirming its uniqueness.[33] Yet that does not mean that his argument can be dismantled altogether; additional reasons for the peculiarity of Being have to be found instead. Even if we dispute Heidegger's claim that "Being" is the only word lacking a strict reference to a thing, one can plausibly state that this word is an apt companion to every noun or substantivized term. Being is, in this sense, a readily accepted complement: applicable to every word and, thereby, to every thing. It is, in this sense, a perfect "all-rounder." But what is its specific effect on the words it is accompanying? How may it serve them?

The Being of something depends on language, on a linguistic complement that is nothing but the petty gift of saying "it is" (compare 70, 138). This claim may seem trivial or even senseless, but it has a polemical value that turns out to be the decisive point of this theory of naming: this value cannot be set forth on the level of things; as a linguistic one, it has to evolve its power against nothing but other linguistic options.

The only plausible and positive effect of the "it is," of the enactment of Being, *consists in a corroboration of naming.* This reconstruction of Heidegger's argument goes along with a devaluation of the "question of Being" treasured by Heidegger and his disciples. Its main point is not Being itself; even if Heidegger seems to be captivated by it, it does not play a leading role. Being, rather, serves as a kind of a bodyguard for all the names that are the starring actors in the play. Guarding or protecting the name means, in this case, prohibiting its entanglement with other names. Heidegger says in the *Introduction to Metaphysics* that he wants to reveal "beings . . . in their full scope" (21). In this "full scope" *(Umkreis)* other words are certainly present and welcome, since otherwise the landscape surrounding a being would resemble a desert. Yet that scope, context, world, cosmos to which a thing belongs (the German word *Umkreis* is related to the Greek *kosmos*) is not to be populated with other things all too eagerly. Heidegger pleads for caution.

It is exactly that "scope," "room," or "space" (21, 145) that is provided or founded by Being, and this is the point where the difference between ordinary naming and naming in Heidegger's sense becomes evident. Whereas the former naming makes things available that may appear in different perspectives, the latter is a temporary suspension of all afterthoughts, of every further activity; it is an act of resistance against concatenation, or, to put it even more dramatically, an act of liberation. By adding an "is" to a name, by saying, for example, "the tree is," one acts like the coach calling for a time-out at a critical point of the game. The most succinct and decisive articulation of the impact of this naming is to be found in the following passage from the *Introduction:* "The word, the name, sets the self-opening beings out of the immediate, overwhelming assault, back into their Being, and preserves them in this openness, delimitation, and constancy" (131).

Taking Heidegger's statement that the language of Being creates a "room" or "space" for "beings" (145) literally, and sticking to that same metaphor, one may say: usually, language is not roomy enough. Language appears cramped when every word is tied to others, when no room for play is left. Facing this almost cataleptic state, the task of Being or the "is" as a linguistic bodyguard or servant of the name is nothing but to allow movement, to make language, as it were, roomy again. This is made possible by the demonstrative turn, by the inhibition of contextuality. The room of which Heidegger speaks is certainly not a spatial sphere but a virtual room or realm made accessible through a language that gives way to a thought (or a thing) by enhancing the interspaces. For the time being, the longing for the completion of a phrase like "the tree is," that is, the longing for a predicate, remains unsatisfied. The tacit complements to Heidegger's Being are space-bars creating emptiness between scattered names. Though in *Being and Time* that turn is a privilege of Dasein, and though in the later writings individuals are surrendered to a dubious whole, the *Introduction to Metaphysics* maintains the individual character of naming, without limiting self-assertion to a single Dasein. The relation between name and context is not affected or damaged at the outset.

The particular status of the name and the subordination of Being as its servant: this figure is not found only in the *Introduction to Metaphysics*. Heidegger discovers some of his relatives among the poets Arthur Rimbaud and Georg Trakl,[34] and this list has been expanded to include René Char and Guillaume Apollinaire.[35] A glance at their poems make clear that the effect of the "is" benefits not only things in Heidegger's limited sense but events, experiences, and feelings, too; they are, as it were, immobilized by the interruption of the stream of language brought about by the obstinately repeated "it is." This enhancement of the competence attributed to the "it is" confirms its plausibility as a language-game beyond the realm yielded by Heidegger. We might illuminate Heidegger's conception by comparing it to those of Walter Benjamin and Robert Antelme. Benjamin stresses the saving function of naming, and he seeks to come to terms with a question Heidegger cannot help being puzzled with—the question of how isolated and isolating names may be accompanied or complemented by a language based on associations, qualities, and correspondences.[36] Robert Antelme distinguishes between two different types of naming: on one hand, a naming that makes a person available (one may say: a naming as taking prisoners), on the other, a naming as saving, as creating a refuge. This distinction mirrors Heidegger's distinction between objectifying concepts and the "preserving" name (compare 131).[37]

I hope that my reconstruction of Heidegger's approach to naming sounds plausible so far (and I will give some further arguments supporting my claim shortly). But, to be just, one has to say that it is a rather incomplete account of Heidegger's theory of language in the *Introduction to Metaphysics*. It is, to be precise, an examination (and approval) of its first step. Heidegger's second step is far less suggestive and suffers from difficulties that become obvious in his later writings. Since most of them are already discussed above (see section 3), I confine myself to stressing one crucial point.

With his second step, Heidegger seeks to recover from what he himself takes as the destructive effects of the first step. The liberation from an "overwhelming assault" (131) goes along with the destruction of the superficial, inauthentic language that covers things up like a "blind mirror" (35). But Heidegger is not content with laying things bare, which he regards as a mere preparation for the new "gathering" or "gatheredness" (95, 131), where finally the "beings" shall come together in a new order: "In originary saying, the Being of beings is opened up in the structure of its gatheredness. . . . [T]he word governs what holds sway, *phusis*. Human beings, as those who stand and act in logos, in gathering, are the gatherers. They take over and fulfill the governance of the sway of the overwhelming" (131–132). Heidegger rejects sheer naming as insufficient, but the status and justification of the "gathering" that is supposed to overcome it are questionable, and the source of the "rules"[38] of this assembly of beings is unfathomable.

In the *Introduction to Metaphysics,* Heidegger's terminology is still indecisive, which, in this case, is a relief. The most obvious symptom of his reluctance is the term that stands for the overcoming of naming itself: "gathering" *(Sammeln)*. In its most innocuous meaning, *Sammeln* is nothing but collecting, and the profession of a collector does not encompass the job usually done by a curator in a museum: whereas the latter has to come to terms with a lot of material that is to be put in order, a passionate collector may be satisfied with a wild assortment of his gems (and, as a matter of fact, he often is). Heidegger is prone to a reading of *Sammeln* that already encompasses the establishment of a newly recuperated order. He thereby simply overcharges this term and blurs the difference between individually picking things, situating them idiosyncratically on one hand and putting findings in order on the other. Demonstrative naming, being an activity of a different kind, cannot comprise the arrangement of the material. Although this difference is at least conceivable in the *Introduction,* it is lost in the fusion of "saying" and "showing" that is brought about in the later writings.

Heidegger's ambivalence with regard to the relation between naming and context, or rather showing and ordering, has to do with his political involvement in 1933–1934, and the *Introduction* is instructive in this regard, too. One may keep in mind that the *Sammeln* ("gathering") traced back to *logos* by Heidegger is also familiar in a political and military context. (Think of the command: *Sammeln!*—"Assemble!") But I am far from substituting speculations about semantic similarities for philosophical analysis. What is illuminating, though, is the quotation from the Rectoral Address that is to be found in the *Introduction;* Heidegger borrows his own phrase from the address regarding the "knowing resolution to the essence of Being" (37–38) and specifies the latter as the "originary realm of the powers of Being" to which the German people has to expose itself (29). This political allusion to a diffuse whole is accompanied by the neglect of the difference between naming and context. Yet though the symptoms of this tendency are noticeable in the *Introduction,* too, the text remains ambivalent in this regard, and this makes it interesting. On one hand, it alludes to a whole that abolishes the distinctiveness of phenomena; on the other, it exposes naming as a unique mode of approaching single beings.

With Heidegger, one may say: sheer naming is defective; it does not render an adequate picture of how language works and what it is about. But his own account of the farther-reaching aspects of language is misleading, and his attempt to present some of these aspects ("showing" and "gathering") as implications of naming is confusing. In order to explain those complex aspects of "how to do things with words," I would rather rely on other conceptions (and by quoting that title I already indicate that the tradition I have in mind was fathered by Wittgenstein, in his late writings, and by J. L. Austin). Yet I think that, with his appeal to an ambitious kind of naming, Heidegger makes an intelligible and convincing contribution to the philosophy of language, and I want to conclude my remarks by giving some arguments for this assessment.

A name is a linguistic proxy for a demonstrative gesture. It insists on the uniqueness of something and withholds any further information about the qualities that could be attributed to it. This is obvious with regard to proper names: they apply to one person, and even if there is a namesake, a proper name can be traced back to a baptism that stands at its origin and excludes any confusions. Yet in the context in which Heidegger introduces naming, it applies not only to proper names but to denominating words in general (in the sense of the Greek *onoma*). Hence one may doubt whether, with this kind of naming, the unique existence of something may be saved and recognized in the sense I have in mind here. Words or "names" in a broader sense comprise a multitude of examples (or copies) that fit into the same category, belong to the same species. Yet even in this case, the demonstrative aspect of naming is not lost altogether; it merely shifts to another level.

On this level, insisting on a name can be explained as designating something and thereby rejecting any further predicates. Hence if, on the first level, the difference between "This is Martin" and "Martin is a human being" is to be regarded as a conflict between naming and predication, this procedure can be repeated on the second level: here, the statement "This is a human being" confronts statements like "A human being is selfish" or "A human being is a rational animal." Either way, an objection can be made against the second statements, namely, the question: "That's it? That's all you have to say about it?" Without being able to tell the whole story of something or somebody, one is aware of the limits that are drawn by the statements on that second level of predications, and, in order to indicate this skepticism, one goes back to a poor or thin expression: the name.

One of the most illuminating examples of the suspicion that incites to this turn is to be found in Rousseau's *Emile:* "Let my student be destined for the sword, the church, the bar. I do not care. . . . Living is the job I want to teach him. On leaving my hands, he will, I admit, be neither magistrate nor soldier nor priest. He will, in the first place, be a man."[39] And it is no accident at all that, in a rather different context, Rousseau invented the notion of the "sentiment of existence bared of every other sensation" that makes him a powerful predecessor, or rather stepfather, of Heidegger's concept of Being and existence.[40]

If an ecologist says, "Look, first of all, this is a tree!" his point can be explained as follows: "Please don't regard that tree only as raw material useful for the paper industry, but take into consideration all its complex qualities: that it produces oxygen, offers aesthetic pleasures, produces nuts, shelters squirrels, and so on." Hence, the ecologist's apparently empty claim is a container for further explications and associations. Yet one should rather say: it *can* be such a container. Obviously, the effects of "This is a tree" or "This is a human being" would be null and void if the speaker did not say anything more than that, if he wrapped himself in silence henceforth. The name *can* be the incentive for a process that leads beyond it, and it is by this very process that naming unfolds its positive effects. The name itself enables the attempts to overcome it; it announces, so to speak, its own defeat. Its harvest is to be brought in on the field of language, and its fruits depend on the readiness of speakers to engage the widespread associations linked to a thing or a person. Insisting on the name itself does make this process possible, but, in the worst case (as depicted by Robert Antelme, see above and note 37), it remains a helpless reminder and remainder of a richness that may be threatened or destroyed.

The name that serves as a kind of shelter or refuge can be accompanied by a complex linguistic practice that deals with something or somebody without pretending completely to conceive or grasp it, him, or her. The interpretations belonging to the linguistic process ignited by the name and leading beyond it are diverse attempts to trace something or somebody, to describe plausible surroundings, to set the stage for persons who do not want to be miscast. The examination and confirmation of all these different interpretations must take place on different layers and refer to different criteria: truth-claims are involved, but so are pragmatic intentions and aesthetic biases. All these efforts aim at the extension or completion of diverse language-games—with naming on their edge.

In this process, language beyond naming is necessarily involved. Moreover, it belongs to a practice that is not confined to the realm of language. The particular kind of naming that I take as the most convincing aspect of the theory of language in the *Introduction to Metaphysics* depends on additional conditions. Naming can succeed in fulfilling the assignment provided by Heidegger only if it is accompanied and endorsed by a certain behavior toward things or persons that is guided by attentiveness and tolerance, that is, by certain *virtues*. Hence this very *practice* of naming, here promoted in the context of a thinking of Being, belongs to nothing but the *heart of ethical theory*. The domain of naming as depicted by Heidegger is something he shies away from: it is an ethical realm.

I mentioned two examples of possible actualizations of the idea of naming: Rousseau's defense of humanity against a variety of occupations and the ecologist's somewhat clumsy considerations regarding the tree. It is obvious that, first and foremost, the true domain of this *ethical* naming is the interaction among humans. Here, naming is brought back to a realm where it is dedicated to an "object" that is, by that linguistic act, authorized to be more than that. Although Heidegger is mainly concerned with things in the *Introduction,* naming in his sense is actually most aptly applied to a person, to her behavior and bequest. The multitude of qualities attributed to a human being is overwhelming; hence a name, that is, a linguistic gesture insisting on indeterminacy, is particularly in place here.

I explicitly mention a person's bequest here since remembering is a good example of the particular function and strength of naming. The widespread traces of a life, the surprising entanglements and correspondences form an almost infinite labyrinth, yet they are bound together by the appeal to the name. This is most evident in the case of mourning, which is unthinkable without a linguistic gesture (a name) that stands for the irreplaceability of the deceased. Naming, in this case, is not intended to determine an agent that is held accountable and responsible for a single deed in a moral framework; instead of formally identifying a perpetrator ("It was he . . ."), naming in the context of mourning preserves the image of a unique person who otherwise would be likely to dissolve in historical totality. Mourning does not depend on specific honorable qualities of a person; one may say instead that it simply revolts against her absence or non-Being. The naming that recalls the Being of a beloved person echoes the Heideggerian liaison of naming and Being.

In the *Introduction to Metaphysics,* Heidegger unfolds a conception of naming that goes beyond mere denomination and is to be embedded in a complex behavior toward a thing or a person, yet he does not take the step that eventually leads into an ethical realm that is, in my opinion, the true homestead of that conception. Heidegger opens a door but does not cross the threshold. Yet this gesture is one of the major rewards that are to be expected from the reading of the *Introduction to Metaphysics.*

Part II

HEIDEGGER AND THE GREEKS

Chapter 7

WHAT'S IN A WORD?: HEIDEGGER'S GRAMMAR AND ETYMOLOGY OF "BEING"

GREGORY FRIED

When Chapter 2 of *Introduction to Metaphysics* opens, Heidegger reminds us that he has just concluded a long exposition of the fact that "for us Being is just an empty word and an evanescent meaning" (40). According to Heidegger, Being, *Sein,* has almost completely lost its force and meaning as a word, and more important, as a *question* that arises in the form of a word within the context of a particular language. The lecture course began with the question, "Why are there beings at all instead of nothing?" Heidegger quickly shows that this question about beings and nothing is in fact a question about Being (which must be distinguished from *beings*). But the force of the argument in Chapter 1 is to show that the question of Being as such has been obscured in the unfolding of Western history and thought, and that, indeed, the loss of sense of the *question* of Being is the mark of a profound and nihilistic "spiritual decline" (29) in the West. According to Heidegger, because we have forgotten that authentically responding to this question of Being constitutes "the spiritual fate of the West," Europe lies on the brink of disaster, with the German people at once most at peril (caught in "the great pincers between Russia . . . and America") and also most called to historical responsibility as the people with the "vocation" to uphold the spiritual and geographic "center" of Europe and the West (28–29).

In this chapter, I will attempt four things: (1) to explain how Heidegger arrives at a discussion of the grammar and etymology of the word "Being" in the development of his larger argument; (2) to make sense of Heidegger's analysis through a synopsis of his treatment of this grammar and etymology; (3) to evaluate Heidegger's argument with respect to our current understanding of philology and linguistics; and (4) to close with a prospectus on the work

125

that remains to be done. My efforts here will be, for the most part, propaedeutic, which is to say that I do not expect to lay the issue to rest but rather to clarify Heidegger's position for the new reader and to call on advanced scholars to take up the philosophical challenge of the history of the word "Being."

1. THE ROLE OF THE "LINGUISTIC" ARGUMENT
IN *INTRODUCTION TO METAPHYSICS*

Heidegger's claims about the word "Being" may appear exaggerated, to say the least. How can a word, or a concept, lie at the basis of the history of the West? But this is precisely the point Heidegger has been trying to make in Chapter 1. We have lost our sense that what is said in one word, *this* word, may well underlie everything that is worth thinking about, that the question of Being is indeed the question of meaning per se, and that a failure to respond to the question of what it means "to be," to take it as settled or as merely meaningless (an "empty" word, a "vapor"), is to fail in our calling as human beings, or, more properly, as "Dasein." As Heidegger makes clear in his plays on the German word *Einführung* (15), his lecture course aspires to a kind of philosophical *Führung,* a leading-in to the reawakening of the question of Being for the German people, "the metaphysical *Volk*" (29).

For Heidegger, the question of Being is a question about language because meaning itself, the way we understand the world as the home for our own "to be," is constituted *by* language. As Heidegger says famously in a later essay, "language is the house of Being."[1] Although Heidegger is concerned with language *as such,* just as he is with Being as such, language is always concretely manifested in particular languages, as Being is in beings. In 1935, the date of the *Introduction to Metaphysics* lecture course, Heidegger is in particular concerned with the *German* language and its role as the home for a thinking that might save the West. With this we see the import of Heidegger's effort at a *Führung,* a leadership of his own, in the context of the National Socialist regime. He gives a quick bow to the "organizations for the purification of language and for defense against its progressive mutilation"—and here, of course, he means the efforts of Nazi-oriented groups working against the "degeneration" of the German language. But in the next breath he takes this praise away: "Nevertheless, through such institutions one finally demonstrates only more clearly that one no longer knows what language is all about" (39). To treat language as a *thing* misapprehends the matter. Because the relation of a people, a *Volk,* to its language is grounded in that people's relation to the question of Being, a language can never be rescued merely by organizations or by laws devoted to its preservation. The preservation of language as a vital home depends on the rekindling of the question of Being, for Being and language are intimately intertwined in the question of what it means to be.

This is why Heidegger turns to the problem of the grammar and etymology of the word "Being" in Chapter 2. In order to understand why "Being" has become a virtually meaningless word to us, nearly incapable of inciting serious questioning and thought, Heidegger suggests that we begin by looking at the formal use of "Being" in language (its grammar) as well as its history as a word (its etymology). Linguistics may at least give us some "remnant of a connection" (40) to the meaning of this word, and so it may help us break open unanticipated avenues for philosophical questioning and for restoring its meaning.

2. HEIDEGGER'S ARGUMENT CONCERNING THE GRAMMAR AND ETYMOLOGY OF "BEING"

Heidegger begins with the grammar taught to us all in childhood ("grammar school"). His initial point is that the basic categories of grammar in the West have been treated for more than two thousand years as simply self-evident (40–41). The Greek and Latin grammarians established the concepts of grammar as one of the domains of philosophy, but once established, these categories dropped out of philosophical debate and became taken for granted.[2] Heidegger does not intend simply to toss this tradition away, but he does want to lay language radically open to question again, and to do so, he needs to dislodge the sedimentation of two thousand years of uncontested grammarian dogma. In this sense, Heidegger's "destruction" of the history of grammar mirrors in miniature the "destruction" of the history of philosophy that he has argued is necessary to revive the question of Being (SZ, 19–27). In particular, he wants to emphasize that language is *not* simply just another being, like an animal or a mineral, readily accessible to the circumscribed study of a scientific discipline. Language is not a being at all, but, like Being itself, it is what gives us access to all beings in the first place (41). The attempt to circumscribe language as if it were just another being is more than a category error. This is what Heidegger means by saying that an undertaking such as the grammarians' dissection of language "depends on the fundamental conception of Being that guides it" (41).

Heidegger begins his reflection on the specific grammar of the word "to be" with the observation that *das Sein* (Being) in German belongs to a class of words that produce a substantive, or noun, on the basis of the infinitive form of the verb, in this case, *sein* (to be) (42). Here arises a discrepancy between English and German that might lead to confusion. English, unlike German, does not form nouns on the basis of the infinitive, although other Indo-

European languages do (the French *l'être,* for example); English uses the gerund, as in "Running is her favorite sport." So *being,* rather than *the to be,* is the substantive of the verb. German also produces substantives from participial forms: *das Rennende* is "that which runs," whereas *das Rennen* is the activity of running in general. *Das Seiende* is "that which is in being," a particular "being," to be distinguished from *das Sein,* Being in general—whatever that is! As we shall see, Heidegger insists that our sense of Being as something *general* is part of the problem.

Because the German noun *Sein* is based on the verb *sein,* Heidegger's next step is to examine these two grammatical forms: the substantive *(das Sein)* and the infinitive *(sein).* Here, Heidegger says, we seem to have stumbled onto one of the essential questions about language: whether the "primordial form" of any word is the noun or the verb (43). But he argues that this is in fact a pseudo-question generated by the classification system of the Greek and Latin grammarians (44), a system that has not received a "thoroughgoing investigation" for millennia (43).[3] The grammarians' distinctions were inaugurated philosophically by the discussion of *onoma* and *rhēma* in Plato's *Sophist* (261e ff.)

As Heidegger argues (44–45), *onoma* and *rhēma* in the context of Plato's *Sophist* do not yet mean the "noun" and "verb" of the grammarians' academic categorizations. In ordinary Greek, *onoma* means "name" (and *onoma* is in fact etymologically cognate with the English "name," as well as "noun"), and *rhēma* means "that which is spoken," from the verb *rheō,* to say. Hence: "We call *rhēma* that which reveals actions [*dēloma . . . praxesin*]"; "And an *onoma* is a spoken sign applied to things that do these actions"; finally: "Hence no statement [*logos*] is ever constructed by speaking *onomata* alone, and also not by *rhēmata* spoken without *onomata*" (*Sophist,* 262a). The grammarians have taken this to mean that no statement (*logos*), no speech about what may be true or false, can be constructed merely by stringing together nouns alone or verbs alone. What we now call a "sentence" requires both noun and verb. According to Heidegger, though Plato's meaning is more complicated than this, the need is clear enough for a distinction between words that make manifest the beings with which we have doings and words that make manifest the doing itself. Aristotle (*De Interpretatione,* 2–4) codified this distinction between words that signify without time *(onoma)* and those that indicate time *(rhēma).* Only when this distinction falls into the hands of the grammarians, becoming the familiar "noun" and "verb," does philosophical reflection gives way to mere academicism (44–45). Philosophy once investigated the Being of the things named, whereas grammar merely adjusts established categorizations.

At issue here is the nature of one form of the verb: the infinitive. This term is derived from the terminology of the Roman grammarians: *modus infinitivus verbi,* the mode of the verb that is *not* finite, that is *not* bound or definite. Heidegger displays his animus against the Latin translation of Greek: the "bland" Latin term *modus* (mode, manner) is the Romanization of the much more evocative Greek word *enklisis,* "an inclining to the side" (45), which in turn is related to *ptōsis,* which means "any kind of inflection of the fundamental form . . . not only in substantives but also in verbs" (45). The Greek *ptōsis* becomes the Latin *casus* (as in our *case* of a noun), and *enklisis* becomes *declinatio* (as in our *declension* of a verb). But the original force of meaning in the Greek has been lost.

Here Heidegger begins his real work. He has argued that the understanding of language is intimately related to the understanding of Being. His argument now is that the Greeks understood Being as "taking and maintaining a *stand*" (46). That which takes a stand is necessarily con-stant; it endures, at least for a while, but in order to endure, it must delimit itself, must set itself within its own limits. For Heidegger, this Greek conception of limit *(peras)* and end as finitude *(telos)* is not the mark of deficiency or failure, but rather that which allows whatever is, to be. The end and the limit complete what stands there in itself, preventing it from slipping back into an undifferentiated muddle. "Limit and end are that whereby beings first begin to *be*" (46). Limit is what allows the differentiation that makes the being one thing rather than another (for example, "to sit" rather than "to fly"). Limit allows difference to take a stand, and so makes room for identity and constancy.

We might well ask what all this has to do with the infinitive as a grammatical form. We need to jump ahead here. Heidegger writes, "*Ptōsis* and *enklisis* mean to fall, to incline, that is, nothing other than to depart from the constancy of the stand and thus to deviate from it" (49). The *declension* of a verb describes this falling-away from the *delimitation* that maintains a being in its Being, in its constancy. Inflected forms of the verb, such as the present, the subjunctive, and so on, supposedly *add* something, as it were, to the word. Besides the infinitive "to speak," for example, we have "you speak," "they spoke," "I will speak," "it was spoken," "were he spoken to, he would speak," and so on. In Greek, says Heidegger, this declension of the verb is "an *enklisis paremphatikos,* a deviation, which *is* capable [as opposed to the putatively raw 'infinitive'] of making manifest *in addition* person, number, tense, voice, and mood" (51).

The Greek word *paremphainō* means "to show oneself along with something," and so the Greek sense of the inflected forms is that they "make something else manifest in addition, [they] allow it to arise and be seen in addition" (50). But the *enklisis a-paremphatikos* allows nothing to be seen "in addition" to the basic meaning of the verb. The Romans translated *enklisis aparemphatikos* as *modus infinitivus* (51), a rendering that implies that, against the inflected forms that say something *definite,* the infinitive marks a deficiency, a lack of meaning. But Heidegger argues that in the Greek understanding, the *enklisis aparemphatikos* is what grants us access to what the verb per se "means and makes manifest" (51). The Latin grammarians' treatment of the *modus infinitivus,* by contrast, indicates an *abstraction* from definite meaning; the infinitive eventually becomes the most abstract, the least meaningful form of the verb (51–52), useful perhaps as the name for a particular verb because it conveys only this generalized meaning.

This demotion of the importance of the infinitive as the site for reflection on the full meaning of the verb as such constitutes, for Heidegger, one of the chief causes for the modern notion that "to be" (*das Sein,* Being) is the most empty and general of words and concepts. The development of language, especially once the self-conscious reflections on grammar have taken hold, leads to innovations such as the verbal substantive based on the infinitive, such as *to einai* in Greek and *das Sein* in German. For Heidegger, this leads to the most telling confusion of all, the failure to distinguish *Being* from *beings:* "The substantive *Sein* implies that what is so named, itself 'is.' '*Das Sein*' [Being] now itself becomes something that 'is,' whereas obviously only beings are, and it is not the case that Being also is" (53). What Heidegger says here about the noun formed on the infinitive is equally true of the gerund "Being" based on the participial form of "to be." For the unwary English reader, this "Being" is almost impossible to take as anything but a being, a thing, and thereby all sense of what might be at issue in the question of what it means to be may easily be lost. And English is even further at a remove than other Indo-European languages; we cannot even speak of "the 'to be.' " "Can it be any wonder to us now that Being is so empty a word . . . ?" asks Heidegger, ironically. "This word 'Being' stands as a warning to us. Let us not be lured away into the emptiest of forms, the verbal substantive" (53). At the very least, Heidegger's sarcasm here should warn us against thinking that he considers *Sein* a kind of sacred word in and of itself, like *Om* in Sanskrit, whose mere verbal form and sound can yield enlightenment upon meditation or devotional repetition.[4] That is to say, there is nothing about this *particular* word as a *particular* phoneme, with its own particular sound and form, that makes it somehow the key to all understanding. Of course, the details of this word's *history,* in German and more broadly in the Indo-European languages, have great significance for its meaning, and in this sense the specific word in question is crucial. But far more important than the word itself is what language, in its Being as a historical process within which we have our "home," is trying to bring to thought *through* the word. And though this is not Heidegger's point here, this matter-for-thought ought in principle to be available in any language.

The warning concerning the empty verbal substantive leads Heidegger to attempt an examination of Being through other *definite* forms of the verb, such as "I am," "you are," "he is," "they were," and so on (53). But now Heidegger runs into new problems. First of all, does saying "I am" bring me or you any closer to an understanding of Being itself? Our own Being is so close to each one of us that Heidegger says that indeed each is "furthest from himself." Saying "we are" is no more transparent, for it is unclear what unites "the plurality of I's" in Being (53). Moreover, it is unclear in what sense "Being" unites the many definite forms of the verb. Another puzzling feature of the verb augments this bewildering multiplicity, namely, that the various forms do not even seem to be based on the same root: I *am*, you *are*, he *is*, we *were*, they have *been*, and so on (similar variations are found throughout Indo-European languages). Whence this motley collection of forms that seem to bear no immediate relation to the "general" form of the verb in the infinitive (53–54)?

This brings Heidegger to the question of the etymology of "Being," and the several roots, or stems, of the various forms of the verb. Heidegger points to three stems for the morphemes of the German *sein*, and these have close correlates in English. The first stem is the Indo-European root *es*, which shows up in the English forms "am" and "is," as well as the Greek *einai* (to be) and the German *ist* and *sein*. Heidegger suggests that the root meaning of this stem is "life, the living . . . the self-standing" (54). The second stem is the Indo-European root *bhū* or *bheu*, from which the English "be" and "been" arise, as well as the Greek *phusis* (that which grows and shows itself forth; nature) and the German *bin* and *bist*. Heidegger suggests that the sense of this root is "to emerge, to hold sway, to come to a stand from out of itself and to remain standing" (54). Finally, the third stem is visible in German forms such as *war* and *wesen*, and the English *was* and *were*. The Indo-European root here is *wes*, to which the Greek *astu* (town, citadel) is related, and so we can see that lexically, this root does seem based in a sense of *abiding*. Modern linguistics supports Heidegger's treatment of the three roots, and, giving him some latitude, also his interpretation of the three basic meanings of the three roots *es*, *bheu*, and *wes* as "living, emerging, abiding" (55).[5]

The next question, of course, is, what *unites* these three root meanings in the verbs *sein* and "to be"—even if the infinitive form has become, as Heidegger so forcefully argues, drained of all but the most general meaning? Heidegger goes on to ask a chain of nine questions about the historical development of the verb "to be," asking, for example, why the three initial meanings were brought together, how they were blended, what "dominant meaning" emerged, and then how the verb lost its vigor and became the abstract, vapid infinitive of today (55–56). Heidegger does not answer these questions here, in part because he cannot without further linguistic research, but also because he wants to emphasize that linguistics can take thinking only so far; his goal has been to reawaken a sense of Being as a *question* (55, 57). The subsequent chapters of the *Introduction to Metaphysics* now trade on our growing appreciation for how radical this question is.

But we may still venture an answer as to what unifies the three root senses of the verb "to be." A fair guess would be that "living, arising, abiding" are united in the Heideggerian notion of "coming to presence" *(anwesen)* (46), which indeed he identifies as one of the senses of the Indo-European root *wes* (55). Being as coming to presence embraces the meaning of "to be" as "living" in the sense that presencing is not an inert *present* object, a timeless *thing* present-at-hand, but rather a process of dynamic unfolding. This unfolding, as coming to presence, also includes the sense of the arising, the appearing, the self-manifesting of Being as nature *(phusis)*. Coming to presence is also what abides. What abides is not the beings that temporarily endure in their stand and thereby reside as present if only for a little while before departing, but rather the temporal coming to presence *of* these beings. Intimately connected to such coming to presence is going into absence, the falling-away, the not-Being-there, the departure into impermanence and absence, and so we have returned to the guiding question about Being and Nothing with which Heidegger began the lecture course.

Before concluding this section, we should return to something we passed over. We saw that in Heidegger's account, the Greeks understood Being as a kind of taking-a-stand, a coming to presence that endures precisely *not* because it is general and unlimited (or, for that matter, eternal), but rather because it establishes a limit *(peras)* and an end *(telos)* for beings. According to this interpretation, Being is precisely *not* a "vapor" but rather that which grants beings their specificity and distinctness. Heidegger's point about the infinitive as a name for Being is that, as a result of the development of grammar, this name has conditioned us to think of Being, in the form of the "to be" *(das Sein),* as that which is the most empty, the most indefinite, the most general (56).

But this "decline" of the infinitive has much more than academic significance for Heidegger, according to whom, as we have seen, failure to respond properly to the question of Being defines the historical decline of the West and, more broadly, the crisis of nihilism in the modern epoch.[6] For Heidegger, citing Heraclitus' Fragment 53,[7] Being must happen, must "take place," as a struggle, a *polemos,* in which beings, in their coming to presence, are set forth into their limits (47). Heidegger declares: "Confrontation does not divide unity, much less destroy it. Confrontation builds unity; it is the gathering *(logos). Polemos* and *logos* are the same" (47). When Being as the infinitive declines into mere generality, all distinctions of rank, difference, limit, and position become blurred. Confrontation and struggle *are* the *logos,* which is to say, *logos,* or language itself, forms a meaningful world for us to inhabit precisely because we are responding to this call to confront Being through our struggle to interpret the world in language, thought, and action. True ontological struggle must then be upheld by a triad of great "creators, by the poets, thinkers and statesmen" (47).

For Heidegger, the way we understand and inhabit our world is forged in language by poetry, questioned and unfolded by thinking, and preserved by statesmanship. This triad is *creative,* not because they produce Being and beings ex nihilo, but because their struggle with Being both reinvests the world with meaning and sustains it. "Where struggle ceases, beings indeed do not disappear, but world turns away" (47). The world "worlds," to use a Heideggerian idiom, only when the limits of beings in their coming to presence remain open to an interpretative confrontation in language, thought, and deed. But to the extent that the original motive force of Greek philosophy has been lost, and Being has been reduced to either the vapid infinitive or a name for a particular entity (an ultimate substance, a final essence, or a "Supreme Being"), then nihilism has set in. As a consequence, beings—both human beings and nature as a collection of inanimate entities and energies—"become objects, whether for observing . . . or for making, as the fabricated, the object of calculation" (47). The onset of nihilism casts the *question* of Being into oblivion by objectifying Being as a *thing,* an object of knowledge as the mere accumulation of information. Such objective information about Being then promises an accumulation and deployment of power for the sake of dominion over nature, both human and otherwise. Heidegger's delusion in the 1930s was that a modern triad of poet, thinker, and statesman—Hölderlin, Heidegger, and Hitler—could withstand this nihilistic onslaught.

A final point: as much as Heidegger valorizes Greek language and thinking, we must emphasize that he also holds the Greeks in part responsible for the decline into nihilism. Greek philosophers developed words based on forms of the verb *einai* (to be), such as *ousia* and *parousia,* in which they experienced the question of the meaning of Being without fully carrying it through (46).

Heidegger attempts to recapture this experience of Being by rendering these words as modes of coming to presence. But he also asserts that precisely such Greek terms readily lent themselves to an interpretation of Being as an eternally enduring essence or substance: *coming* to presence becomes objective presence-at-hand; the dimension of time is lost, and so is the sense that absence (the Nothing) belongs to Being in the temporal play of the coming-to-, enduring-in-, and departing-from-presence of beings. Heidegger discerns this loss in the Greek treatment of language as a being (41, 49), rather than as the realm of Being itself, its "house." Hence the Platonism of subsequent Western thought, which interprets Being as a being in the search for a reality that is everlasting and unchanging. For Heidegger, because the Greeks were unable to uphold the question of Being *as* a question, the philosophically originary experience of Being as the polemical domain of coming to presence lapsed into oblivion. The decline of the infinitive becomes a decline not only in grammar but also in language itself, as well as in thinking, and indeed in history, culture, and politics. It seems that only a revolution in thinking can bring the genuine question back to its stand.

3. EVALUATION OF HEIDEGGER'S GRAMMAR AND ETYMOLOGY OF "BEING"

From the perspectives of linguistics and the philosophy of language, there are any number of avenues we might take to evaluate Heidegger's interpretation of the grammar and etymology of the verb "to be," but space limits us severely. We may grant that Heidegger's broad points about the role of the Greek and Latin grammarians in codifying linguistic forms and his discussion of the etymology of the Indo-European roots of the verb "to be" are basically sound (allowing him some license in interpreting the roots). In this section, then, I concentrate on one philosophical problem concerning the verb "to be," and I take as a guide the work of Charles Kahn. Over the course of his scholarly career, Kahn has set the standard for a detailed investigation of the philosophical significance of the linguistic meaning of the verb "to be," producing numerous articles on the topic as well as his distinguished work *The Verb 'Be' in Ancient Greek*. Anyone with an interest in the linguistic foundation for ontology must confront Kahn.[8] He has understood his own work on *einai* and its various forms in ancient Greek as a necessary propaedeutic and corollary to the *philosophical* investigation of the very meaning of "Being."[9]

The question of whether there should be any doubt as to the validity (or perhaps more precisely, the *universal* validity) of philosophical inquiry into "Being" is addressed by Kahn as the problem of *linguistic relativism*.[10] Kahn, of course, did not invent this term. Its roots go back as far as Herder, Hamann, and von Humboldt; linguistic relativism had its greatest impact in the twentieth century through the writings of Benjamin Lee Whorf and Edward Sapir. As Whorf puts it, "the 'linguistic relativity principle' [means] that users of markedly different grammars are pointed by their grammars toward different types of observations and different evaluations of externally similar acts of observation, and hence are not equivalent as observers but must arrive at somewhat different views of the world."[11] The doctrine of linguistic relativism is epitomized by the following quotation from the linguist Emile Benveniste: "It is what one can *say* which delimits and organizes what one can think" (PGL, 61). For the linguistic relativist, since there is no *lingua mentis,* no nonverbal language of pure thought, and no such thing as language "as such," then all thinking beyond raw emotion and the processing of sensory data, that is, everything that we might call reflection upon concepts and ideas, depends utterly on the *specific* language that one happens to speak. More to the point, the language that one happens to speak conditions what philosophical problems one is likely to think *about:* "Linguistic form is not only the condition for transmissibility, but first of all the condition for the realization of thought" (PGL, 56). Benveniste takes particular delight in demonstrating that Aristotle's famous ten categories "do not refer to attributes discovered in things, but to a classification arising from the language itself" (PGL, 58). For Benveniste, Aristotle's categories (substance, quantity, relation, and so on) do not describe the a priori categories of Being, but rather *linguistic* entities and *linguistic* categories for classifying objects whose basis is the specificity of the *Greek* language. Aristotle may have noticed that " 'Being' is spoken of in many ways" (*Metaphysics* Gamma 2): Being is addressed as accidental, in the categories, as truth, and as actuality. But for the linguistic relativist, these multiple senses of "Being" are a peculiarity of *one* language family, and Aristotle was misguided to believe that they can or should be *philosophically* reconciled "to something that is one and single by nature" (1003a33–34).

The linguistic relativity of Aristotle's categories, then, is meant to serve as an example for the larger proposition that the very question of Being itself is an accident of the Indo-European family of languages. The morphology of modern forms of "to be" includes, as we have seen, several roots: *es, bheu,* and *wes.* These are distinct root words, having separate original meanings. Heidegger interpreted these as "living, abiding, arising" (a more conventional reading takes *es* as "to be" in the sense of "to exist," "to be objectively real"). The linguistic relativist will argue that it is simply an accident that these three roots are brought together in this one word in Indo-European languages, and, furthermore, it is because of the perplexities caused by the conjunction of these roots that the philosophical problems arose in the first place; in Benveniste's words, "the linguistic structure of Greek predisposed the notion of 'being' to a philosophical vocation" (PGL, 63).

Linguists and philosophers of language have adduced two primary usages of forms of "to be" in Indo-European languages: Being as the copula ("The sky is blue"; or, the predicate Y may be affirmed of subject X) and Being in its existential use ("The sky is"; X exists). As Benveniste points out (PGL, 61), the fact that Indo-European languages allow for the substantivization of the verb (such as *to einai* in Greek, *das Sein* in German, or "Being" in English) compounds the confusion, because such substantives induce one to think that there is a realm of "Being" as objective reality that could be analyzed as the basis for all possible predications as either true or false, and also as the touchstone for determining what truly exists, or is. In reference to the roots of the verb, the philosophical problem becomes: What is it that exists eternally, that dwells and abides without interruption, and of which everything that by nature truly exists can be predicated? We see this already in the didactic poem of Parmenides and in the nature-philosophy of the pre-Socratics. But as Benveniste points out, there are other language families in which the various functions of the verb "to be" are divided among totally different verbs and even linguistic forms that are not verbs (PGL, 62–63). His point is that in such languages, the question of how to combine the concepts of "existence" and "predication" does not even arise *as* a problem. It is only because Indo-European languages combine several concepts into one word, such as "Being," that we inherit a predisposition to discerning a problem in fully reconciling these senses to one another. The sinologist A. C. Graham has put it this way: "There is no concept of Being which languages are well or ill equipped to present; the functions of 'to be' [sc. as verb of predication in Indo-European] depend upon a grammatical rule for the formation of the sentence, and it would be merely a coincidence if one found anything resembling it in a language without this rule."[12]

The analytic school of philosophy has been similarly dismissive of a "general" problem of "Being." This position might be traced back to Kant's refutation of the ontological proof of God's existence, in which he famously argues that " '*Being*' is no real predicate" and that "the little word 'is' " in sentences such as "God is omnipotent" leads us into a confusion between existence and predication (*Critique of Pure Reason*, A598/B626). John Stuart Mill denounced "the frivolous speculations concerning the nature of Being . . . which have arisen from overlooking this double meaning of the word *to be;* from supposing that when it signifies *to exist,* and when it signifies to *be* some specified thing . . . it must still, at bottom, answer to the same idea; and that a meaning must be found for it which shall suit all these cases." The failure to detect this ambiguity as a mere accidental peculiarity of a family of languages has meant that "even the strongest understandings [such as Plato's and Aristotle's] find it difficult to believe that things which have a common name have not in some respect or other a common nature."[13] The general criticism of "Being" and "metaphysics" in what historically has been dubbed the Anglo-American school of analytic philosophy is no longer just a version of linguistic relativism but rather a broad philosophical attitude held in the light of it. Charles Kahn has summed up succinctly the prevailing view of the analytic school: "Since Russell, most philosophers of logic have agreed that we must distinguish at least three and perhaps four senses of 'to be': (1) existence as expressed by the quantifiers, (2) predication, as in Fx, (3) identity, as in $x = y$, (4) class inclusion, symbolized as $x \in y$. Russell once described it as 'a disgrace to the human race' that it has chosen to employ the same word 'is' for two such entirely different ideas as predication and identity."[14]

To put this in Wittgensteinian terms, the whole problem of "Being," and so, to a large extent, the concerns of the first two and a half millennia of philosophy, are not just a matter of language going on holiday but of its going completely out to lunch.[15] The problem of "Being" as a search for the "metaphysical" grounds for a reality that would, a priori, reconcile existence, predication, and truth to one another is simply a chimera induced by the ambiguity of the seductive "little word 'is.'" Giving philosophy a properly rigorous basis in logic and in the analysis of ordinary language depends above all on dispelling the illusions occasioned by this ambiguity, as does the foundation of a soberly empirical ontology, consistent with the methodologies of the sciences.[16] For Rudolf Carnap, famously, Heidegger's "pseudostatements" about "Being" constitute the high-water mark of the meaningless metaphysical nonsense occasioned by the ambiguities of the word "to be."[17]

Kahn has nothing to do with defending Heidegger, of course; his aim is to correct and to refine the understanding of the role of "Being" in the history of philosophy. But his work for the sake of "Being" shares something with Heidegger, who was first moved to philosophy by Franz Brentano's 1862 dissertation, *On the Manifold Meaning of Being in Aristotle*.[18] Kahn's great endeavor, in his study of "to be" *(einai)* in Greek, has been to show that the question of Being is not a pseudoproblem generated by a mere linguistic accident. In this, he shares Heidegger's first intuition that in Aristotle's *to on legetai pollachōs* there resides a *genuine* question, perhaps the one most proper to thinking. A major thread of Kahn's argument is that the existential and predicative uses of the verb are not the only significant ones for the dawn of Greek philosophy and so for the subsequent history of thought. To these two he adds the "veridical" use: *esti tauta houtō hōsper su legeis:* "Things are as you say." (In English, we see this veridical use in "That's the way it is!" or to use Kahn's example, "Tell it like it is!"). This is the sense of "to be" as "to be true," "to be so," or "to be the case."[19] Kahn's thesis is that when the proper place of this third element is understood, the verb does have a certain unity, and the problem of Being then regains its dignity.

We may summarize Kahn's argument for this unity of Being, beginning with the predicative use of "to be" in the copula. He notes two critical forms of the copula: the *locative* and the *durative,* as in "We are in this room," for the former, and "I am human" rather than "I am hungry," for the latter. The durative aspect marks the distinction between *being* something enduringly and *becoming,* or between the *stative* and *mutative,* as Kahn puts it, a difference that Spanish denotes by separating "to be" into *ser* and *estar,* for example (*soy americano* versus *estoy cansado*). So far, we have three uses of the copula in its predicative form: the locative, the durative (which is equivalent to the stative), and the mutative. Next, the existential use should be clear: "There is a city called Paris." Here the "is" does not ascribe a state or quality (that is, a predicate) to an existing thing; rather, it underlines the very existence of the thing, that this thing is present in some sense and so may be the subject of predication. But it is the veridical use ("Tell it like it is!") that Kahn sees as unifying these other two (the predicative and the existential): "the concept of truth involves some kind of correlation or 'fit' between what is said or thought, on one side, and what is, or what is the case, or the way things are, on the other side."[20] Being, as "what happens to be the case," that things are just so and not otherwise, is then a name, in a rough and ready way, for truth as *reality.* Without this third, veridical sense of Being we could not make statements that assert such a reality as the ground for claiming that certain facts are so (the existential use) and that we may correctly say things about these facts (the predicative use).

For Kahn, philosophy's primary impetus has always been to seek knowledge, to search out this veridical sense of Being as reality, and we can see that the existential use (*X is*) and the predicative (*X is Y*) depend on reality's being the way it is for the truthfulness of any statement. Kahn does not want to offend the antimetaphysical sensibilities of analytic philosophy: "I am using 'reality' here not in any large metaphysical sense but simply as a convenient term in the hermeneutical metalanguage: as a mere name or counter for the facts that make true statements true and false statements false."[21] As for the durative and locative aspects of the copula, this is where, he asserts, the first real work of philosophy began: in teasing out the implications of this *unified* set of concepts. Parmenides, for example, argues that "what is" not only endures for a while, it also can *never* change and become "what is not." For Parmenides, "what is" still *is somewhere,* and he ascribes to this place the form of a perfect sphere (fr. 8). Only with Plato does philosophy attempt to divorce Being as reality from location in place to the nonspace of the realm of the Idea.

For Kahn, the answer to "What is the question of being a question about?" is that, from Parmenides on, it "is a question as to what reality must be like—or what the world must be like—in order for knowledge and true (or false) discourse to be possible.[22] By identifying reality, in the veridical use of "to be," as the key to Greek ontology, Kahn argues that he has answered the linguistic relativists:

> The concept of being in Parmenides and Plato cannot be regarded as an illegitimate confusion of existence and predication, since it does not rely initially and fundamentally on either notion, nor on their special connection in the uses of the Indo-European verb *to be.* Instead, the concept of being must be understood by beginning with the notion of truth and its correlate, the notion of knowledge or inquiry and its object. But the connection between these three notions—truth, knowledge, and reality in the general sense entailed by the other two—is in no way a peculiar feature of Indo-European. The connections here are firmly grounded in the logical structure of the concepts of truth and knowledge, and similar connections must turn up in every language where human beings try to acquire information or try to test the reliability of what is told them. . . . No language can do without these basic notions of truth, reality, and fact.[23]

In other words, Kahn is suggesting that, even if they do not exactly reproduce the various meanings of "to be" in a *single* correlate word, *all* languages must reproduce somehow the questions surrounding "truth, reality, and fact." For this reason, the philosophical problem to which the West gives the name "Being" can in principle be "translated," even if this single word cannot be translated with one exactly parallel word. Language in general, as a way of communicating about the world, must in principle (if not as a matter of universal practice) be able to raise the question of how we can speak truly about the underlying reality that allows us to posit the existence of certain things and their qualities; it is only a matter, then, of actualizing this possibility, latent in all language. Even our champion of relativism, Benveniste, bears Kahn out here, for he says, "every language, no matter what its structure, is capable of producing finite assertions" (about "reality" in Kahn's terms)—and that nominal sentences, as the bearers of such assertions, present "a truth offered as such, outside time, persons, and circumstances" (PGL, 134, 143). To the extent that Kahn agrees with the linguistic relativists that the particular array of concepts brought together in Indo-European forms of "to be" is simply an accident, he also goes further to assert that this was a *serendipitous* accident for philosophy: "the language spontaneously brought together concepts which genuinely belong together."[24]

Here Kahn comes surprisingly close to Heidegger, who says that "along with the German language, Greek is (in regards to the possibilities of thinking) at once the most powerful and the most spiritual of languages" (43), although Heidegger would never say that the key to language is the ability to make assertions about reality. Kahn writes: "I would suggest that ancient Greek is one of the most adequate of all languages [to philosophy], and that the possession of such a language was in fact a necessary condition for the success of the Greeks in creating Western logic and philosophy."[25] But Kahn has not much use for Heidegger, saying that the Greek concept of Being "also turns out to be very different from the questions of personal existence and the human condition which dominate that other school of modern ontology associated with the name of Heidegger,"[26] as opposed, presumably, to the analytic school represented by Frege, Russell, Wittgenstein, Quine, and so on. By falling prey to the common misinterpretation of Heidegger as an "existentialist" and a humanist, Kahn fails to realize just how much he has in common with Heidegger.[27] Of course, Heidegger *is* interested in the human being as Dasein, but only to the extent that analysis of Dasein will give thinking access to Being itself. Kahn and Heidegger do agree that the question of Being is a valid *question* and not a pseudoproblem generated by the quirks of language. They agree that Greek has some particularly illuminating usages of *einai,* such as the locative (the *chōra* for Heidegger: 50–51) and the durative (in Heidegger's sense of coming to presence, which then hardens into the metaphysical notions of *constant presence* as *idea,* substance, and so on). They can also be said to agree that the question of Being turns on the problem of truth, but here they part company.

For Kahn, the problem of truth relates to *reality* as a totality of "the facts" about the world, a totality that forms the basis for all true statements. In his attack on linguistic relativism, Kahn shows himself to be a defender of commonsense notions of truth. For Heidegger, despite Kahn's protestations to the contrary, this notion of truth as the reality that allows statements to correspond to the facts is a supremely metaphysical view, for it does indeed interpret Being as a *being,* in this case, the set of facts called "reality." Kahn's Being loses the verbality and temporality of the "to be." More to the point, for Heidegger, *truth* is a temporal *event* of disclosure, not a correct correspondence (or even a coherence) of statements and facts. Understood ontologically, rather than metaphysically, truth is the *eventuating* that opens up a world of significance and meaning to human interpretation; truth is this opening itself, the primordial openness of our understanding in grasping beings as they are given to be and our own Being as what it was, is, and can be. Metaphysical truth as "reality" is derivative from this ontological truth as *alētheia,* or unconcealment.

4. CONCLUSION

Whereas Kahn may well be right in saying that the particular conjunction of meanings of the word *einai* in Greek led to the dawning questions of Greek philosophy, Heidegger is almost certainly wrong in saying that *only* German and Greek can "speak" philosophy because only in these two languages does the language itself intersect so forcefully with Being to engender the *question* of Being. This is Heidegger's linguistic relativism. As Kahn implies, *all* languages, each in their own way, ought in principle to be able to engender the fundamental questioning that Heidegger dubs the "question of Being," even if there is no proper equivalent in all languages for the verb "to be." The point is not to grind a politically correct ax for the cause of linguistic equality but rather to *become* open and to *remain* open to the inexhaustible richness that language encompasses as the domain of meaning, or the "house of Being," to use Heidegger's idiom.[28] Linguistic relativism rejects the idea of a common matter for thought; openness to linguistic multiplicity, by contrast, should remain alive to the way in which each specific language may reveal new pathways, each with its own unexpected insights and vistas, into this matter for thought.

I indicated at the outset that it would be impossible to provide anything but the most preliminary commentary on the adequacy of Heidegger's own argument. If we are to take Heidegger seriously, then only a complete *philosophical* history of the development of grammar and philology since the Greeks, *plus* a philosophical study of the linguistics of the role of the verb "to be" not only in Greek (as Kahn has done), not only in German, and not only in English, but also in *all* language, must be undertaken first.[29] This is, to say the least, the labor not of a book but of a lifetime. That all language in its multiplicity must be brought into the question is required by the Heideggerian presumption that "language is the house of Being." For Heidegger's questions to be taken seriously as anything more than the parochial products of certain Indo-European languages, it must be shown that the "matter for thought" that stands forth in his question of Being can be translated, as it were (and not by finding exact equivalents for *Sein* in other languages, for these equivalents do not exist), into a question that makes sense *in* and *about* all language. The question of language and the question of Being both turn on the problem of *meaning*. Briefly, language allows things to have meaning for us; that is clear enough. But how? The question of what it means to be is a question of how any being can be meaningful to us. We can take this as the question of how is it possible that we can know (epistemology), or how the brain processes input (neuropsychology), and so on. But all of these constructions of the problem rely on a particular *answer* to the question of Being itself, and so may be reduced to this question *as* a question that must be held open as such. Or at least, this is what is at issue in the complete justification of Heidegger's project on the scale that he advocates. And that scale is anything but modest. There is a vast realm to explore here, and at best we stand only at the threshold. The challenge that a philosophical linguistics must take up, if properly conducted, is one that could do much to bridge the lamentable gap between the "analytic" and the "Continental" schools of contemporary academic philosophy. For this endeavor to succeed, we scholars with sympathy for Heidegger's *questions* must learn to make these questions speak in our *own* languages, independent of Heideggerese. This too is no small task, and one hardly yet attempted.

Chapter 8

HEIDEGGER'S INTERPRETATION OF *PHUSIS* IN *INTRODUCTION TO METAPHYSICS*

SUSAN SCHOENBOHM

1. ORIENTING REMARKS

The task of this chapter is not a simple one. Heidegger's interpretation of *phusis* in *Introduction to Metaphysics* is as complex as any of his interpretations in his work in the history of philosophy.[1] Following his thought is difficult in part because his German is often convoluted. This makes the rendering of his thought into English especially challenging. But the most difficult aspect of Heidegger's thought is always the matter for thinking that he attempts to address in his writing. I will attempt to lay out his thought as straightforwardly as possible by following the structure of his text. The reader, of course, will herself need to follow Heidegger's thought and text in order for my chapter to make any sense at all.

On the basis of early Latin translations of *phusis* as *natura, phusis* is commonly translated into English as "nature." A general definition of this word as we find it in a collegiate dictionary reads:

> *n.* [ME, fr. MF, fr. L *natura,* fr. *natus, pp. of nasci* to be born . . .]
> 1a: the inherent character or basic constitution of a person or thing:
> ESSENCE b: DISPOSITION, TEMPERAMENT 2a: a creative and
> controlling force in the universe b: an inner force or the sum of such
> forces in an individual 3: a kind or class usu. distinguished by fundamental or essential characteristics . . . 4: the physical constitution or drives of
> an organism . . . 5: a spontaneous attitude (as of generosity) 6: the
> external world in its entirety 7a: man's original or natural condition b: a
> simplified mode of life resembling this condition 8: natural scenery.[2]

Not only do the meanings in the above list not appear to have a common meaning, there is also no meaning in the list that, at least on first analysis, would take priority over the others. Is "nature" simply equivocal, that is, does the word indicate a variety of things that don't have any inherent connection? Furthermore, some of the meanings listed appear to contest others. It is not clear, for example, whether temperament is or is not to be thought of as belonging to the essence of a thing (another listed meaning of "nature"). Thus, if we are looking for the meaning of "nature," merely following such a dictionary definition leaves us unsatisfied.

Would a dictionary of philosophy be more helpful? Consulting such a dictionary, we also find included under the heading of "nature" various definitions, such as "the origin (or foundation) of everything; the ground for the explanation of things," and see listed a statement of Aristotle's definition of "nature" *(phusis)* as "that which is not made by humans . . . in contrast to *technē,* . . . the cause (principle, law, source) of all change (motion, movement)."[3] Such a definition is also unsatisfactory. For example, it seems to exclude what otherwise might be thought necessary to a definition of "nature," namely, temporal phenomena. We might wonder how we are to reconcile the apparently paradoxical relation of natural (that is, temporal) phenomena to that which is supposed to be their (natural, that is, permanent) source. Questions like these, among many others, motivate us to join in an attempt like Heidegger's to reenter and raise again the question of *phusis.*

The interpretation of *phusis* that Heidegger gives in his *Introduction to Metaphysics* is a rigorous attempt to understand the way in which the word *phusis* comes to be thought in terms of definitions such as those cited above. In the process, Heidegger reopens questions, unresolved difficulties, and ambiguities of meaning at the heart of such definitions. Why, for example, does *phusis* come to mean something like a permanent being that gives rise to beings? And how is it that physical things stand out both from each other and from their source, indeed, appear to be independent from and in conflict with each other, without, however, being able to fall entirely out of their togetherness? When Heidegger writes his "introduction to meta-physics," then, he is turning toward a question of *phusis* that also attempts to retrieve the earliest Greek experiences of being.[4] His project has revolutionary consequences for our understanding both of "nature," in the more restricted modern sense, and of beings as a whole, including ourselves. As we shall see, at the very least, his attempt leads to a way of thinking of the meaning of *phusis* that points beyond the ambiguities of the meaning of the word (but not beyond the questioning) to an understanding of being without substance that transforms an interpretation of being as permanent nature.

2. THE AMBIGUITY OF THE ENTERPRISE OF METAPHYSICS

Phusis enters Heidegger's discussion of metaphysics early in the text, as he first turns to a consideration of the ways in which the ancient Greeks conceived of beings. For the Greeks, Heidegger says, "beings were called *phusis*" (10). In the context of the concern to recover an originary question concerning the being of beings, Heidegger points out the need to attempt to understand the meaning of *phusis* for the Greeks and thus for philosophy in its first inception. Since the meaning of *phusis* has to do with beings, it also has in some way to do with being. We must be careful, then, not too quickly to assume the later, Latinized way of thinking of *phusis*, namely as *natura*, which basically means "birth" or "to be born." Doing so may result in "the isolation and alienation of the originary essence of Greek philosophy" (10–11). Heidegger's interest in the question of the being of beings works to retrieve an originary dimension of Greek thought that is obscured by later metaphysical interpretations of being whose primary focus is on beings and not on being. Because these interpretations of being and of *phusis* already assume too much, they understand too little of the difference between beings and the meaning of being and of *phusis* that Heidegger wishes to retrieve. In order to clarify the meaning that *phusis* bore for the Greeks, we must attempt to return and explore for ourselves ancient Greek texts where it appears. Language, translation, and interpretation, then, are all already clearly foregrounded as matters for concern in this text.

In a fashion that is itself questionable given his caution regarding interpretation, Heidegger proceeds to venture an initial, elaborated interpretation of the meaning of *phusis* for the Greeks: "It says what emerges from itself (for example, the emergence, the blossoming, of a rose), the unfolding that opens itself up, the coming-into-appearance in such unfolding, and holding itself and persisting in appearance—in short, the emerging-abiding sway [*das aufgehend-verweilende Walten*]" (11). In order to support this interpretation, Heidegger refers to the etymology of one of *phusis*' cognates, *phuein*, in its meaning of "to grow or make grow." Although this "emerging" character of *phusis* "can be experienced everywhere" (11), Heidegger's claim is that *phusis* was not first experienced by, in, or as natural processes, "but the other way around: on the basis of a fundamental experience of being in poetry and thought [*dichtend-denkend*], what [the Greeks] had to call *phusis* disclosed itself to them" (11).

Here it appears that Heidegger thinks of an experience of being as in some sense grounding the Greek experience of *phusis*. The implication is that *phusis* disclosed itself on the basis of a (still more?) fundamental experience of being.

Accordingly, an experience of being would have an even more primordial status, at least in this interpretation, than would *phusis*. In turn, the disclosure of *phusis* becomes a basis for experiencing natural things *(ta phusika)* as natural or as belonging in and to *phusis*. The priority that Heidegger appears to assign to being in this initial statement of the relation between being and *phusis*, which in many respects he maintains throughout the text, turns, however, into a virtual equivalence such that we cannot clearly determine which word has priority in his interpretation of the Greeks.

Phusis may be thought of as process, but not as a process among others. *Phusis* means "process" in a different sense from any particular process or the combination of processes that beings can be observed to undergo in their physical careers. *Phusis* means "process" in an originary sense of that eventfulness that enables or allows the processes of things to come into appearance, to take a stand "for the first time" (12). Neither is *phusis* a collection of processes that physical beings exhibit. *Phusis*, for the Greeks, according to Heidegger, meant something like the continuous emerging or coming into being of beings that then, in a derivative sense, could be thought to exhibit differentiated and interrelated processes. Far from—and far greater than, in the sense of "more originary than"—the conception of nature that modern science investigates, *phusis* names for the Greeks "what is, as such and as a whole" (12). An originary meaning of *phusis* remains, he says, in Aristotle when Aristotle speaks of "the grounds of beings as such" (12).

Out of, or on the basis of, this originary conception of *phusis*, a variety of narrower meanings of the word arise. *Phusis* comes derivatively to mean something as contrasted with or opposed to counterphenomena such as "the psychical," "*thesis*," "*nomos*," "*ethos*," "*technē*," and "the historical" (13). Yet, for the Greeks, all these continue until much later to be included in an "originally broader sense of *phusis*" (13). Both being "in the [later and] narrower sense of fixed continuity" (12) and becoming are still included in that which the word *phusis* originally says. The distinction between being and becoming, then, was a later, subsequent interpretation of being and *phusis*.

Like the words "being" and "metaphysics," the word *phusis* is susceptible of more than one meaning. Along with various narrower meanings, it also carries a wider one that ought not to be forgotten. Whereas a delineation of the narrower definitions of *phusis* is achieved through contrasting them with counterphenomena ("the psychical," and so on),[5] its wider meaning embraces both "sides" of the narrower oppositions and enables these opposites to relate to each other both as opposites and as "same."[6] The question of the way in which this wider sense of being and of *phusis* is to be thought and articulated is one of the central questions that Heidegger is wrestling with throughout this text.

Heidegger can thus make the following two claims: (1) "Beings as such and as a whole are *phusis*" (13), that is, in the wider sense of *phusis*, and (2) the word *phusis* "means the being of beings" (14).[7] The entire discussion, then, clearly "is in itself already beyond *ta phusika*, on beyond beings, and is concerned with being" (14). In this way, Heidegger begins to use the words "being" and "*phusis*"—in their wider meanings—as synonyms. Just as *phusis* cannot only be thought of in terms of physical or natural things, so also being cannot be understood by thinking only about beings. The traditional meanings of both these words need to be called into question in such a way that the originary—for Heidegger the *unitary* (47)—meaning of these words is able to emerge.

In attempting to understand the way in which Heidegger thinks of *phusis* in this text, then, we need to keep several points firmly in mind. (1) The meaning of the word *phusis*, like that of the word "being," is ambiguous; it has wider and narrower meanings, which we must not confuse. (2) If we are to be able to think the full meaning of *phusis*, we need not collapse the wider meaning of *phusis* into any of its narrower ones. Rather, we need clearly to understand these narrower meanings as embraced by the wider one. (3) For Heidegger and, according to Heidegger, for the Greeks, the word *phusis* in its wide and more originary meaning denotes "the emerging-abiding sway" *(das aufgehend-verweilende Walten).*[8] It thus also means the same as the being of beings.

Heidegger's virtual equation of being and *phusis* is elaborated, at least initially, by characterizing both in terms of cognates of "standing." *Phusis*, he says, "is the *event* of com*ing*-to-stand, aris*ing* from the concealed and thus enabl*ing* the concealed to take its stand for the first time" (12, translation modified; emphasis added). Further, as Heidegger suggested earlier in the discussion of the Greek experience of *phusis*, knowing *(Wissen)* "means to be able to stand in the truth . . . to be able to stand in the openness of beings, to stand up to it" (16). Restated, the question of being becomes, "How does it stand with being?" (25). The discussion then focuses increasingly on the question of the meaning of the word "being." Although we do not know what, if anything, the word means, this "is counterbalanced by the fact that we still understand being and distinguish it with certainty from not-being . . ." (62). Being contrasts with not-being insofar as beings are clearly other than nothing. Nevertheless, "the being that we are asking about is almost like nothing . . . [and is] undiscoverable" (27) and "indeterminate" (30).

Heidegger argues that *ptōsis* and *enklisis* (inflection) designate "a falling, tipping, or inclining . . . a dropping-off from an upright, straight stance" (46). In contrast, the meaning of the infinitive "to be" *(sein)* has to do with "standing-there . . . taking and maintaining a *stand* that stands erected high in itself" (46). On the basis of his etymological excursus, then, Heidegger interprets the meaning of the word "being" for the Greeks as follows: "Whatever takes such a stand becomes *constant* in itself and thereby freely and on its own runs up against the necessity of its limit, *peras*. . . . [The being of beings is] the self-restraining hold that comes from a limit, the having-of-itself wherein the constant holds itself" (46). In short, "for the Greeks, 'being' fundamentally means presence" (46). In a similar way, Heidegger further infers that "*phusis* means the emergent self-upraising, the self-unfolding that abides in itself. In this sway, [opposites such as] rest and movement are closed and opened up from an originary unity. This sway is the overwhelming coming-to-presence that has not yet been surmounted in thinking, and within which *that which* comes to presence essentially unfolds as beings" (47)

Phusis names the originary, unitary, eventful process—the "sway abiding in itself"—that yields the beingness of beings; *phusis* names the eventfulness out of which beings emerge as beings. Within this occurring, all things that are presencing come to pass as beings. *Phusis* points, then, not only to physical beings that emerge, nor only to the emerging into being of beings, but, in addition, to that occurr*ing* which "yields" determinate things (or out of which, as it were, determinate things emerge) but which is not itself a thing. That originary "out of which" "is" no thing, since before the yielding of determinate things there "is" neither world nor beings nor names, neither before nor after.

The thought of *phusis* here becomes particularly difficult. The difficulty stems from the radical question that is involved here, namely, the question of the way in which *phusis* and its originary, differentiating determination are to be thought and brought into human language. How, if at all, is it possible to render in words that which "is" previous to any being, word, or name? How to articulate the very coming-into-being of determination for the first time? For according to Heidegger, this is what *phusis* must mean originarily (see again 12). Only secondarily or subsequently can the word mean anything like "something out of which beings emerge," or "the context within which beings come to be," or "the event of the emergence of being," or even "the determination of nothing as something."

If we follow the radicality of Heidegger's thought, we can see that the word *phusis* points not to beings—or even to the being of beings as beings—but to that originary event of the very emerging, for the first time, of some determination.[9] In its most originary meaning, *phusis* means the emerging, for the first time, of something out of no determination at all. It means the occurrence of the originary, determinate emergence of something as other than indeterminate nothing or, in other words, the process of something's coming-to-be-something from nothing. The elaboration of things, of beings in their being, is secondary to this most originary event.

But this formulation, too, is inadequate. *Phusis* is a name for the emerging of the originary difference of determination and no determination, the very occurrence of an articulation of a primordial difference between something and nothing. This originary determining that is but one aspect of the meaning of *phusis* determines "something" to be for the first time; it thus "is" the articulation of originary differentiation as a difference of something and nothing, which occurs "within" or "out of" or "from" what then comes to be thought as that "not yet anything and yet not yet nothing either" which yields it. This originary articulation to which *phusis* points first brings into being something as other than nothing or, one might venture to say, first brings being into being as being and not just nothing. This event of articulation thus occurs somehow both "out of" and "within" *that which* yields it.[10] That within (or out of, or from) which this originary differentiation of something and nothing occurs is not reducible to any thing or determination, neither to (a) the articulation of itself, (b) the beings that emerge "from" it, (c) the event of emerging, (d) what, subsequent to the emerging of something, comes to be called nothing nor (e) the entire constellation of these. The meaning of *phusis* at once embraces and exceeds all these determinations.

We might attempt to approach such a radical meaning of this word by attempting to describe the way in which, according to a phenomenological analysis like that of Husserl, the differentiation between background and foreground occurs in consciousness: the differentiation first discloses itself in consciousness as a differential that simultaneously determines foreground as foreground and background as background. In this differentiation, the background is determined as receding into indetermination as the foreground becomes more or less determinate. The phenomenal movement of foregrounding and backgrounding, the coming to be background and the coming to be determinate foreground, all occur simultaneously. This complex movement of determination is originary in the sense that it makes simultaneously possible (a) the determination of background (however indeterminate) as background and foreground as foreground, (b) the consequent appearing of determinate beings that appear (in the foreground), and (c) the coming into being of the entire constellation as context or world, including background, foreground, and the determinate movements of differentiation. All these aspects belong to an originary event of differentiation of background and foreground.[11] Analogically, the meaning of *phusis* includes (a) the originary event or movement of articulation or differentiation of something and nothing, (b) the indeterminacy of what now can be called "indeterminate nothing," which recedes back or withdraws from the field of determinate beings, and thus both serves as phenomenological background for the emerging of those beings and as that over against which beings come to stand, (c) the emerging of particular beings into being, and d) the entirety of this complex.

Our language misleads us, then, if we say *phusis* "is": *phusis* does not name a being, the being of beings, indeterminate nothing, the emerging of beings into being, nor all of these. Rather, *phusis* names at once that originary not-yet-even-background yielding a determination of "itself" *and* the originary event of differentiations that are articulated in and by that determination.

In the paragraphs immediately above, I am struggling, as Heidegger was struggling, to think and to articulate *phusis* in its most radical, originary, unified meaning. And, as Heidegger has already indicated, insofar as the word "being" functions as a synonym of *phusis,* it likewise points, on one hand, to *that before which* there "is" nothing, and on the other, to the originary differentiating event of something and nothing. Thus, although in this text and in his later work Heidegger appears to continue to prioritize the question of the meaning of being over that of *phusis,* both words indicate a dimension of originary eventfulness that is forgotten in the history of metaphysics. In both cases, Heidegger compels us to remember the originary differentiation of being(s) and nothing and thus to think also of *that which* "is" not yet even determinate enough to call "it" anything, including "being."

The meaning and status of originary *phusis,* then, is determinately ambiguous. Only on the basis of the originary determination of *phusis* as *phusis* can "it" come to be thought at all; only on the questionable basis of this originary determination can *phusis,* in a highly questionable and still ambiguous way, come to be thought, as Heidegger thinks of it here, as the "abiding sway." This physical sway can subsequently be thought in relation to the beings that come to be in and from it and yet can also be thought to "have" or "be" that sway which holds sway in and through, over and beyond beings. *Phusis* names "that which originarily worlds" or "that which originarily holds sway" (48). "This sway [*phusis*] first steps forth from concealment, that is, in Greek, *alētheia* (unconcealment) happens, insofar as the sway struggles [*erkämpft*] itself forth as a world" (47). *Phusis* "abides" in this sense, that is, as the emergence of world as world and as interworldly beings in their difference from nothing as well as from each other.

Here again there is, however, a problem, namely, understanding *phusis* as abiding. The name *phusis* originarily names—and so originarily determines—not-yet-anything, so that "it" (which is not yet even an "it") becomes something, becomes determinate. A determination comes to be and names "something" that is then characterized as abiding. But the abiding character of this determination, like the standing or enduring character of things that the Greeks called beings, is indeed highly questionable, since having arisen from nothing, what arose *was not always,* and certainly not always *so.* What, if anything, abides, then? We will leave this question open.

The originary, opening, and determining power of *phusis* that Heidegger elaborates in terms of "worlding" involves a differentiation that, with the aid of Heraclitus, he proceeds to think of in terms of *polemos,* struggle. *Phusis,* characterized by Heraclitus as strife, confrontation, is that which abidingly "allows what essentially unfolds to step apart from each other in opposition [and] first allows position and status and rank to establish themselves in coming to presence. . . . [It] allows those that struggle [within it] to originate as such in the first place" (47).

Aside from the question of the standing of what *phusis* names, we might ask also the following questions: How is the status—the standing—of physical things to be thought? What power enables different things in their differences to stand at all and to last for a time both against each other and against the unified "overwhelming sway" in terms of which Heidegger characterizes what *phusis* names?[12] How do particular beings preserve themselves in their over-againstness so that they appear constant? As far as I can tell, these questions remain largely unanswered by Heidegger. He does speak, however, of a kind of struggle that "first projects and develops the un-heard, the hitherto un-said and un-thought. This struggle is then sustained by the creators, by the poets, thinkers and statesmen. . . [who] throw the counterweight of their work and capture in this work the world that is thereby opened up. With these works, the sway, *phusis,* first comes to a stand in what comes to presence. Beings as such now first come into being. This becoming-a-world is authentic history" (47–48). A strange mixture of being and not being, we might say, characterizes what *phusis* names. Heidegger's thought is that a power of giving names brings something first into being. This power of naming, which, Heidegger says, belongs to "creators,"[13] struggles within "the overwhelming" *(phusis)* to enable something that was no thing to appear for the first time. What appears is delimited by this originary physical (in the sense of belonging to *phusis*) power of naming. It is this originary delimitation of something rather than nothing that Heidegger will later say remains at once a mystery (119, 125) and susceptible to degeneration into a prototype for reproduction and copying (48).

The way in which the power of creators functions remains largely unaddressed by Heidegger. We glean only that creators "work" within the sway of *phusis*. The implication appears to be that they (or something) *must* work for the sake of making real *(verwirklichen)* ever anew the emerging of something from and in opposition to nothing, as well as for the sake of preserving things in their being. The meaning that being acquired for the Greeks, then, as the constant, the standing, *ousia,* was originally—and that means historically—effected through a physical, poetic power of naming. This power came to be in and by delimiting that indeterminacy of the unnamed for the first time. "It" called "itself" *phusis* and then subsequently called *phusis* other further delimited things. By virtue of originary naming, then, things could have—could be—their "stands" in—and in contrast or opposition to—the overwhelming sway, *phusis*. According to Heidegger, poetic naming *(Dichtung)* is an originary power that holds the otherwise indeterminate sway of *phusis* at bay, as it were, so that a site for the being of beings clears. This siting is the originary occurrence in a delimited way of something over against or in differentiation from an indeterminate background. Yet this delimitation also enables the indeterminate background to be both indeterminate and background in relation to a foreground. Naming gives some "constancy" of determination, gives determination constancy, constantly gives determination in the sense of originarily delimiting something as different from nothing. "For the Greeks, 'being' says constancy" (48) in such a way that falling, not standing, comes to mean notbeing. Thus, by virtue of the name and the effect of naming in first bringing something to a stand, the contrast of this standing with not-being (notstanding) also was made inevitable, since delimiting, bringing something to a stand, drew some thing out from what before this was not (any thing) at all named or delimited.

Heidegger's attempt to return to the realm of questioning concerning both *phusis* and the being of beings here indicates that we are obliged to approach the meaning of these words indirectly. Thinking must always approach the question of the meaning of being (and of *phusis*) from within that meaning, from among beings. The questioning proceeds, for example, from asking a question concerning beings toward something like what Heidegger refers to as the ground of beings (2, 18) or the universal essence *(allgemeines Wesen)* or the "as-suchness" that originarily enables us think of such beings as being (61). In our approach, however, we discover a "necessity" that we already understand the word "being" (62), albeit in an indeterminate manner. That is, we are already in some way consequent to that which we seek to understand in our attempt to understand being. This "fact" gives us an inkling, albeit indirect, of originary being, as well as of its remove from us. "[T]hat we understand being, if only in an indefinite way—has the highest rank, insofar as in *this,* a power [*Macht*] announces itself in which the very possibility of the essence of our dasein is grounded" (63).

3. RESTRICTED BEING *(PHUSIS)*

In order further to expose the wider meaning of the word "being" that embraces its narrower meanings, Heidegger now undertakes an examination of four interrelated respects according to which being is delimited in opposition to an other. According to these delimitations, the word "being" (like the word "*phusis*") came historically to have not just a wider but also narrower meanings. A further discussion of *phusis* also recommences within the discussion of this fourfold delimitation of being. We should bear in mind as Heidegger proceeds that he has been occupied with being in contrast to nothing. As we saw in the context of Heidegger's previous discussion of *phusis,* however, there is a sense in which "being" and "*phusis*" both name an opposite or other to nothing and another sense in which they name a "unity" that also embraces these "opposites." The meaning of both these words, "being" and "*phusis,*" is ambiguous, and it is their wider meaning that is most questionable because, apparently, it most conceals itself in our attempt to approach it, hiding, as it were, behind the various narrower meanings that these words historically have acquired. Because our access to the wider meaning of these words is indirect, as noted above, we must pass back through the narrower meanings toward the wider meaning. Heidegger states that his discussion of the fourfold delimitation of being is intended to indicate the ways in which "contrary to the widely accepted opinion, being is anything but an empty word for us. Instead, it is determined in so multifaceted a fashion that we can hardly manage to preserve this determination sufficiently" (71).

For Heidegger, Parmenides stands as the preeminent thinker of being as "self-collected perdurance of the constant" (74) in contrast to becoming. Parmenides views becoming as not-being. Although the thought-pathway toward not-being, "the path of nothing," cannot be traveled, it must nevertheless be considered, if only in order to be recognized as unviable (85). In addition to these two sharply opposed paths (toward being and toward not-being or nothing), there is, according to Heidegger's reading of Parmenides, a third way, the way of seeing, of *doxa*. This is the way along which the view of things always changes. Yet, along this way, according to Heidegger, "seeing is experienced *as* belonging to being" (86), that is, there still *appear* to be things and not just nothing. Although seeing or appearing changes, within that changing it is possible for a thinker nevertheless to distinguish being, as that which endures, from seeing. Interpreting this third way, Heidegger says without further elaboration only that it can be avoided. In addition, knowing it as one of the three ways enables humans to come to a decision *(Entscheidung)* for or against them so that, depending on the character of this decision, either dasein comes to stand, to endure in and against seeming, which is to "tear away both seeming and being from the abyss of not-being" (84), or . . . not.

It is important to note, as Heidegger does, the way in which seeming (appearing) and being as the constant belong together (106). Indeed there are at least some senses in which "seeming means exactly the same as being" (76), insofar as both mean self-showing, for example, in stars' shining. This would indicate that, beyond the meaning of being in opposition to becoming and seeming (appearing), a wider meaning of being is the togetherness of constancy and change.

Here, Heidegger remarks that *phusis* names being's opening itself, appearing. "Being means [*heißt*] appearing" (77). "The emerging-abiding sway is in itself at the same time the seeming appearing" (77). *Phusis,* the emerging sway, is also appearing; this is an event of disclosure *(alētheia)* wherein something comes to be revealed. Yet, there is also, simultaneously, a concealing occurring. Being or *phusis* is not only appearing or what appears but the *event* of appearing or concealing. Here, being, *phusis,* and *alētheia* all mean the same: Heidegger's equation of these terms is particularly evident in this passage.

In what way, if any, are we able to think enduring and changing together? If we think in a more originary way, that is, in terms of the belonging together of what the opposing terms name, this opposition—according to which being and becoming, as well as being and appearing, are contrasted—might enable us to think of *that which* being and *phusis* name in their wider meanings. With echoes back to our earlier explication of the strangeness of *that which phusis* names, perhaps as an abyss at the very root of our questioning, the further question again opens up: How, if at all, can anything, of *phusis,* of being, of dasein, endure? Does that no thing which *phusis* or being names endure? If so, in what sense?

At least it seems clear that, according to Heidegger's interpretation, enduring was the value assigned by Parmenides, as well as by many thinkers who followed him, to being over against becoming and seeming. The latter two were, in contrast, both names for change. Yet, being *(phusis)* also names that in and out of which anything arises, comes to be, or appears. What, in short, do these names mean? Don't they name not only that out of which things appear but also that into which they disappear? And how are we to think of this "that"? So far Heidegger has heavily stressed appearing, opening, coming to stand. But do being and *phusis* also mean the opposite of these determinations? Do they also mean disappearing, closing, and falling? We shall see that his emphasis on this other becomes more emphatic in the latter part of the text, where Heidegger begins to discuss death in the context of the ode from Sophocles' *Antigone*. We must follow the way in which his reading of the Greeks—and if he is correct, the characteristic Greek manner of thinking of being as "the constant"—covers over the opposite of constancy. The emphatic insistence on constancy in such a way of thinking, that is, its assumption of the meaning of being as constancy *and not as the opposite of constancy,* obscures a meaning of being that is the paradoxical togetherness of constancy and change. So, we might raise the additional question: does either that which shows itself or that which conceals itself ever really *stand?* Or is the character of beings as appearing not even more mysterious in the sense that any standing is also a falling? Isn't the falling of beings as constant as their emerging and thus equally disclosive of both being and *phusis?*

In Heidegger's reading of Heraclitus, too, we find that, rather than putting equal stress on the inclination toward concealment or the movement of striving aspects falling apart, Heidegger stresses, as he did in his reading of Parmenides, primarily if not exclusively the importance of constant persisting, the "glory" of standing in repute (78). His stress is on the gatheredness of the gathering,[14] the *constancy* of strife and of the gathering (96–97), and the straightness and prominence of being. It is the constancy of the *gathering* and not falling apart that Heidegger interprets as the meaning of *phusis* for Heraclitus (98). It is the rank and dominance of being in the sense of constancy and the maintenance of it that appear to be in the foreground of his concern (101–102). To what extent, then, is Heidegger glossing over differences between Parmenides and Heraclitus when he states that he wants to think of Heraclitus as saying "the same as Parmenides" (74)? Perhaps, we may suspect, Heidegger's unevenness stems from the way in which this thought of constancy is not immune to opposition, and thus, perhaps, is one of the most contested, most questionable characterizations of being.

4. BEING *(PHUSIS)* AND THINKING

Heidegger's third pair of opposites, in which being is thought not primarily in terms of its wider meaning as embracing the opposites but rather in terms of its meaning in opposition to an other, is being and thinking.[15] This involves him in a discussion of logic as the historically preeminent "science" of thinking, and in the question of the originary meaning of *logos* in relation to its subsequent interpretations. How does Heidegger continue his discussion of *phusis* in this section?

There is an ambiguity of meaning in the word *logos* that corresponds to the ambiguity of the meaning of the words "*phusis*"and "being." *Logos* also has both a narrower and a wider meaning.[16] Heidegger is referring to the wider meaning of *logos* when he states that "being and *logos* [are] originally and unitarily the same for the Greeks" (95) and thus that "we find an originary connection between being, *phusis* and *logos*" (94). Because " 'being' means for the Greeks: *phusis*" (96), and because both being and *phusis* are originally the same for the Greeks as *logos* in its sense of gathering, we can understand all three more fully when we see the connection between *logos* and *phusis*. To do this, Heidegger turns once again to Heraclitus, then to Parmenides. In Heidegger's interpretation, *logos* in Heraclitus' fragment 1 means that which "constantly remains itself and which essentially unfolds as the together [*Zusammen*] in beings" (98, translation modified). The *kata ton logon* in this fragment means the same as *kata phusin*, and hence, *phusis* and *logos* are the same. The gathering of *logos* is also that which contends: *polemos*, struggle, originary *Auseinandersetzung*. Being is *logos*, *harmonia*, *alētheia*, *phusis*, *phainesthai*. Change, Heidegger says, is not a matter of "pure inconstancy, but instead it means: the whole of beings in its being is always thrown from one opposite to the other, thrown over here and over there—being is the gatheredness of this conflicting unrest." *Logos*, in this sense, "has the character of pervasive sway, of *phusis*" (102). *Logos* and *phusis* originally belong together as *same;* only on the basis of this relation is it possible to comprehend "the inner necessity and possibility of their division" (103).

To demonstrate the process of the disjunction between *phusis* and *logos*, Heidegger turns again to Parmenides. Although the customary translation of Parmenides' Fragment 5 reads "thinking and being are the same," this, according to Heidegger, is a misinterpretation. *Noein* (which Heidegger translates as *Vernehmen*, apprehension) originally belongs to *phusis*, to being. It is "the receptive bringing-to-a-stand of the constant that shows itself in itself." *Noein* happens "for the sake of being," which "essentially unfolds as appearing, as stepping into unconcealment only if unconcealment happens, only if a self-opening happens. . . . Apprehension [*Vernehmen*] also necessarily occurs *along with* appearance" (106). Along with any (delimited) appearing of something, there is also a dimension of being and *phusis* that, although not itself appearing as a being, "holds around" that which appears, occurring beyond it, as it were, as the taking in or hearkening perception of it.[17] Taken in its meaning of (human) thinking, *noein* therefore is a narrowing of the meaning of *noein* in its originary sense as the other of appearing. *Noein,* then, does not originarily mean either "thinking" or "apprehension" as a (human) faculty (107). Rather, being human happens within that more originary apprehension that occurs in differentiation from and together with the appearing of beings in being or *phusis.*

The next segment of Heidegger's discussion turns to the ode in Sophocles' *Antigone,* which thematizes *phusis* as uncanny and man as "the uncanniest."[18] He elaborates his interpretation of the ode in terms cognate with *Walten* (which he has already introduced as his translation of *phusis*) as follows: "The violent, the overwhelming is the essential character of the sway itself" (115). In this section of the text, Heidegger elaborates his earlier discussion of *phusis* as *polemos* by thinking of *phusis* in terms of the violence enacted on one another by each participant in the struggle. *Das Überwältigende* (the overwhelming) and *das Gewaltige* (the violent) are, both, together, *phusis,* in such a way that both "the overwhelming" and "the violent" point to the physical breaking in *(hereinbrechen)* on each other, as it were, of the sides of the *polemos* that *phusis* is, and thus the breaking in of *phusis* upon itself. *Das Gewaltige* (the violent) is *phusis* breaking in on itself, which enables a "keeping" of its power *(Macht)* "to" itself (116). As human, the violent is a power of *phusis* (the overwhelming sway), indeed, *the* power of *phusis,* which uses violence *against* itself; that the overwhelming turns against itself characterizes the power of *phusis.* By asserting that the sway *is* overwhelming violence, Heidegger is saying that both *phusis* and being human are *deinon* because being human is derivative of *phusis.* Human being remains a determinate, physical way of being given by *phusis,* which, however, is itself determined or destined in its being to use violence in setting itself against other physical things by differentiating itself from them through language and action. Human being stands out violently from and against sea, earth, animals, and so on, all of which are named, delimited things other than human. This means, however, that human being is also always in relation to other beings. Human being's power is dependent upon as well as in conflict with other physical things. To be humans, humans must use their physical power to make a "venturing" way through other beings (116). This venturing, however, is also inevitably a tearing displacement of the lives of other things out of *their* given physical order *(Fug),* which then becomes a matter of "capturing" and "subjugating" and thus "surmounting" them (118).[19]

But though it may *seem* that "it is he [the human] who has [the other powers of *phusis*] at his disposal," we need to understand this seeming by reference to the ways in which human being remains "disposed" into the uncanniness of *phusis* (120). Thus, although human being may arrogate to itself the power to invent language, understanding, building, and poetry, human being does not originally bring these about. Rather, the origin of these remains shrouded in a mystery that humans can neither create nor understand. Genuinely historical knowing, in Heidegger's sense, is understanding the character of this origination as mystery (119).

The power "granted" by *phusis* to humans as human, which Heidegger has called "violence," though not belonging originarily to humans, does produce a sense in which humans can be thought to "co-create" paths into other beings. Language, understanding, constructing, and building are powers due originarily to *phusis* that nevertheless can be thought also, in a secondary sense, to be used by and useful to humans (119–120). "Human" power, granted originarily in and through the mysterious, originary, opening up and differentiating power of being or *phusis*, is also always already delimited. It is always also over against that of *phusis*, which exceeds it. This over-againstness makes inevitable the shattering of the delimited power that is "human" against the delimiting power of that over against which it stands. Thus, death is inevitable. Death originally occurs as the closing up or shattering of the "breach" that originarily occurs in the breaking open of *phusis* (124–125).

Heidegger's discussion then becomes an interpretation of the physicality of *technē*, which he translates as "knowing" *(Wissen)* and takes to mean "being out beyond [that which] sets to work . . . [that which] first gives to what is already present at hand its relative justification, its possible determinateness, and thus its limit" (122). *Technē* means "to work out [*er-wirken*] being in a being . . . to bring [*phusis*] into the work . . . within which, as what comes to appear, the emerging that holds sway, *phusis*, comes to appear" (122).[20] *Technē* in this sense is doubly uncanny (115): it is at once determinative and derivative of *phusis*. It is a physical power that takes up delimited power and uses it against other physical powers; its power is at once the very power of unitary *phusis* and a delimitation of both itself and other things in an over-against structure. The physical power of delimitation that is "human" determines beings to stand in their differentiations over against each other. It thus is the "knowing struggle to set being, which was formerly closed off, into what appears as beings" (122).

This struggle entails, according to Heidegger, a question of fittingness *(Fug)*, joint or fit *(Fuge)*, structure *(Gefüge)*, arrangement *(Fügung)*, and direction *(Weisung)*. Any manner in which human fittingness or direction happens is always highly contested and contestable. Although being or *phusis* urges *(nötigt)* human being(s) to stand in and out of it so that it can be something rather than (only) nothing, the relative duration depends, it would seem, solely upon the physical strength of the originary urge. And inevitably, the physical strength of any being weakens, wanes, and dies. Heidegger says that, for humans, knowing the inevitability of undergoing disaster while also experiencing the urge and urgency to be constitutes "the deepest and broadest Yes to the overwhelming" (125). Through human being, being "confirms itself in works as history," to which belong *both* arising and going under. We see that the stress on standing with which Heidegger initially is preoccupied yields to a reciprocal stress on the inevitability that any standing will fall. However enduring a stand may be in and against *phusis,* its fall is also inevitable by virtue of its belonging to *phusis.* Being, as gathering fittingness, as *phusis,* thus "becomes the necessity [*Notwendigkeit*] of the essence of historical humanity" (130).[21]

Dasein, being-there, then, is to take a relatively lasting, although always mortal, always temporal, always contested, stand in and against being or *phusis.* This is the pivotal meaning of disclosure as Heidegger is working it out in this text. When this stand occurs, it is in a historically decisive *(entscheidende)* manner that opens up a determinate site for beings within being or *phusis* (the overwhelming). The abiding possibility and inevitability of defeat, of not-being, for dasein announces itself together with an ever renewed resurgence of being-there as the opening of sites of disclosure of beings within being (136).

Throughout the entire course that this text traces, Heidegger attempts to follow the way in which the wider meanings of being, *phusis, alētheia,* and *logos* are transformed into narrower meanings (144–145). His primary interest is in following the transformation of an originary thought of disclosiveness of being to the closure or collapse of this way of thought of origin. In the course of his discussion, however, he also shows the way in which, no matter how much human beings might like to be able to represent things as permanent in language, and to "count on" things, this is not possible, because of the temporal, eventful character of *phusis.* Phusis, in an original sense, prevents—does not allow—such a familiarity but remains strange, withdrawing from familiarity so that human dasein is urged again and anew into the question of itself, of its meaning—which it always "is." Heidegger's attempts in *Introduction to Metaphysics* to expose and to rethink originary, physically powerful ways of thought and being that have been forgotten therefore can only have limited success. His later work, nevertheless, takes up in various ways the themes which he addresses in this text. Indeed, in his later works, he will call the closure or collapse of originary thought of origination the abandonment of being *(Seinsverlassenheit)* and articulate this in terms of the forgetfulness or oblivion of being *(Seinsvergessenheit).* This collapse, Heidegger will say, also occurs out of an inevitability. It occurs because originary disclosiveness, "the inception, as incipient, must, in a certain way, leave itself behind. . . . [In the way it initiates, originary disclosiveness] can never directly preserve its initiating" (145–146). The only way that a thought of originary disclosiveness may be preserved in its originality is "by re-trieving it more originally," by following how it occurs, by articulating it, and by displaying its collapse "as far as possible in its historical course" (146). Following this inevitability out, we ourselves participate, perhaps, in the enactment of . . . another beginning.

Chapter 9

HEIDEGGER'S *ANTIGONES*

CLARE PEARSON GEIMAN

Heidegger's interpretation of the choral ode from Sophocles' *Antigone* is one of the best known, or perhaps most notorious, passages in the *Introduction to Metaphysics*. His reading has been frequently critiqued not only for doing violence to Sophocles but also, and more important, for the way in which it appears to glorify actual violence in its heroic-tragic assessment of the nature of human knowing and in the consequent role of "violent" creators (priests, poets, thinkers, statesmen) in founding historical communities. The lecture course was given in 1935, relatively soon after Heidegger resigned his post as the first National Socialist rector of the University of Freiburg, a position for which he assumed party membership and during which he was involved in the restructuring of the university (at least in name) along party lines. The date of *Introduction to Metaphysics* and its occasional but striking political remarks have drawn attention to the course and to its interpretation of Sophocles in particular as a key articulation of Heidegger's political thought and its possible relation to National Socialism.

As most commentators have recognized, however, this interpretation must be read from within its context in the long-term development of his thought. Recently, more attention has been given to comparing it with Heidegger's second interpretation of *Antigone* in the 1942 lecture course *Hölderlin's Hymn "The Ister."* A number of interpreters have noted the striking differences in tone and emphasis in Heidegger's second reading, though most argue that these changes do not amount to a revision or retraction of the core of the *IM* account, which concerns the violence inherent to human knowing as *technē*, or of the understanding of history and politics that derives from this account.[1] In what follows I argue that, read against the backdrop of Heidegger's long-term engagement with the concept of *technē* in the history of metaphysics, his later reading of Sophocles reveals a decisive shift in his thinking and in his approach to praxis and politics, making it evident that he abandons the earlier model of knowing and its violence when in the second interpretation he moves to reconceive poetry and poetic thinking as offering a possibility of knowing outside of and opposed to all *technē*.

This shift in Heidegger's thought sheds light on the philosophical basis of his adherence to National Socialism in the thirties. It suggests that those of Heidegger's defenders who would like to exonerate him based on the distinction he draws between the inherent potential that he saw in National Socialism and its actual historical development are misguided; the potential for violence and totalitarian politics belongs inextricably to the attempt to conceive human knowing through the working of *technē*. At the same time, it indicates that the approach to Being and knowing that Heidegger developed in the poetic thinking of the later writings succeeds where *technē* failed, attains the nonsubjectivist stance that had been the aim of his work from the beginning, and articulates a philosophical understanding that is no longer compatible with any kind of totalitarian politics. The path to this later perspective is itself of interest; Heidegger insisted that his later thinking developed out of the earlier and did not in any simple way invalidate it. What poetic thinking is and what is at stake in the move to such a thinking become clear only when the full consequences of the approach to Being in terms of *technē* have been brought to light.

TECHNĒ AND PHRONĒSIS BEFORE 1934

Heidegger's first extended discussion of *technē* occurs in the reading of Book 6 of the *Nicomachean Ethics* that occupies the first half of the 1925 lecture course on Plato's *Sophist*. Aristotle, in distinguishing *technē*, the understanding that guides the skill of the craftsman or artist, from *phronēsis*, the understanding that guides appropriate human action or *praxis*, insists that action is essentially different from making and that *phronēsis* is not reducible to *technē*.[2] In his critical appropriation of Aristotle, Heidegger does not directly challenge Aristotle's distinction between *technē* and *phronēsis* or his privileging of *phronēsis* over *technē*.[3] In fact, although he does blur the distinction later by referring to *phronēsis* as a kind of making, a *poiēsis* specifically concerned with disclosing the acting human being, the stress of his reading falls on the essential difference between the two, in a way that parallels Aristotle's own distinctions and clearly privileges *phronēsis*. Even if both *technē* and *phronēsis* are concerned with bringing something into existence in time and space, Dasein exists in a fundamentally different way than do things in the world, and so requires a different kind of understanding. Heidegger points out that though *technē* is a mode of knowing or revealing *(alētheuein)* concerned with the production of present-at-hand beings, *phronēsis* is a mode of knowing in which the object or aim of knowing, the deed, is not present-at-hand but "has the same character of being as the *alētheuein* itself";[4] that is, it is a discovering of Dasein, not of things, and so relates to Being in a fundamentally different way. This distinction, and the priority of *phronēsis*, are brought home when Heidegger comments that "Aristotle has here hit upon the phenomenon of conscience. *Phronēsis* is nothing else than conscience set into that motion which makes an action clear" (GA 19, 56).[5] Just as, for Aristotle, one of the critical points of distinction between *technē* and *phronēsis* is that *technē* is open-ended or morally neutral, whereas *phronēsis* first of all grasps the natural goal or fulfillment of human nature and only then also shows how to achieve this fixed goal, Heidegger similarly stresses that whereas *technē* is a knowing that can lose its essential measure or orientation by losing its essential relation to Being, this is not possible for *phronēsis:* "one cannot forget conscience" (ibid.). The relation between *technē* and *phronēsis* as Heidegger interprets it here underlies the later distinction between everydayness and authenticity in *Being and Time.* At the same time, in this early analysis, we already find the argument that *technē* (which here is still clearly identified with craftsmanship or production) is the basis for the Platonic concept of the *eidos,* the form or idea. In the ideas (and in a related way in Aristotelian metaphysics), *technē,* here conceived as a secondary form of knowledge whose scope is limited to nonhuman ways of being, becomes the dominant model for conceiving human Being and human knowing.[6]

This dominance of *technē* and the distortion of the conception of human Being and action that arises from it become an important focus for Heidegger's work in the late 1920s and early 1930s. In the work on Kant that dominates the years 1927–1930, and similarly in the work on Aristotle and Plato in 1931–1932, Heidegger is engaged in a concerted attack on what he sees as Western metaphysics' consistent reliance on models that grasp thinking and being by analogy with making, and specifically, with craftsmanship. This model results, on one hand, in the very real development of all forms of thought aimed at calculating with and manipulating existent beings, and so in the rise of logic and mathematics as well as mathematically based natural science and technology, on the other. But it is unjustifiably carried over to the human being, whose action can then only be made sense of in terms of producing, whose knowing is only validated so long as it is a calculating with representations, and whose embodied existence becomes, with the rest of material nature, an object for manipulation. When handicraft as one limited and derivative form of human action is taken to be paradigmatic of all acting and knowing, then that form of knowing that is proper to the knowledge of human beings and human action and that, as something like conscience, orients human action to its proper essence and measure, is lost.

Heidegger attempts to address this issue by looking for a unified account of human knowing that is appropriate to the specifically human way of being in time and that does not reduce the difference between human beings and things to that between makers and made objects. In the late twenties and early thirties, Heidegger attacks the productionist model by thoroughly inverting the traditional relation of activity and passivity and then reconceiving both as a unified capacity for responsiveness that is always dependent on a prior reception of something that comes from "outside" and that cannot itself be understood in terms of some purely "active" power.[7] The intent of this is to undercut the subjectivist and technological stance of contemporary human beings by depriving it of its metaphysical foundation, and to provide an ontological foundation that brings human finitude and dependence to the fore. This new model of knowing would not invalidate natural science and technology but would encompass them, first genuinely establishing them by setting them, as one limited and derivative relation to beings as present at hand in the world, into their proper relation to a fuller and more original account of appropriate human action, one that is itself grounded in a relation to Being and not just beings. Heidegger's work in the decade preceding *Introduction to Metaphysics* was thus shaped in important ways by a consistent search that might reasonably be described as an attempt to uncover an original unity to human knowing that overturns the dominance of *technē* and grounds it essentially in a phronetic knowing, one that rests in an understanding of human Being in its difference from beings and relation to Being.

RECLAIMING *TECHNĒ*: THE INTERPRETATION OF SOPHOCLES IN *INTRODUCTION TO METAPHYSICS*

In 1934 and 1935, Heidegger, having developed the critique of the role of *technē* as model for metaphysics, moves away from his earlier attempt to address this issue through fundamental ontology (the ontology of Dasein) and, in a way that remains nonetheless resonant with fundamental ontology and the constructs of *Being and Time,* instead articulates a positive alternative to the productionist model through a deconstruction of *technē.*[8] The interpretation of Sophocles in *Introduction to Metaphysics* articulates a critical stage in the development of this project. Prior to 1934, Heidegger consistently interprets *technē* as the know-how that pertains to handicraft; after 1934, Heidegger turns to *technē* itself, and to his original blurring of *technē* with *phronēsis,* to find the possibility of a higher knowing that unifies them in a reconceived *technē.* Based on this, he explicitly attempts to disentangle the concept of *technē* from that of handicraft, arguing that this "technical" concept is only one of many derivative applications of the original sense of thoroughgoing practical un-covering. Heidegger now turns his attention increasingly to thinkers who, in blurring the line between philosophy and poetry, break with the prevailing mathematical model of reason and the idea of philosophy as science and open a possible connection to a thinking that orients itself on human Being rather than on things. Beginning with the first course on Hölderlin in 1934 and continuing through the 1935 *Introduction to Metaphysics* and "The Origin of the Work of Art" and the 1936 lecture course on Nietzsche *(The Will to Power as Art),* he now looks for the solutions to the problems of the productionist model in the sense of *technē* that led it also to be applied to poetry and high art. Unlike the making of use-objects, the making of artworks might come together with *phronēsis* as the "making" of authentic *Dasein* and appropriate human actions, since artworks do not exist in the same way as tools or as objects of natural science but are meant to reveal and sustain human Being amidst beings in the world. Heidegger now suggests that human knowing in general is grounded in the kind of knowing that guides the "work" in this sense, in particular, the works of great artists and poets but also of thinkers, of priests (here in the sense of mythological, theological, and liturgical founders), and of political founders.

The critical role of the interpretation of Sophocles in this project is high-lighted by its placement and set-up in the *Introduction to Metaphysics.*[9] Heideg-ger introduces the ode from *Antigone* in the context of his reflections on "Being and thinking," the third of the four oppositional polarities under which the reflection on Being has been historically subsumed in the West. This polarity between Being and thinking, he argues, sums up "the entire Western tradition and conception of Being, and accordingly the fundamental relation to Being that is still dominant today" (156), and he emphasizes that it is "the real target of our attack. It can be overcome only *originally,* that is, in such a way that its inceptive truth is shown its own limits and thereby founded anew" (89). As he makes abundantly clear, what is under attack here is one specific consequence of the productionist model for metaphysics: the Western reduction of thinking to representation and of *logos* to logic and *ratio* (calculation and reason on a mathematical model), a development whose clearest (though not first) origin he finds in the Platonic ideas and whose "inceptive end" he finds in Hegel (144). Also under attack is thus the corresponding dominance of reason and representation as "court of justice" over Being (138), a development that makes not only possible but also necessary the definition of the human being as rational subject. The outcome of this way of conceiving human knowing is, for Heidegger, the contemporary crisis of "global technology" (152);[10] in order to overcome this, he must return to the pre-Platonic roots of the polarity between Being and thinking in Heraclitus and Parmenides, whose "still poetic" thought of *logos* and of "the belonging-together of apprehension and Being" reveals an essentially different relation, one that comes together in the understanding of the human being that Heidegger finds at the root of Greek poetry and philosophy (110, 126). This more original definition of human Being, determined "on the basis of the essence of Being itself" (110), is in turn "authentically founded" in the poetry that corresponds to the poetic thinking of Heraclitus and Parmenides, that is, in tragedy, and specifically in the tragedy of Sophocles (110).[11] Heidegger's reading of the Sophoclean ode is presented as an explicit attempt to "win back" the truth of this understanding of being human in its vision of the original unity of thinking and Being, and in winning it back to "unfold [it] in a still more originary way" (111), so that it can then become the means for overcoming metaphysics and for responding to the modern crisis in a new historical grounding.

In Heidegger's reading of the ode, the relation between Being and thinking is encapsulated in the key word *deinon* and in the manifold tensions expressed in this word. *Deinon,* a Greek word that connotes "strange" and "terrible," expresses for Heidegger at once the essential character of (1) the totality of beings that confronts the human being, challenging and enveloping and sustaining him, (2) the Being of this totality, and (3) the human being's essential relation both to beings as a whole and to Being; hence it also expresses the characteristically human way of knowing and acting, the definition of human Being itself. In his interpretation of *deinon,* Heidegger foregrounds the meaning of power or force, and in essential connection with this, the use of force or violence in the expression or actualization of power and in the confrontation of powers. It is only in terms of power that we can understand Being, since Being in its difference from beings can never be grasped through any given actuality (whether an actual being or a given totality of beings) but only as the source of potentiality that is prior to and exceeds all actuality. It is, similarly, only in terms of power that we can understand human Being, since human Being in its temporality is given only in and through possibilities or potentialities. For Heidegger, *deinon* expresses a power-manifold, dynamically driven by essential inner tensions and conflicts that characterize the relations between the human being, beings as a whole, and Being. He tries to capture this interplay of power in an extensive wordplay that involves variations on the stem *walt-*, whose root meaning is "force" and whose German compounds include common words for government and authority, for being mighty or powerful or forceful, and for violence and violation. The tension that comes to light in the *deinon* is a complex struggle between governance and violence, a struggle that defines the specifically human way of being and the human embeddedness in the difference between Being and beings.

The first sense of the *deinon*, and the fundamental force or power here, is the power of beings as a whole (later ascribed also to Being); it is *das Walten*, the "sway" or the sovereign force, the activity of power in its most naked and direct sense. Its essential character is that it is *das Gewaltige, das Überwältigende*, ultimately forceful and overpowering. The *ge-* prefix on *Gewaltige* indicates a gathering of elemental forces, and the *über* indicates not only the relation to the human being, for whom the might of Being is overpowering, but also the "excess" that belongs to Being (in that it "exceeds" any given actual being or totality) and drives its temporal expression. This sense of the *deinon* is summed up for Heidegger in the Greek *dikē*, whose meanings include customary practice, right or proper order, and legal judgment. Heidegger interprets *dikē* as *Fug*, or "fittingness," not in a juridical or moral sense, he emphasizes, but in the sense of the "originary gatheredness." By this he means the structure or articulation of the forces that confront the human being in their might, as well as the direction or orientation that this arrangement of forces gives to the movement of power within the whole, and the way in which this arrangement "compels fitting-in and compliance" (123).[12] Deinon as *dikē* is a dynamic ordering of original forces as the *logos* of nature or *phusis*, where we have moved away from a static systemization of nature in a set of mathematical laws to a dynamic concept of nature as emergent force whose ordering *(logos)* is thus also necessarily a temporal structuring.

Arising out of *deinon* as *dikē* and opposing it is the second sense of the *deinon*, captured in the definition of human Being as *gewalt-tätig*, as at once using or actualizing the collected force of beings as a whole (and of Being) and as doing violence in this use or actualization. This violent actualizing of force, the essential activity of human Being, is *technē*, here understood as it is applied to high art, as a knowing that "[puts] Being to work [*er-wirkt*] in a being," or "brings Being to stand and to manifestation in the work as a being" (122). *Technē* in this sense is not about the production of particular beings but about "opening up" Being itself in works that establish a particular ordering of and perspective on beings as a whole. This makes it possible to understand and relate to beings "as" a particular being and in a particular way (122), and so opens up and establishes a particular definite structure of human possibilities. Being can only be revealed in the human relation to particular beings, to the extent that, in using them, exploiting them, forming them, the human being looks beyond the particular being to a set of particular relational possibilities that are offered by the actual being and that transcend its actuality. In the act of damming the river, the river is at once made into a source of electric power and revealed as having always harbored this; this act changes the human understanding of the river and ways of relating to it and to nature in general. In seeing and actualizing new possibilities of relating to beings, the human being actualizes and manifests different potential articulations of the totality of beings and so "works out" the manifestation of Being in history. In the language of "The Origin of the Work of Art," which was written immediately after *Introduction to Metaphysics* and develops its conception of *technē,* the work reveals Being in setting up a "world."[13] This world rests on and is in tension with the powers of "earth," with the *deinon* in the sense of *dikē,* which on one hand (as *das Zubewältigende* [119]) must be mastered, brought under human ordinance and governance, if the human being is to have a "home," and on the other (as *das Überwältigende* [119]) exceeds and resists all attempts to master it in a definite and stable form.

Heidegger's interpretation of the ode is broken into three phases, which, in a circling movement, build to and gradually unfold the full and many-sided violence of human knowing as *technē* in a characterization of the human being as *das Unheimlichste,* the most unsettling,[14] who is denied any essential home, any ultimate reliance on a constant and familiar order of things, because *technē* itself requires constant and violent unsettlement and reworking. At the same time, the movement of interpretation traces a movement from an everyday or inauthentic homelessness, which is an entanglement in *technē* in a derivative sense and a loss of essential relationship to Being, to an authentic homelessness, which is a knowing embrace of the dynamism and temporality of Being and of the role of *technē* as creative knowing in the face of this temporality, or, in other words, an embrace of *technē* as historical knowing and as the working out of Being in and as history. The first phase of the interpretation sketches the violent actualization of force that defines human Being in relation to the overpowering might of beings as a whole. It also indicates the "extent" and "destiny" (117) of this essential human activity by extending the interpretation of the *deinon* into the two paradoxical pairings *pantoporos-aporos* ("all-resourceful"— "without a way") and *hupsipolis-apolis* ("high-citied"— "citeless"), which point to the two possible ways in which human Being, in its characteristic violence, is unsettling and homeless. The second phase is the central one here, since it

168

unfolds these pairings into their inherent movement, and in doing so opens out the full meaning of each aspect. The third phase is meant, by its own violent interpretative disclosure, to accomplish the renewed grounding of a definition of being human that regains the connection to Being, and so to achieve the movement from an inauthentic *technē* to an authentic one on a historical scale.

The interpretation moves first of all from *technē* as the violent conquest and appropriation of a place for human habitation to *technē* as the disclosure and mastery of inherent human potentiality as the ground for the disclosure and mastery of a world. The ode begins with the violent incursions into sea and earth, which Heidegger describes in terms of the human activity of forcibly making a place by heading out into the "placeless" sea and by breaking into and controlling the seasonal cycles of the earth's growth, and in terms of forcibly domesticating this place by subjugating living things and fitting them into the human order. This concerns *technē* in its most immediate and direct sense, as the know-how that governs the basic mastery of nature through the power of making. The force that *technē* confronts and actualizes is identified at this point as belonging to beings as a whole; *technē* in this sense concerns itself with beings and their totality and does not yet fully reveal the Being of this totality. The key movement comes in the second strophe, which Heidegger has broken into two in order to emphasize the turning that he finds here. The first half of the strophe moves us, as Heidegger indicates, from violent mastery of the forces that envelop the human being to violent mastery of the forces of understanding ("language, understanding, mood, passion, and building" [119]), the forces that pervade and define the human being and so lead us to a more essential understanding of *technē*. Heidegger stresses that the human being is not, or does not possess, a separate power that she brings to bear against the collective force of beings as a whole but actualizes and comes to master forces that belong to beings as a whole and to the Being of beings. It is the relation to Being and to beings that defines human Being, rather than existence as some separate faculty, and it is a sign of the difficulty of fully understanding and mastering the characteristically human way of being that the human being misinterprets herself as the possessor and inventor of language and understanding, building and poetry. Correspondingly, the power of *technē* that is involved in the mastery of nature in the first sense belongs to the emergence of Being, and is essentially a power of understanding, of disclosing of nature and Being through human Being in "disciplining" and "disposing" of the forces that belong to beings themselves (120). Heidegger's choice of words emphasizes that human understanding and engagement with the disclosure or truth of beings involves forcibly imposing a structure or order on the forces that confront the human being and bringing them under his governance in a way that makes them at once accessible and serviceable to human ends: the violence of *technē* as disclosure is a "*Bändigen*" and a "*Fügen*," bringing under control by binding together in a particular articulation or structure; at the same time, it is a "*Bahnen*," forcibly laying out paths, making habitable by making accessible and familiar (120–121). Human knowing as *technē* imposes an interpretive structure on nature that is necessarily at the same time a "construction" and "co-creation" of a humanly habitable world. Disclosure, rather than mastery or creation, is primary, but this disclosure is itself possible only as forcible mastery and co-creation.

This inherent tension between disclosure and creation, necessary to the actualization of Being in works, means that the activity of making a human habitation, whether it succeeds or fails, is pervaded by respective possibilities of "disaster," of loss of self or loss of home in the very attempt to master and win self and home. At this point in his interpretation, Heidegger raises the "unsettling" character of human activity in its first, inauthentic sense. The characteristic human activity of forcible world-creation and disclosure in *technē* carries with it essentially the possibility of becoming lost in the very success of this activity, such that in making beings accessible and familiar and serviceable, this ordering of the world comes to seem ultimate, and it and beings within it become too familiar and unquestionable. As a result, the human being loses access to the Being that this world discloses and loses access to the very forces that pervade and envelop and sustain him, mistaking these forces for his own possession or creation. The fundamental activity of human Being, *technē* as violent disclosure in world-creation, is no longer possible, and the human being is lost in the inessential, without orientation. The turning point in the strophe for Heidegger is the mention of death as the sole thing that the human being cannot master by *technē;* Heidegger translates the strophe in a way that highlights this differently from the Greek and emphasizes death as that which shatters all mastery and ultimacy.[15] In doing so, death reconnects human Being to the essential forces of Being and so to the essential human activity of violent disclosive creation, though now in a new sense, in a sense that is mindful of the excessive power of Being (no longer just of beings). The mention of death makes it possible for the unsettling character of *technē* to be grounded and to come into its own proper essence and limits.

It now becomes possible for Heidegger to bring out the authentic homelessness and unsettling character of human Being. In this sense, the human being is homeless because he is, first of all, the creator of order and governance for human beings, and as such unable to be bound by his own created order. In the first phase, Heidegger tells us that such creators "rising high in the site of history, . . . also become *apolis,* without city and site, lone-some, unsettling, with no way out amidst beings as a whole, and at the same time without ordinance and limit, without structure and fittingness, because they *as* creators must first ground all this in each case" (117). In the second phase, he expands this idea to emphasize the relation of the creators to the creative-disclosive process and so to time and history in this creation. Precisely to the extent to which the human being is authentically and appropriately engaged in *technē* as violent creative disclosure, he is also homeless and unsettling, because in holding to Being (beyond all particular beings), he despises all "seeming fulfillment," all ultimacy, and affirms the "shattering of the wrought work" as necessary to the process (125). Being is held open by a continual questioning that actualizes definite potentialities of, or responses to, Being in the continual re-creation and restructuring of the human historical world. Human activity as *technē,* then, is caught in a paradoxical necessity. On one hand, it must order and stabilize the forces of nature and of human life itself into a world, creating the possibility and standards of justice and governance on a human level. On the other, it must respond to a higher ordinance that compels the continual destruction and reforming of such orders. Tragically caught in this paradox and defined by it, the human being is sacrificed to the temporal disclosure of Being in history; human Being is the "site of openness" (124), the "in-cident [*Zwischen-fall*] in which the forces of the released excessive power of Being arise and go to work as history" (125, translation modified), and "the breach into which the excessive power of Being breaks in its appearing, so that this breach itself shatters against Being" (124, translation modified).

It is in this conception of *technē* as the working out of Being in history that Heidegger means to find a new phronetically grounded model for human knowing that can overcome the modern inauthentic lostness in a totalizing technological mastery by replacing it with full human self-realization and self-appropriation. This interpretation does violence to the Greek understanding of the human being in that it brings to the fore for the first time the temporality of Being and the historical nature of human knowing and acting, which the Greeks, despite a "deep intimation" of the nature of human Being, were never able to fully bring to light (125, 90). But though Heidegger here emphasizes the human dependence on Being and the forces of beings as a whole and the necessity of responsiveness to these forces, the concept of history as the temporal expression of Being in works that are the violent co-creations of human beings leaves the line between responsiveness and willful self-assertion dangerously thin, and it also leaves unclear the extent to which this responsiveness to

Being could ever resemble anything like responsible acceptance of limitation. The disclosure of Being is at the same time a decision that engages human will in an ultimate act of self-making, whereas the responsiveness to Being is in fact a struggle against Being in the self-consciously tragic attempt to wrest form from formlessness, measure from measurelessness, and stability from flux. The disclosure of Being remains decisively in human hands, and the distinction between appropriate and inappropriate violence rests entirely on the degree to which the historical character of setting into work is appropriated. As result, the sole measure of essentiality in a given work is the depth and success of its engagement with the past and its discovery of new possibilities in the historical tradition. In addition, the authenticity of the creators is visibly marked only by their willingness to sacrifice themselves to the destructive forces of history in refusing all rest and ultimacy. In an explicit echo of Nietzsche's *Zarathustra,* Heidegger remarks that for the authentic creator, "disaster [*der Untergang*] is the deepest and broadest Yes" to the dynamism of Being (125).[16] At the same time, only authentic creators can distinguish between appropriate and inappropriate violence, and though their violence is primarily a restructuring of the human understanding of the world, human community is itself one of its works, so that political violence is left to be legitimated or not according to the judgment of the founders and the radicalness of its historical founding.

FROM *TECHNĒ* TO *DICHTEN:* REREADING SOPHOCLES AND HÖLDERLIN

There are some indications that Heidegger himself may have seen fundamental problems in this formulation of human knowing as history as early as the fall of 1936, and in the years 1936–1942 was engaged in a radical reworking of various aspects of the relation of human knowing to *technē* and to history. Jacques Taminiaux has argued that the lecture "The Origin of the Work of Art," originally given in 1935 and revised for a second lecture in 1936 and subsequent publication, shows a process of revision that moves toward downplaying the role of historical peoples and the role of decision in human co-creation of the work and hints at a move away from the violence of knowing.[17] The direction of these revisions is telling, although the final version of lecture remains entirely in agreement with the conception of *technē* and of setting-into-work developed in *IM*. Heidegger's 1956 addendum to the final version highlights this *technē*-based understanding of human knowing as an ongoing ground for dissatisfaction with his own formulations: he comments that "in the heading 'the setting-into-work of truth,' in which it remains undecided but decid*able* who does the setting or in what way it occurs, there is concealed *the relation of Being and the human being,* a relation that is unsuitably conceived even in this version—a distressing difficulty, which has been clear to me since *Being and Time,* and has since been expressed in a variety of versions."[18] The 1934–1936 retrieval of *technē* as setting Being into the work proves incapable of providing a genuinely nonsubjectivist orientation for human action and a nontechnological conception of historical human community, and its failure requires a radically new approach.

By 1942, when Heidegger revisits *Antigone,* he confronts this failure in an interpretation of the ode that stands in stark contrast to the 1935 version and at times reads like explicit self-criticism of both this and his related earlier reading of Hölderlin.[19] The scope of this revision is such that it can only be broadly outlined here; despite a sometimes deceptive similarity of language and a core focus on the human being as *deinotaton,* "most unsettling," almost every key term bears an essentially different meaning. The core of the revision concerns the ontological difference (the difference between Being and beings) itself. Although human beings are still defined by their situatedness in this difference as the site of the historical disclosure of Being, Heidegger has in the meantime reconceived the exclusive centrality of time in this disclosure, such that space can no longer be seen as derived from original temporality but must give way to a concept of place or locality that is co-originary with temporality. This move is central to the shift from Heidegger's early approach to history as the historicity of Dasein to his later approach to history as the destining *(Geschick)* of Being, and it is made possible by his development of the concept of *Ereignis* (appropriation) in 1936–1942.[20] Reflecting back on this move, Heidegger comments that "Since time as well as Being can only be thought from Appropriation as the gifts of Appropriation, the relation of space to Appropriation must also be considered in an analogous way. We can admittedly succeed in this only when we have previously gained insight into the origin of space in the properties peculiar to site and have thought them through adequately. . . . The attempt in *Being and Time,* section 70, to derive human spatiality from temporality is untenable."[21] In defining human Being as the site of the historical disclosure of Being through the working of *technē,* as he does in both *IM* and "The Origin of the Work of Art," Heidegger is still deriving this site solely from human historicality, with the result that place and history are seen as won in the violent attempt to compel Being into disclosedness in the structure of the work, and ultimately authentically won when temporality itself is embraced as the source of historical dwelling and working. When Heidegger returns to *Antigone* in 1942, he embeds the discussion of the ode in an interpretation of Hölderlin that centers around the attempt to "poem" *(dichten)* the original unity of place and temporality (*Ortschaft* and *Wanderschaft*) in a way that simultaneously reconceives poetry and gives a new "law of history."[22] Redefining the place-character of human historical situatedness as co-originary with temporality has serious ramifications for the entire attempt to conceive human knowing as *technē*. If this place is given, then it can no longer be conceived as something that must be or can be violently wrought and won. In addition, because, alongside time, place belongs equally to Being, the purely temporal difference between power and actuality (as "workliness" or *Wirklichkeit*), even given Heidegger's attempts to rethink the concepts of power and the work, cannot adequately grasp the difference between Being and beings. Consequently, the disclosure of Being in history can no longer be conceived as setting Being into the work. The knowing that discloses Being, and so gives proper measure and orientation to human action, must then be essentially different from all *technē*. Heidegger finds this knowing in Hölderlin's "new founding" of the essence of poetry (no longer thought of as a form of "art" or *poiēsis*) and in the way in which this poetry "takes measure" in the mindfulness of Being.[23] This measure is to be found in poetry's appropriate orientation on the "not" and "nothing" that, beyond temporality, indicate the concealed source that "gives" place and time for human dwelling.

The differences in the two interpretations of the ode are immediately striking, especially with respect to the core pairing *deinon-deinotaton,* which expressed the human situatedness in the ontological difference in the *IM* interpretation and was interpreted primarily as violent actualization of force. Here, Heidegger gives only the barest nod in the direction of his previous interpretation when he lays out the range of meanings captured in the *deinon* as "the terrible, the powerful, and the unaccustomed," and again when he concedes that Hölderlin's early translation of *deinon* by *gewaltig* "indeed brings one essential trait of the *deinon* to appear" before rejecting it in favor of the "riper" and "more poetic" *ungeheuer* (GA 53, 85). But far from foregrounding power as the core meaning, the later interpretation is striking for the extent to which all discussion of power and violence has vanished; indeed, the words themselves scarcely appear, and then largely in the context of the reflection on the fall into an inauthentic conception of human Being. Neither Being nor human Being is defined here as power or in terms of the interplay of power. *Technē* and *dikē* have similarly disappeared, at least in the positive characterizations given them in *IM; technē* is consistently referred to metaphysical thinking and to the loss of self in the forgetfulness of Being, whereas *dikē* is mentioned only once, when Heidegger stresses that Antigone's fate is not ascribable to *dikē* but comes from "beyond" *dikē* (GA 53, 147). The discussion of setting into work has been replaced by a series of remarks aimed at critiquing the reduction of reality to *Wirklichkeit* (continuing a theme of the previous semester's course on "*Andenken*"). In addition, the interpretation of the final antistrophe is critically different, both in its assessment of the antithetical pairing *hupsipolis-apolis* and the relation to politics that it implies, and in its assessment of the critical closing words of the chorus, which here occupies the largest part of the interpretation and requires that Heidegger go beyond the choral ode to take up Antigone in her difference from Creon.

In the new interpretation of the juxtaposition *deinon-deinotaton,* the previously defining violent confrontation between beings and human Being has dropped away. The juxtaposition is here read purely comparatively and indicates that human Being differs from the Being of beings in the way in which, for human Being, the "un" belongs essentially to Being. Not the interplay of power and actuality but the interplay of concealment and unconcealment—and, relatedly, of "*Wesen*" and "*Unwesen,*" of essential presencing and of confusion, disorder, and loss of essentiality—comes to define the inherent tension and movement that belong to the human being as the essentially most unsettling being, who is "un-at-home" amidst what is "homely." Heidegger sets up this interpretation of the ode by citing the call to the rising sun in the opening words of the choral entrance song, in which "the rising light gives space to the unconcealed and is at the same time a recognition of the darkness, of twilight and of shadows. All this is not in simple opposition to the bright and transparent, but rather that which is penetrated by counterpresencing [*Gegenwesen*]" (GA 53, 64). This interplay of light and dark, of disclosure and concealment, can define the human being in two essentially different ways, revealed in the figures of Creon and Antigone. It is also captured for Heidegger in the structure of the poetry itself, which speaks directly only about the inauthentic expression of this tension embodied in Creon while it expresses the authentic possibility that belongs to Antigone only in what it keeps silent and does not say, but whose silent force pervades the entire ode and gives it its dramatic impact and meaning. The ode thus gives expression to a human relation to Being that is rooted in the interpretation of Being captured for Heidegger in the word *pelein,* a pre-Socratic word for "to be" that Heidegger relates to the neighbor *(pelas),* whose dwelling near is marked by a constant coming and going, and to the sea *(pelagos),* that "does not flow away, but remains and rests in its waves"; *pelein* indicates "the concealed presence of stillness and rest in the unconcealed constant presencing and absencing, and that means, in the appearing of change. . . . [It] does not mean the empty presence of what merely exists, but remaining, which is precisely what it is in journeying and flowing" (GA 53, 88). Being has its defining and orienting force precisely in what is present only as absence and concealment. The human ways of being unsettling, then, will be determined according to the relation to this absence, according to whether one mistakes it for mere negativity and thus forgets Being and loses the historical situatedness and orientation that it grants or whether one maintains a relation to this absence and takes it up as essentially defining.

This interpretive reorientation requires a corresponding shift in the interpretation of the movement of the ode and in the way it locates the difference between authenticity and inauthenticity. Heidegger begins with an assessment of inauthentic homelessness that on the surface echoes that developed in *IM:* the fundamental danger for human Being, that which bars access to reflection on Being and so to proper limitation and measure in human activity, is the very success of technical versatility as it comes to light in the oppositional characterization *pantoporos-aporos.* In this technical versatility, however, what is now stressed is that the human being's search for a "home" does not aim at stable and familiar access to things and mastery of a world but at essential self-understanding. The human being who is essentially un-at-home in an inauthentic sense mistakes the place of this understanding, "seeks herself but does not find herself, because she seeks herself by way of a distancing and alienation from herself" (GA 53, 103). This takes the form of the "violent passage through the inhabitual" (GA 53, 89), in which human beings become lost in the total management of beings and are driven out of Being, "however much beings as real [*Wirkliches*] in their operation [*Wirksamkeit*] may be influential [*einwirkend*] and 'effective' [*wirkungsvoll*]" (GA 53, 93). Echoing the Hölderlin verse "Poetically man dwells," Heidegger comments that the human being thereby seeks himself in seeking to "amount to something" and to earn a "means" ["*Vermögen*," *poros*], but precisely in this focus on earning and effecting, "comes to Nothing" *(kommt zum Nichts)* (GA 53, 92–93). Whereas Heidegger earlier used the mention of death in "coming to Nothing" to provide a transition to the knowledge of temporality and so to authenticity, here he focuses on the human relation to the concept of the nothing *(das Nichts)* as the decisive factor. In getting lost in the technical mastery of beings, human activity and the human way of Being are essentially defined and driven by the "un" in "unsettling" and "un-at-home"; "deprivation," Heidegger tells us, "is the way in which the homely possesses the unhomely one" (GA 53, 92), constantly driving human beings from one activity and accomplishment to the next, without offering any possibility of rest or meaning. They are possessed and governed by the "not" without being able to orient themselves to this source of their being, so that even the indication given by death is not necessarily saving; rather, "the 'nothing' to which they come is that which, turning counter to Being, immediately excludes human beings from Being as such [*schlechthin*]" (GA 53, 93). Thus "the human being in his own essence is a *katastrophē*—a reversal that turns him away from his own essence" (GA 53, 94). Heidegger concludes his discussion of these lines with a warning that our metaphysical understanding of negativity and our tendency to devalue every negative into "that which ought not to be" (GA 53, 95) prevents us from properly grasping the meaning of the *deinon* expressed in the opposition *pantoporos-aporos*. This is meant not only to warn us not to read "catastrophe" as an ethical judgment but also, and more important, to indicate that it is the very reduction of the "not" and inability to think it that underlies the errancy of technical versatility.

When Heidegger moves to the next paradoxical pairing, *hupsipolis-apolis,* it is no longer to show the positive appropriation of self in the tragically contradictory work of world-creation and disclosure; instead, he now reads this as revealing the essential ground of the catastrophic turn away from essentiality expressed in the previous verse. This ground is the way in which human beings are situated in and by a grounding relation to the "not." The explication of the paradoxical character of the human relation to the *polis,* by sketching the possibilities and parameters of this relation, will thus reveal the full range of human possibility, from the most complete fall into delusion to the turn into an appropriate self-understanding and historical belonging, from a fundamentally different perspective. Gone is the reference to violent creators and violent acts of historical founding that defined human historical situatedness in the earlier interpretation. In its place, Heidegger stresses the way in which the *polis* as the space of history is given or self-emerging, and as given, itself gives place and ordering and orientation to human beings, is "destining." It is "the open site of dispensation [*Schickung*] out of which all relations of human beings to beings, and that always first of all means the relations of beings as such to human beings, determine themselves" (GA 53, 102). The *polis* is neither the structure of human community nor a particular interpretive articulation of beings in a world that grounds such community but is the original disclosure of Being itself in its difference from beings: "the character of the human abode [amidst beings] has its ground in that Being has generally opened itself to human Being and is this open, as which open it takes human Being into itself and so determines it to be in a site" (GA 53, 113). What is distinctive about human dwelling is that human beings are placed or situated negatively, located in an "open" space, in a dis-closure, which on one hand binds them uniquely to errancy, to the loss of order and home in confusing and mistaking beings, and on the other does offer a measure and a genuine "rest" and "home," but only as absent and in the human relation to what is absent. Thus the *polis* is the "pole," the "vortex," the invisible center of gravity that draws all things about it and determines their movement and relations; it is the essence of the "question-worthy," which "must be acknowledged and guarded in this worth" (GA 53, 100).

Being in this sense no longer must or can be kept open as the site of history by the process of reformation and the constant interchange of answers in works. Instead, it already opens itself, prior to all works and formation, in the very absence and inaccessibility of ground, stability, and transparency in the inconstant interchange of appearance and illusion that comes to light in the processes of nature and the shifting forms of the human world. This absence provides a structuring and orienting force in human life to the extent that it calls human beings into an attitude of essential questioning. With the displacement of human situatedness in the difference between Being and beings, the questioning that marks the human relation to the *polis* as the site of the history of Being is also displaced, so that though the emphasis on questioning is not new, this questioning can no longer be taken in the previous confrontational sense to be a "challenging forth." Questioning now must be understood as a self-opening or a stance of receptivity that relates to beings by looking beyond them, in an attitude of wonder or reverential expectation, to their source and ground in concealment and mystery. Force, and specifically the attempt to compel Being to disclosure in works, now becomes precisely what closes off the relation to Being and "turns counter" to the given place for historical dwelling (GA 53, 202). In a striking revision of his earlier reading of the Rhine hymn, a reading that laid the groundwork for the interpretation of creative founding in *IM*, Heidegger now marks his own earlier understanding as a "catastrophic" errancy. The Rhine abandons the vicinity of the source, abandons appropriate situatedness, and, like Oedipus with his "eye too many,"[24] "means to plunge into the heart of the native mother" with force (GA 53, 201); the works of violent founding are driven by an excessive desire to know and amount to a violation of the concealment of Being. They are a *Vermessenheit*, a presumptuous mistaking of the standard or measure, in the attempt to "force a stead" amidst beings, a stance that "is only what it is from out of a forgetfulness of the hearth, that is, of Being" (GA 53, 202).

Given that the *polis* as the site of historical dwelling is the disclosure of Being, reconceiving the nature of this disclosure means simultaneously reconceiving the nature of human knowing. The shift in the way Heidegger understands human knowing in general and the particular knowing that holds open and preserves the relation to Being comes to light in his reconsideration of the final words of the chorus, which refuse the unsettling human being a place at the hearth and a belonging to the home. Whereas Heidegger previously dismissed this judgment of the chorus as revealing their inauthentic understanding and everydayness, he now disparages his own earlier interpretation and emphasizes that the chorus can only speak these words out of the highest and most essential knowledge, the knowledge of the "hearth," or the knowledge of Being itself and of the way in which human beings are granted a site and a home by the "not" in belonging to Being (GA 53, 121). The knowledge of the chorus is a *phronein,* a "sensing and reflecting which comes from the *phrēn,* that is, out of the 'heart,' out of the innermost center of human Being itself" (GA 53, 134). This knowledge is "of another essence" from the knowledge of the one who, forgetting or mistaking the difference between Being and beings, wants to secure the home by creating orders and statutes and whose form of knowledge is "madness" or "delusion" (GA 53, 132). It is "poetic," but though this echoes his earlier stress on poetry as the highest art form and the ultimate way of grounding truth in works, in the working of the word, here, in contrast to his earlier interpretations, he says that poetry is a form of knowing that is fundamentally different from all art and *technē* and that has nothing to do with works and working. It is this displacement from inauthentic knowing as *technē* into poetry as authentic knowing that guides the chorus's expulsion of the violent founder from the home or hearth. They understand that

> in their working and in their works, human beings are capable of an abundance. It is almost impossible to survey what they accomplish, whereby they establish themselves on this earth, in that they use it, wear it out, and work it, in that they protect and secure it and further their "art," that is, in Greek, *technē.* "Yet" all this does not reach into the essential ground of their dwelling on this earth. . . . This dwelling, authentic being at-home, is "poetic." *The center and ground of dwelling, that is, the "hearth of the house," is nothing which could be grasped and determined within the real [Wirkliche] by making and producing.* (GA 53, 171, emphasis added)

Hölderlin is now understood to be the poet who founds a new "destiny" and an "other beginning" of history precisely because he founds a new understanding of poetry that removes the knowing and saying of poetry from the relation to art and works and so achieves the step out of metaphysics.[25] Poetry and poetic thinking are not some deeper level of *technē;* the displacement to a more original understanding is only achieved in a fundamentally different kind of knowing, a knowing that in turn achieves a profound reorientation of human self-understanding and relation to beings. Poetry and poetic thinking "require of us a conversion of the way of thinking and experiencing that concerns the whole of Being" (GA 53, 205). Specifically, poetry requires of us that we "perceive . . . that something can be without effecting [*wirken*] and being a thing worked, that something other is with [*mit-ist*], without being worked by another and exhausting Being in such being worked . . . that the authentic Being consists precisely in this no-longer-working, in whose truth our being-with all beings rests and from which it arises" (GA 52, 100–101). *Technē*, although it does disclose Being in beings, approaches Being in the effort to force what is hidden into the light. In doing so, it turns counter to Being, cannot achieve a knowing that appropriately orients itself on Being as it gives itself in its concealment, and so can offer no phronetic measure to human life. Poetry, on the other hand, addresses itself to this very concealment, takes it up in a mode of saying that preserves it in its mystery, and orients human beings to this mystery as grounding source and as what is to come. In this, poetry comes to be understood not on the model of art but on the model of prophesy. Unlike *technē*, poetry is conceived as a receptive knowing that is fundamentally non-violent, as Heidegger once again stresses with his quotation of Hölderlin's "The Journey" at the close of the lecture course: "To a dream it turns, if one would / Ambush it and it punishes him, who / Would equal it with force. / Often it surprises him, / Who scarcely even thought it" (GA 53, 206).

With the move to poetic thinking, Heidegger's characterization of the "destiny" of the West thus turns decisively away from the violence of creative founding in the direction of the later *Gelassenheit,* the "releasement" toward beings that belongs to meditative thinking and "lets beings be."[26] Although the implications of this move cannot be fully drawn out within the limits of the present discussion, a brief sketch may help ward off a few common misunderstandings. In his reinterpretation of the poetic, Heidegger means to overcome metaphysics, and specifically Hegel and Nietzsche, by thinking the relation between Being and the nothing in a way that does not reduce the nothing to some positivity. His reading of Taoism is likely to have been significant here, and the way in which poetic thinking and poetic dwelling take measure from the "nothing" has more in common with Asian philosophy and its concepts of emptiness and nonaction than with the practical philosophy of the West.[27] As is the case in Taoist thought, poetic thinking displaces political action entirely from the realm of authentic knowing and authentic praxis, and this displacement itself is understood as transformative of the practical and political realm; it would be a mistake to read this as mere resignation or fatalism, as has often been done, and to argue that the rejection of normative standards in favor of a negative measure amounts to nihilism.[28] Since political action must be concerned with works, with measurable effects and accomplishments, it remains within the parameters of a technological conception of reality; any attempt to counter the violence and totalizing tendencies of modern politics from within politics itself is correspondingly shaped and driven by its own counterviolence and its own forms of totalization. The only effective response to "global technology" would be found, then, in a thinking and action that removes itself resolutely from all attempts to control.

Poetic thinking achieves this as "remembrance" *(Andenken),* as a thoughtful engagement with the roots of one's own tradition and with what is different in that tradition, in order to reveal what properly belongs to one's historical situation and to open up new possibilities of response to that situation.[29] Difference is specifically not appropriated or overcome but preserved in "guest-friendship" (GA 53, 171–181); poetic thinking is thus meant to lay the ground for a nonappropriative dialogue with otherness, by means of which it first becomes possible to come into one's own historical place. In this, poetry is a historical transition. At the same time, it is a transition in another sense: poetry can only situate historically, it can only be measure-taking, to the extent that in this opening of this historical place, it recovers the concealed ground and inherent negativity that appears in the past relation to divinity as wonder and as destiny and holds this ground open. Poetry awakens an attitude of reverential expectation and so is a kind of prophesy; it announces a destiny (GA 52, 101) and mediates between human beings and "gods" (GA 52, 69). It is crucial to understand, however, that these "gods" are not and cannot be existing divinities. They are accessible only in their withdrawal, and it is precisely in this withdrawal and concealment that they have power for human life; consequently, the "advent" of the gods cannot mark an actual historical event. The transition that poetic thinking marks is not a transition between two actualities but is the original disclosure of Being and of human Being in their relation, which first allows them to "be" (GA 52, 98). To subordinate this thinking to a future actuality would "destroy the coming in its coming and draw the possible into a presumptuous and accidental reality" (GA 52, 127).[30] Poetic thinking is thus not the path to an "other beginning" of history but is itself that other beginning, that destiny, as a way of relating to beings that is rooted in mystery and in a questioning that refuses all closure. This destiny, Heidegger emphasizes, "does nothing and makes nothing of beings, but it ordains [*fügt*] in that it lets beings be" (GA 52, 101). Poetic thinking as remembrance aims to reclaim divinity in absence by reawakening the sense in which all human Being and acting is shaped by and bound to something essentially ungraspable and beyond it and to orient human life on the "un" in opening up what is unfamiliar and unusual at the core of all everyday familiarity.

What Heidegger is calling for here is a radical departure from politics as we have understood it up to now, that is, as the human agent's personal or collective attempt to systematically order and control both physical and human nature. Heidegger offers no principles of justice, no treatise on the proper organization of institutions, no way to guarantee a better future—in short, no systematic guidelines for action whatsoever. The utter indeterminacy of what Heidegger is calling for leads many to accuse him of a reckless and stubborn quietism in the face of pressing issues facing humankind. But it is precisely Heidegger's point that the conception of politics (and of thinking itself) as the violent and willful imposition of a "program" on Being is what we need to let go of. He calls us to consider that the factors that drive our modern politics, in all its plurality, in the direction of the consolidation of power and control and (sometimes subtly but often violently) in the direction of conformity and homogenization cannot in turn be effectively overcome by exerting a counter force, by attempting to control and secure the human drive to control, by demanding conformity to another universal norm. *Gelassenheit,* on the other hand, means, in part, letting politics as the *polos* come to us. Heidegger argues that the "being-with" and interaction that would make up a more vital and essential human community require that we risk "exposure" to the other (a word he ties to "care") and suggests that it is a mistake to think that we can properly engage and listen to others so long as we are simultaneously protecting and advancing our own separate spheres and identities. The openness that would appropriately situate human Being is only possible in the move away from all attempts to systematize and control, from all attempts to fix the historical appearance of Being in some manageable form. Heidegger is calling for a new kind of *respons*-ibility, one that has its measure and only safeguard in the willingness to risk openness and let be. This of course entails a very real political risk, yet it remains compelling that the best way to confront large-scale violence is to reshape our personal and political action in such a way that it is fundamentally nonviolent. Poetic thinking points to just such a move.[31]

Part III

POLITICS AND ETHICS

Chapter 10

THE ONTOLOGICAL DECLINE OF THE WEST

MICHAEL E. ZIMMERMAN

The inception is what is most uncanny and mightiest. What follows is not a development but flattening down as mere widening
out . . . it makes the inception innocuous and exaggerates it into a
perversion of what is great.

—*Introduction to Metaphysics*

In the following chapter I describe, contextually situate, and critically appraise Heidegger's conception of history in *Introduction to Metaphysics*. In
section 1, I show that Heidegger rejected efforts to read Western history either
in terms of the metaphor of progress or in terms of the collective events of
peoples and nations. Instead, he tells a saga of the West's eruption through the
ancient Greek encounter with Being and of the West's subsequent decline into
technological nihilism, characterized by the darkening of the earth and the
flight of the gods. This decline resulted from the gradual self-concealment of
Being, a process that began with Plato and Aristotle and that was hastened by
the translation of crucial Greek philosophical terms into Latin, such as the
Latin *natura* for *physis*. Because language lets things be, this decay of language
enables things to reveal themselves only one-dimensionally, not in their depth,
complexity, and rank. Western history has become increasingly governed by
the "metaphysics of presence," whose combination of anthropocentrism, foundationalism, and representational concepts of truth led to the contemporary
view that in order for something "to be" it must be present as raw material for
enhancing the power of the technological system.

In section 2, I argue that in some—but by no means all—respects Heidegger's account of the West's history accorded with the belief of "cultural

185

pessimists" such as Oswald Spengler, author of *The Decline of the West* (1918). In section 3, I offer some critical remarks about Heidegger's view of Western history. These remarks take into account his links with National Socialism.[1] At the outset, I wish to emphasize that despite my critical remarks, I continue to hold important aspects of Heidegger's ontology in great esteem.

1. *INTRODUCTION TO METAPHYSICS'* ACCOUNT OF THE RISE AND FALL OF THE WEST

The immediate context for *EM* was the National Socialist movement, with regard to which Heidegger tried to establish a leading position for his own philosophy.[2] To Nazi ideologues who asserted that philosophy "did not contribute to preparing the revolution," Heidegger replied that genuine philosophy is "a thoughtful opening of the avenues and vistas of a knowing that establishes measure and rank, a knowing in which and from which a people conceives its Dasein in the historical-spiritual world and brings it to fulfillment" (8). Regarding the situation in 1935, Heidegger wrote: "The spiritual decline of the earth has progressed so far that peoples are in danger of losing their last spiritual strength, the strength that makes it possible even to see the decline [*Verfall*] and to appraise it as such" (29). Caught in the pincers between Russia and America, both of which are governed by "the same hopeless frenzy of unchained technology and of the rootless organization of the average man" (28), German (and European) Dasein could be saved from technological nihilism only by a world-founding renewal of Dasein's relation to Being.[3] That renewal would be carried out by a few thoughtful and lonely creators—poets, statesmen, and philosophers—who were anointed for this task by Being itself.

Such individuals must tread the insecure path of repeating and retrieving *(wieder-holen)* "the inception of our historical-spiritual Dasein, in order to transform it into the other inception" (29). This retrieval begins with posing a question—"How does it stand with Being?"—that precedes the fundamental question of metaphysics, "Why is there something rather than nothing?" Being has been so emptied of meaning that the prior question, "How does it stand with Being?," seems pointless to scientists, engineers, and politicians. For Heidegger, however, posing the prior question is essential to the ontological happening *(Geschehen)* of history *(Geschichte)*, and thus central to the "spiritual fate of the West" (28). "In this questioning," we are told, "our Dasein is summoned to its history in the full sense of the word, and is called to make a decision in it" (34).

For Heidegger, human Dasein is endowed with a unique relation to the Being of beings. Dasein constitutes the clearing or the opening—temporal, historical, linguistic—in which beings can manifest themselves *as* beings. For something "to be," then, means for it to reveal itself or to show up within the clearing opened up through Dasein. Animals can encounter beings, but only Dasein can explicitly note that things *are* and that Dasein itself *exists*. Different historical epochs involve determinate ways in which beings manifest themselves, that is, different ways in which people understand what things *are*. The modern epoch lacks depth because beings have been so emptied out ontologically that they can manifest themselves only one-dimensionally, as raw material for the technological system. Such a condition, in Heidegger's view, is demonic and nihilistic.[4] Nihilism amounts to positivism, "where one clings to current beings and believes it is enough to take beings, as before, just as the beings that they are" (155). Oblivious to Being, positivists assume that beings are everything, whereas Being itself is empty, "nothing," *nihil.*

Describing Europe's descent into nihilism, Heidegger resorts to a striking metaphor: "All things sank to the same level, to a surface resembling a blind mirror that no longer mirrors, that casts nothing back" (35). Things have been leveled to a flat plane, because Being has withdrawn itself from them and from human Dasein. Deprived of its relation to Being, Dasein can no longer act as the ontological-linguistic mirror through and in which things can manifest themselves and thus "be."[5] The empirical symptoms of decline, including cultural decay and social disorientation, are to be distinguished from the *source* of decline *(Verfall)*, namely, the self-withdrawal of Being, which is discernible in the process by which key metaphysical terms were translated from Greek to Latin (47).[6] The term *Verfall* is derived from *verfallen*, "to fall," a term that plays a central role in *Sein und Zeit's* concept of inauthenticity.[7] To be inauthentic means not to own oneself, that is, not to be the mortal openness that one always already is. *Being and Time* maintains that such inauthenticity involves a lack of individual resoluteness, but *EM* suggests that the decline of the West stems not only from a lack of resoluteness on the part of Dasein but also from the impersonal withdrawal of Being from language, earth, world, and Dasein. Because *EM* retains some voluntaristic vocabulary, it is often said to stand midway between Heidegger's "early" and "later" phases. In his chapter in this collection, however, Thomas J. Sheehan contests the claim that Heidegger's thought underwent a "turn" *(Kehre)* in any such chronological sense.

In Heidegger's opinion, a linguistic and spiritual revolution is needed to renew German history and to save the *Volk* from modern decadence (41). Such a revolution is not to be confused with political reaction, in which people flee to the past in order to defend themselves from the present situation (93). Authentic revolution involves *polemos,* the dangerous struggle by which creators bring Being to a stand in works that open up a world in which beings can come to be (47). "*This becoming-a-world is authentic history*" (48, emphasis added). The meaning of history can be understood neither in terms of Divine Providence nor in terms of progressive human self-actualization, for such views presuppose an illusory metaphysical foundation. Instead, history takes on significance in the rare and insecure moments in which human Dasein experiences Being "from the bottom up and in the full breadth of its possible essence" (155). Today, this experience would constitute a new beginning for the metaphysically exhausted West, a beginning that could be as great as the one initiated in ancient Greece.

Before attempting to encounter Being anew, however, German Dasein must address the prior question, "How does it stand with Being?" This question can first of all be understood as asking: How are things going for Being? The answer is that things are not going well at all. Indeed, things are virtually disappearing *as* things, insofar as Being has withdrawn from them. A related way of understanding the prior question is this: Is Being standing erect, or is it falling? The answer is that Being has practically toppled over, as evidenced both by the one-dimensionality of beings and by the ontological spinelessness of Dasein. Without Being in our ontological marrow, we have lost the ability to stand erect ontologically; hence, "We are staggering" (154). The modern world-clearing has become so constricted that Dasein moves about like an animal on all fours, totally absorbed by the beings that confront it.

The prior question, "How does it stand with Being?," invites an invidious contrast between ancient Greek and modern Dasein. In ancient Greece, Being stood fully erect, in part because ontologically virile Dasein brought it to a stand in its full magnificence, fury, and overwhelming power. The ontological orgasm resulting from this encounter between Dasein and Being engendered a great historical world in which beings manifested themselves in their articulation, rank, and order. Today, in contrast, Being has become flaccid, leading Dasein itself to become impotent, ontologically and linguistically. In matters of ontology, all movement from the origin involves degeneration and decline. Far from being primitive, protomodern scientists, then, ancient Greek philosophers were inordinately great, having been touched by an ontological radiance that has been reduced to an ember 2,500 years later. Technological control over and scientific knowledge of entities cannot compensate for what has been lost through Being's self-concealment. For Heidegger, the positivists and Nazi ideologues who praise "hard science" as opposed to "soft-headed" metaphysics are ontologically impotent, incapable of getting it up with regard to Being.

Although *EM*'s sexual metaphors sometimes suggest that human Dasein is the active (male) party who brings Being to a stand, Dasein's actions also involve a seemingly feminine, receptive aspect. After all, Dasein's efforts are not self-owned but instead are inspired by *logos,* which itself is an aspect of *physis,* or Being (88–104). Hence, Greek Dasein's creativity was grounded in the willingness of great thinkers and poets to *submit* to ontological violation *(Gewalt)* by Being (124–126). As Heidegger indicated in lectures from 1931 to 1932, ontological eros, the striving after Being *(Seinserstrebnis),* drew Greek philosophers and poets toward their violent lover, Being.[8] Once impregnated by the ontological power to which they were thus attracted, they engendered a new world. In 1935, however, in the gloomy epoch of *Seinsdämmerung,* the twilight of Being, Germans had to experience Being anew, *not* as the ancient Greeks had experienced it.

Faced with overpowering Being, the ancient Greek mood was astonishment. Faced with the utter meaninglessness of the modern industrial wasteland, the modern German moods are horror and boredom.[9] Despite *EM*'s manly rhetoric about the Greeks' bringing Being to a stand, Heidegger insists that modern Germans need courage to submit to and thus to experience their ontological *pain.* Again, such submission may be read as involving a feminine dimension that seems incompatible with *EM*'s masculinist account of the violence and homelessness of the lonely creator. Heidegger believed that Hölderlin's poetry could help transform the moods of horror and boredom into one of "holy affliction, mourning but prepared."[10] The mood of holy affliction would free the German *Volk* from the rigid, control-oriented Apollinianism of modern technology and would thus bring an end to the productionist metaphysics that had reduced modern Dasein to the world-conquering laborer, which Ernst Jünger described in *Der Arbeiter.* Eventually, Heidegger would speak approvingly of the same home and hearth that were spurned by the violent creators, but in 1935, his continuing fascination with the martial discourse of Jünger and Spengler led him to favor the rhetoric of hardness, violence, and courage.[11]

In *EM,* we read that the "concealed history" (70) of the West's decline lies in how the verb *sein* (to be) is gradually restricted according to four historically definitive Others: becoming, seeming, thinking, and value. For the sake of "future historical Dasein," we are told, the philosopher must face "the decision [*Entscheidung*] regarding the concealed powers in these distinctions [*Unterscheidungen*] and [bring] them back to their own truth" (72–73). In order to experience these powers, we must break out of the steel net of grammatical forms (40). Heidegger starts this liberating process by analyzing the grammar of the verb *sein,* the infinitive whose substantive form, *Sein,* is rendered as

"Being" in English. Before reviewing that analysis, which Gregory Fried examines in more detail in this anthology, let us recall that it comes *before EM*'s discussion of the encounter between ancient Greek creators and the overwhelming power of Being. *EM*'s intent is to contrast the merely grammatical account of Being with an *originary* encounter with it. Grammar impoverishes Being by treating *it* like a being, whereas an originary encounter allows Being to stand erect so that beings may manifest themselves in new ways.

According to Heidegger, by defining the infinitive *(modus infinitivus)* as the mode of unboundedness and indeterminacy, the Romans failed to understand Greek reflection on Greek language, and thus contributed to the process of emptying *sein* of meaning. The Greek term for *modus* is *enklisis,* meaning "to incline to the side." Similarly, the Greek word *ptōsis,* translated as *casus* (case) in the sense of the inflection of nouns, originally meant "any kind of inflection of the fundamental form (deviation, declension), not only in substantives but also in verbs" (45). Heidegger describes how a verb "declines":

> The terms *ptōsis* and *enklisis* mean a falling, tipping, or inclining. This implies a dropping-off from an upright, straight stance. But this standing-there, this taking and maintaining a *stand* that stands erected high in itself, is what the Greeks understood as Being. Whatever takes such a stand becomes *constant* in itself and thereby freely and on its own runs up against the necessity of its limit, *peras.* . . . The self-restraining hold that comes from a limit, the having-of-itself wherein the constant holds itself, is the Being of beings; it is what first makes a being be a being as opposed to a nonbeing. For something to take such a stand therefore means for it to attain its limit, to de-limit itself. . . . Limit and end are that whereby beings first begin to *be.* (46)

Far from lacking a limit, Being—that which the infinitive "to be" names—is that which lets beings be by bringing to them limit, order, rank, and structure. The ontological decline of the West is related to the decline (declension, sagging, falling over) of Being into a mere grammatical infinitive, that is, into that which cannot establish limits. The Greeks themselves played a role in this process, since they treated language as one being among others and since they never *questioned* the meaning of Being even though they *experienced* it (45,46). For the Greeks, Being means "1. standing-in-itself as arising and standing forth *(phusis),* 2. but, as such, 'constantly,' that is, enduringly, abiding *(ousia)*" (48). *Physis* appropriates human Dasein, endowing it with the *logos* required to bring *physis* itself to a stand in what presences. "Beings as such now first come into being" (47). Once this momentous struggle *(polemos)* ceased, however, beings became what simply stands around, available to anyone. "That which originally holds sway, *physis,* now degenerates *(fällt . . . herab)* into a prototype for reproduction and copying," that is, into what we call "nature" (48). Now that Being has deserted beings, their only constancy *(Ständigkeit)* derives from their being treated as objects by the human subject (48).

Now returning to his examination of verbal inflection, Heidegger notes that the basic position of the verb is the first-person singular present. Generally, *enklisis* involves the process by which "the word that stands straight inclines to the side," thereby making something manifest in its number, voice, tense, and person (50). The Greek term *enklisis paremphatikos* refers to a deviation that can make manifest, which capacity is in turn grounded in the fact that "a word as such *is* a word to the extent that it lets shine forth *(dēloun)*" (51). The infinitive constitutes an inflection, deviation, *enklisis,* in the following sense: Compared with the basic position of the verb, the infinitive is deficient in the sense that it does not manifest number, person, tense, and so on. Hence, the infinitive is *enklisis a-paremphatikos,* poorly translated as *modus infinitivus* by Roman grammarians. Heidegger notes that *paremphatikos* is related to *paremphainō,* one of whose meanings is defined by Plato as "the medium in which something builds itself up while it is becoming and from which it then stands forth once it has become" (50). Things become within *chōra,* usually translated as "space." Heidegger asks whether *chōra* might be understood as "that which separates itself from every particular, that which withdraws, and in this way admits and 'makes room' precisely for something else" (51). This understanding of *chōra* amounts to Heidegger's own conception of Being as that which conceals itself precisely so that things can become present: *Abwesen* (absencing) makes possible *Anwesen* (presencing). Focusing on Being as constant presence, the Greeks did not inquire into the temporal condition for presencing as such.

In defining the infinitive as *enklisis a-paremphatikos,* the Greeks meant that it deviated from the capacity for other forms to reveal additional aspects of a verb by inclining away from its basic (first-person singular present) position. The Roman translation as *modus infinitivus* emphasizes the abstract quality of the infinitive, while dropping out the notion of manifesting included in the Greek notion of *enklisis.* Moreover, grammarians regard the infinitival form as perhaps the latest in the chronological development of a language. As a result, the infinitive "to be" has come to be regarded as an almost complete abstraction and thus as an empty vapor.

Approaching in a very different way the status of the Greek infinitive for "to be," *einai,* Heidegger argues that standardized grammar derives "from the speech of dialects that originally stand rooted in soil and history" (52). Even though in Greek and Latin the *modi finiti* had become fixed, the infinitives *(enklisis aparemphatikos)* tended to retain the peculiarities of their various dialects. Heidegger considers this to indicate "*that the infinitive has a preeminent significance in language as a whole*" and suggests that the infinitive "names something that lies at the foundation of all inflections of the verb" (52, emphasis added). In other words, *enklisis a-paremphatikos,* far from being the abstract latecomer in language, constitutes that which makes possible all the revealing of beings that occurs in the inflections of verbs. The infinitive *einai* in particular is *a-paremphatikos* not because it is deficient in manifesting in comparison with other verb forms but because it obliquely reveals something entirely *different:* Being, not beings. Ancient Greek interpretations of the nature of language and subsequent Roman translations of them made it impossible to understand the world-opening relation between language and Being. Instead, language was reduced to the status of one thing among others, while Being was regarded as meaningless. The decline of the West, then, occurs because language deviates from its world-historical disclosive power. The self-concealment of Being occurs in such deviation.

2. THE HISTORICAL CONTEXT FOR HEIDEGGER'S VIEW OF THE DECLINE OF THE WEST

As one of the first works by Heidegger to be translated into English (1959), *EM* played an important role in Heidegger's reception in the English-speaking world. Most American readers were unaware that *EM*'s electrifying discussion of the darkening of the Western world was part of a widespread German conversation. *EM*'s account of nihilism struck a chord with 1960s counterculturalists, many of whom were introduced to Heideggerian themes through *One-Dimensional Man,* written by Herbert Marcuse, one of Heidegger's students. More recently, Heidegger's bleak view of modernity began arriving in the form of French poststructuralism. Years ago, I myself portrayed Heidegger as a precursor of what is now called the deep ecology movement, which condemns modernity's drive to dominate nature. Only in the late 1980s, after unsettling disclosures about Heidegger's involvement with National Socialism, did I fully understand the extent to which his thought accorded in many respects with the views shared by many cultural conservatives and National Socialists, as Hans Sluga explains in this collection.

German discussion about cultural despair was heightened by defeat in World War I, which further eroded the leading status of the liberal-progressive view of history propounded by the influential neo-Kantians. Affirming Germany's appropriation of Enlightenment cultural, political, and scientific values, neo-Kantians interpreted history as the gradual development both of more effective ways of controlling nature and of more enlightened modes of social organization and cultural self-expression. Opposed to the progressive view of history were two groups: those who believed that history had no direction and those who believed that history involved a decline from great beginnings. According to the former group of historians, influenced by Herder and other neo-romantics, each historical epoch had to be understood in its own terms, as a unique manifestation of a possible mode of social organization and cultural self-expression. According to the latter, history was a story of decline and fall from the achievements of earlier peoples, especially the Greeks and Romans. By comparison with the cultural flowering of ancient Athens—with its organic web of drama, sculpture, architecture, philosophy, rhetoric, and politics— modern commercial society seemed tawdry and mediocre to many German academics. Heidegger's approach to history has affinities with the view that Western history involves decline from noble origins. Explaining that decline not in terms of either racial or biological degeneration *(Entartung),* but rather in terms of ontological degeneration *(Herabfallung, Fallen),* he believed that other approaches to the meaning of history were obstacles to appropriating Germany's heritage through a new encounter with the Being of beings.

The idea that the West is degenerating has a long history, going back at least to Gibbon's famous *Decline and Fall of the Roman Empire,* which helped give currency to the notion that European civilization was bound to imitate the collapse of classical Rome. As Arthur Herman explains, even in the heyday of optimists such as Hegel, Marx, and Comte, social critics became concerned that the same civilizing processes that had brought Western civilization to its heights were now conspiring to corrupt it.[12] These critics often maintained that degeneration was the outcome of commercial culture, which removed people from contact both with instinctive forces and with noble ideals. The Swiss historian Jakob Burckhardt, admired by both Nietzsche and Heidegger, criticized modern mass humanity and democracy for destroying an already decadent European culture. Like many other cultural conservatives, he believed that the French Revolution had led the way to cultural mediocrity by unfettering "all passions and selfishness."[13] From such a debased mass society, so Burckhardt predicted, a military-industrial complex and totalitarian states would arise. Later on, Paul de Lagarde "saw progress as the Trojan Horse of a soulless bourgeois future. Mechanization, philistinism, socialism, and liberalism were all of a piece: true spiritual health meant escaping from their malign influences."[14] Although racists spoke openly of the "yellow peril" threatening Western vitality and dominance, even some progressive thinkers believed that people needed to reestablish contact with nature, improve personal hygiene, become more physically fit, and establish a better sense of community, in order to avoid psychological decay, physiological collapse, suicide, alcoholism, crime, and the other symptoms of urban civilization.

Nietzsche offered perhaps the most influential critique of decadent European society. Though admiring Schopenhauer, Nietzsche distinguished between the earlier thinker's resigned nihilism and his own active nihilism. True, European culture was in dreadful condition and Western man had been reduced to a herd animal, but Nietzsche said "yes!" to the possibility that a healthy instinct for the Will to Power could be recovered. He envisioned a "blond beast" who could annihilate feeble institutions and beliefs, in order to pave the way for the new, the vital, the powerful, and the creative.[15] Many German intellectuals adopted Nietzsche's Zarathustra as the symbol for rejuvenating soul-inspired *Kultur* and for overcoming the effects of calculating, commercial, and technological *Zivilisation*.

Nietzsche's thought is clearly at work in the writings of two cultural pessimists, Ernst Jünger and Oswald Spengler, each of whom influenced Heidegger. Unlike some conservatives who condemned modern industry, Jünger claimed that the soft, decadent, and unmanly European bourgeoisie was being displaced by *der Arbeiter* (the Worker), a new type of humanity combining the steely hardness of modern technology with the iron will of a proto-Nietzschean blond beast. Jünger foresaw a powerful new upsurge of Will in the face of Western decrepitude. Even while adopting Jünger's rhetoric of struggle and hardness, Heidegger called on Germans to submit to the technological Will to Power in order to overcome *(überwinden)* it, in the sense of "getting over" it.[16]

Having examined elsewhere Heidegger's relation to Jünger, here I explore Heidegger's critical appropriation of Spengler's book *The Decline of the West (Der Untergang des Abendlandes)*, which was "a great summing-up of a half-century of historical pessimism and cultural discomfort."[17] This book was labeled "the most popular philosophical work" of the interwar era. Some academics extolled it, while others panned it.[18] Spengler was inspired to write his account of the organic rise and fall of world cultures because of a storm of national protest that occurred when Germany appeared to back down from a 1911 confrontation in Morocco between France and Germany.[19] Perceiving this event as heralding a "world-historical shift," Spengler concluded, "The European civilization that rational science and the Enlightenment had made, and that France and Britain represented, was breaking apart. Germany may have lost the battle, but it was destined to win the war that was certainly coming, a struggle between cultural life and death, that is, between Germany and the liberal West."[20] Writing between 1914 and 1917, Spengler presupposed that Germany would be victorious in the Great War. The inconvenient fact of Germany's defeat did not discourage him from asserting that Germany was about to ascend into an era of world-dominating Caesars in the final two centuries before the last gasp of Western civilization. Although pessimistic about the long-term fate of the West, Spengler was optimistic that a final flowering of power could occur in Germany. Indeed, denying that he was a pessimist, Spengler said that he preferred speaking not of the West's decline *(Untergang)* but rather of its completion *(Vollendung).*[21]

Attacking progressive views of history, Spengler maintained with Nietzsche that world history is an ultimately meaningless but aesthetically sublime spectacle generated by irrational and insatiable cosmic Will. John Farrenkopf observes that "[f]or Hegel world history is the triumphant march of the *Weltgeist,* for Spengler, a student of Hegel's archrival Schopenhauer, it is the march of the *Weltwille,* the tragic, irrational odyssey of human will towards catastrophe."[22] Spengler claimed that there have been eight great cultures—Western, Greco-Roman, Indian, Babylonian, Chinese, Egyptian, Arabian, and Mexican—each of which has displayed a cyclical sequence characterized by the mounting up of and the slackening of creative tension. As Jeffrey Barash points out, for Spengler great "cultures 'live' like other organic realities. Like all life-units, they are individually distinct. Each can be characterized as an individual type. . . . Spengler proposed his vital cultural types as hypostatizations of a metaphysical life-principle making possible the primary forms *(Urgestalten)* through which cultural reality is constituted."[23] All civilizations pass through the same sequence of childhood, youth, manhood, and old age but are otherwise autonomous and thus not influenced cross-culturally. Since human history lacks any overall meaning or purpose, each civilization views things from its own perspective, establishes its own table of values, and thus constitutes a type. Each great culture has an *Ur-symbol* that "governs the style of the whole expression of life. It lies in the form of state, in religious myths and cults, in the ideals of ethics, the forms of painting, music, and poetry, the basic concepts of every science."[24] Decline sets in as this primal symbol loses its force. Unlike those who regarded the modern West as but a decadent offshoot of ancient Greece and Rome, Spengler maintained that modern culture did not derive from the classical world but instead is a completely new and demonic manifestation of world-conquering Will.[25]

The alleged incommensurability and perspectivalism of great cultures posed a certain problem for Spengler. Unlike previous cultural interpreters, who were always influenced by their culturally specific standpoint, he claimed that he effected a Copernican revolution in historiography by achieving the objectivity of the natural sciences.[26] Based on his allegedly objective standpoint, he confidently predicted the decline of the West. Spengler, however, did not adequately address two performative contradictions. The first involves his supposing that he could provide a culture-transcending interpretation of *all* cultures, even though he himself was a member of one particular culture.[27] The second involves his description of his own work as objective, even though he declared that natural science itself—the model for Western objectivity—has no grounds for making ultimately valid truth claims but instead is "a working hypothesis" and is "the servant of the technical 'Will to Power.' "[28]

According to Spengler, it was in the nineteenth century that the West entered into old age, wintertime, and sterility, the final stage of every historical culture. Mummified and parasitical, Western culture had degenerated to a mere civilization, which "clings to the once living roots of culture, which are its own forebears."[29] In "the metaphysically exhausted soil of the West," Spengler observed, a vital new philosophy can scarcely take root.[30] Modern civilization has become rigid, petrified, incapable of reconciling humankind and nature, human being and *Volk,* individual and community.[31] Denying the existence of the sacred, the West experiences the collapse of values and identity, just as other extinct cultures did previously. In order to conceal the decline, "Facile philosophies of optimism—Comte, Herbert Spencer, and Marx—sprang up . . . , only to be negated by the skeptical pessimism of Schopenhauer, Wagner, and Nietzsche. The nineteenth century had to face 'the cold, hard facts of a late life. . . . Of great paintings or great music there can no longer be, for Western people, any question.' Spengler does not use the term 'degenerate,' but that certainly describes his civilized man."[32]

As Herman points out, the "type" embodied by Western civilization is Faustian, for Western humankind "restlessly pursues knowledge and change. [The West's] chief product, science, is merely the concretization of the indomitable Western will, which it then projects onto the rest of the world in mechanical, rather than organic, terms."[33] The time- and space-conquering appetites of the Faustian imperialists are merely "the prelude of a future which is still in store for us. . . . The expansive tendency is a doom which grips, forces into service, and uses up the late mankind of the world-city stage."[34] Enslaved to his own creation, modern industry, modern man sacrifices the globe in his insatiable lust for money and power.[35]

Spengler believed that only the rise of a new Caesarism could break "the dictature of money and its political weapon democracy."[36] Unless Germans sacrificed their own blood by siding with a new Caesar who could overthrow the money-machine, they too "would be dragged into extinction along with the rest of the West."[37] Seeking to reconcile German nationalism with socialism, he believed that "[t]ogether workers, soldiers, engineers, and right-wing intellectuals would team up to crush the international financiers and the mob. They would substitute a 'dictatorship of organization' to replace the 'dictatorship of money' in postwar Germany."[38] Rejecting decadent liberal individualism, Spengler believed that "[t]he Prussian tradition of discipline and self-sacrifice could build a modern, unified community of equals, men joined together by obedience, service, and instinct. This 'true socialism' would destroy capitalism *and* Marxism, since both were false and degenerate ideologies of the past."[39] Important aspects of Spengler's vision of a "nationalist socialism," which so influenced future Nazis such as Strasser and Goebbels, were also echoed in Jünger's writings. To transform Germany into "a single totality of state, man, and machine," Jünger and Spengler alike believed that a fearsome elite must adopt "Roman hardness."[40] Spengler proclaimed: "We do not need ideologues anymore, we need hardness, we need fearless skepticism, we need a class of socialist master men . . . . Once again, socialism means power, power, and yet again power."[41]

Let us now briefly consider Heidegger's critical appropriation of Spengler's thought, including his thesis of decline. Heidegger's *ontological* interpretation of the decline of the West differed from Spengler's view, but Heidegger and Spengler had much in common.[42] Indeed, during the disoriented era of the 1920s, Karl Barth, Spengler, and Heidegger were generally viewed as offering analogous diagnoses of Western decay.[43] Agreeing with Spengler that history could not be understood as the progressive self-realization of rational Spirit, and that Western technological civilization was nihilistic, Heidegger nevertheless criticized Spengler for several reasons. First of all, he portrayed Spengler as an inferior popularizer of Nietzsche's thought, and worse, as a follower of Schopenhauer.[44] Such a dismissive evaluation conceals the extent of Heidegger's debt to Spengler, however, which may even include the concept of technology as *Gestell*.[45] Heidegger's own critique of Nietzsche, which began in the mid-1930s, may have been prompted in part by misgivings about Spengler's own use of Nietzschean categories. Like Spengler, Heidegger described modern science as being driven by the Will to Power, but he did not regard the Will as an ultimate metaphysical category. Something akin to Spengler's notion of a culture's *Ur-symbol* is discernible in Heidegger's claim that each epoch of Western history (ancient, medieval, early modern, technological) is governed by a particular mode of Being that organizes all cultural practices and institutions. In "The Origin of the Work of Art," for example, Heidegger described the

Greek temple as a work of art that "first fits together and at the same time gathers around itself the unity of those paths and relations in which birth and death, disaster and blessing, victory and disgrace, endurance and decline acquire the shape of destiny for human being. The all-governing expanse of this open relational context is the world of this historical people."[46] For Heidegger, however, Spengler's concept of *Ur-symbol* lacked any notion of works of art as poetic events that open up the world in which beings can manifest themselves and thus "be." Still operating within the confines of metaphysical thinking, Spengler tended to treat language as a kind of being, not as the "house of Being."[47]

Heidegger regarded Nietzsche as the last metaphysician, that is, as the last thinker working out the quest to find a foundation or ground for beings. In the grip of the metaphysical naturalism that Heidegger despised, Nietzsche interpreted humankind as a clever animal, driven by the Will to Power to seek world dominion. Heidegger controversially portrayed Nietzsche's Zarathustra as the apotheosis of modernity's world-conquering subjectivism. Influenced by a Nietzsche-inspired *Lebensphilosophie,* Spengler viewed humankind as a symbolic animal, driven by the Will to Power like every other life form. Spengler anticipated Heidegger's view in the 1930s that humankind had become a power-seeking animal. Herman notes that for Spengler, "once the vital force was dead, 'all that remains is the struggle for mere power, for animal advantage per se.' The post-Western world appears on Spengler's speculative horizon as a frozen, savage landscape, an atavistic struggle for life and death between uprooted nations and classes. 'In late civilization even the most convincing . . . idea is only the mask of purely zoological striving.' "[48]

Spengler maintained that the source of decline of the West is estrangement of self from its meaning-giving acts, but he did not view the self as truly responsible for those acts. Rather, the self was a function of deterministic cultural categories.[49] It was Heidegger's view that Spengler, not unlike other ideologues of the twentieth century, concealed the disturbing fact that humans must assume some responsibility for forming and sustaining great cultures.[50] Of course, Heidegger himself subscribed to a certain kind of determinism. If Hegel argued for the teleology of Western history, the final actualization of a hidden potential, Heidegger argued for the *eschatology* of Western history, the eventual exhaustion of possibilities laid out by the Greek encounter with Being.[51] He maintained that a genuinely new beginning was possible precisely at the point of depletion, but only if Dasein encountered Being in a primordial manner. Whereas Spengler regarded the Will to Power as the foundation for all cultures, Heidegger regarded it as the mode of metaphysical understanding characteristic of the near-final phase of Western history, which is governed by the foundationless destiny *(Geschick)* of Being.

Like Nietzsche and Schopenhauer, Spengler regarded philosophy as nothing more than an expression of a particular culture. Heidegger insisted, however, that far from being such an expression, philosophy makes culture itself possible. According to Barash, Heidegger concluded that Spengler operated according to a kind of inverted Platonism: "Here meaning arises [not from transcendental ideational structures, but instead] in the generative matrix of the historical process, and any possibility of transcendence of the historical is negated. Consciousness does not retain an autonomous base of coherence in the midst of the historical material it analyzes: consciousness, meaning, and value all are determined by the historically evolving cultural soul."[52]

Spengler asserted that Germany could temporarily forestall decline and bring Western history to perfection or fulfillment *(Vollendung)* by becoming a world-dominating military power. For Heidegger, however, such an idea only demonstrated the extent to which Spengler's thinking was characterized by metaphysics of the Will to Power. Already in 1921–1922, Heidegger remarked: "Spengler's basic lack: Philosophy of history without the historical, *lucus a non lucendo.* That Spengler does not understand what he wants shows itself in the fact that he becomes anxious before his own position and now sounds the retreat and weakens everything and pacifies those for whom the decline-perspective—even if merely in the 'as if'—has gotten into their bones. It was really not meant so grimly, business [*der Betrieb*] can peacefully continue (expression of the soul of the time)."[53]

From Heidegger's perspective, taking nationalistic pride in world domination was an indication of *hubris,* since German Dasein would not at all achieve historical greatness in Spengler's industrial Caesarism. Instead, by becoming a warring animal using high-tech weapons to annihilate other cultures and to plunder the planet, German Dasein would bring to a dreadful culmination *(Vollendung)* the nihilistic history of the West.

Spengler believed that by conceiving of the Will to Power at work behind the scenes in all cultures, he could understand their common patterns. For Heidegger, however, the Will to Power is a uniquely Western phenomenon that reflects ontological degeneracy. In his view, projecting the Will to Power onto non-Western cultures was the height of folly, because only European history was characterized by the history of Being. Whether in fact non-Western cultures began gloriously and then declined was not one of his concerns. In contrast, Spengler spoke of the uniqueness of each great culture but postulated the Will to Power as the metaphysical foundation shared by each of them. In this respect, at least according to Heidegger, Spengler did not fully appreciate the truly unique and radical character of Western history: that it began as a life-risking response to the groundless presencing of beings. Unfortunately, this original response degenerated into a search for a permanent foundation that would guarantee the security and survival of that culture. In that moment, human Dasein turned away from the risk and insecurity required for truly historical existence. Whereas Spengler sharply differentiated between Apollonian and Faustian culture, Heidegger insisted that the modern West is the ontically powerful but ontologically impotent dissipation of the destiny articulated by Plato and Aristotle.

For Heidegger, a key indicator of the West's ontological decline is that virtually all beings are disclosed as phenomena that are best comprehended by the methodology of natural science. Spengler's reference to his own methodological "objectivity" reveals his connection with this constricted ontology, despite his insistence that some of his "intuitions" could not be understood adequately in terms of natural science. Heidegger's critique of Spengler about this matter occurred in the context of the methodological dispute (*Methodenstreit*) that occurred among early twentieth-century German historians. Some favored explaining human history through natural scientific (*naturwissenschaftlich*) methodology, whereas others insisted that only mental-spiritual or "humanistic" (*geisteswissenschaftlich*) methodology was appropriate for interpreting human history. The latter group refused to treat human history as analogous or reducible to physical, chemical, or biological processes. According to Heidegger, "Spengler is the consequential and sure expression" of the mode of historical consciousness that views history as a kind of natural science.[54] Barash has argued, however, that Heidegger ignored the terms of the methodological dispute and rejected not just Spengler's approach but all other efforts to establish history as an independent scientific discipline of *any* kind. Instead, he insisted that philosophy alone could provide historical understanding of the kind needed for eventful cultural renewal.[55]

Heidegger maintained that by treating history as an objective framework that constrains the present, historians disburdened the current generation of its responsibility for encountering Being in a way that would set into place a new historical world. Such an approach to history is the culminating moment of *inauthentic* historical consciousness.[56] Gripped by metaphysical foundationalism, historians sought a firm ground for historical events, whether it be Hegelian *Geist* or natural types. Just as later Christians forgot the radical character of early Christian faith and replaced it with the firm foundation of Christendom, so too modern Dasein ignores the extent to which modernity's apparently firm foundations straddle the abyss of finitude. Seeking to rescue his generation from the dead hand of history, Heidegger summoned German Dasein to the responsibility of *making* history by radically renewing culture.[57] In the early 1920s, he proclaimed that "In our Dasein, we are today unlike every generation before us . . . insofar as through ourselves we have an expressly historical consciousness, live in this consciousness, see ourselves in it, with and from it see or await the future."[58] Although deserving to be taken seriously because he depicts so effectively the degenerate *Zeitgeist,* Spengler's focus on typology and morphology prevented him from gaining access to the authentic problems of the "historical," defined as the ontological conditions that make historical cultures possible.[59]

According to Heidegger, modern Dasein's striving for certainty and control is the late outcome of the Greek tendency to define Being as permanent presence (*Wesen,* essence), and thereby to occlude the historicity of Being and the temporality of Dasein. Being's increasing self-concealment of its own abysmal character constitutes the "errancy" to which the decline of the West may be attributed. Despite frequently criticizing Plato and Platonism, Heidegger himself drew on the Platonic metaphor of recollection, *Erinnerung.*[60] Only by recollecting what has been forgotten, namely, Being as such, can human Dasein enact the authentic repetition *(Wiederholung)* of the original Greek encounter with Being. Such repetition is impossible for those who seek to represent history as something given in the past, rather than as a heritage that opens up future possibilities.

Insofar as Heidegger believed that a new beginning was possible for the West, he did not consider himself to be a cultural pessimist of Spengler's variety. Indeed, he remarked that the darkening of the world, the flight of the gods, and the destruction of the earth had reached such proportions that "such childish categories as pessimism and optimism have long become laughable" (29). Although here seeking to separate himself from the run-of-the-mill pessimist, in effect Heidegger implies that such pessimists had no idea how terrible the situation really was. They saw only the *symptoms* of decline (collapse of values, loss of the sacred, and so on), whereas he identified its ontological *source.* Nevertheless, he shared with leading cultural pessimists at least two convictions: first, that under the condition of technological nihilism, the future of the West was grim; second, that existing ideologies and institutions were incapable of rescuing the West from that nihilism.

3. CRITICAL EVALUATION

Having personally experienced cultural loss, social dislocation, and environmental destruction, Heidegger regarded technological modernity as the horrendous outcome of a long decline from noble origins. Critiques of modernity as totalizing as Heidegger's, however, fail to distinguish between modernity's dark side and its undeniably positive achievements. The dark side is well known to people living in the twentieth century, but the noble aspect is often insufficiently appreciated. Heidegger ignored it completely.

The nobility of modernity involves its effort to foster individual personal development by emancipating humankind from material deprivation, political authoritarianism, and religious dogmatism. As Kant, Jürgen Habermas, and more recently Ken Wilber have noted, these goals could be achieved only by differentiating among the spheres of science, art, and ethics or politics. These spheres are undifferentiated in premodern cultures, in which all knowledge must be consistent with the truth claims made by religious authorities who are the basis for the legitimacy of the ruling class. Individual experience, including appreciation of works of art, must also be consistent with the kinds of judgments permitted by governing institutions. The Enlightenment project sought to differentiate among the truth claims made by the three spheres, in order that (1) scientific research could occur freely, without being impinged on by ecclesiastical authority; (2) political decisions and moral judgments could be made on the basis of free rational judgment, rather than on the basis of dogmatic pronouncements of the kind that encouraged religious warfare; and (3) individual persons could develop their own modes of subjectivity, including judgments of taste, independently of collective expectations.

Unfortunately, the noble achievement of this differentiation did not long endure.[61] One of the three spheres—scientific and technological knowing—soon began to dominate the other two. In comparison with the truth claims of modern science, whose validity was borne out by the extraordinary technological achievements made possible by them, the truth claims of morality, politics, and art became portrayed as merely emotive responses, not as having any truth validity of their own. The scientific-technological mode of knowing was supposed to serve the worthy goals of freeing humanity from material deprivation and pacifying human social relations. Once the status of the moral-political and aesthetic-personal spheres was almost completely eroded, however, science and technology began to serve not only goals consistent with the emancipatory aims of the Enlightenment but also goals consistent with the striving after power for its own sake. Heidegger, too, concluded that Enlightenment modernity's talk of emancipation and progress was merely a mask for modern humanity's quest for infinite power. This quest makes humankind brutelike, deprived of an ontological *ethos* that assigns limit, order, and measure to human existence.

The suffering made possible by unbounded science and technology—including industrialized Nazi death camps, nuclear ICBMs, totalitarian social control mechanisms, and planetary ecological destruction—is enough to make almost anyone suspicious of the Enlightenment's "progressive" vision of history. Faced with the potentially species-destroying power of technological modernity, a number of people reject modernity's ideals and institutions, preferring instead to envision a society that reunites what modernity put asunder. Some radical ecologists, for example, seem to call for a return to premodern ways of life, such as that of horticulturalists or gatherer-hunters. Because premodern cultures do not differentiate among the above-mentioned three spheres, such cultures enjoy an internal cohesion that is understandably envied by modern people whose lives are characterized by fragmentation and conflict. Although denying that he wanted Germany to reproduce ancient Greece, Heidegger admired its internal cohesion made possible by a shared *ethos*. Seeking to de-differentiate what modernity had set apart, he yearned for a culture-unifying *ethos* that would come from a new dispensation of Being. Seeking to accomplish de-differentiation in another way, National Socialism generated a totalizing society that achieved unity first by excluding and later by annihilating otherness. That Heidegger never publicly repudiated Nazism and continued to speak of its "inner truth and greatness" when he published *EM* in 1953 does not mean that he agreed with its genocidal practices, but it does suggest that he favored some form of antimodern de-differentiation that would supposedly restore Being to its proper role in Western affairs.

Heidegger is often brilliant when it comes to interpreting the work of thinkers such as Aristotle and Kant, but his interpretation of Western philosophy and history has shortcomings. For one thing, his account of Western history inexplicably omits Hebrew, Stoic, neo-Platonic, early medieval, and Renaissance thought.[62] For another, his interpretation of some thinkers, perhaps especially Nietzsche, is flawed by his effort to fit them into the Procrustean bed of the history of Being. Finally, he does not adequately justify his view that the West has declined but instead presupposes the truth of that view. In some respects, Heidegger was a cultural pessimist. For such pessimists, as Ken Wilber writes,

the spiritual universe is running down. In the actual unfolding of the universe's history, we humans (and all creatures) were once close to Spirit [Being, for Heidegger], one with Spirit, immersed in Spirit, right here on earth. But through a series of separations, dualisms, sins, or contractions, Spirit became less and less available, less and less obvious, less and less present. . . . [H]istory itself is the story of spiritual abandonment, with each era becoming darker and more sinister and less spiritual. For pre-modern cultures, in short, history is devolution.[63]

A pessimistic evaluation of history highlights the faults of the present age, while ignoring those of the past. Hence, Heidegger never mentioned ancient Greece's slavery, nor its portrayal of women as half-human.[64] In some postwar essays, he surrendered his notion that some cultures are closer to the ontological origin than others, but in 1935 he surely believed that the ancient Greeks were closest of all to Being.[65] Heidegger's account of the overarching influence of Being on Western history is so idiosyncratic that it has prevented him from being taken seriously even by those who share his pessimistic view of the future of the West under the regime of metaphysics. Indeed, some critics have accused him of inventing his own private religion. Furthermore, although many philosophers have given language top billing in this century, few can accept his claim that translating Greek philosophical terms into Latin sent the West into a nihilistic tailspin.

Aspects of Heidegger's conception of Being were shaped by his rejection of the Jewish-Christian idea that transcendent Providence plays a central role not only in human history but in cosmic history as well. His transcendent Being functions somewhat analogously to Providence in Western history but plays no role in the creation or metaphysical origin of beings. If he had developed a theology, it would probably have been close to Schelling's. Nevertheless, Heidegger resisted the claim of German idealism, which was itself influenced by neo-Platonism, that human history is the manifestation of Spirit in time, whereas nature is the manifestation of Spirit in space. Informed by contemporary cosmology, a number of thinkers are currently trying to integrate scientific, historical, and spiritual understanding by developing a post-Hegelian, evolutionary narrative of Divine *involution,* in the form of the sudden emergence of matter-energy (Big Bang), and *evolution,* in the form of the evolved carbon-based life that enables the Divine to recognize itself.[66] Heidegger would not have countenanced such a reconciliation, in part because of his suspicion of science, which for him was largely equivalent to positivism. Such a reconciliation is not impossible, however, for those willing to regard modernity as an important but by no means the final step in the progressive process through which humankind strives to put into practice the freedom promised by Spirit.[67] Defining that process, however, must be left to a future essay.

Chapter 11

"CONFLICT IS THE FATHER OF ALL THINGS": HEIDEGGER'S POLEMICAL CONCEPTION OF POLITICS

HANS SLUGA

Nowhere does Martin Heidegger speak of politics in a more emphatically philosophical tone than in his *Introduction to Metaphysics* of 1935. Though devoted, in name and substance, to the question of Being, the lecture course turns again and again to questions of politics. It cites political concerns as motivating the metaphysical investigations and claims that a genuine engagement with the question of Being has political bearing. The resulting fusion of metaphysical and political themes is hardly surprising when one considers that Heidegger delivered these lectures fresh from his hasty political engagement in 1933 and his equally hasty withdrawal a year later—still conscious of the urgency of the political but sufficiently removed from it to test once again the philosophical waters.

This does not mean that he had altogether lost faith in Hitler and his movement. He was certainly disillusioned by the proliferating bureaucracy and the pettiness of the party state, but he still held hopes for a purer version of National Socialism. In 1936 he confided to Karl Löwith that he still believed it to be "the path mapped out for Germany."[1] He was conscious, however, of the need for "an inner self-collection" and "renewal of the people, and a path toward the discovery of its Western-historical purpose," as he wrote after the war. In the rectorate he had "risked the attempt to save and to purify and to strengthen what was positive" in the Nazi movement.[2] Such were presumably also his motives in 1935, when he felt dismayed by colleagues who were fishing for a philosophy of National Socialism in the "troubled waters" of a theory of objective value and organic unity. To their attempts he wished to oppose his own conception of "the inner truth and greatness of this movement," as he declared dramatically toward the end of his lecture course (152).

Not that he was sure of his powers to do so. In a letter to Jaspers, written on July 1 while he was still in the middle of his lectures, he described his new work as a "laborious groping" and a "feeble stammering" that moved dutifully through interpretations of other thinkers and thus established "only a further occasion to experience how great the distance is to the possibilities of a real thinking."[3] There is no doubt that the *Introduction to Metaphysics* is a transitional work, relying on philosophical thoughts first voiced in his inaugural lecture at Freiburg in 1929 while gesturing toward the later conception of a history of Being. Politically, too, the lectures mark a point of transition. One is struck by their continuity with the political pronouncements of his rectoral address of 1933, to which they make a direct and positive reference (37 f.).[4] The two texts have, indeed, several things in common. Both speak darkly of a spiritual crisis endangering the West and of Germany's historical mission in its resolution. Both recognize the importance of philosophical questioning to the political dilemmas at hand and the need for spiritual leadership in establishing a true order. Both engage in the search for an "essential knowledge" on which to ground man's political Dasein. And both texts argue that such knowledge can be found only by turning back to early Greek thought, "only if we again place ourselves under the power of the *beginning* of our spiritual-historical existence."[5]

It is true, at the same time, that the *Introduction to Metaphysics* evinces none of the passion for practical politics so evident in the rectoral address. In 1933 he had accepted a "commitment to the *spiritual* leadership of this institution of higher learning" (RA, 5). Two years later he seconded Nietzsche's statement that philosophy is "essentially untimely" (6). He was sure now that philosophy "can never *directly* supply the forces and create the mechanisms and opportunities that bring about a historical state of affairs" (8). Somewhat later he added that Plato's call for philosopher-kings "does not mean that philosophy professors should run the business of the state."[6] Still, he held on to the certainty that "what is useless can nevertheless be a power" (7). For philosophy was, in his words, "a thoughtful opening of the avenues and vistas of a knowing that establishes measure and rank, in which and from which a people conceives its Dasein in the historical-spiritual world and brings it to fulfillment" (8). Or, as he put it more simply in the Nietzsche lectures: "The basic attitudes which support and direct the community must be founded on essential knowledge."[7]

THE QUESTION OF BEING AND THE DARKENING OF THE WORLD

Heidegger's opening query, "Why are there beings at all instead of nothing?," stimulates him initially to reflect on the philosophical business, on

Nothingness and Being, and on the Greek understanding of Being as *phusis,* but then moves him swiftly to "the spiritual destiny of the West." Europe, he declares, is struck by an "awful blindness" as it lies "in the great pincers between Russia on the one side and America on the other" (28). We are witnessing, more generally, a "decline of the earth" and a "darkening of the world" (29). In a "flattening-out" of the world all things have sunk "to the same level, to a surface resembling a blind mirror," and a "measureless so-on-and-so-forth of the ever-identical and the indifferent" dominates; there is an "onslaught of that which aggressively destroys all rank and all that is world-spiritual," and with it an "onslaught of what we call the demonic (in the sense of the destructively evil)" (35). Surprising as this trajectory from the introductory question to these stark observations may seem, it is warranted, Heidegger tells us, because the question of Being is not just "a vapor" and an idle intellectual pastime but "one of the essential fundamental conditions for awakening the spirit, and thus for an originary world of historical Dasein" (38). The question of Being and the historical condition of the world belong inextricably and intimately together.

It is crucial to understand, however, that Heidegger is not concerned here with providing a dispassionate, historical analysis of the current age but is speaking *politically* as someone concerned with turning the destiny of the West around. For he wants to "restore the historical Dasein of human beings . . . back to the power of Being," and specifically to restore "our ownmost future Dasein," by which he means presumably Western, European, and German Dasein (32). But he also wants to show that the political problem is historical in nature and as such spiritual and therefore ultimately metaphysical in character.

Heidegger speaks of four distinct misinterpretations of the spirit that have led to the current darkening of the world: (1) its reinterpretation as intelligence, (2) its reduction to a mere instrumentality, (3) the interpretation of the spiritual world as a cultural value, (4) and the use of spirit as a showpiece and spectacle (35–37). The first two, with their "technological" interpretation of spirit, form in effect a single group, and the third and fourth, with their appeal to the notions of culture and value, form another group; we can therefore say that Heidegger has essentially two types of misinterpretation in mind, of which the first is directly responsible for the darkening of the world and the second offers a false remedy for this decline. The two misinterpretations move "along the same decadent path," but the former has, at least, "the merit of open and clear consistency," whereas the latter is a "reactionary interpretation" and an "unconscious mendacity" (36 f.). Heidegger therefore concludes that with the assumption of values, "the maximum in confusion and deracination has been reached" (151).

That conclusion also explains Heidegger's most notorious and most explosive statement in the whole course of lectures: "In particular, what is peddled about nowadays as the philosophy of National Socialism, but which has not the least to do with the inner truth and greatness of this movement [namely, the encounter between global technology and modern humanity], is fishing in these troubled waters of 'values' and 'totalities'" (152). The sentence was obviously meant as a provocation when Heidegger spoke it in 1935, for it made, in fact, four polemical claims: (1) that National Socialism *has* an inner truth and greatness, (2) that this must be distinguished from its outer and possibly flawed manifestations, (3) that the speaker himself possesses a unique insight into the inner truth of the movement, and (4) that National Socialism cannot be grounded in a theory of value and organic unity. Each of these claims had its own specific polemical target: the first, opponents of the system who dismissed it as small-minded and based on illusion; the second, petty officials who were turning the movement into a bureaucratic regime; the third, party ideologues who claimed to possess the truth of National Socialism; and the fourth, some of Heidegger's own philosophical colleagues. We cannot go wrong when we assume that in speaking such provocative words Heidegger must have wanted to underscore his attack on the theory of value as one of the central concerns of the whole lecture course and of his attempt to determine other and more adequate foundations for National Socialism.

When Heidegger published the *Introduction to Metaphysics* after the war, this sentence provoked an immediate outcry. He presumably let it stand in his text not in order to stir up debate about his Nazi past but in order to renew his critique of the philosophy of value and the political appeal to it. For the theory of value was once again in vogue in Germany in 1953, Nicolai Hartmann and Max Scheler were read as authorities in this field, and values were widely invoked in the conservative political climate of the time. The appeal to values is still ubiquitous in politics. Political reactionaries regularly call on "traditional" and "family" values to bolster their economic and power interests. Progressives consider it necessary to draw on "moral" and "human" values to support their reformist causes. Heidegger's critique of values has therefore lost none of its gravity. Our problem is still the one he sought to address in 1935: do we need to choose between a politics based on "objective," "transhistorical" values and one that takes all decisions to be arbitrary? What if the appeal to values proves philosophically untenable? Are we then left only with a flattened-out world in which everything is at the same level, in which only "a measureless so-on-and-so-forth of the ever identical and indifferent" obtains? Or can we make sense of distinctions of rank and position (in politics and elsewhere) without having to draw on values?

FROM THE ORIGINARY *POLEMOS* TO HUMAN POLITICS

"Precisely because we dare to take up the great and lengthy task of tearing down a world that has grown old and of building anew, that is, historically, we must know the tradition. . . . Only the most radical historical knowledge brings us face to face with the unfamiliarity of our tasks and preserves us from a new onset of mere restoration and uncreative imitation" (96). For that reason we must, in particular, return to the early, pre-Platonic conception of Being that still reigns, though unrecognized and flattened-out, in the West. Only by recuperating this beginning of our spiritual-historical existence and what is most uncanny and mightiest in it can we account for the origins of distinctions of "position and status and rank" in the world.

The early Greeks thought of Being dynamically as an "emergent self-upraising," a "self-unfolding that abides in itself" (47). Under its "sway," its forceful rule, divisions, oppositions, and distinctions appear.[8] Heidegger draws attention to the Heraclitean fragment 53, according to which "Conflict *(polemos)* is the father of all things and king of all. Some he shows to be gods and others men; some he makes slaves and others free." He declares this *polemos* a cosmic strife, not just a human war, "a strife that holds sway before everything divine and human, not war in the human sense. . . . In such a stepping apart, clefts, intervals, distances and joints open themselves up" (47). And, thus, the struggle "sets the essential and the unessential, the high and the low, into their limits and makes them manifest" (87).

It is not, then, that Heidegger denies a separate realm of values in order to inscribe value as a fixed character into Being itself. It is, rather, that Being dynamically gives rise to a distinction between the high and the low, and does so through cosmic strife that is not merely a human quarreling and feuding. But the cosmic strife is not altogether independent of human action. Heidegger's account of how Being and human Dasein are interwoven remains, however, complex and elusive. He speaks of the originary struggle as that which "allows those that struggle to originate as such in the first place" (47). He believes, therefore, that "*the essence and the manner of Being-human can be determined only on the basis of the essence of Being*" (106). What it means to be human is, accordingly, "not an anthropological question, but a historically meta-physical question" (107). But he reminds us also that to be human is to be a sayer, and that "in the word, in language, things first come to be and are"

(11). The crucial point is that "Being essentially unfolds *as* appearing" (77) and that the Greeks struggled to make Being appear. "Only by undergoing the struggle between Being and seeming did they wrest Being forth from beings, did they bring beings into constancy and unconcealment" (80). The riddle that Heidegger sets before us in speaking of the interlacing of Being and human Dasein is, as he puts it also, the difficulty of understanding "the unity and antagonism of Being and seeming" (81). And though he confronts us with this riddle, he does not resolve it either here or elsewhere and thus leaves the relation of Being and Dasein in question. This is as he may intend it to be, but it introduces uncertainty into our picture of how the originary *polemos* gives rise to human struggle and how the "clefts, intervals, distances, and joints" (47) that open themselves up in the cosmic strife relate to distinctions of position, status, and rank that result from human action.

It is, in any case, by undergoing the struggle between Being and seeming that the early Greeks brought "the gods and the state, the temples and the tragedies, athletic competition and philosophy" into being (80). This human struggle is sustained "by the creators, by the poets, thinkers, and statesmen." Against the overwhelming sway of *phusis,* "they throw the counterweight of their work and capture in this work the world that is thereby opened up" (47). The world that comes thereby into being is "genuine history" *(eigentliche Geschichte),* and its site is the *polis* (48). Everything genuinely historical is placed in that site: "the gods, the temples, the priests, the celebrations, the games, the poets, the thinkers, the ruler, the council of elders, the assembly of the people, the armed forces and the ships" (117). The polis becomes thereby "the ground and place of human Dasein itself, the spot where all these routes cross" (117).[9]

The polis as the place in which Being opens itself up requires a distinction of status, position, and rank, for "rank and dominance" must belong to Being. "If Being is to open itself up, it itself must have rank and maintain it" (101). Heraclitus' attitude that the many are dogs and donkeys belongs therefore essentially to Greek Dasein. "If people today from time to time are going to busy themselves rather too eagerly with the polis of the Greeks, they should not suppress this side of it; otherwise the concept of the polis easily becomes innocuous and sentimental. What is higher in rank is what is stronger. Thus Being, logos, as the gathered harmony, is not easily available for every man at the same price, but is concealed, as opposed to that harmony which is always mere equalizing, the elimination of tension, leveling" (102). Drawing on Sophocles' *Antigone,* Heidegger endorses its characterization of man as the most awe-inspiring or (as he says) the uncanniest being. Quoting the famous words of the chorus: "Many things are uncanny, but nothing uncannier than man," he comments that this means also that man "uses force in the sense of one who needs to use force—and does not just have force at his disposal, but is violent, insofar as using force is the basic trait not just of his doing, but of his Dasein" (115).[10]

Violence is for Heidegger man's basic trait insofar as he uses force against what is overwhelming. His force is a "knowing struggle to set Being, which was formerly closed off, into what appears as beings" (122). The characterization of man as the uncanniest of beings provides therefore the authentic Greek definition of man. His use of force is to be understood not merely as brutality and arbitrariness in a domain where compromise and mutual assistance are thought to set the standard. Man, the force-doer, "knows no kindness and conciliation (in the ordinary sense), no appeasement and mollification by success and prestige and by their confirmation" (125). There is violence in poetic saying, in thoughtful projection, in constructive building, and (last, but not least) in state-creating action, and this violence is not an application of faculties that man has but "a disciplining and disposing of the forceful forces by virtue of which beings disclose themselves as such" (120, translation modified). Emerging through *polemos* from the sway *(Walten)* of *physis,* the *polis* is thus produced by force *(Gewalt)* through the acts of violent *(gewalt-tätige)* men.

In a radical (mis)construction of the Sophoclean text, Heidegger makes it say that those who are set above the state must at the same time act outside its laws. Where Sophocles seems to *contrast* the man who is high in the city *(hypsipolis)* as someone who applies "the laws of the earth and the justice of the gods" to the outcast from the city *(apolis)* with whom the ignoble consort, Heidegger *identifies* the two in a daring but grammatically questionable move and translates the Sophoclean verses as saying that man becomes *both* high above the city and without city by "driving between the law of the earth and the sworn justice of the gods." It is obvious for him that real poets, priests, and rulers must "use force as violent men and become those who rise high in historical Being as creators, as doers. Rising high in the site of history, they also become *apolis,* without city and site, lone-some, un-canny, with no way out amidst beings as a whole, and at the same time without ordinance and limit, without structure and fittingness, because they as creators must first ground all this in each case" (117). It is not surprising, then, that Heidegger has no place in his reading of the Sophoclean text for the decisive distinction between human and divine law. He takes the gods themselves, their temples, and their ordinances to be human and political creations and hence unable to serve as constraints on the life of the city's creators.

Heidegger goes on to assert that the creative act of force through which everything historical and political is founded must not be thought to belong only to a mythical past. It is, rather, an act that needs renewal at every moment, if the vigor of the creation is to be maintained: "When the creators have disappeared from the people, when they are barely tolerated as irrelevant curiosities, as ornaments, as eccentrics alien to life, when authentic struggle ceases and shifts into the merely polemical, into the intrigues and machinations of human beings within the present-at-hand, then the decline has already begun" (48). Everything given calls, thus, for a creative transcendence through force. It calls also for men of force able to bring about such transcendence. In this conception the state is not to be conceived as the joint endeavor of free and equal citizens but as the creation of the "real" statesman who is responsible only to the call of Being. This statesman originates and maintains political order and stands as such both above and outside the law. Charismatic and sovereign leadership (in politics as well as in poetry and philosophy) is thereby affirmed as essential to the well-being of the commonwealth and, in particular, to the health of the polis.

POLITICS AS ART

Heidegger speaks in one breath of "poets, thinkers, and statesmen" (47), of "the poets, the thinkers, the ruler," of "real poets, . . . real thinkers, . . . real priests, . . . real rulers" (117). The casual bracketing together of these distinctive figures indicates that he thinks of their respective work in closely corresponding ways. The state must, according to this view, be conceived in analogy to the work of art, to the thought of the original thinker, and to the sacrifice of the priest. Just as the paradigmatic poetic action is that of making a poem and the paradigmatic act of thinking that of conceiving a thought, so the paradigmatic political act is an act of founding a state, not a mere operating within fixed political boundaries and institutions. Real artists and real thinkers are able to break through the conventions and ordinances of their time to generate new rules that may prove compelling for the whole culture. Real statesmen will likewise produce new forms of political existence.

The correspondence between poetry, thought, and politics remains, however, largely unthematized in the *Introduction to Metaphysics,* and is only made explicit a year later in Heidegger's essay "On the Origin of the Work of Art," where we read: "One essential way in which truth establishes itself in the beings it has opened up is truth setting itself into work. Another way in which truth occurs is the act that founds a political state. . . . Still another way in which truth grounds itself is the essential sacrifice. Still another way in which truth becomes is the thinker's questioning, which, as the thinking of Being, names Being in its question-worthiness."[11] It is for this reason natural to think of this essay as the direct sequel to the 1935 lectures. But this does not mean that we are entitled to read its views back into the *Introduction to Metaphysics*. "The Origin of the Work of Art" represents, rather, the next step in Heidegger's thinking: one in which concern with politics is pushed increasingly aside and subsumed under a concern with the work of art.

Still, there are evident continuities that invite the reader to expand on Heidegger's 1935 account of the polis in terms of these later reflections. Both the polis and the work of art are conceived in the essay as "opening up a world," and both are thought of as products of strife. Heidegger writes in "The Origin of the Work of Art": "Setting up a world and setting forth the earth, the work is the fighting of the battle in which the unconcealedness of beings as a whole, or truth, is won" (WA, 55). Although he is speaking here primarily of the work of art, his words correspond precisely to what he had previously said of the polis. He also writes: "As a world opens itself, it submits to the decision of an historical humanity the question of victory and defeat, blessing and curse, mastery and slavery" (WA, 63). And he refers us once more to Heraclitus' fragment 53 as revealing that "every living word fights the battle and puts up for decision what is holy and what unholy, what great and what small, what brave and what cowardly, what lofty and what flighty, what master and what slave" (WA, 43).

These analogies justify talk of an "aesthetic" conception of politics, but given the broad sense of the term, such a characterization is not without its dangers.[12] Flags and uniforms, ceremonies and parades, rhetoric and propaganda belong straightforwardly to the aesthetic side of politics, but Heideggerian politics is, evidently, not focused on these phenomena. His understanding of politics is "aesthetic," rather, in the sense that he takes the state to be a creative product, something originated and maintained by great political leaders, and that he thinks of these leaders as creators of rules and norms, not as merely implementing fixed (moral or political) principles. This conception of politics owes, perhaps, more to Nietzsche than to the Greeks. What he says in the *Introduction to Metaphysics* suggests, in any case, familiarity with Nietzsche's early essay on the Greek state. Nietzsche speaks there of the Greeks as the "political men in themselves" and discerns, by contrast, "dangerous atrophies of the political sphere" in the present.[13] The Greeks, he claims, had understood the "mysterious connection . . . between the State and art, political greed and artistic creation, battlefield and work of art" (GS, 12). They had recognized that all right is at bottom "presumption, usurpation, force [*Gewalt*]," that war is "the true divinity for consecrating and purifying the State," and that in the military genius we come to recognize "the original founder of states" (GS, 10, 15, 16). Human beings have dignity only insofar as they are tools for this genius and we must, therefore, abandon the claim to "the alleged 'equal rights of all' " (GS, 5). Instead, we must come to see that "slavery is of the essence of culture" (GS, 5). In most of these respects Heidegger's views in the *Introduction to Metaphysics* seem closely akin to Nietzsche's, and it may not be too much to say that his understanding of ancient Greek politics is influenced by Nietzsche just as much as it is by his reading of the early Greek thinkers and poets.

TWO CONCEPTIONS OF A POLEMICAL POLITICS

Still closer to Heidegger's political thinking in 1935 are ideas advanced by Carl Schmitt, who, in turn, is likely to have drawn on Nietzsche. Although Schmitt came to a general critique of value-thinking only much later, he had by 1929 developed a view that detached politics systematically from questions of value. In his essay *The Concept of the Political* (first published as a separate treatise in 1929) he had argued that "in contrast to . . . the moral, aesthetic, and economic, the political has its own criteria."[14] A professed Hobbesian in outlook, he had, moreover, characterized man as "by no means an unproblematic but a dangerous and dynamic being" (CP, 61). In consequence he considered conflict endemic to human life. From this we try to protect ourselves by banding together with those who share "one's own form of existence" *(Art Existenz)* and by distancing ourselves from those who are "existentially something different and other" (CP, 27). Schmitt argues that from this all political phenomena arise. "The specific political distinction to which political actions and motives can be reduced is that between friend and enemy" (CP, 26). All genuine politics is therefore polemical in character and must at all times maintain the potential for forceful struggle. "A world in which the possibility of war is utterly eliminated, a completely pacified globe would be a world without the distinction of friend and enemy and hence a world without politics" (CP, 35). Such a world is, however, inconceivable given the existential role that conflict plays in human life.

Although the distinction between friend and enemy is, as indicated, not meant to be arbitrary but based on real and prepolitical affinities and differences, it is also not determined by these prepolitical facts. Rather, political order requires human decision, and this decision is not ultimately guided by normative constraints. All political distinctions are therefore human creations. We may call this an aesthetic conception of politics, but only in the narrow and precise sense in which we have characterized Heidegger's politics as aesthetic: both men assume that political order is the work of (individual or collective) creators, that it is produced and maintained only through human agency, and that these creators reveal themselves, particularly in moments of true exception, to stand outside the norms of established law. At the same time, Schmitt rejects the application of specifically aesthetic notions to politics as incompatible with the peculiar autonomy of the political sphere.

Heidegger was well acquainted with these ideas when he delivered his 1935 lectures. Two years earlier Schmitt had sent him a copy of his essay *The Concept of the Political* and Heidegger had responded: "Respected Herr Schmitt, I thank you for sending me your brochure which I know already from its second edition and which contains a proposal of very great significance."[15] He had also expressed his hope that they would be able to discuss the work at some time, without, however, setting a date for such an occasion. Instead he had asked for Schmitt's help in his efforts to rebuild the law faculty at Freiburg.[16] More generally, he had added: "Things here are, unfortunately, very disheartening," and he had spoken of the urgent need "to gather the spiritual forces that should lead us into what is to come," closing his letter with "friendly greetings" and a resolute "Heil Hitler."

In expressing his intellectual kinship with Schmitt, he had noted with particular pleasure that Schmitt had inscribed his copy of *The Concept of the Political* with the Heraclitean fragment 53: "In your quotation from Heraclitus I liked particularly that you did not forget the *basileus* who alone gives the total saying its full meaning when one spells it out completely. For years I have had such a reading prepared in relation to the concept of truth—the *edeixe* and *epoiese* which occurs in fragment 53. But now I stand myself in the middle of the *polemos* and literary activity must take a back seat."

That Heidegger and Schmitt should have sought each other's company at this moment is not surprising since they had, indeed, much in common. They had both risen from marginal cultural and social conditions to be among the leading minds of the Weimar period. In contrast to most of their intellectual peers, they had allied themselves with the Nazis in early 1933 and had joined the party on May 1 of that year. At the time he sent Heidegger his brochure, Schmitt had just been appointed a professor of law in Berlin and a member of the Prussian State Council, a newly created consultative government body. He was also soon to occupy a high position in the Nazi organization of German lawyers.[17] Neither of the two had been linked to the Nazis before 1933, nor did they see themselves now as party faithful. They understood themselves, rather, as independent minds who had (at least temporarily) joined in with the new regime. Both believed that the system needed experienced hands, and both were convinced of their indispensability at this moment of national destiny.

Though both subscribed to the polemical conception of politics expressed in Heraclitus' fragment, they nevertheless read it, from the start, in two very different ways, and thus their respective accounts of the nature of politics remained, despite their analogy, at odds. Schmitt took the fragment to be speaking exclusively of human conflict. The polemical character of politics was grounded for him in the dynamic nature of man, and this was in accord with his view that every conception of politics is based on an anthropology.[18] Heidegger, on the other hand, understood the Heraclitean *polemos* to be primarily a cosmic strife; always wary of anthropological explanations, he perceived a more fundamental principle at work in politics than human strife, one that "holds sway before everything divine and human" (47). Hence, Schmitt could consider the friend-enemy distinction basic to politics, whereas Heidegger held that "the essence and manner of Being-human can be determined only on the basis of the essence of Being" (106).

This led them, in turn, to speak of political leadership in two different ways. Schmitt's sovereign is in essence the modern autonomous individual, whereas Heidegger shuns altogether the language of modern subjectivism. The political leaders must "first and foremost and at any time themselves be led," he had declared already in the rectoral address (RA, 4). And in his lectures of 1935, he speaks accordingly of the Heraclitean *polemos* as a struggle in which human beings "originate as such in the first place" (47). The point is made even more forcefully in "The Origin of the Work of Art," where Heidegger writes: "It is precisely in great art . . . that the artist remains inconsequential as compared with the work, almost like a passageway that destroys itself in the creative process for the work to emerge" (WA, 40). He accuses modern subjectivism of having misinterpreted creativity "as the self-sovereign [*selbstherrliche*] subject's performance of genius" (WA, 76). Against this, he affirms that creation must not be thought of as "the performance or act of a subject striving toward himself as his self-set goal" (WA, 67). These are profound conceptual differences that have quite different philosophical implications: whereas Schmitt is, in effect, an existential political thinker, Heidegger's conception of politics can only be called metaphysical and ontological. But it must be admitted that this difference, important as it may be philosophically, did not affect their respective political judgments. As far as Adolf Hitler's leadership was concerned, they could still be of one mind.

POLITICS AND THE HISTORY OF BEING

Their philosophical differences must also not obscure the fact that Heidegger owed to Schmitt one crucial idea that was to shape his thinking on politics in 1935 and his whole subsequent thinking about the history of Being. Schmitt had been led by his polemical understanding of politics to postulate the essential instability of all political order. In a lecture titled "The Age of Neutralizations and Depoliticizations" (1929) he had, in consequence, laid out an epochal history of modern European politics that had sought to delineate a natural sequence of historical stages leading to the current decline of politics and to the current urgency of restoring politics to its genuine place.

Still earlier Schmitt had postulated a structural correspondence between "the metaphysical image that a specific epoch forges of the world" and "what the world immediately understands to be appropriate as a form of political organization." And he had argued in a Hegelian flourish that this was so because "metaphysics is the most intensive and the clearest expression of an epoch."[19] His 1929 lecture expands on this insight and claims that modern European history has passed through a number of distinct phases in which different concepts occupied the central domain of the culture and in which therefore different conceptions of politics dominated. The cultural and political preoccupation with religion in the sixteenth century gave way in the seventeenth to a preoccupation with rational science and metaphysics, then in the eighteenth to one with universal morality, and in the nineteenth to dominant concern with economic facts and notions. Schmitt writes: "Above all the *state* derives its actuality and power from the given central sphere, because the decisive disputes of friend-enemy groupings are also determined by it."[20] He goes on to say that the succession of stages signals at the same time a progressive political neutralization of the conceptual spheres that have shifted away from the center, and that this whole process was driven by the search for a neutral domain in which there would be no conflict at all. This search was, however, doomed to fail because "in the dialectic of such a development one creates a new sphere of struggle precisely through the shifting of the central sphere" (AND, 138).

In the unfolding historical development, a decisive point was reached, as Schmitt has it, with the appearance of modern technology, which seems to offer an absolute and ultimate neutral ground. Political problems appear now as solvable by technical, instrumental, or bureaucratic means. This development has given rise to a vulgar faith in technology as promising a human paradise "predicated on the apparent neutrality of technology." In the face of the neutralizing tendencies of the modern technological state, the challenge is now to recapture an authentic sense of the political. Schmitt insists that we will succeed in this only by distinguishing between technology as a legitimate tool and technological thinking. The latter is still a form of spirit, he writes, even though an evil and perverted one, and this spirit must and can be countered by a strong politics. The question is, therefore, now "which type of politics is strong enough to master the new technology and which type of genuine friend-enemy groupings can develop on this new ground" (AND, 141).

It is to this task that Schmitt devotes his essay *The Concept of the Political*. It must accordingly be read as a *political* undertaking aimed at restoring an authentic conception of the political, not as a work of dispassionate scholarship. For, as Schmitt emphasizes: "All political concepts, images, and terms have a polemical meaning," and this polemical character above all "determines the use of the word political" (CP, 30, 32). The polemical target of his undertaking is the imminent threat he perceives to politics itself. He charges, in particular, that modern liberalism signals a dissolution of the political struggle and seeks to replace the state by society: "In a very systematic fashion liberal thought evades or ignores state and politics and moves instead in a typical always recurring polarity of two heterogeneous spheres, namely ethics and economics, intellect and trade, education and property" (CP, 70). He adds that "these dissolutions aim with great precision at subjugating state and politics, partially into an individualistic domain of private law and morality, partially into economic notions. In doing so they deprive state and politics of their specific meaning" (CP, 72). But he assures us at the end of his essay that such efforts will fail because "state and politics cannot be eliminated" (CP, 78). To this he adds in his 1929 lecture that every genuine rebirth (of the kind now required in politics) needs to return to some original principle and must grow silently and in darkness. When it finally manages to become apparent, it will face the inevitable prospect of decline, for "the moment of brilliant representation is also at once the moment in which every link to the secret and inconspicuous beginning is endangered" (AND, 141).

Such formulations must have echoed in Heidegger's mind.[21] One can see this in the later sections of the *Introduction to Metaphysics,* where he seeks to explain the current decline in politics, and the confusions produced by value-theoretic attempts to stem it, in terms of an epochal history of Being. But though he has appropriated Schmitt's historical scheme, he has, at the same time, polemically transformed it from an existential to an ontological account. Where Schmitt describes the neutralization of politics in existential terms as the outcome of an epochal history of modern Europe, Heidegger argues ontologically that an authentic politics must reflect the genuine order of Being, that an appropriate understanding of Being can be found only in the beginnings of Greek philosophy, and that the current decline in politics is the result of a forgetfulness and flattening out of the notion of Being.

For him, the determining fact is that the original Greek understanding of Being is now "rendered unrecognizable" (45). This transformation signals "a fall away from the inceptive inception" of Greek philosophy (144). And there arises, thus, the possibility of a "plunging into what has no way out and has no site: perdition" (124). In Heidegger's history the original Greek understanding of Being as *phusis* was covered up first by Platonic idealism, then by the Christian doctrine of creation, then by the conception of Being as that which is calculable. The outcome is that Being is no longer "what provides the measure" (150). And from this loss there emerges finally the separation of Being and the Ought and the attempt to found a philosophy of National Socialism on the murky assumptions of a philosophy of value. Now, "values provide the measure for all domains of beings" and history becomes "nothing but the actualization of values." With this "the maximum in confusion . . . has been reached" (151). This is because such an account "takes humanity out of the urgency of its essence . . . . Such an appraisal posits the human being as something present at hand, deposits this thing into an empty space, and appraises it according to some table of values that is attached to it externally" (125).

WHAT'S WRONG WITH VALUES

Heidegger's discussion of values in these lectures is too sketchy for the decisive significance he attaches to it, that is, the destruction of the philosophy of value and the mapping out of an alternative vision of the inner truth and greatness of National Socialism. Still, he makes some compelling points and hints at others. What he offers certainly illuminates how he sought to interpret politics philosophically. But it is also of current interest given that talk of values is still pervasive.

Heidegger argues that the introduction of the notion of value is due to a separation of Being and Ought that was foreshadowed by the determination of Being as idea in the Platonic sense. The process came to fulfillment, however, only with Kant, who, in accordance with modern ideas, conceived of beings as "whatever can be determined and is determined in mathematical-physical thinking" (151). To nature, understood in this way, he opposed the categorical imperative determined both by and as reason. Heidegger suggests that Kant's attempt to establish that imperative by means of a transcendental argument proved insufficient. His objections to Kant, barely hinted at in the text, seem to come to this: the categorical imperative demands that we act as rational beings and, hence, on universalizable principles. If, however, we are necessarily and always rational, the formula can have no imperative force. It can only state a natural and universal fact about us. If, on the other hand, we take the formula (more realistically) to have the force of a real injunction, then it must be possible for us to act either rationally or not, and then it tacitly presupposes that being rational is desirable, is a good for us. We may assume that Heidegger would have reasoned similarly against a latter-day neo-Kantian like Jürgen Habermas, who also seeks to ground a moral Ought transcendentally. His point would be that in each case the conclusion proves unstable. If it expresses a real necessity and universality, it can have no injunctive force, and if it has an injunctive force, the Ought, argued for transcendentally, will tacitly presuppose the assumption of a substantive good. Heidegger makes this complex and difficult point very simply and elegantly by reminding us that Kant's followers in the nineteenth century found it necessary to postulate values as a grounding for Kant's categorical Ought. At first, he recalls, they opposed these values to facts by maintaining that they are only valid and have no Being. This proved, however, insufficient to guarantee their supposed objectivity. "Validity is still too reminiscent of validity for a subject. In order to prop up yet again the ought . . . one attributes a Being to values themselves" (151). In other words, the moral imperative's claim to objective authority must be grounded in something else that will need some kind of ontological status, and it is to this consequence that Heidegger's critique of value philosophy addresses itself.

We may find that critique appealing, because an ontology of values has, indeed, few attractions. Both metaphysically and epistemologically, such an ontology strikes us now as implausible. In the light of modern physics and anthropology, we have come to think of what is as material and spatio-temporal and of ourselves as creatures whose senses and capacities have been shaped by interacting causally with the physical world. Nowhere does this picture have room for an ontology of values and, if such a realm existed outside the material and spatio-temporal world, we would have no reasons to consider our organs equipped to discern it. Heidegger did not, of course, subscribe to such a naturalism, but everything we have learned during the last half-century seems to confirm it. The considerations he advanced against the assumption of a realm of values are different, perhaps more "philosophical" in character, though certainly compatible with a naturalistic conception of the world and ourselves. Heidegger's point is this: we consider it necessary to introduce values because Being itself no longer provides the measure. But then, in order to secure their authority, we find ourselves forced to ascribe Being to values. Values turn out to be a particular kind of being. And now we find ourselves in an impasse. For if Being can provide no measure, as we assumed at the outset, then the particular mode of Being that is the Being of values cannot do so either. There remain only two ways out. The first would be to deny nihilistically all significance and meaning; the other is to allow that Being itself can, after all, provide us with measure, that distinctions of position, status, and rank, of the high and the low, are grounded in Being itself. This should not be seen as a relapse into another kind of theory of value according to which value rests in Being itself, but as a fixed and ready-made characteristic. Heidegger's view is, rather, and increasingly so in the course of his lectures, that Being is dynamic in nature and that distinctions of position, status, and rank will open themselves up only in the originary struggle that characterizes Being.

Heidegger's critique of objective values has been a target of attack since he first voiced it in *Being and Time.* After 1933, such assaults came, in particular, from philosophers who sought to ground National Socialism in a philosophy of value and organic unity. Bruno Bauch, one of Heidegger's most politically engaged and most powerful opponents, wrote in 1934 in defense of German nationalism and racism: "Only on the assumption of values that hold supra-individually, generally, and objectively can one speak of the meaning of a folkdom, of a nation as a meaning-structure, can one distinguish between superior and inferior races and nations, can one even make the distinction between good and bad genetic endowment."[22] For Bauch and his followers, Heidegger was not a true National Socialist but a nihilist. For others, opposed to National Socialism, his denial of objective values explained his falling in with the Nazis. This was first charged by Karl Löwith, one of Heidegger's former students, who in 1935 accused both him and Schmitt of an unprincipled, opportunistic, and "occasionalistic" decisionism that was due to their denial of objective values in politics. According to his diagnosis: "What Schmitt defends is a politics of sovereign decision, but one in which content is merely a product of the accidental *occasio* of the political situation which happens to prevail at the moment; hence content is precisely not a product 'of the power of integral knowledge' about what is primordially correct and just, as it is in Plato's concept of the essence of politics, where such knowledge grounds an order of human affairs."[23] Löwith went on to compare Schmitt's analysis of the political with Heidegger's analytic of Dasein, claiming to find an agreement between Schmitt's concept of political Being and Heidegger's existential ontology (ODS, 147, 150). In a later addition to his essay he also spoke of Schmitt's attachment to a "pathos of decision" that had "paved the way for decision in favor of Hitler's decisiveness" and had "made possible political overthrow in the sense of a 'revolution of nihilism'" (ODS, 159). Such a decisionism, he added, was not confined to Schmitt but equally characterized "dialectical theology and the philosophy of resolute existence" (ODS, 160). Löwith's conclusions are clear: Schmitt's and Heidegger's philosophical views are attuned to each other. They are both guilty of an opportunistic decisionism. Their political engagement in 1933 can be fully explained in terms of their failure to recognize absolute values.

This criticism has had a lasting effect on the long and cantankerous debate about Heidegger's politics. What is more, not only Heidegger and Schmitt but also Hannah Arendt and Michel Foucault are today attacked as opportunistic decisionists for their refusal to speak the language of objective value. By the logic of association, even these later thinkers are thereby indirectly tarred with the brush of Nazism. None of these assaults, however, can overcome the inherent philosophical weaknesses of the doctrine of objective value. Löwith and those who follow his banner seek to obscure this by putting before us the following dilemma: either there are absolute norms and values or all actions are arbitrary, all decisions opportunistic. The claim is, however, unsatisfactory on both phenomenological and theoretical grounds. When I act (to take some examples) to assure my survival, to satisfy a need, or to gain a pleasure, I do not thereby choose in terms of objectively existing values. The appeal to values appears in these cases as idle because life, needs, and pleasures have their own motivating and legitimating force. The objection that they cannot have this force by themselves but only in terms of some outside value or norm returns us to the beginning of Heidegger's argument and to his compelling conclusion that values cannot give meaning to beings, if Being itself is without meaning and measure.

Both Schmitt and Heidegger, in fact, rejected the claim that they were opportunistic decisionists. Schmitt complained after the war that the polemical debate had distorted the decision "into an arbitrary act, decisionism into a dangerous ideology, and the word 'decision' into a slogan and term of abuse."[24] Although it is true that for him all political order derives from the making of distinctions between friends and enemies, these are by no means meant to be arbitrary; they are meant to derive, rather, from the reality of preexisting social bonds and alienations. Political notions, as he had said elsewhere, are "not normative but existential" (AND, 134). Heidegger's was an analogous view. He had asked already in *Being and Time* on what basis Dasein discloses itself in its resoluteness and had answered: "Only in what it is to resolve. *Only* the resolution itself can give the answer." And he had insisted that it would be a mistake "to suppose that this consists simply in taking up possibilities which have been proposed and recommended." Human resoluteness had, thus, certainly an "*existentiell indefiniteness*." But, though "resoluteness never makes itself definite except in a resolution; yet it has, all the same, its *existential definiteness*" (SZ, 298). We may take this to mean that human choice is, in

Heidegger's view, not normatively determined by substantive and objective values—this makes resoluteness "existentielly" indefinite—but that there are metaphysical constraints on human resoluteness that derive from the nature of Being itself and, hence, make resoluteness "existentially" definite. This is because an authentic Dasein will have to face "the existence of its Situation," which discloses for it its "current factical possibilities of authentic existing" (SZ, 300, 383). Heidegger takes these suggestions up again in the *Introduction to Metaphysics* where he calls for a genuine struggle "*for* Being *against* Nothingness" (128, translation modified), for a political renewal of the West out of the spirit of early Greek thinking, and for resistance against forms of politics and political thought that would lead to a "plunging into what has no way out and has no site: perdition" (124).

His arguments in 1935, however, not only assail the doctrine of objective value but equally reject Nietzsche's belief in historical and created values. This is decisive for Heidegger's understanding of both politics and creative action in general. He certainly agrees with Nietzsche's critique of fixed, timeless values, but he has no more liking for the idea that values are created by great artists, philosophers, and legislators. He says almost nothing in 1935 about his reasons for rejecting this view. But in his support we can note that Nietzsche clearly misdescribed what artists, philosophers, and legislators do. They do not create values but rather poems and paintings, thoughts and theories, laws and institutions. This may sound like a mere quibbling over words, but it is of the greatest philosophical significance, for works of art, works of thought, and works of politics are, of course, in this world; they are historical in character; they are certainly not standards and measures that exist outside the world, but they are also not created "values" that can be used to judge whatever is. A particular historical poem may set a tone that will sharpen the ears of other and later poets, a particular historical painting may exhibit a style that will change the way later painters see, a philosophical thought may prove so exemplary that a whole epoch begins to think in its terms, a political order may seem so attractive that whole societies will seek to adopt it. But this does not mean that the poem, the painting, the thought, the order have now become values. It means, rather, that these concrete and particular creations have the power to serve as paradigms for other creations. And as paradigms they stand before us not in the role of judges, not as something we *must* imitate, but as something that permits and makes possible new ways of hearing, seeing, and thinking, new ways of accommodating ourselves in the world.

To think in paradigms means to think historically. But historical paradigms allow many different uses. They are not like rules that demand one kind of application. They must be read, interpreted, and brought to life. They may sometimes be objects of imitations, but what they then generate will prove to be dead and without interest. They will produce something vital and new only if we learn to confront them, struggle with them, transform them, and polemically make them our own. *Heidegger's practical thinking in ethics (if you will) and in politics is, in this sense, paradigmatic in nature* and not based on the assumption of transcendental Oughts or of absolute or created scales of values. To live a worthwhile life means, for him, to struggle with history and the paradigms it provides. We can see this mode of thinking clearly at work in the *Introduction to Metaphysics,* where Heidegger draws on the early Greeks—thinkers such as Parmenides and Heraclitus, poets such as Sophocles—as his philosophical and political paradigms. In turning to them, his goal is, however, not to make them the historical standard by which we must measure ourselves. In the early 1940s he would say accordingly, "The Greeks appear in most 'research reports' as pure National Socialists. In their zeal the scholars seem unaware that such 'results' do no service to National Socialism and its historical uniqueness and that National Socialism is not in need of them."[25] National Socialism is, rather, in need of the Greeks as that other with which it has to engage in struggle to find itself, for "Greekness is not equal to and not the same as Germanness" (GA 53, 67). Hence, Heidegger's own continued confrontation with early Greek thought and poetry; hence, also, his willingness to forego philological correctness and his striving for an original appropriation. Heidegger's *Introduction to Metaphysics* is, for that reason, no scholarly treatise on the polemical element in man's political, historical, and spiritual existence; it is an exercise in polemics in which the moderns are confronted with the ancients and in which such creative strife is meant to produce new distinctions of position, status, and rank in what Heidegger perceives to be a flattened-out and measureless world.

What remains attractive in all this is, of course, not Heidegger's attempt to salvage National Socialism. He himself came to see this (belatedly) as a vain effort. It is, rather, the project of an "ethics" that shuns authoritative oughts and goods and sets out, instead, to find particular and historical paradigms to follow—an "ethics," we might say, that envisions possibilities of living rather than injunctions, constraints, fixed and unquestionable blueprints for life. The limit of Heidegger's insight lies in his inability to find historical paradigms anywhere but in early Greece. And that limitation is due, in turn, to his peculiar and never-reasoned belief that only the beginning is great and that only ancient Greece can be such a beginning for Western man.

In drawing on this particular historical paradigm, Heidegger sees himself standing up not only against Germany's foreign enemies, America and Russia, but also against those at home who claim to be speaking on behalf of National Socialism. All these powers "have long determined, dominated, and pervaded our Dasein and keep it in confusion regarding 'Being'" (156). The inner truth and greatness of National Socialism can, however, only be sought in polemical confrontation with these opponents. In this we must come to recognize that "the question of how it stands with Being also proves to be the question of how it stands with our Dasein in history, of whether we *stand* in history or merely stagger" (154). To take a stand, Heidegger says, means metaphysically to concern oneself with such ultimate matters as the notions of Being and nothingness, and this we can do only by going back to early Greek thought. "We are staggering," he writes, "even when, as in recent times, people try to show that this asking about Being brings only confusion, that it has a destructive effect, that it is nihilism" (155). And with a last flourish he declares that "Being must therefore be experienced anew, from the bottom up and in the full breadth of its possible essence, if we want to set our historical Dasein to work as historical" (ibid.).

The lectures break off abruptly at this point, without having fully disclosed a conception of the inner truth and greatness of National Socialism. Heidegger ends, instead, with the admonition that "being able to question means being able to wait, even for a lifetime." What is essential is "the right time, that is, the right moment and the right endurance" (157). The significance of the new national departure, this clearly meant to say, will emerge only through a prolonged philosophical struggle with the question of Being. And with this we are back to the Heraclitean dictum that everything true, great, and original can come about and can be maintained only through cosmic strife. Referring us once more to Nietzsche's characterization of philosophy as untimely, Heidegger concludes his lecture course accordingly with Hölderlin's warning that "the mindful god detests untimely growth" (ibid.).

Chapter 12

HEIDEGGER'S PHILOSOPHICAL GEOPOLITICS IN THE THIRD REICH

THEODORE KISIEL

Heidegger's lecture course of the summer semester of 1935, *Introduction to Metaphysics,* first appeared in a German edition in 1953. In its measured pace and expressive power, its telling examples and hermeneutic exegeses especially of ancient Greek texts, the 1935 lead-in *(Ein-führung)* to metaphysics is one of Heidegger's finest and most crucial courses, the very first course that he published as such. Several late courses were soon to follow under Heidegger's direct editorial control, along with other courses from the Nazi thirties. The ongoing publication of the virtually posthumous Collected Edition (starting in late 1975) promises to provide the full panoply of course-length examples of Heidegger's vaunted teaching. The slightly retouched first edition of the 1935 course manuscript immediately sparked a firestorm of controversy in a postwar Germany divided by the war's aftermath and still very much in the throes of reconstruction and reconstitution. Erupting into a national scandal in the German newspapers, the controversy took its toll especially across the generation gap of postwar university students of West Germany, who were only beginning to learn of the widespread and deep complicity of their teachers in the twelve-year reign of the "millennial" Third Reich. Heidegger's *Einführung* thus served to re-cite the charge raised by the Athenian court against Socrates (and a university committee against Heidegger in 1945) of his complicity as "seducer" *(Verführer)* of the German university youth (thus the "future leaders of the nation") of the thirties in his official capacities as lead teacher of his philosophical seminar and rector-leader *(Führer)* in the German university system. Virtually by Heidegger's own admission (14–15),[1] intro-duction is se-duction deliberately designed to mislead the leaders and readers, to lead them astray into all of the errancy that the term "metaphysics" (if not "Nazism") has historically come to invoke.

Heidegger's public philosophical support of the Nazi regime began at the University of Freiburg in May 1933 with his rectoral address, whose proposals are still cited with approval in the 1935 course. This continuing albeit qualified support is especially manifest in a single sentence near the end of the course that became the focus of the public controversy and national scandal in 1953: "In particular, what is peddled about nowadays as the philosophy of National Socialism, but which has not the least to do with the inner truth and greatness of this movement [namely, the encounter between global technology and modern humanity], is fishing in these troubled waters of 'values' and 'totalities'" (152). By the summer of 1935, virtually all elements of life in Germany, including the university, had been "brought into line" *(gleichgeschaltet)* with the politics and policies of National Socialism. Its totalitarian form of domination allows us to identify the "Germany" of 1935 with National Socialism. This equation of a nation with a tendency or "movement" (not to say "party" or "worldview")—Heidegger stresses the exceptional status of Germany in the polity of nations in this uniquely chauvinistic course—has inevitably led the discussion of the above sentence to a comparison of Germany (= National Socialism = NS = Nazism) with two other modern global responses to planetary technology that Heidegger criticizes in several memorable passages early in the course. The following excerpts are especially telling and are contextualizing for the entire course (and so for the sentence singled out above):

This Europe, in its unholy blindness always on the point of cutting its own throat, lies today in the great pincers between Russia on the one side and America on the other. Russia and America, seen metaphysically, are both the same: the same hopeless frenzy of unchained technology and of the rootless organization of the average man. When the farthest corner of the globe [*Erdball*] has been conquered technically and can be exploited economically; when any incident you like, in any place you like, at any time you like, becomes accessible as fast as you like; when you can simultaneously "experience" an assassination attempt against a king in France and a symphony concert in Tokyo; when time is nothing but speed, instantaneity, and simultaneity, and time as history has vanished from all Dasein of all peoples; when a boxer counts as the great man of a people; when the tallies of millions at mass meetings are a triumph; then, yes then, there still looms like a specter over all this uproar the question: what for?—where to?—and what then? . . . We lie in the pincers. Our people, as standing in the center, suffers the most intense pressure—our people, the people richest in neighbors and hence the most endangered people, and for all that, the metaphysical people. We are sure of this vocation; but this people will secure a fate for itself from its vocation only when it creates *in itself* a resonance, a possibility of resonance for this vocation, and grasps its tradition creatively. All this implies that this people, as a historical people, transpose itself—and with it the history of the West—from the center of their future happening into the originary realm of the powers of be-ing. Precisely if the great decision regarding Europe is not to go down the path of annihilation—precisely then can this decision come about only through the development of new, historically *spiritual* forces from the center. (28–29)

This unabashedly Eurocentric and Germanocentric text—combining the two adjectives, the Frenchman Derrida calls it "central-europo-centric"[2]— reflects, virtually to a cliché, the geopolitics of beleaguered *Mitteleuropa* in the first third of the twentieth century, which quite naturally became the guiding idea of the Nazi foreign policy of expansionism in portraying Germany as the "endangered nation in the middle."[3] But Heidegger transposes this squeezed "German Dasein" in the landlocked viselike grip imposed by the "lay of the land" *(Lage)* of Europe first to the metaphysical level, which means to assize Germany, along with Russia, America, and related geographical entities, "in regards to their world-character and their relationship to spirit" (34). The facticity of geography and the geopolitics that it has induced in the course of the "world history of the earth" (34) become questions of metaphysics by way of the concepts of spirit, spiritual world and the world history of spirit. Geographical location *(Lage)* is thereby transposed into the unique "spiritual position" (*geistige Lage:* 34) in which Germany, "the metaphysical people" most threatened by its abundance of "neighboring" folk, found itself, philosophically and temperamentally, burdened by the traumas of defeat in war and its territorial-economic aftermath. On one front, Germany is threatened by the "spirit of capitalism" (Max Weber's phrase) and, on the other, by its metaphysical kin, the "specter" (the Communist Manifesto's opening line: compare *Introduction to Metaphysics,* 29) of Bolshevism then "haunting" Europe and the entire planet. "But geopolitics conducts us back again from the earth and the planet to the world and to the world as a world *of spirit*. Geopolitics is none other than a *Weltpolitik* of spirit."[4]

Heidegger's portrayal of the decline of the West thus begins with the change in "spiritual position" of the "metaphysical folk," threatening its deracination, that resulted from the "collapse of German idealism" (34). The collapse implicates all of continental Europe in the ensuing "disempowering of spirit" and the "slide into a world that lacked that depth from which the essential always comes and returns to human beings, thereby forcing them to superiority and allowing them to act on the basis of rank" (35). The bleak picture of mass man in a technologically leveled world so prevalent in the early twentieth century has its roots in European scientism, positivism, and other identifiable versions of nihilism incurred by the industrial revolution. But the most extreme forms of revenge afflicting the present age are being exacted by Anglo-American "liberal" utilitarianism and Russian state "regulation and mastery of the material conditions of production" (36), which have gone to "demonic" extremes in this "onslaught of that which aggressively destroys all rank and all that is spiritual about the world [*welthaft Geistiges*], and portrays these as a lie" (35). Since "world is always *spiritual* world," the "darkening of the world" is accordingly a "disempowering of the spirit," which entails its "dissolution, exhaustion, suppression, and misinterpretation" (34). In its full nihilistic detail, this includes "the flight of the gods, the destruction of the earth, turning human beings into masses of 'humanity,' the preeminence of the mediocre [that is, antipathy to the creative and free]" (34, 29).

Heidegger chooses to analyze only the very last phase of this situational happening of technological nihilism, the *misinterpretation* of spirit, in detail, rendering it into four subparts of "spiritual decline" or disempowerment (35–38). This is because "the spiritual decline of the earth has progressed so far that peoples are in danger of losing their very last spiritual strength, the strength that makes it possible even to see the decline and to appraise it as a decline" (29). This capacity to see is the spiritual strength of "willing to know" and "being able to learn" that is necessary for authentic questioning, spearheaded by philosophy. It is the "authentic strength of seeing and questioning and saying" (15–17) that Heidegger had already made central to the "essence of the university" in his rectoral address two years earlier. For the will to know, learn, question *is* the self-assertion of the German university, the way in which it is to fulfill its "spiritual mission" in the service of knowledge for the Reich and its people. The problems facing the German university are from Heidegger's philosophical perspective no different two years later: the global degradation of spirit, through misinterpretation, to "spirit" as utilitarian intelligence (ingenuity of calculative planning), with its "spiritual world" being reduced to "culture," finds its university equivalents of degradation in science as a mere technical and practical specialty and science as a cultural value in accord with standards of production ("for art's sake") and consumption (self-fulfillment, propaganda displays). When the spiritual world becomes culture, it is divided up into regions of distinct values or "symbolic forms," thereby dissolving the original unity and interplay of its spiritual powers, "poetry and fine arts, statescraft, and religion" (36, 34), with thought. The university is no longer an "originary unifying spiritual power exacting obligations from its various faculties in accord with this unity." It is instead the nominal unity of an "arrangement of the amalgam of the specialized sciences in accord with the practical purposes of teaching and research." Heidegger here cites the passage from his 1929 inaugural lecture regarding the purely "technical organization of universities and faculties," which he later recognizes as his earliest expression of concern over the sweeping tide of technology inundating the twentieth century. "In all its areas, science today is a technical, practical matter of gaining and transmitting information" (37).

The will to know, learn, question that is crucial to leading-into philosophy in this university course (1935) as well as to fulfilling the mission of the university (1933), when it is regarded as a "spiritual strength," remains terminologically tied to a metaphysical analysis ("will," "spirit," "power," and so on). But the reversal of the drift toward the disempowerment of spirit simply by seeing through its late modern misinterpretation, along with the reawakening of spirit that the will to question portends, also promises to take us a step closer to the leap into the pre-metaphysical level of radical questioning, toward which this quasi-metaphysical analysis has been pointing since the concrete geopolitical situation presaging the decline of the West was first introduced (25–28). Textually, this takes place just after the middle of the opening chapter (1–49), whose basic aim turns out to be to introduce the fundamental question of metaphysics (Why beings rather than nothing?) by gradually concretizing a more radical prior question (first mentioned on 25) that leads into it. To put the matter simply in the most rudimentary of Heidegger's terms, the leap in questioning toward which the chapter has been moving is across the ontological difference of beings and their be-ing,[5] from metaphysics (the science of beings as a whole) into its ground in be-ing. And the concretization that is to bridge the leap is historical human Da-sein (being-here-now), which is in each instantiation mine, or ours when it serves to instantiate a particular people in its particular historical situation, as it by and large does in this geopolitically oriented course. The leap of crisis and decision, of radical transition—and as essentially temporal (ek-static = non-static) and *historically* situated, Dasein is transitional through and through—is executed by the basic turning action of open resoluteness or resolute openness (*Ent-schlossenheit:* 16). This pivotal existential notion overtly drawn from the analytic of Dasein of *Being and Time* (BT) naturally puts a more concretely situational and fundamentally ontologi-cal, therefore a less traditionally metaphysical and epistemological, accent on the terms of the historical decision posed by the threatening demise of the West. Resolute openness is the originary human response to the epochal hap-pening of the decline of be-ing from its great inception as it is concretely encountered in the present situation of action. "Whoever wills, whoever lays his or her whole Dasein into a will, *is* resolute. . . . Open resoluteness is not a mere final resolution to take action, it is the decisive inception of action that reaches ahead of and through all action" (16). Heidegger sometimes called it the protoaction of letting-be. In a bracketed addendum that postdates the course, Heidegger interjects a bit more of the deep ontology of temporal truth implicit in BT: "But the essence of open resoluteness lies in the unconcealed-ness [*Ent-borgenheit*] of human Dasein *for* the clearing of be-ing and by no means in the reserving of strength or energy [*Kraft*] for 'activity.' . . . But the relation to be-ing is letting. That all willing should be grounded in letting is a thought that is offensive to common sense" (16).[6] This is the clearest statement in the published text of the lecture course of the disengagement of the proto-practical action of resolute openness, understood as responsiveness to the de-mands exacted by the unique historical situation of be-ing in which we find ourselves (in formulae of receptivity such as "listening to the call of conscience" and "letting beings be"), from metaphysically misleading activist terms such as "will to power" and "strength/energy."

Yet Heidegger's "Nazi" period, with a press that celebrated the "triumph of the will" and resurgence of the "German spirit," from 1933 to 1935 teems with examples that mix the discourses of an activist metaphysics of spirit and the crisis ontology of the be-ing of Da-sein. In a striking bit of intertextualizing that suddenly frames the situation of the university in 1933 between the analytic of Dasein of 1927 and the geopolitically historical analyses of 1935, Heidegger cites a pivotal statement from the rectoral address that for him distills the "essence of spirit" from the late modern misinterpretations that have rendered it impotent, thereby preventing it from rejoining a "history of archaic be-ing" now drifting toward oblivion: "Spirit is neither empty acuity, nor the noncommittal play of wit, nor the boundless pursuit of rational dissec-tion, nor even world reason, but rather spirit is originally attuned, knowing, open resoluteness to the essence of be-ing" (37–38). Spirit is no longer a vaporous impotence but concrete Da-sein in its full potential-to-be, *Seinkönnen:* an attuned letting-be of the facticity of its situation of action (Dasein's protoaction), a deep protopractical insight into the situational wholeness in which it finds itself (Aristotle's φρόνησις), decisive acceptance of the concrete vocation or mission that it offers, culminating in a pursuit of the evolving historical sense of that situation (a *Be-sinnung:* 41, 70, 91, 156) wherever it might lead, by way of basic questioning and the radical "willingness to learn" essential to philosophy. In 1933, concrete spirit is the resolute "will to the essence" of the university, where science is a questioning of the whole of beings and truth is the violence of unconcealment. In 1935, the resolute questioning of be-ing is "one of the essential fundamental conditions for awakening the spirit, and thus for an originary world of historical Dasein, for subduing the danger of the darkening of the world and taking over the historical mission of our people, the people of the center of the West" (38). In 1933, the originary and constant decision of a people is "between the will to greatness and the acceptance of decline: which is to become the law of the tempo of the march that our people has begun into its future history?"[7] In 1935, the path-dividing question is "whether [historical] be-ing is to remain a mere vapor or whether it is to become the fate of the West" (38).

The question of be-ing posed by our Da-sein is, accordingly, no abstraction. Here and now, in 1935, it is posing itself concretely in the form of a global challenge to centrally positioned German Da-sein. The concrete historical question of be-ing arising from and for unique German Dasein has already surfaced at the climax of the re-cited passage pervaded by the aura of "hopeless frenzy of unchained technology" and reads: "What for?—where to?—and what then?" (29). This is the historical form that the question of be-ing takes when it is "brought into connection with the fate of Europe, where the fate of the earth is being decided, where for Europe itself our own historical Dasein proves to be the center" (32). Heidegger therefore looks to Germany, "this land of poets and thinkers," this "holy heart of peoples" (Hölderlin), the "metaphysical people" (29) in its currently "squeezed" historical position in beleaguered Central Europe and now under National Socialist rule, to respond concretely to this nonantiquarian, urgent historical question of nonvaporous be-ing, a question whose position and bearing are now "directly defined from the history of the earth's spirit" (32), which is the spirit of late modernity. Its very questioning stands and maintains itself in the happening of Da-sein (the Germany of 1935) "in its essential relations" and so "questions out of this happening and for this happening," for its "futures to come" (34). Resolution of this crisis of the European spirit falls especially on the metaphysical folk at the center to assume its philosophical leadership in Europe by pursuing the essentially *philosophical* mission of a uniquely German National Socialism, where, for the Heidegger of 1935, its "inner truth and greatness" lies. The dark diagnosis of the times is countered by a bright prognosis only by way of the radical prescription that dictates the repetition of the "great inception" (133, 137, 145–146) of European Dasein's happening in Greek Dasein "more originally" (30, 146) in order thereby to transform itself into "another inception" (29).

Is this another revolution by way of the "Greece-Germany axis"—as some have ironically dubbed it in this "geopolitical" context—to supplement the political revolution begun in January 1933? Indeed. In the first week of the course, Heidegger sizes up this hope for a second, more philosophical revolution within a transformed German university by taking his bearings from the first upheaval two years earlier, still a fresh experience for his auditors. The context is the obvious uselessness and untimeliness of a philosophy that endlessly asks the larger questions of sense and direction: radical, thus untimely, and yet necessary questions like "What for?—Where to?—What then?"

> One says, for example, that since metaphysics did not contribute to preparing the *Revolution,* it must be rejected. That is just as clever as if someone were to say that, since one cannot fly with a carpenter's bench, it should be thrown away. Philosophy can never *directly* supply the forces and create the mechanisms and opportunities that bring about a historical state of affairs, if only because philosophy is always the direct concern of the few. Which few? The ones who transform creatively, who unsettle things. It spreads only indirectly, on back roads that can never be charted in advance, and then finally—sometime, when it has long since been forgotten as originary philosophy—it sinks away in the form of one of Dasein's truisms.
>
> Against this first misinterpretation, what philosophy can and must be according to its essence, is this: a thoughtful opening of the avenues and vistas of a knowing that establishes measure and rank, a knowing in which and from which a people conceives its Dasein in the historical-spiritual world and brings it to fulfillment—that knowing which ignites and threatens and compels all questioning and appraising. (8)

An honorific title bestowed on German professors in the Second Reich and borne by some of Heidegger's teachers, for example, Paul Natorp and Edmund

Husserl, was that of *Geheimrat,* privy counselor. Prominent thinkers such as Max Weber and Max Scheler had recently played dominant roles as government counselors, joining a long line of German intellectuals going back to Goethe and the Humboldt brothers. Heidegger, as a world-renowned professor of a state university in the "land of poets and thinkers," had, ever since his assumption of the rank of rector or "spiritual leader" of the "life of the Mind *(Geist)*" in the Third Reich, some philosophical counsel that he wanted to impart to the Führer, whom he ranked among the few "creative transformers," the potential creator of a new German Reich, virtually on the same level as the nation's poets and thinkers. The unlikely dialogue between "statesman" and "thinker" never took place, and Heidegger was no longer rector, but in 1935 he was obviously still trying to make his counsel known in the public domain of the state university. Now almost as a warning against impending disaster in a time of world upheaval that begged the larger question "What for?—where to?—and what then?," he was intent on imparting the "longer view" of originary philosophy on the avenues and vistas open to German Dasein, to his students from the university podium and to his colleagues in committee meetings, private seminars, and other venues available to him.[8]

The practical uselessness of the longer view of philosophy, raised as an accusation against Heidegger's ontology by narrow-minded party functionaries, is an old plaint. "Uselessness" has even been eagerly assumed as an honorific title by the traditional "perennial philosophy" of "eternal" truths, which accordingly regards itself as "timeless." But Heidegger's revolution in philosophy is precisely the displacement of this perennial philosophy by a philosophy that finds its priority in a wholly temporal and historical Dasein, "being here and now for so long." It thus takes its starting point in the Great Fact of Life in its irrevocable finitude, in the basic experience of already finding oneself ineluctably under way in life and situated in a world not of one's own making and yet called upon to make it, in the unique and urgent human situation of my and our having to be here-and-now at this time within the bounds of its allotted temporal stretch: the Dasein of an individual and, especially in this lecture course, the Dasein of a people, of a state, of a historical world. (53: "But today the We is what counts. Now it is the 'time of the We' [*Wirzeit*] instead of the I. We are. What be-ing do we name in this sentence?") Despite its overtly temporal and historical orientation, such a philosophy still finds itself to be *un*timely in regard to its own times, as Hölderlin and Nietzsche did in theirs. Its larger view of the historical situation does not and never can find "an immediate resonance in everydayness" (7), for example, in the day-to-day *Realpolitik* of National Socialism in which Rektor Heidegger failed so miserably. The urgent philosophical questioning that arises from the full scope of the Dasein experience is always untimely in regard to everyday concerns, because it "either projects far beyond its own time, or else binds its time back to this time's earlier and *inceptive* past" (6). The larger temporal view of philosophy will always be too "visionary" and out of phase, too useless in the narrow time span of the practical world of everydayness:

> But what is useless can nevertheless be a power—a power in the rightful sense. That which has no direct resonance [*Widerklang*] in everydayness can stand in innermost harmony [*Einklang*] with the authentic happening in the history of a people. It can even be its prelude [*Vorklang*]. What is untimely will have its own times. This holds for philosophy. Therefore, we cannot determine what the task of philosophy in itself and in general is, and what must accordingly be demanded of philosophy. Every stage and every inception of its unfolding carries within it its own law. (7)

Heidegger clearly regarded the Revolution of 1933 as an "authentic happening" of the German people as well as a European event of world magnitude, in its conservative contrariness on a par with the French Revolution of 1789. He was deeply engaged in amplifying the resonances of his own philosophy of Dasein, itself born of the aftermath of World War I, that are in "innermost harmony" with this "happening" of "German self-assertion." The formal ontology of Dasein, in its inception drawing its examples from questions of existential self-identity, now begins to raise questions of historical group identity. Dasein applied to a people now assumes a nationality (German Dasein, Greek Dasein) and seeks to situate itself as a nation and to define its unique place within a world polity. We shall conclude this re-citing of the 1935 course with a quick look at a pair of its more prominent examples of a "political" ontology, each bearing on the creative art of statecraft concerning which Heidegger was seeking to develop some untimely philosophical advice.

In the first of two litanies on the many senses of the word "is," in which the examples tend toward the institutional, that is, forms of "objective spirit" à la Hegel[9] (a high school, a church door, a painting in a museum), one example in particular is reflective of the political "realities" of the institution called "Germany" in 1935: "A state—it *is*. What does its be-ing consist in? In the fact that the state police arrest a suspect, or that in a ministry of the Reich so and so many typewriters clatter away and record the dictation of state secretaries and ministers? Or 'is' the state in the discussion between the Führer and the

English foreign minister? The state *is*. But where is its be-ing situated, where does it reside? Is it situated, placed, secreted anywhere at all?" (27). Seemingly a random example, left without an answer in the interrogative air of ontological wonder, however much it also remarkably reinforces some of our most enduring stereotypes of the National Socialist state: the terror of a police state under Gestapo rule sustained by an efficient bureaucracy notorious for its thoroughness *(deutsche Gründlichkeit)*, thereby filling archives too voluminous to be completely shredded at war's end, and the ultimate identification of the state with the will of the Führer, his "resoluteness" ("The Führer himself and alone is the present and future German reality and its law," concludes one of Rektor Heidegger's hortatory addresses to "German students").[10] The example recalls two of Max Weber's ideal types of legitimation of state authority: the rational-bureaucratic and the charismatic. The third type, the traditional, is evoked by Heidegger's meditations on Hölderlin's poetic sense of "fatherland" and "homeland." The three together reflect, respectively, the temporal unity of the present, future, and past of the state, its "clearing" of be-ing. But hours later in the course, this example does receive its answer in an extended Greek counterexample which in some of its wording develops a striking resonance with the first example drawn so presciently from the German Dasein of 1935.

Much of the course can be regarded as a linguistic fusion of horizons between German and Greek Dasein, as Heidegger seeks to revive modern German's power to name be-ing and its delimiting correlatives—appearance, becoming, and thinking—which in this course's return to their Greek inception yield its equiprimordial names for be-ing: ἀλήθεια (truth as unconcealing concealing), φύσις (nature as abiding emerging), and λόγος (speech as discriminating gathering). This is a return to the first inception of ontology in the Western language which, "next to German, is at once the most powerful and the most spiritual of languages (in regard to its possibilities of thought)" (43). In the example that we shall now quickly track in its historical sense *(Besinnung)*, it is a matter of restoring the originative power of one of the most influential words in the Greek language, πόλις, the root of the political, its politics, polity, policy, police, and so on in so many Western languages and overly exploited in the politicized time of 1935 (102). In the context of the tragic fate of humanity that is drawn in the foreboding lines of the chorus of Theban elders in Sophocles' *Antigone,* Heidegger finds that πόλις is not merely a geographically located state *(Staat)* or city *(Stadt)* but, more basically, a historical site *(Stätte:* 156) virtually identical to the ontological site of Da-sein in which a unique humankind (for example, Greek being-here, German being-there) "takes place" *(statt-findet, statt-hat),* is "granted stead" (*gestattet* = permitted), and in this "leeway" *(Spielraum)* of allotted time and historical place makes a unique "homestead" *(Heimstatt)* befitting its historical destiny.

The *polis* is the site of history, the Here, *in* which, *out of* which and *for* which history happens. To this site of history belong the gods, the temples, the priests, the celebrations, the games, the poets, the thinkers, the ruler, the council of elders, the assembly of the people, the armed forces and the ships. All this does not first belong to the *polis,* is not first political, because it enters into a relationship with a statesman and a general and with the affairs of state. Instead, what we have named is political, that is, at the site of history, insofar as, for example, the poets are *only* poets, but then are actually poets, the thinkers are *only* thinkers, but then are actually thinkers, the priests are *only* priests, but then are actually priests, the rulers are *only* rulers, but then are actually rulers. *Are*—but this says: use violence as violence-doers and rise to eminent stature in historical be-ing as creators, as doers. Rising to a supreme stature in the site of history, they also become *apolis,* without city and site, lone-some, un-canny, with no way out amidst beings as a whole, and at the same time without statute and limit, without structure and fittingness, because they *as* creators must in each of their situations first ground all this. (117)

The creators of the political are not only politicians but also the apolitical ones. Poets and thinkers, statesmen and prophets are gathered together in unity and lonely, untimely, tragic, and contentious dialogue at this core of history, Da-sein. The very example, Heidegger's choice of Hölderlin's translation of Sophocles' *Antigone,* itself illustrates this unity and peculiar interchange among the creators of the πόλις. To be truly political is to be at the site of history, Da-sein in its root facticity and possibility, which in each of its epochal instantiations is ours here-and-now. The epochal history of the West begins with the ancient Greek Da-sein (retrieved incipiently in the passage above from the Greek tragedy of conflict between family piety and royal ediction) and is now ending in the global epoch of technological geopolitics. In each instantiation of Da-sein, "the human being is then related in an exceptional sense to this pole [of the πόλις], insofar as human beings, in understanding be-ing, stand in the middle of beings and here necessarily have a 'status' in each of their historical instantiations, a stance in their states and their circumstances. Such a 'status' is the 'State.' "[11] Geopolitics is now to be regarded, not geographically or metaphysically, but in its purity as a "site" within the *seynsgeschichtliche* politics of Dasein as it instantiates itself in the epochal history of archaic be-ing, now on the verge of the revolution of a new and radically different inception. This " 'politics' in the supreme and authentic sense,"[12] as the above re-cital shows, thus takes place at the supreme site of radical historical transition displayed by the Greek tragedy, which glosses the oxymoronic status of the tragic heroine (Antigone) as ὑψίπολις ἄπολις, at once far beyond and without home and site, unhomely, lone-some, un-canny, singled out for lofty greatness by creating a new home for her people, as well as for the precipitous destruction that was also the fate of Heidegger's more contemporaneous heroes: Hölderlin, Nietzsche, Van Gogh, and Schlageter.[13] Throughout this "Greek-German mission of transmission [*Sendung*]" (GA 39, 151) across the history of be-ing by way of Hölderlin's translation of Sophoclean tragedy, Heidegger repeatedly alludes to the counteressence of the tragic hero, his hubris in arrogating power (GA 53, 116/93), but without ever truly confronting the inhuman possibilities of this lonesome superiority and uncanny "greatness" that yields another kind of hero, or antihero (Creon, Hitler). The Greek-German mission focuses instead on a repetition of Hölderlin's transmission of a poetic sense of the "fatherland" and the "national" and "home" that Heidegger had originally hoped to find resonating in the folkish mythos of a uniquely German National Socialism and guiding the decisions of the statesmen in the "land of poets and thinkers."

With this rapid rehearsal of Heidegger's other repetitions of Hölderlin's literary work, we have just signaled a need hitherto suppressed in our largely straightforward, synchronic exegesis of the text of *Introduction to Metaphysics (IM)*. Despite its unique insights, *IM* is a transitional text, on the way from Heidegger's rectoral address to his *Beiträge zur Philosophie* (1936–1938), which is purported to be Heidegger's second magnum opus, displacing his first major work, *Sein und Zeit*. The *Introduction to Metaphysics* thus implicitly assumes the findings of post-rectorate courses such as the *Logic* course of SS 1934,[14] which first came to terms with the Dasein of a people in the question "Who are we?," and the Hölderlin course of WS 1934–1935, quasi-geographical in its poetic focus on "The Rhine" and "Germanien," reinforced by the seminar on "Hegel und der Staat." The *Introduction to Metaphysics* anticipates the central theme of the forthcoming *Beiträge* in its passing single mention of "another inception" (29) and in its practice of the "overcoming of metaphysics" by going back to its ground in an epochal "history of be-ing," without calling it that, in its "use" without a single "mention." Thus the themes highlighted in our synchronic rendering of the 1935 course will need to be subjected to a diachronic reading of surrounding texts that would schematize their developmental inter-textual context.

EDITORIAL RECITATIVE

To further frame these themes, we begin with how they were highlighted in the more journalistic intertext that developed in postwar Germany in the first public reaction to some of the troublesome and still politically charged sentences that stood out in this course given in the first years of the Third Reich.

The question first raised in the German press was posed in a hermeneutic mode: "How are we to read sentences from 1935 in 1953?" This question evolved in part into an editorial question that was answered only years later: "Were these the sentences actually delivered in 1935, or do they also incorporate explanatory correctives added in 1953?" This editorial and interpretive battle was perpetuated by Heidegger's letters to the editors of various newspapers, a 1966 journalistic interview published posthumously in the popular news magazine *Der Spiegel* in 1976, and the publication of the original lecture course in the Heidegger *Gesamtausgabe* in 1983 (GA 40).

The first salvo came with a review in the *Frankfurter Allgemeine Zeitung* on July 25, 1953, by the young Jürgen Habermas, in a career-defining move that turns him away from his youthful Heideggerianism toward a lifelong philosophy of modern democracy. As he puts it, "It appears to be time to think with Heidegger against Heidegger" (75/197).[15] Habermas's main concern is with Heidegger's political influence then and now, still verging on the charismatic, in the "formation of the wills of students prone to be excitable and enthusiastic" (67/190), through a philosophical conviction that seemed "to coincide with what would later be expected of them as officers" (74/196). This is because the "conditions established by this technologically determined situation" that modern man and National Socialism, "in its inner truth and greatness," must ineluctably encounter, "are still very much in effect" (74/196: even more "globally" ripened today, we might add). Largely unaware of the rich intertext around the notorious statement of praise that Heidegger couples with blame of a mediocre "fascist intelligentsia" (67–68/191) for perverting "the movement" into a rigid *Weltanschauung,* Habermas nevertheless has access to a few texts that locate this fateful encounter with technology within a history of be-ing, serving to explain not only Heidegger's "errancy" but also that of the Nazi leadership in a way that "takes the place of a moral clarification." This prompts Habermas to ask, in a postwar Germany "in rehabilitation": "Can the planned murder of millions of human beings, which we all know about today, also be made understandable as a fateful errancy within a history of be-ing? Is it not the factic crime of those who, with full accountability, committed it—and the bad conscience of an entire people? Have we not had eight years to assume the risk of confronting what was, what we were? Is it not the foremost task of thoughtful persons to clarify the accountable deeds of the past and keep the knowledge of them alive?" (75/197). This in lieu of the statement on the "inner truth and greatness of this movement" that Heidegger was trying to "peddle" in 1953. (It is only later that we will learn that Heidegger had already, in a talk first given in 1949, placed the "fabrication of cadavers in gas chambers and death camps" on the same level as any other manifestation of global technology.)[16]

A newspaper article quickly appeared in response to Habermas's accusation that Heidegger, by allowing the offensive sentence to stand in his published lecture course, is seeking "to rehabilitate the infamous system of National Socialism philosophically, indeed metaphysically." A more careful reading uncovers other sentences in the course that suggest that Heidegger in 1935 regarded the Hitler regime to be one more symptom of a long history of the demise of metaphysics rather than a "sign pointing to a new salvation." For example, in the famous "pincers" passage, the phrase "when the tallies of millions at mass meetings are a triumph" (29) inevitably had to evoke for its student auditors images of the annual party rally at Nuremberg conducted with great pomp under the banner of "The Triumph of the Will" in German newspapers and newsreels since 1933. And on page 36 of *Introduction to Metaphysics,* we read that the counterfeit of spirit called "intelligence" is perverted not only to the goals of capitalism and communism but also "to organizing and directing the vital resources and race of a people," thus to the goals of the Nazi state, "which Heidegger naturally did not name explicitly, but which was recognizable to all his auditors."[17] Thus the practice of German National Socialism is, already in 1935, "metaphysically the same" as that of Americanism and Russian Communism. The notorious sentence shows that Heidegger found that the NS "philosophers" were a parody and that therefore the NS movement was a characteristic result of the encounter of technology and humanity. "The NS-movement is a symptom of the tragic collision of technology and humanity and, as such a symptom, it has 'greatness,' because its effect reaches out to the whole West and threatens to drag it into decline."

In a letter published in *Die Zeit* on September 24, 1953, Heidegger concurs with this interpretation of the sentence in its connection with other sentences in the course as a "correct characterization of my political bearing since 1934. . . . What could be said then in such a lecture course and what not, how far one could go, can scarcely be grasped today. But I know that those among the auditors who really listened understood quite well what was being said" (GA 40, 232–233).[18]

A similar tack on the disputed passage is taken in a letter that Heidegger wrote to a scholar in Jerusalem in 1968. If one takes the entire course into account, it becomes evident "that my position toward National Socialism at that time was already unequivocally antagonistic. The auditors who understood this lecture course thus also grasped how the sentence was to be understood. Only the party informers who—as I knew—sat in my course understood it otherwise, as well they should. One had to throw these people a crumb now and then in order to preserve the freedom of speech and the freedom to teach" (GA 40, 233). As Leo Strauss has pointed out, freedom of speech in times of oppression and thought control involves the freedom to mislead, that is, the practice of the art of *Tarnung,* camouflage, the cloaking of an esoteric teaching by way of an acceptable exoteric doctrine. In this way, Heidegger could say of his Nietzsche courses from 1936 to 1940 "that every auditor understood them unequivocally as a fundamentally critical 'polemical contestation' of National Socialism" (GA 40, 233).

By 1966 and the *Spiegel* interview, editorial questions about the offensive sentence began to surface publicly. Thus, the editors of *Der Spiegel* ask Heidegger whether its parenthetical remark was already there in 1935 or added just before publication "to explain to the reader of 1953 how you in 1935 saw the 'inner truth and greatness of this movement,' i.e. of National Socialism." Heidegger's unequivocal reply: "It was in my manuscript and corresponded to my sense of technology at the time, but not yet to my later interpretation of the essence of technology as artifactual 'com-posite' [*Ge-Stell*]. I did not read the passage aloud because I was convinced that my auditors would understand me correctly. The stupid ones and the informers and spies understood it differently—as well they might" (204–206/54).[19]

This reply has evoked two corrections, the first an editorial-archival one and the second an extensive correction on the topic of technology in Heidegger's development:

First, each of the three student assistants who worked on the page proofs of *IM* with Heidegger has come forth and flatly contradicted their teacher, noting, moreover, that the sentence in the proofs first contained the phrase "greatness of N. S." before it was finally changed to the "greatness of this movement" and immediately followed by the newly added parenthetical insertion.[20] This is now confirmed by the editor of the *Gesamtausgabe* of the course, who, moreover, reports that the original manuscript page containing the offensive sentence is "missing" (GA 40, 234, 231)!

The correction is as follows: "What is certain is that the explanatory parenthesis was not uttered in 1935 and that—even if he was already 'thinking' it then—Heidegger had in no way made his thoughts on technology explicit for his student audience. . . . Heidegger would surely have required exceptional and divinatory clairvoyance on the part of his students in 1935 if he expected 'those who knew how to listen' to understand a 'profession of faith' made in an unspoken parenthesis!"[21] By 1953, Heidegger had given his talk "Ge-Stell" or "The Question of Technology" more than once, culminating years of commentary on ever-new manifestations of the global thrust of technology with the onslaught of World War II and the subsequent postwar geopolitics. But the first hours of the 1935 course, with the dramatic "pincers" passage, was Heidegger's very first public venture into the topic, with essentially no reference to "the question of technology" between this cluster of texts (chap. 1) and the offending sentence near the end of the course. Subsequent semesters talk of the essence of science as mathematical and not (quite) as technological. It would take Hitler's announcement of the Four Year Plan in September 1936 and the impact that this "total mobilization" of the German military-industrial complex, tacitly in preparation for a total war in four years, would have on the universities before we find the first true evidence of wholesale, albeit (as usual) discreet, resistance to state policy and planning on the part of Heidegger. This resistance is sustained by a full-scale deliberation-of-sense *(Besinnung)* on the essence of science (thus of the university) as technological, that is, of the institution of scientific research as a "business" activity, in which method takes precedence over the domain of objects that is itself being projected by the particular scientific specialty. It is within such a deliberation that the essence of modern metaphysics is seen to culminate in the essence of modern technology.[22]

The courses from SS 1937 hence display increasing concern over the technical organization of the sciences toward useful results for the "benefit of the people and nation" (362/103)[23] and over the "superpower" of technology and the total technical mobilization of the entire planet (451/186). This takes place against the background of the Four Year Plan impacting on the university, whereby even the human sciences are being made into pedagogical tools to inculcate a political worldview, and the "technology of vast libraries and archives" is placed at the disposal of news media and information services or used primarily to avoid unnecessary duplication of costly lab experiments (268/16–17). "Today the major branches of industry and our military Chiefs of Staff have a great deal more 'savvy' over 'scientific' exigencies than do the 'universities'; they also have at their disposal the larger share of ways and means, the better resources, because they are in deed closer to the 'actual'" (268/16, translation modified).

Consternation over the Four Year Plan, especially among the younger faculty members at Freiburg, led to a series of "working meetings" among them, independent of the party-sanctioned discussions of the matter, beginning in the fall of 1936. Heidegger took over such a working session meant especially for instructors in the natural sciences, mathematics, and medicine in 1937–1938, launching it on November 26 with a keynote lecture titled "The Threat to Science."[24] Long before the external threat of the Four Year Plan, there has been an internal threat to science that comes from itself in its modern modality, in its giving of primacy to method over its matter, which has led to the progressive technization and specialization of the sciences to the detriment of their relation to their domain of beings. The resulting threat of groundlessness is only amplified by the "unusual emergency of our people" (8), which confirms the political need for further technical organization. Industry now takes over science, after the American way of scientific pursuit and in competition with it. Scientific organization "is becoming a world process, such that in the future, it is no longer the countries with the richest natural resources, but the countries and peoples with the greatest and most impressive inventions that will seize world leadership" (9). As industry takes over science, science in its fulfilled form of abundantly equipped facilities no longer finds any deep and inner roots within the university. Yet it is not just industry that takes science away from the university, but also the absence of the long overdue "self-assertion of the German university." Self-assertion here does not mean clinging to the past, nor does it mean the political organization of the university, but rather "the will to put itself under question and thereby, and only thereby, to win back its proper task *for itself,* and in a higher form: thus to be the site in which science itself, on the strength of an original knowledge of itself, secures and continually renews and augments itself. This knowledge of itself can only grow out of the communal deliberation-of-sense on the different albeit interrelated domains of science and groups, out of the will to an historically spiritual ground" (10). Without such a self-assertion, the escalating threat to science is further intensified nowadays by the necessity of political education and of the creation of a new generation of leaders in the party. The recent announcement of plans for a new kind of technical supreme school, "with the will of the Führer behind it" (11), need not make the university superfluous, but it will dilute its initiative. With the invention of new departments for the university such as military science, racial science, ethnology, Germanic prehistory, and space research, and the establishment of new chairs in them, "the great will toward a deliberation-of-sense on what is essential will become more and more impossible" (11). But ultimately, the essential threat to science comes not from political measures against it nor from the new utilitarian goals set for it but solely from itself, its inability and unwillingness to renew and transform itself from within.

Heidegger's notes for and from these working meetings turn again and again on the political constellations that relate science to the National Socialist "worldview" (and not the "movement," as in 1935!). One choice example: "There is not even a transformative will for this new organization [of science as a *spiritual* power]. The farcical 550th jubilee celebration at Heidelberg University: forced and inflated without ground and background. And the Führer? Stays away! Instead, on August 16 [1936] he closes the Olympic games in Berlin; on the same day, he organizes the preparations for the Tokyo games! . . . The Olympic games are better suited for foreign propaganda. The sports greats from all lands are courted for their approval—one is more among one's own kind! 'University people' of the old style also know too much" (22). One of his greatest mistakes in the rectorate: "I did not know that the ministry cannot be approached with creative projects and large goals" (24). Now that the "coarse and nonsensical and naive outburst of a 'new *völkischen* science' has totally gone awry," the pendulum has swung the other way. In demanding undisturbed quiet for supratemporal science, one finds a new common ground for compromise: From the side of science, one concedes that there is no such thing as pure theory, that there is room for a worldview. From the side of the *völkischen* representatives, one concedes that one must concentrate work on the "matters themselves," but also that the demand for a worldview is indispensable. Both sides are now saying the same thing, but the compromise thereby diffuses all the forces of questioning that would bring us to "the moment of true inception and a real change" (24). What to do in this stalemate? Running away solves nothing. Best to remain and exploit the possibility of meeting like-minded individuals while willing one's own individuality. "This not to prepare the university—now hopeless—but to preserve the *tradition,* to provide *role-models,* to inspire new demands in one or another individual— somewhere, sometime, for someone. This is neither 'escape' nor 'resignation' but the necessity that comes from the essential philosophical task of the second inception" (24 f.). In this situation, "we must put on the mask of the 'positivists' and be confused with them." We thereby enter into the "circle of the λανθάνοντες [secret ones]. But these *Lanthanontes* can only be those who know that and why they must be secretive. Not the game of the misunderstood or those passed by or the 'longsuffering.' Resignation? No. Blindly agreeing with everything? No. Accommodation? No. Solely *to build for the future*" (25). The university is at the end and so is science, "but this is precisely because philosophy has its second essential inception before itself. That what we have called science is running its course and technologizing itself, perhaps for a whole century, proves nothing to the contrary!" (26). In view of its uselessness, philosophy's university positions and chairs are being reduced or canceled. "But with the abolition of philosophy, the Germans—and this with the intention of fulfilling their essence as a people!—are committing suicide in world history" (27).

With this "total" entry into the industrial and arms race in preparation for war, National Socialism, purportedly in search of geopolitical "living space" and scarce natural resources, has unequivocally placed itself on the same plane as capitalism and communism. The "movement" in search of its uniquely German roots has become, like them, a technological worldview. At this point, Heidegger gives up his fading hope in a difference in the decisions made by narrow-minded party functionaries and by Hitler himself, the statesman whose originative deeds might have created a new state and a higher order. After he develops a more refined sense of the essence of technology as completed metaphysics, Heidegger will characterize Hitler as the supreme technician of a system that is as much imposed on him as manipulated by him, by way of a shrewd calculative thinking totally devoid of any vestige of the deliberation-of-sense required of the statesman.[25] In his first approximation of the metaphysical essence of technology in "The Age of the World Picture," which revisits the pincers passage three years later in order to characterize the situation as a "struggle of worldviews" ("Die Zeit des Weltbildes," 87/134–135), Heidegger identifies the "National Socialist philosophies . . . the laborious fabrications of such contradictory products" (92/140), as among these worldviews (but as usual, discreetly, in an appendix that was not read!). He singles out the phenomenon of the "gigantic" (*das Riesige:* also the "titanic, colossal, mammoth . . . monstrous!") that appears in various guises and disguises in the course of the technological conquest of the "world as picture"— referring not just to the oversized machines but also to the gigantic numbers of atomic physics, annihilation of mammoth distances by the airplane and radio, and so on—and observes that this manifold phenomenon of giganticism cannot be explained by the catchword "Americanism" and its presumed worship of bigness (87–88/135). This is because "Americanism itself is something European" (103/153), and the modern worldviews that come from Europe develop their own gigantic displays . . . "when the tallies of millions at mass meetings are a triumph"! Giganticism is but one of the results of the "global" thrust of modern technology, already manifesting its totalizing consequences in the early twentieth century in global phenomena such as the world war and the worldwide economic depression.

In fact, globalization continues to define the history of the twentieth century, as Heidegger notes in his 1966 *Spiegel* interview (206/54) and as we who managed to survive him to the very brink of the millennium know all too well, at least by way of acclimatization. Is it a sign of Heidegger's thoroughly backward peasant provincialism when he confesses his fright on seeing the first pictures of the earth beamed from the moon by satellites? We now truly have the "world as picture" constructed by human subjects, the lords of the earth. "We don't even need an atom bomb; the uprooting of human beings has already occurred. All we have is purely technological relationships. There is no longer an earth upon which man now lives" (206/55), but only a global *Erdball*, a planet. In the same context (which discusses the key sentences in *IM*), the old Heidegger poses another question that is still quite relevant today, after the fall of the Wall (but not Wall Street), in a time of super-globalization: "How can any political system be coordinated to the technological age, and which political system would that be? I know of no answer to this question. I am not convinced that it is democracy" (206/54). Clearly, terms such as globalization and its totalizing effects, the political, democracy, the earth (local-mythical versus planetary-technical), modern versus postmodern, the world and its worldviews still need clarification and thoughtful coordination. With the emergence of the category of the gigantic, even the favored Heideggerian term "greatness" *(Größe)* has acquired ambiguity in becoming quantitative magnitude (also *Größe*).[26] Is this now Hitler's and so National Socialism's "greatness"? Does the Führer's response to his time thus reach the "stature" (again *Größe*) of the hero of a Greek tragedy? Or is this a travesty of language, its "monstrosity," a parody inflicted by the global inflation of publicity, such that "a boxer counts as the great man of a people" (*IM*, 28)? An examination of the growing Heideggerian intertext is the first step toward clarifying the development of the constellation of some of these basic terms. We conclude with a brief listing of some of the more pressing tasks now made viable by the expanding intertext of publications by and on Heidegger.

INTERTEXTUAL DIMINUENDO

First, a final dimension to the "journalistic" intertext that spells out the immediate sources of influence on Heidegger's passages of 1935. It is only with the world depression of 1929 that Heidegger openly admits the importance to his situation-oriented philosophy of the "higher journalism of our age," whose interpretations "are in part borrowed second- and third-hand and configured into an overall picture" in order to "create the spiritual space" that immediately defines the moods and shapes the decisions of a particular Dasein at a particular time (GA 29/30, 106/71, 114/77).[27] Two of the four examples of the higher journalism that Heidegger reviews in 1929, Oswald Spengler's *The Decline of the West* (1918) and Max Scheler's "Man in the World Epoch of Balance and Compromise" (1927),[28] will have a direct impact on Heidegger's own ventures into "higher journalism," such as the passages in *IM*. In 1930, a "higher journalist" with the gift of literary elegance, the front-line war hero Ernst Jünger, wrote his influential essay "Total Mobilization,"[29] whose title names a trait of global technology first made manifest when World War I became a total war of material attrition; this essay is the prelude to the configuration of the "The Worker" (1932) turned soldier, fated to dominate the globe through technology. In the *Spiegel* interview (196/44), Heidegger also refers to the classical geopolitician of the *Großdeutsches Reich*, Friedrich Naumann, whose reflections sought "to find a national and, above all, a social orientation" for a German identity in Central Europe.[30] All of these dated diagnoses of the early twentieth century imitate the spirit and strategies of Nietzsche's cultural diagnoses to outline a "grand politics done in the grand style."

Heidegger's passing comments on the current events of his immediate times, in the manner and style of a newspaper columnist, proliferate in his lecture courses from the early thirties and continue unabated until the end of his life, especially with each new major advance in science and technology. One recurring and thus obsessive streak, his prejudicially charged remarks on Americanism and its English cousin, liberalism, is worth an article or two: "Heidegger Meets the Ugly Amerikaner."[31]

Some of the themes coursing through the period of the thirties, such as the Dasein of a people and the technologizing of science, receive sustained treatment in the *Beiträge* (1936–1938), despite its aphoristic structure and staccato style.[32] The giganticism of technology is further developed there, its machinations are emphasized, its totalizing tendency is touched on, but globalization is never mentioned. The "political" is mentioned on occasion, but almost always in the inauthentic sense imparted to it by National Socialism and never in relation to the "site of the moment" *(Augenblicks-Stätte)*, its ultimate site in the second inception of Dasein's history of be-ing.

Further work is required to bring out the developing sense of the "political" in Heidegger, from its rhetorical-phenomenological sense in the early twenties,[33] based on Aristotle's *Rhetoric,* to its metaphysical sense around the time of the rectoral address, based loosely on Plato's *Republic,* and its final *seyns-geschichtlichen* sense, based on Sophocles' *Antigone.* Coursing through all three Greek senses of the political would be the theme of *Kampf* (struggle, for example, of worldviews) and "polemic" disputation (*Auseinandersetzung,* also "contention, contestation") as rhetorical, as metaphysical, and as the articulative work-play of the history of be-ing.[34]

The titular guiding thread of this essay, geopolitics, has likewise appeared on these same three levels (a state in its geographical location, spiritual position, and poietic-ontological site). It can now be used as a thread to summarize what we have uncovered. We have re-cited the geopolitical passages in *IM* and glossed them in full philosophical and journalistic detail, first in close proximity to their initial context in the 1935 course, then in the context of the multifaceted controversy that they later ignited over the nature, extent, and duration of Heidegger's involvement in and commitment to the National Socialist state. A close examination of the intertextual context of the mid-thirties reveals that Heidegger is still promoting the European philosophical mission of a uniquely German National Socialism. This would be a National Socialism made aware of its inherited roots and instilled with the unifying ethos[35] of thoughtfulness in a "land of poets and thinkers," prophets and statesmen, and prepared to use the full array of the "natural [spiritual] resources" of its tradition to stem the tide of technology indiscriminately stripping nations of their roots. Conservative of its own roots going back to the Greeks, conscious of its status as a metaphysical folk with the most philosophical of languages (43), and prescient of its mission as philosophical vanguard of the European spirit, an enlightened German people under creative leadership could make its wholly home-grown "movement" of autonomous self-assertion, under way since 1933, into an exemplary bulwark against the disruptive and uprooting new "superpower" of technology, not necessarily by rejecting technology wholesale but by holding it in reserve while subjecting it to a careful deliberation of its historical sense. Clearly, Heidegger's provincial university agenda and Hitler's "world power" agenda for National Socialism were totally at odds. With the entire nation, and especially that "site of science" called the university, placed in the service of the total mobilization of the military-industrial complex in 1936 in preparation for total war, the "movement" goes high-tech and becomes an unbending worldview. As such, it comes into contention with the worldviews of capitalism and communism for the status of dominant world power within the calculative scheme of an abstractive global geopolitics that levels all ethnic uniqueness and its pluralism, even one's own.

Its leaders become supreme technicians and its people the worker-soldiers of a gigantic global artifact. Fundamental questioning and deliberation on the sense and roots of one's home situation are put on hold. As early as 1937, Heidegger can predict, albeit *privatissime,* that "with the abolition of philosophy, the Germans—and this with the intention of fulfilling their essence as a people!—are committing suicide in world history."

Chapter 13

AT THE CROSSROADS OF FREEDOM: ETHICS WITHOUT VALUES

FRANK SCHALOW

We speak of "values" almost uncritically to designate either preferences that are culturally relative or norms that are grounded in the natural order of things. Yet the concept of value that to us is so innocuous was for Martin Heidegger particularly troublesome. If only because of this disparity, Heidegger's treatment of values *(Werte)* in *Introduction to Metaphysics* is among the most puzzling and problematic of any of his writings. Toward the conclusion of this work, he criticizes Nietzsche for his philosophical approach to values and thereby reinforces a suspicion of value-thinking *(Wertdenken)* he demonstrated more than a decade earlier in opposing both Max Scheler's phenomenology and Heinrich Rickert's brand of neo-Kantianism. Heidegger's critique of values unfolds on two fronts. On one hand, he reproaches his contemporaries for embracing value-thinking. On the other, he construes the concern for values as an offshoot of metaphysics, which originates from Plato's idea of the Good and culminates in Nietzsche's philosophy of the will to power. As the forgetting of Being, metaphysics polarizes the "ought" and the "is" and upholds subjectivity as the domain of values in opposition to the valueless sphere of inanimate things ("nature").

Insofar as the turn to values stems from metaphysics, Heidegger criticizes value-thinking as one stage in his overall attempt to "overcome metaphysics." Since he draws a parallel between ethics and metaphysics, the question inevitably arises whether the overcoming of the latter would undermine the possibility of the former. On the contrary, I illustrate how it is possible to reorient ethical inquiry from another direction, that is, by displacing the centrality of the "subject" as the heart of value-thinking. To reopen the question of ethics, it is necessary to uncover its possibility beyond the scope of the moral subject-agent. And the presupposition of ethics, or freedom, must be rediscovered at the historical juncture where Being reveals itself to human existence. I argue that the retrieval of a more original insight into freedom governs Heidegger's critique of value-thinking. This retrieval seeks to prevent either dismissing ethics altogether or subordinating it to ontology. Thus Heidegger's inquiry into ethics reemerges as a path of thought, a signpost to another beginning for philosophy.[1]

This chapter is divided into three sections. I begin by examining the historical factors that shape Heidegger's critique of values. Then I outline the way in which *Introduction to Metaphysics* advances this critique. Finally, I examine the nature of freedom that facilitates an authentic response to the *ethos*, as well as ask about what kind of "governance" Heidegger leaves open, having foreclosed normative ethics in the traditional sense.

Heidegger's approach to values can be considered idiosyncratic, for it deviates from almost every other treatment of that issue, whether viewed from the standpoint of the history of philosophy, of his contemporaries, or even of our worldview. For example, in our American culture we emphasize "personal" and "family" values; we speak of values in a positive sense to suggest certain "priorities" that govern our actions. Although Heidegger does not deny that such priorities are important, he denounces the uncritical acceptance of values, the presumption of their givenness as either culturally determined preferences or norms rooted in the natural order of things. Because of its unquestioning nature, value-thinking can foster an attitude of either relativism or dogmatism. As such, the devotion to values reinforces biases that members of a culture uncritically accept. Given that Heidegger's primary aim in *Introduction to Metaphysics* is to rekindle the question of Being, his effort to criticize value-thinking never becomes more evident than in that work.

In both German culture and in our own, through the appropriation of Max Weber's thought, ethics and values become inextricably interwoven. To denounce values as completely as Heidegger does would seem to leave ethics in a precarious position. How can a philosophy that forsakes all concern for values still address the perennial concern for good and evil? Heidegger's decoupling of ethics and values in this way becomes most ominous in an infamous remark from *Introduction to Metaphysics,* where he distinguishes between the truth of National Socialism and the works of its impostors, which are flawed due to their absorption in values (152). In this context, Nietzsche also bears the brunt of Heidegger's criticism, as he prepares for his extensive dialogue with his predecessor in the late 1930s and 1940s. But whether Heidegger turns a critical eye to the value-theory of his dissertation supervisor, Heinrich Rickert, between 1916 and 1919, or Max Scheler's value-philosophy in the 1920s, Heidegger remains consistent throughout in his assault on values.[2] In *Being and Time* (1927), he refers to values as an attempt to assign or impose significance as opposed to a process of discovering meaning.[3] In the "Letter on 'Humanism' " (1947), he formulates his most concise albeit emphatic rejection of *Wertphilosophie* in stating that "thinking in values is the greatest blasphemy imaginable against Being."[4]

In circumventing the minefield of values, Heidegger finds a constant signpost in his critical appropriation of Kant's thought. Yet this signpost can point in many different directions and can suggest various ways of returning to the origins of Western philosophy. At the outset of his career, Heidegger undertakes a "confrontation" or critical exchange *(Auseinandersetzung)* with his mentor, Rickert, who incorporated an interest in values as the hallmark of transcendental thinking, of a "critical" methodology. Later, Heidegger would defend the so-called formalism of Kant's ethic of the good will against Scheler's criticism of it; Scheler advocated a material ethics of values, a phenomenology of the feelings that displays higher levels of worth. And finally, when Heidegger pits his thinking against Nietzsche's thought of the will to power, the eternal recurrence, and the reevaluation of values, he embarks on a new path to "destroy" the philosophical tradition. By "destroying" the tradition, Heidegger intends to appropriate it in a more radical way, as he first illustrated in his dialogue with Kant in the late 1920s.[5]

To the extent that ethics came to be associated with values, it is not difficult to see why Heidegger refrained almost from the outset from engaging in ethics. Although ethics may not have been Rickert's primary emphasis, his appeal to values reflects an attempt to redesign the philosophical project. Rickert upheld the banner of neo-Kantianism, the "back to Kant" movement at the beginning of the twentieth century that sought to transform Kant's thinking in order to correct the imbalances of positivism. Specifically, Rickert opposed the positivistic attempt to absorb all disciplines into the valueless sphere of natural science. By contrast, he argued that the so-called objective thrust of natural science was still colored by values, and that these values displayed the stream of life from which all inquisitiveness (even into nature) and knowledge emerged. Rickert not only influenced Heidegger but also provided the key for Max Weber to argue in his sociological reflections that value cannot be reduced to fact.[6]

While endorsing the intent of Rickert's project, Heidegger questioned its methodology and fundamental assumptions. According to Heidegger, the shift in the direction of values conceals the *ethos* of ethics by subjecting it to a metaphysical dichotomy already in place: the split between freedom and nature, ought and is. The question that Heidegger raises, however, is not whether a place should be reserved for values but why we should compensate in the first place for construing everything nonhuman, that is, nature, as valueless. According to him, the attempt to upgrade our insight into reality by considering it as value-laden stems from a deficient understanding of Being. We can ask "What is the origin of values?" provided that we recognize that this is only a provisional question. More important, we must consider what changes in our understanding of Being have led to construing nature as a static realm of things, rather than as the dynamic event of self-emerging presence. What changes transpire historically that culminate in polarizing our understanding of Being into the division between fact and value, is and ought, matter and spirit, nature and freedom? In raising these questions, Heidegger indicates that Rickert's attempt to resurrect values only reinforces a prior problem rather than solves it.

In contrast to Rickert and then Scheler, Heidegger undertakes a philosophical investigation that moves in the opposite direction to his contemporaries, namely, the attempt to rekindle the question of Being. This is the enigma that had guided the inquiries of the ancients but subsequently had become dormant. In the face of this forgetting of Being and the forgetting of this very omission, Heidegger develops a plan to "destroy" or to unbuild the layers of philosophical sediment. Rather than emphasizing the spiritual side of humanity in order to uncover the source of values, he formulates a new concept of human being as Dasein to resonate with the Greek experience of nature as self-emerging presence. By the same token, Dasein is not just a natural being, an entity embedded within nature. Instead, Dasein is that being through which the self, nature, and beings as a whole can be revealed both in their emergence into presence and their withdrawal into absence. Dasein is unique not only because it embodies the movement of temporality and exhibits its trajectory (transcendence), but also because it directly participates in the "openness" engendered by the interplay of its temporal ecstases (future, past, and present).[7]

For Heidegger, transcendence is not a religious experience, a surpassing toward a divine being;[8] nor is it a moral issue, a movement toward a higher value, as is the case for Scheler. And yet, it does not necessarily follow that Heidegger's analysis of Dasein's transcendence and its corresponding freedom is devoid of ethical implications. On the contrary, through its self-transcendence, its surpassing of beings-in-totality, Dasein can cultivate a response to the other. Such a response is an extension of its own Being as care *(Sorge),* the structural totality of Dasein. Heidegger suggests that it is Dasein's finitude—the governing of its freedom by its limitations—that first disposes the self to address ethical concerns.[9] The reciprocity between freedom and governance, decision and lawfulness, sets the boundaries in which a concern for the good can first arise.

To be sure, there is an element of formality in this exposition of the good. Yet, as Heidegger argues in his 1930 lectures on Kant, "the essence of the [moral] person, personality, consists of self-responsibility [*Selbstverantwortlichkeit*]," through which we can first experience a concern for others.[10] In Heidegger's terms, the formal element that Kant upheld as the key to all morality—respect for the moral law, self-respect, and respect for others—presupposes the voice of conscience, the call to my own openness that enables me to address my kinship with the other. Insofar as Heidegger recasts Kant's "metaphysics of morals" in phenomenological terms, he upholds the spirit of a Kantian ethic. Correlatively, Heidegger defends Kant against Scheler's charge of "formalism" and maintains that the latter's appeal to values mislocates the concern for the good.[11] As Heidegger states in *Being and Time:* "Even the theory of value [*Werttheorie*], whether it is regarded formally or materially, has as its unexpressed ontological presupposition a 'metaphysics of morals'—that is, an ontology of Dasein and existence."[12]

But what is it precisely about values that inhibits the disclosure of Dasein's Being as care? The answer is not as obvious in Heidegger's thinking as one might suppose. For him, authenticity entails the self-disclosure of care, the revelation of one's own possibilities. In contrast to authenticity, Dasein displays a tendency to "fall," to become absorbed in the concerns of the "they-self." As fallen, Dasein measures its worth or determines its "value" according to a standard of approval or disapproval upheld by the anonymous "crowd." The "they-self" establishes its measure of worth according to external assessments, e.g. social position, power, prestige. In contrast to the authentic self, the "they" assesses worth by appealing to pregiven cultural preferences in reference to which all differences in viewpoints arise. This way of assessing worth according to degrees of approval or disapproval is the "existentiell" root for Dasein's tendency to seek values. In short, the search for values is predicated upon the comparative mentality of the "they-self." Values in this sense reflect Dasein's "subjectivity" and hence its tendency to impose on others arbitrary standards of behavior, for example, the "moral majority."

But what about values that are supposedly "objective," as Scheler emphasizes, values that have an objective basis like God or the Platonic Good? As indicated in the above quotation from *Being and Time,* Heidegger maintains that the subjective and the objective, though significantly different in many respects, are still two sides of the same coin. This is why he still opts for the "formalism" of self-responsibility or acting in accord with one's nature as care, in a way compatible with the Kantian ethic. In this regard, Kantian autonomy as the self-legislation of the law equals self-responsibility. That is, the comportment of the authentic self relinquishes any external guidelines to direct it, since its direction comes from the voice of conscience that cuts through the comparative mentality of the "they-self." In the *History of the Concept of Time* (1925), Heidegger states: "If Dasein in forerunning can bring itself into such an absolute resoluteness, it means that in this running forward toward its death Dasein can make itself responsible in an absolute sense. It 'can' *choose the presupposition of being of itself,* that is it can choose itself. What is chosen in this choice is nothing other than *willing to have conscience.*"[13] Five years later in his lectures on Kant's transcendental philosophy (1930), Heidegger remarks: "Practical freedom as autonomy is self-responsibility, the essence of the personhood of the person, the authentic essence, the humanity of man."[14]

As Heidegger turns his attention to problems posed by science and technology, he resurrects his dialogue with transcendental philosophy in a lecture course delivered in 1935–1936 *(What Is a Thing?).*[15] But within a year, the linchpin of his destructive-retrieval of the tradition shifts from Kant to Nietzsche, whose encounter with nihilism poses a new challenge: the nothingness of a world emptied of meaning and value. Heidegger's *Introduction to Metaphysics,* written in 1935, proves crucial to this transition.

What is the origin of values? On the surface, this seems to be an innocuous question. And yet, all those who have philosophized under the banner of values have failed to ask it in a radical way. Initially, we might turn to ethics in order to find an answer. Yet from Heidegger's perspective, we must consider first what seems almost alien to values, namely, Being itself insofar as our understanding of it arises prior to the schism between ought and is, value and fact. This "origin" does not arise in a vacuum, for the question of Being always unfolds historically through a thinker's belonging to an epoch and the tradition that he or she inherits. Thus, Heidegger investigates the origin of values by traversing the beginning and end of metaphysics, its emergence from Plato's idea of the Good and its consummation in Nietzsche's reevaluation of values.

The fact that a concern for values dominates the end of metaphysics suggests that the relation between Being and values is an inverse one. The emphasis on values implies an indifference toward (the question of) Being, or more precisely, the historical withdrawal of Being prepares the way for an interest in values. Why is this the case? According to Heidegger, values arise with the translation of the dynamic experience of Being into a static concept.

After the pre-Socratics, philosophers such as Plato allow a longing for eternity to govern their understanding of Being, which in turn gives rise to the designation of reality according to an ideal (150). A restricted appearance of Being, or its overdetermination by one dimension of time, namely, the present, prefigures the development of a sense of perfection. Given this penchant for perfection, for the ideal, a standard or exemplar arises in comparison to which all change, becoming, and perishing are deemed imperfect. Insofar as Being manifests itself in terms of time, and the metaphysical tradition misunderstands time as a mere flux that is inferior to eternity, metaphysics subordinates Being to an ideal of perfection. The determination of a standard of perfection constitutes the source of values, which in turn originates from the forgetting of Being, from overlooking the "concealing *projection* of Being upon time."[16] As Heidegger remarks in *Introduction to Metaphysics,* "Plato conceived of Being as idea. The idea is the prototype, and as such it also provides the measure. What is easier now than to understand Plato's ideas in the sense of values, and to interpret the Being of beings on the basis of the valid?" (151).

In *Introduction to Metaphysics,* Heidegger refers to the division between Being and the ought as one of the four "restrictions" of Being (149):

> We need no far-reaching discussions now in order to make it clear that in this division, as in the others, what is excluded from Being, the ought, is not imposed on Being from some other source. Being itself, in its particular interpretation as idea, brings with it the relation to the prototypical and to what ought to be. As Being itself becomes fixed in its character as idea, it also tends to make up for the ensuing degradation of Being. But by now, this can occur only by setting something *above* Being that Being never yet is, but always *ought* to be. [150]

We can see the extent to which Plato's idea of the Good, the exemplar of all exemplars, provides the first step in shifting thinking in the direction of values. In Plato's terms, the Good defines the movement of meta-physics over and beyond nature *(physis),* so as to mark the zenith of a hierarchal scheme by which everything else is measured. As a metaphysical notion that supplies the pattern for all norms, the Good can ground other evaluative principles and moral guidelines.

There is, however, a two-thousand-year interval separating Plato and Nietzsche, a lengthy transition from the objective grounding of norms to the subjective determination of values through the will to power. Plato elevates the supersensuous ideal over its inferior, sensuous counterpart. Nietzsche maintains that the result of this chasm is to empty this world of value in such a way as to cast doubt on the other world's ability to supply the needed guidance. When the otherworldly ideal is shown to be unsustainable, when the idols themselves ring hollow, we enter a climate in which God is dead and nihilism reigns. In the *Will to Power*, Nietzsche defines nihilism as a historical occurrence in which "*the highest values devaluate themselves.*"[17] As a pivotal event in history, nihilism clears the way for rediscovering the sensuous source of evaluation in the affirmation of life, the vitality of desire as will to power.

Whereas Nietzsche criticizes Plato for ushering in the initial phase of nihilism, Heidegger maintains that the two thinkers represent two sides of the same coin, the larger tendency to "forget Being." Far from thinking the origin of values, the unthought source of the Good, Heidegger claims that Nietzsche merely inverts Platonism.[18] Thus Nietzsche in fact perpetuates the problem of nihilism rather than overcomes it. But just as Heidegger seeks a more primeval root of the idea of the Good, so he conceives nihilism in a different way than does Nietzsche. Heidegger understands nihilism as the outgrowth of the forgetting of Being, as a shadow cast by Being's withdrawal that abandons humanity to find meaning in a meaningless world. Herein lies another key development in tracing the origin of values, namely, the metaphysical shift in the direction of the "subject." With the emergence of the subject as the new ground for the determination of beings, the evaluative principle that Plato located in the Good reemerges from the human will. Humanity's will then subordinates beings to its precepts of representation, imposing its design on what can manifest itself.

In relocating the source of both "Being" and values in the will to power, Nietzsche maintains that the basic thrust of his thought is to overcome the metaphysical constructs of the self, free will, substance, and the good, which have plagued philosophy since Plato. According to Heidegger, however, Nietzsche's metaphysics of the will to power unleashes the extreme possibilities of Western philosophy by prefiguring the organization of all beings in the service of technology, the global drive toward control, manipulation, and domination. Insofar as the will wills only itself, that is, its own accrual of power, technology unfolds as the "frame" *(Gestell)* in which the organization and compartmentalization of everything can occur.[19] Yet Heidegger also emphasizes that technology can only emerge within a history that shelters the origin of the West in its concealment and thereby yields to the process of an unconcealment that inscribes each historical epoch. Given this Janus-like character of technology, the interpretation of Nietzsche's thought admits a double gesture. In other words, not only does Nietzsche's thinking constellate all the negative implications of the will, it also points to an alternative way of addressing its corollary phenomenon, namely, human freedom.

In the late 1930s, Heidegger accepts the challenge posed by Nietzsche's thought to develop a new topography of questioning, that is, to view freedom and Being as reciprocal concerns. Accordingly, Heidegger no longer considers freedom to be a possession of the subject. In accord with a new emphasis that first emerged in 1930, he instead relocates the origin of freedom in the ecstatic realm of openness, in reciprocity with the process of unconcealment itself. Freedom can no longer simply be reduced to a specific volition but rather originates within the open expanse of Being, directing whoever decides to participate in this disclosive event. The anthropocentric form of willing that Nietzsche criticizes must give way to a willing which is really a nonwilling, that is, an invitation to participate in openness. In *The Will to Power as Art,* Heidegger points toward a deeper root of the will than Nietzsche recognizes: "Willing proper does not go away from itself but goes beyond itself; in such surpassing itself the will captures the one who wills, absorbing and transforming him into and along with itself."[20] Willing in this sense defers its power to the openness prompting it, rather than reducing its capacity to an addendum of a simple presence to self. The self-aggrandizement of the will to power yields to the dynamics of thrownness, which transposes the will's "power" into the wider compass of the emergence of beings themselves. From as early as *Being and Time,* Heidegger describes this participatory role of de-cision *(Ent-scheidung),* of un-locking the possibilities of a situation, as "resoluteness" *(Entschlossenheit).*

We cannot ignore Heidegger's analysis of resolve in his attempt to reorient ethics from the *ethos* of Dasein's historical situation. Yet at the same time critics from Hans Jonas to Richard Wolin have sought the precarious convergence between Heidegger's philosophy and politics in a strain of "decisionism" found in *Being and Time* (1927).[21] Not surprisingly, eight years later in *Introduction to Metaphysics,* Heidegger addresses the character of historical decision, freedom, and politics in a new way when he begins to question his involvement in National Socialism. In one of the more provocative passages, Heidegger addresses the nature of freedom and decision: "But such essential de-ciding, when it is carried out and when it resists the constantly pressing ensnarement in the everyday and the customary, has to use violence. This act of violence, this de-cided setting-out upon the way to the Being of beings, moves humanity out of the homeliness of what is most directly nearby and what is usual" (128). Freedom cultivates the historical possibilities by which human beings unfold the promise of the future. For Heidegger, the "moment" *(der Augenblick)* of ethical and political decision emerges at the crossroads between future and past. Let us then address Heidegger's concept of freedom insofar as it bears on the danger of his encounter with National Socialism on one hand and on the possibility of ethics on the other.

"No one can leap over his own shadow," remarks Heidegger in observing that Nietzsche never extricated himself from value-thinking. "Because Nietzsche was entangled in the confusion of the representation of values, because he did not understand its questionable provenance, he never reached the genuine center of philosophy" (152). In this provocative way, Heidegger concludes his discussion of values in *Introduction to Metaphysics*. His remarks follow on the heels of questioning the message of National Socialism in light of a recent proliferation of propaganda whose rhetoric is laden with values. Does value-thinking, then, become a universal scapegoat on which Heidegger can blame all aspects of philosophy that he finds objectionable and which allows him to disguise his failure to recognize the destructive nature of National Socialism? Does his wavering on how to redirect ethical inquiry, or how to seek moral guidance apart from any reliance on values as predetermined cultural preferences, suggest a shadow over which Heidegger himself could not leap?

We must recall that Heidegger, like Nietzsche, addresses ethics at that point in history when its crisis becomes most pronounced. Heidegger does not develop another ethical theory but instead brings ethics and its possibility into question.[22] In questioning ethics in this radical way, he evolves new distinctions to address the *ethos* so as to dismantle the conventional concepts that have defined ethical inquiry previously, for example, freedom. As Kant recognized, freedom is the crucial presupposition for morality. Heidegger does not deny this presupposition but instead reexamines freedom insofar as it is divested of any trace of the metaphysical concept of subjectivity. But what then becomes of morality once it has been purged of its concept of agency? For the most part, Heidegger does not explicitly raise this question. But he does point to the dislocation in the ethical problematic in which freedom ceases to be a capability we have and instead becomes a power we receive. This radical shift from freedom as a possession to freedom as an endowment proves crucial in Heidegger's attempt to seek the roots of ethics in the *ethos,* in a way of dwelling in harmony with Being's manifestations. As he remarks in his 1930 lecture course on Kant, "Human freedom henceforth ceases to mean freedom as a property of human being," and instead human being becomes a "*possibility of freedom.*"[23]

The tradition of the Enlightenment construes freedom in its isomorphism with reason, that is, as pure spontaneity, as self-determination. In this regard, Enlightenment figures such as Kant consider freedom primarily along an axis of identity. Heidegger, on the other hand, conceives freedom as the unfolding of a relationship, the reciprocity between Being and Dasein. Insofar as human beings receive the gift of Being's unconcealment, they reciprocate for having been granted this opportunity to participate in the disclosive process. One example of this stewardship occurs when human beings receive the bounty of nature and seek to protect it in all its diversity through ecological awareness.[24] Given this relational dimension of freedom, the power proper to it is one that resides in its allocation. That is, freedom is preserved precisely through its distribution.

But for Heidegger freedom has primarily an ontological meaning. Indeed, the relation between Being and humanity provides the vector for distributing the power of freedom, insofar as the "there" of Dasein provides the historical site for Being's manifestation. There is, however, a dangerous aspect to this portrait, insofar as human being becomes subordinate to Being as a servant to its random disclosure versus a manager of its endowment. If freedom is exclusively a property of Being, then in what sense can it correlate with the ethical and political concerns raised by human beings and designate the possibility of good as well as evil? As Michel Haar remarks: "Therefore a human freedom can exist, but only when the effacement of every practical or theoretical relation to entities will have extracted it from all subjectivity. . . . Yet is not this strange freedom born of the quasi-disappearance of man?"[25] Undoubtably, this ontological thrust in Heidegger's concept of freedom provides fuel for Levinas's criticism that Heidegger subordinates ethics to ontology.[26]

If Heidegger's concept of freedom is to include a social dimension, then a second level for allocating its power must be operative within human choice. Just as Being and thinking occur through their belonging together, so society and individual unfold through a relation of reciprocity. That is, the essential character of freedom as a gift, an endowment for which human beings reciprocate, means that the power of freedom is distributed in the way of sharing, that is, through a partnership between self and other. Put in ethical and political terms, the self is free to the extent that it welcomes, promotes, and safeguards the freedom it has in common with the other.

In section 26 of *Being and Time,* Heidegger points to "authentic solicitude" as that enactment of care by which the self acknowledges its reciprocity with the other by upholding the other's capacity to pursue his or her possibilities. As an extension of freedom, we can describe this act of freedom as "letting be," seeking the other's emancipation in such a way as to let the other be as other.

Despite displaying different aspects of freedom, "letting be" and resolve are not opposing concepts, for letting be can also include the vigilance of resolve as a way of guarding the gift of freedom with which human beings are endowed. Such emancipatory or authentic solicitude develops the differences within a relationship (between self and other) versus a totalizing will to conform as embodied in the "they-self." Insofar as Heidegger accentuates the open dimension of resolve both in *Introduction to Metaphysics* and in his 1936 Schelling lectures,[27] his concept of freedom is already multifaceted, evolving just as his thought does.

Given the polyvalency of his concept of freedom, Heidegger overcomes the traditional dichotomies that impede our understanding of that phenomenon: spontaneity and receptivity, reaction (affect), and action (self-direction). For him, the exercise of freedom may include affects. In letting the other be, freedom is a way of responding to the other through an act of solicitude. Affects are not involuntary reactions but instead are modalities of openness that orient the decisions that we make. Though critical of Scheler's concept of empathy,[28] Heidegger nevertheless recognizes that affects contribute to the facticity of the situation in which human action unfolds. Given this factical orientation, acting translates into a way of responding insofar as Dasein cultivates precisely those possibilities that speak to its current predicament. Choosing is also a way of heeding, for example, the call of the other or the voice of conscience. Thus, the affect of compassion can be an instance of Dasein's ecstatic openness, a way of being attuned to the other's situation. This reciprocal attunement, or way of co-responding to the other, lies at the heart of any ethical awareness.

In summarizing Heidegger's destruction of traditional ethics, we can say that responsibility and responsiveness become co-extensive. Although Heidegger denounces traditional ethics, he leaves open the possibility of an "original ethics," which can foster a cooperative spirit among human beings who view the earth as their common habitat.[29] In order to exist in harmony on the earth, Dasein must reciprocate for having received the gift of freedom. In this way, the self acquires the "power" to choose in proportion with its willingness to safeguard it. The adherence to such proportionality would welcome another measure beyond the subjective assessment of worth through the human will's imposition of values. By developing an original ethics, Heidegger proceeds in his quest to dismantle the philosophical tradition and to redirect thinking toward another beginning.

We can trace Heidegger's destruction of ethics and thereby unfold the ethical implications of his thought. But his reticence about the Holocaust and reluctance to recant his Nazi views, along with his earlier allegiance to the Nazi party in 1933, make us wonder if the above portrait of ethics is a chimera. Given the historical situation of the twentieth century, it becomes difficult to separate ethics and politics. In this respect, can the restoration of a concern for the other implied in a Heideggerian ethic set new parameters for addressing Heidegger's politics? We cannot ignore this question given his infamous remark in *Introduction to Metaphysics* rejecting "Americanism" and democracy as a whole (34–35).

The key message of the economy of freedom lies in developing a climate in which the exercise of freedom implies its guardianship by those who reap its benefits. That is, a pluralistic, "open" society must not only seek maximum participation among its citizens but must also adhere to a governance that protects that freedom. In his 1930 lectures on human freedom, Heidegger maintains that *Auseinandersetzung* is the key to an open dialogue between different thinkers. "*Philosophical confrontation [Auseinandersetzung] is interpretation as destruction.*"[30] Heidegger, of course, sought the roots of philosophy in the prephilosophical wonder *(Erstaunen)* of Being-in-the-world.[31] But the factical corollary of a thinker's membership in a community seems to have escaped him, namely, that philosophical exchange presupposes a political climate of dissent and tolerance—of safeguarding the voice of the other. As our historical and cultural horizons expand, we can recast the key motifs of Heidegger's philosophy within a pluralistic context in a way that he could not envisage. Given that we stand at the crossroads of a new century, we can develop parallels between his description of freedom and the form of democratic governance he so vehemently rejects.

Perhaps recalling the historical distance that separates us from the political crisis of Heidegger's time is part of the challenge we face in undertaking an *Auseinandersetzung* with his thought at the beginning of a new millennium. For the graver the crisis of our age appears to be, the more we can benefit by returning to the historical crucible of Heidegger's ethical and political thinking.

NOTES

Chapter 1. *Kehre* and *Ereignis*

1. *Einführung in die Metaphysik,* GA 40. Hereinafter the various volumes of Heidegger's *Gesamtausgabe* are abbreviated as GA plus the volume number. Citations in these notes frequently refer to texts by page and line. The line count does not include the "header" or any empty lines on the page but does count the lines of section titles.

2. "*Die* Kehre, die eben das Wesen des Seins selbst als das in sich gegenschwingende Ereignis anzeigt": GA 65, §40, 261.25–26. "Das Ereignis hat sein innerstes Geschehen und seinen weitesten Ausgriff in der Kehre": §255, 407.7–8. Compare (1) the *Kehre operative in Ereignis:* "Die im Ereignis wesende Kehre": §255, 407.8 and "die (im Ereignis wesende) Kehre": GA 9, 193, note a = Martin Heidegger, *Pathmarks,* ed. William McNeill (Cambridge: Cambridge University Press, 1998), 148, note a. Compare within GA 65: (2) the *Kehre in Ereignis:* §10, 30.2–3, §13, 34.10–11, §22, 57.10, §141, 262.3–4, §146, 267.12, §197, 320.19, §202,325.9–10, §255, 407.6; (3) the *Kehre of Ereignis:* §190, 311.4, §217, 342.25, §226, 351.22, §227, 354.9–10; (4) the *Ereignis of the Kehre:* §190, 311.13–14; (5) *Ereignis and its Kehre:* "Ereignis und dessen Kehre": §11, 31.18–19, and "Die Er-eignung in ihrer Kehre": §217, 342.22.

3. "Das Denken der Kehre": cited from Martin Heidegger's "Vorwort" (hereinafter cited as "Vorwort") to William J. Richardson, *Heidegger: Through Phenomenology to Thought* (The Hague: Martinus Nijhoff, 1963): xvii.25, 28; "[das] Sagen dieser Kehre": GA 9, 328.3 = *Pathmarks,* 250.3.

4. Compare "eine Wendung. . . , die seinen [d.h. des Denkens] Gang der Kehre entsprechen läßt": "Vorwort," xix.27–28.

5. "Vorwort," xvii.25 (see also Richardson, *Heidegger,* 243, n. 86). Compare "eine Wandlung des Denkens": "Vom Wesen der Wahrheit," GA 9, 187.21–22 = *Pathmarks,* 143.33; and "Wandel des Fragens," ibid., 202.4–5 = *Pathmarks,* 154.18.

6. Richardson, *Heidegger:* "breakthrough": 243.17; "Heidegger I becomes Heidegger II": 254.12; "With EM [*Einführung in die Metaphysik*] Heidegger II has taken full possession": 296.15.

7. Richardson, *Heidegger,* respectively 243.19 and 624.28 ("shift of focus") and xxvi.17 ("reversal").

8. "Auf einen Stern zugehen, nur dieses. / Denken ist die Einschränkung auf einen Gedanken, der einst wie ein Stern am Himmel der Welt stehen bleibt": GA 15, 76.8–11 (Martin Heidegger, *Aus der Erfahrung des Denkens,* 2nd ed. [Pfullingen: Neske, 1965], 7.6–9) = Martin Heidegger, *Poetry, Language, Thought,* trans. Albert Hofstadter (New York: Harper & Row, 1971), 4.8–11. Compare "Jeder Denker denkt nur einen einzigen Gedanken": Martin Heidegger, *Was heißt Denken?* (Tübingen: Max Niemeyer, 1954), 20.24–25 = Martin Heidegger, *What Is Called Thinking?* trans. Fred D. Wieck and J. Glenn Gray (New York: Harper & Row, 1968), 50.5.

9. "Die Kehre ist in erster Linie nicht ein Vorgang im fragenden Denken; sie gehört in den durch die Titel 'Sein und Zeit', 'Zeit und Sein' gennanten Sachverhalt selbst. . . . Die Kehre spielt im Sachverhalt selbst. Sie ist weder von mir erfunden, noch betrifft sie nur mein Denken": "Vorwort," xix.1–3 and 6–8, emphasis added. "Vorwort," xvii.29–31, shows that the pairing "Sein und Zeit" / "Zeit und Sein" does *not* indicate that the *Kehre* was to "take place" between Divisions 2 and 3 of Part 1 of SZ, but only that Division 3, "Time and Being," was to spell out the *Kehre.*

10. The term *die Kehre* made its debut on Thursday, 12 July 1928, in Heidegger's course *Die metaphysische Anfangsgründe der Logik:* GA 26, 201.30, 35 = Martin Heidegger, *The Metaphysical Foundations of Logic,* trans. Michael Heim (Bloomington: Indiana University Press, 1984), 158.30, 34. There it described the transformation (not "overturning"! cf. GA 9, 249.21–29 = *Pathmarks,* 191.8–15) of the received ontology of entities into a meta-ontology or metaphysical ontics (including the metaphysics of Dasein qua ontic), grounded in temporally interpreted being. This transformation is primarily a matter of the movement intrinsic to being-itself, that is, "the clearing" (its emergence as finite); and as early as 1926 Heidegger saw that the articulation of this "turn in being" would require a "change in thinking" ("Vorwort," xix.25–27). Hence *die Kehre* and *die Wendung im Denken* were distinguished from the beginning. By *Beiträge zur Philosophie,* 1936–38, *die Kehre* had attained the settled sense it would keep for the remainder of Heidegger's career, viz., the inner movement of *Ereignis:* cf. GA 9, 193, note a = *Pathmarks,* 148, note a; GA 9, 328.4–11, and note d = *Pathmarks,* 250.4–10 and note d; GA 79, 69.9 (Wandel im Sein) and 71.17 ff. *(Sich-kehren, Kehre, einkehrt, kehrige),* also in *Die Technik und die Kehre,* 38.11, 40.21 ff. = Martin Heidegger, *The Question Concerning Technology,* trans. William Lovitt (New York: Harper & Row, 1977), 38.12, 41.11 ff.; *Vorträge und Aufsätze,* 182.29–30 (II, 56.29–30) = *Poetry, Language, Thought,* 184.4–5. See also the author's "Time and Being, 1925–27" in *Thinking About Being:*

Aspects of Heidegger's Thought, ed. Robert W. Shahan and J. N. Mohanty (Norman: University of Oklahoma Press, 1984), especially 184–186, 192–193, and 208–216.

11. Aristotle laid the basis for these transgeneric ("transcendental") notions in the *Metaphysics* when he asserted both the universality of being (τὸ ὄν καθόλου μάλιστα πάντων: B 4, 1001 a 21) and the fact that being is not a genus (οὐχ οἷόν τε δὲ τῶν ὄντων ἓν εἶναι γένος οὔτε τὸ ὄν: B 3, 998b 22). In keeping with that: (1) Aristotle asserted the convertibility of εἶναι and ἀλήθεια at *Metaphysics* α 1, 993 b 30–31: ἕκαστον ὡς ἔχει τοῦ εἶναι, οὕτω καὶ τῆς ἀληθείας (cf. the Scholastic axiom "ens et verum convertuntur"). (2) He likewise asserted the convertibility of "being" and "one" at I, 2, 1053b 25: λέγεται δ᾽ ἰσαχῶς τὸ ὄν καὶ τὸ ἕν, and at 1054b 13: ταὐτὸ σημαίνει πως τὸ ἕν καὶ τὸ ὄν (cf. "unum convertitur cum ente": *Summa Theologica* I, 11, 1, resp.). At B 3 he argued that although "being" and "oneness" are the two characteristics most predicated of all things (τὸ ὄν καὶ τὸ ἕν . . . κατὰ πάντων μάλιστα λέγεται τῶν ὄντων: 998b 20, 21; cf. I, 2, 1053b 20–21), neither one of them can be a genus of entities (998b 22), because whatever might serve to differentiate each species within that genus (i.e., each "specific difference") would, of course, itself also have the characteristics of being and oneness (ἀνάγκη μὲν γὰρ τὰς διαφορὰς ἑκάστου γένους καὶ εἶναι καὶ μίαν εἶναι ἑκάστην: 998b 23–24), and that would be illogical (cf. *Topics* Z 6, 144a 36–b 11). Therefore, "being" and "oneness" have to be transgeneric. On that basis Thomas Aquinas in *Quaestiones de veritate* (in *Quaestiones disputatae et quaestiones duodecim quodlibetales,* III–V [Turin and Rome: Marietti, 1942]), qu. I, art. 1, responsio (pp. 2–3), spelled out three other transgeneric characteristics of an entity, each of which adds something over and above what "being" ("*ens* [quod] sumitur ab actu essendi") says, not by supplying what is not included in the notion of being but by articulating a mode or manner of being that is not explicitly expressed in the word "being" ("dicuntur addere supra ens, in quantum exprimunt ipsius modum, qui nomine ipsius [sc. 'ens'] non exprimitur"). He argues that this "exprimere" can happen in two ways: secundum quod consequitur omne ens

A. *in se:*
   1. *res:* quidditas/essentia entis
   2. *unum:* indivisio entis
B. *in ordine ad aliud* (or: secundum ordinem unius ad alterum)
   (B.i) concerning "divisio unius ab altero":
       3. *aliquid* ("aliud quid"): divisio ab aliis (as opposed to "indivisio entis")
   (B.ii) concerning "convenientia unius entis ad aliud" (on the presupposition of "aliquid quod natum est convenire cum omni ente," viz., anima):
       4. qua vis appetitiva: *bonum:* convenientia ad appetitum
       5. qua vis cognitiva: *verum:* convenientia ad intellectum.

See also Heidegger's remarks on the analogia entis: GA 33, 26–48 = Martin Heidegger, *Aristotle's Metaphysics Θ 1–3,* trans. Walter Brogan and Peter Warnek (Bloomington: Indiana University Press, 1995), 21–39, and Martin Heidegger, *Schellings Abhandlung über das Wesen der menschlichen Freiheit (1809),* ed. Hildegard Feick (Tübingen: Max Niemeyer, 1971), 233.20–31 = Martin Heidegger, *Schelling's Treatise on the Essence of Human Freedom,* trans. Joan Stambaugh (Athens: Ohio University Press, 1985), 192.28–38. GA 42 omits these notes, which date from ca. 1941. On *verum* and *ens* see GA 65, §225, 349.30.

12. The formulae abound in Aristotle, *Metaphysics* Λ: αὐτὸν δὲ νοεῖ ὁ νοῦς κατὰ μετάληψιν τοῦ νοητοῦ: 7, 1072 b 19–20; ταὐτὸν νοῦς καὶ νοητόν: 7, 1072 b 21; ἔστιν ἡ νόησις νοήσεως νόησις: 9, 1074 b 34–35; νόησις τῷ νοουμένῳ μία: 9, 1075 a 4–5; οὕτως δ' ἔχει αὐτὴ αὑτῆς ἡ νόησις τὸν ἅπαντα αἰῶνα: 9, 1075 a 10.

13. Compare ἀδιαίρετον πᾶν τὸ μὴ ἔχον ὕλην: *Metaphysics* Λ 9, 1075 a 11.

14. Re "accessibility": See GA 65, §210, where Heidegger links *Sein*/ἀλήθεια as the *Unverborgenheit des Seienden* (334.10) with *Sein*/ἀλήθεια in Aristotle as *Zugänglichkeit/Freistehen des Seienden* (333.28–29; cf. 332.23). Re "ability to be of concern": "Im Sein als Anwesen bekundet sich der Angang, der uns Menschen so angeht, daß wir im Vernehmen und Übernehmen dieses Angangs das Auszeichnende des Menschseins erlangt haben": Martin Heidegger, *Zur Sache des Denkens* (Tübingen: Niemeyer, 1969), 23.33–36 = Martin Heidegger, *On Time and Being,* trans. Joan Stambaugh (New York: Harper & Row, 1972), 23.5–8; see also Heidegger's interpretation of "ereignet" as "concerné," i.e., "getroffen, aufgerüht, umschlossen," cited in Jean Beaufret's contribution to *Dem Andenken Martin Heideggers. Zum 26.Mai 1976* (Frankfurt am Main: Vittorio Klostermann, 1977), 13.11–15. Re "significance": One of Heidegger's earliest titles was "das Bedeutsame" (Tuesday, 18 March 1919, Kriegsnot-semester) in the course "Die Idee der Philosophie und das Weltanschauungsproblem": "nicht Sachen mit einem bestimmten Bedeutungscharakter, Gegenstände, und dazu noch aufgefaßt als das und das bedeutend, sondern das Bedeutsame ist das Primäre, gibt sich mir unmittelbar, ohne jeden gedanklichen Umweg über ein Sacherfassen": GA 56/57, 72.34–73.3.

15. "Sein west *als* Erscheinen": GA 40, 108.31; indeed, "nur als Erscheinen": ibid., 147.29–30.

16. On the Greek νοητόν as "intelligible" in the broad sense, see the author's "Nihilism: Heidegger/Jünger/Aristotle," in *Phenomenology: Japanese and American Perspectives,* ed. Burt C. Hopkins (Dordrecht: Kluwer Academic Publishers, 1998), 287, n. 33.

17. The centrality of being as disclosure *(esse ut verum esse)* in the phenomenological tradition was clear from the beginning: see Erich Przywara, "Drei Richtungen der Phänomenologie," *Stimmung der Zeit* 115 (1928), 252–264, esp. 253–254. Heidegger states the thesis: " '[D]as Sein selbst' ist das Sein in seiner Wahrheit, welche Wahrheit zum Sein gehört, d.h. in welche Wahrheit 'Sein' entschwindet": GA 9, 366, note a = *Pathmarks,* 278, note a.

18. "Das Sein als . . . An-wesen geht das Da-sein an": "Vorwort," xix.24–25, emphasis added. See also *Zur Sache des Denkens*, 23.33–36 = *Time and Being*, 23.5–8.

19. Heidegger is clear that being-as-presence does not mean presence to a *subject:* "Das παρά im εἶναι, das Her- und schon bei-wesen meint nicht, daß das Anwesende als Gegenstand auf *uns*, die Menschen, *zu*komme": *Was heißt Denken?* 144.32–33 = *What Is Called Thinking?* 237.21–24. Rather, it means accessibility for possible significance.

20. "Wenn jedoch zum Sein als φύσις das Erscheinen gehört, muß der Mensch als Seiender diesem Erscheinen zugehören": GA 40, 148.15–16 (cf. ibid., 148.8–10). "Zu ihr [= φύσις] *gehört* Vernehmung, ihr [d.h. der φύσις] Walten ist Mitwalten von Vernehmung": ibid., 147.33–34 (cf. 147.22–25).

21. "Sein west *als* Erscheinen" and "nur als Erscheinen": GA 40, 108.31, 147.29–30. But Erscheinen is ἀλήθεια: "in die Unverborgenheit treten": ibid., 147.30. But that is what φύσις is: "das . . . aus dem Verborgenen sich bringen": ibid., 17.18–19; cf. "Anwesen und Erscheinen": ibid., 76.13. Therefore, Heidegger equates the two: "die ἀλήθεια und die φύσις, das Sein als Unverborgenheit": ibid., 129.9–10, 142.5. Compare "φύσις in sich schon ἀλήθεια, weil κρύπτεσθαι φιλεῖ": GA 2, 282, note a; "ἀλήθεια . . . als Grundcharakter der φύσις": GA 65, §186, 306.7; "Hervorkommen-aus-der-Verborgenheit (im Sinn der φύσις)" equated with "das Aufgehen-in-die-ἀλήθεια": GA 15, 331.5–8 = *Vier Seminare*, trans. Curd Ochwadt (Frankfurt am Main: Vittorio Klostermann, 1977), 69.5–8.

22. Compare "Die Wahrheit des Seins und so dieses [Sein] selbst west nur, wo and wann Da-sein": GA 65, §261.22–23, which echoes "Allerdings nur solange Dasein *ist*, das heißt die ontische Möglichkeit von Seinsverständnis, 'gibt es' Sein": GA 2, 281.1–2, and "Sein aber 'ist' nur im Verstehen des Seienden, zu dessen Sein so etwas wie Seinsverständnis gehört": ibid., 244.5–6.

23. "Denn diese [ontologische] Unterscheidung entspringt ja gerade einem Fragen nach dem Seienden als solchem (nach der Seiendheit)": GA 65, §132, 250.21–23.

24. *Leitfrage, Grundfrage:* GA 65, §2, 6.29–30, §34, 75.26–27, 76.8; §193, 313.23–24. Compare "meine Philosophie, die nicht nur, wie alle Philosophie bisher nach dem Sein des Seienden fragt (l'être de l'étant) sondern nach der Wahrheit des Seins (la vérité de l'être)": Heidegger's private letter to Jean Beaufret, 23 November 1945, cited in Martin Heidegger, *Lettre sur l'humanisme*, 2nd ed, ed. and trans. Roger Munier (Paris: Aubier, Éditions Montaigne, 1964), 182.9–13. See "das Denken, das die Wahrheit des Seins zu denken versucht und nicht wie alle Ontologie die Wahrheit des Seienden": GA 9, 380.23–25 = *Pathmarks*, 289.3–4.

25. "Die Frage, inwiefern es Anwesenheit als solche geben kann": *Zur Sache des Denkens*, 77.17–18 = *On Time and Being*, 70.9–10. See also "die vorgängige Ermöglichung der Offenbarkeit von Seiendem überhaupt": GA 9, 114.26–27 = *Pathmarks*, 90.32; "Grund und Zulassung der Seiendheit," GA 68, 51.5.

26. Heidegger, *Was heißt Denken?* 147.19–20 = *What Is Called Thinking?* 241.10.

27. On "the enabling power" *(das Tauglichmachende)* as τὸ ἀγαθόν, see GA 9, 228.10–11 = *Pathmarks,* 175.6–7 (see also Ermöglichen, Ermöglichung: ibid., 228.8, 24 = *Pathmarks,* 175.4, 19). Compare "die Bedingung der Möglichkeit des Seinsverständnisses": GA 24, 405.12–13 = *Pathmarks,* 286.9–10. Concerning ἐπέκεινα τῆς οὐσίας *(Republic* VII, 509 b 9) and the world as "das Umwillen" see GA 26, 203–252 = *Metaphysical Foundations of Logic,* 159–195. On ontological difference: GA 65, §258, 423.27–424.23.

28. *Verhalten:* GA 9, 184.15–22 = *Pathmarks,* 141.22–28. In this passage Heidegger indicates the "intentional" or "revelatory" aspect of such comportment by the phrases "daß [das Verhalten] . . . je an ein Offenbares *als ein solches* sich hält," "offenständig zum Seienden," and "[das] offenständige Bezug." I am grateful to Charles B. Guignon for helpful discussions on this point.

29. In *Being and Time* the "*preparatory* fundamental" question (GA 2, 24.2) was answered in Part 1, Division 1 (and extended into Division 2), whereas the "fundamental question" itself (die Fundamentalfrage: GA 2, passim) was reserved for the unpublished Part 1, Division 3, "Time and Being."

30. "Es gilt, das Da-sein in dem Sinne zu erfahren, daß der Mensch das 'Da', d.h. die Offenheit des Seins für ihn, selbst *ist,* indem er es übernimmt, sie zu bewahren und bewahrend zu entfalten": GA 15, 415.10–13 = *Vier Seminare,* 145.10–13. Compare "être le là": Martin Heidegger, *Zollikoner Seminare. Protokolle—Gespräche—Briefe,* ed. Medard Boss (Frankfurt am Main: Vittorio Klostermann, 1987) 157.7, hereinafter *Zollikon.* See also Heidegger's private letter to Beaufret, in *Lettre sur l'humanisme,* 182.29–184.3; "Der Mensch west so, daß er das 'Da'. . . ist": GA 9, 325.20–21 = *Pathmarks,* 248.11–12; and "[D]as Menschsein als solches [ist] dadurch ausgezeichnet, auf seine Weise diese Offenheit [= das Da] selbst zu sein": ibid., 157.31–32.

31. "Das *Da* [ist] dort [in *Sein und Zeit*] bestimmt als das Offene": *Zollikon,* 188.14–15. On "das Offene" see also GA 9, 184.11, 184.25, 185.29, 187.32, 188.21 = *Pathmarks,* 141.18, 141.23, 142.26, 144.9, 144.22; *Zollikon,* 9.8.

32. "Das Da, die Lichtung": GA 65, §193, 316.27. "Das *Da-sein* als die Wesung der Lichtung": ibid., §73, 297.25. "das 'Da', das heißt die Lichtung des Seins": GA 9, 325.20–21 = *Pathmarks,* 248.11–12; "das Da als Lichtung des Seins": GA 9, 327.14–15 = *Pathmarks,* 249.22–23; "Wie ist das *Da* dort [in SZ] bestimmt als das Offene? Diese Offenheit hat auch den Charakter des Raumes. Räumlichkeit gehört zur *Lichtung,* gehört zum Offenen": *Zollikon,* 188.14–15.

33. "Der Mensch west so, daß er das 'Da', das heißt die Lichtung des Seins, ist. . . . [D]ie Lichtung des Seins, und nur sie, ist 'Welt' ": GA 9, 325.20–21, 326.15–16 = *Pathmarks,* 248.11–12, 248.36–37.

34. " 'Da-sein' bedeutet für mich nicht so sehr 'me voilà!' sondern, wenn ich es in

einem vielleicht unmöglichen Französich sagen darf: être le-là. Und le-là ist gleich 'Αλήθεια: Unverborgenheit—Offenheit": Heidegger's letter to Beaufret, November 23, 1945, in *Lettre sur l'humanisme,* 182.29–184.3; "ἀλήθεια—Offenheit und Lichtung des Sichverbergenden": GA 65, §209, 331.23 (title); "Wahrheit west nur und immer schon als Da-sein": GA 65, §243, 392.20.

35. "Die Lichtung selber aber ist das Sein": GA 9, 332.3–4 = *Pathmarks,* 253.1.

36. "Das Da, die Lichtung als Wahrheit des Seins selbst": GA 9, 336.27 = *Pathmarks,* 256.23–24.

37. "Der Unterschied als Lichtung, als *Ereignis*": *Zollikon,* 242.12–13.

38. Note the concatenation: "Sein, Wahrheit, Welt, S̸e̸i̸n̸, Ereignis": GA 9, 369, note d = *Pathmarks,* 280, note d. Compare the previous note.

39. "Die sinngemäße Betonung im Deutschen statt *Da*sein: Da-*sein*": *Zollikon,* 157.7–8; and "Da-sein heißt in *Sein und Zeit:* da-*sein*": ibid., 188.13–14.

40. See GA 2, 56.12, with note d. As regards the change of *Zu-sein* to *Sein* at GA 2, 56.8, see Edmund Husserl, *Psychological and Transcendental Phenomenology and the Confrontation with Heidegger (1927–1931),* ed. Thomas Sheehan and Richard Palmer (Dordrecht: Kluwer Academic Publishers, 1997), 298 n. 45.

41. Jean Beaufret, *Entretiens avec Frédéric de Towarnicki,* 2nd ed. (Paris: Presses Universitaires de France, 1992), 17.26, 28.

42. Beaufret, *Entretiens,* 17.29–18.15; cf. GA 65, §193, 313.6–11.

43. ὥστε μηδ' αὐτοῦ [i.e., νόου] εἶναι φύσιν μηδεμίαν ἀλλ' ἢ ταύτην, ὅτι δυνατόν (Γ 4, 429 a 21–22), roughly: "so that [in its capacity to receive] there is no nature of/for it [viz., νοῦς] except this: that it is in possibility." I am grateful to Richard Polt for clarifications on this matter and for pointing out that the receptivity of νοῦς does not contradict its nature as ἐνέργεια: cf. ὁ γὰρ νοῦς ἐνέργεια (*Metaphysics,* Λ 6, 1072 a 6).

44. τὸ γὰρ αἰσθάνεσθαι πάσχειν τι ἐστίν (Β 11, 424 a 1) and τὸ νοεῖν πάσχειν τί ἐστιν (Γ 4, 429 b 24–25). The Latin is *pati quoddam:* Thomas Aquinas, *In Aristotelis librum de anima commentarium,* ed. Angelo M. Pirotta (Turin: Marietti, 1925), liber II, lectio XXIII, p. 182 (text) with p. 186 (no. 547), and liber III, lectio IX, p. 236 (no. 720), respectively. On the possibility that the τι is the *object* of πάσχειν rather than an adverbial modifier, see Aristotle, *De Anima,* ed. and trans. Robert Drew Hicks (Salem, N.H.: Ayer, 1976, 1988) (reprinted from the original 1907 edition), p. 412 f.

45. τὸ δεκτικὸν τῶν αἰσθητῶν εἰδῶν (Β 12, 424 a 18) and ἀπαθὲς ἄρα δεῖ εἶναι, δεκτικὸν δὲ τοῦ εἴδους (Γ 4, 429 a 15). For *susceptivus:* Aquinas, *In de anima* liber II, lectio XXIV, p. 187, text ("susceptivus specierum sine materia") with p. 188 (no. 551), and liber III, lectio VII, p. 224, text ("susceptivum speciei") with p. 226 (no. 676: "susceptivam speciei intelligibilis").

46. For example, Thomas Aquinas, *De veritate,* qu. I, art. 1, responsio, p. 3A (Pirotta, ed.).

47. Aristotle makes the point indirectly: καὶ εὖ δὴ οἱ λέγοντες τὴν ψυχὴν εἶναι τόπον εἰδῶν (ibid.).

48. All these constitute *das transcendens schlechthin* (GA 2, 51.9), which holds a place homologous (and only that) to the transcendental in Husserl. Further examples: *Sinn des Seins, Temporalität des Seins, Entwurfsbereich des Seins, Offenheit, Als, Erwesung der Wahrheit des Seins, lichtende Verbergung, Ortschaft* (τόπος), *Sammlung* (λόγος), *Seinlassen* (ποίησις), *Brauch* (χρή), *Unterschied/Unterscheidung* (διαφορά); cf. "verschiedene Namen für dasselbe": GA 65, §209, 331.24; "Die Vielnamigkeit aber verleugnet nicht die Einfachheit": GA 65, §6, 21.33–34. Re "Zeit" as a title for the *Da/Lichtung:* "Zeit als Vorname des Entwurfsbereichs der Wahrheit des Seins. 'Zeit' ist . . . Lichtung des Seins selbst": Heidegger, *Schellings Abhandlung,* 229.4–6 = *Schelling's Treatise,* 188.38–40; "die Er-eignung des Menschen in die Zugehörigkeit zum Sein und seiner Lichtung ('Zeit')": GA 66, 145.24–25; "die Zeit als der Vorname für die Wahrheit des Seins": GA 9, 376.11 = *Pathmarks,* 285.26–27. Re *Ermöglichung:* "Die vorgängige Ermöglichung [= Ereignis/Seyn] der Offenbarkeit [= Sein/Seiendheit] des Seienden": GA 9, 114.26–27 = *Pathmarks,* 90.32. Re *Unterscheidung:* "Die 'Unterscheidung' als Charakter des Seins selbst; es west als unterscheidend, scheidend einigendes": Heidegger, *Schellings Abhandlung,* 216.29 = *Schelling's Treatise,* 178.21–22.

49. GA 65, §133, 251.24, §141, 262.8, §164, 286.31, and §226, 351.22; see also "*die* Kehre, die eben das Wesen des Seins selbst als das in sich gegenschwingende Ereignis": ibid., §140, 261.25–26. On reciprocity (reci-proci-tas) cf. "die herüber und hinüber schwingende Er-eignung": ibid., §242, 381.26–27.

50. "Sagen wir vom Bezug des Menschen zum Seyn und umgekehrt des Seyns zum Menschen, dann klingt dies leicht so, als wese das Seyn für den Menschen wie ein *Gegenüber* und Gegenstand": GA 65, §136, 256.1–4.

51. Heidegger glosses "Sein ist im Entwurf verstanden" (SZ, 147.30–31) with "Heißt aber nicht: Sein 'sei' von Gnaden des Entwurfs": GA 2, 196 note c. See also "Und demnach nicht 'wir' der Ausgang, sondern 'wir': als ausgesetzt und versetzt": GA 65, §144, 265.19–20; and "Das Seyn nichts 'Menschliches' als sein Gemächte, und dennoch braucht die Wesung des Seyns das Da-sein": ibid., §144, 265.30–31.

52. See Heidegger's warning against the hypostasization of Sein/ἀλήθεια: GA 9, 442.21–22 = *Pathmarks,* 334.21.

53. GA 65, §133, 251.24–25. For the same thing expressed in terms of *Zuruf* and *Zugehörigkeit* see ibid., §191, 311.26; §217, 342.21–26; §239, 372.14–15; §242, 380.16; §255, 407.30–31.

54. GA 65, §140, 261.25–26.

55. GA 65, §141, 262.1–3; ibid., §195, 318.22–23.

56. GA 65, §140, 261.29.

57. GA 65, §144, 265.26–27.

58. Heidegger, *Was heißt Denken?* 6.7 = *What Is Called Thinking?* 9.24. See also GA 65, §129, 246.17.

59. "Was sich uns entzieht, zieht uns dabei gerade mit": Heidegger, *Was heißt Denken?* 5.37 = *What Is Called Thinking?* 9.13–14.

60. Heidegger, *Was heißt Denken?* 5.27 = *What Is Called Thinking?* 9.23, where the sentence is mistranslated "Withdrawal is an event," as it also is in Martin Heidegger, *Basic Writings,* rev. and exp. ed. (San Francisco: HarperSanFrancisco, 1993), 374.17.

61. "Was sich entzieht, versagt die Ankunft": Heidegger, *Was heißt Denken?* 5.25–26 = *What Is Called Thinking?* 9.1–2, with "das Sichverbergen ist das innerste Wesen" and "ist wesentlich": GA 15, 343.24 and 28 (= *Vier Seminare,* 81.24 and 28).

62. "Das Seyn aber 'ist' über solches 'Nichts' hinaus nun nicht wieder 'Etwas' ": GA 65, §164, 286.22–23.

63. Heidegger, *Was heißt Denken?* 70.26–28 = *What Is Called Thinking?* 73.31–33.

64. On τέλος as "circle" and "full circle," see Richard Broxton Onians, *The Origins of European Thought* (Cambridge: Cambridge University Press, 1954), 442 ff.; see also the comment at 443, n. 2, on τελεσφόρος ἐνιαυτός (*Iliad,* XIX, 32f., with parallels): "The sense demanded by the various contexts is rather that of a complete year—'full circle.' "

65. This reading of *Schuldigsein* as unovercomeable lack-in-being is based on GA 2, 375.6 *(mangelhaft),* 376.18 *(Nicht-Charakter),* 376.33 and 34 *(Mangelhaftigkeit, Nichtcharakter),* 378.9 *(Nichtcharakter, geworfene, nicht insofern selbst der Grund seines Seins).*

66. Compare " *Wesung* soll nicht etwas nennen, was noch über das Seyn wieder *hinaus* liegt, sondern was sein Innerstes zum Wort bringt, das Er-eignis, jenen Gegenschwung von Seyn und Da-sein, in dem beide nicht vorhandene Pole sind, sondern die reine Erschwingung selbst": GA 65, §164, 286.29–287.2.

67. "Gegenwart im Sinne des Gegenwärtigens": GA 2, 431.31.

68. "Denn Ontologie ist ein Index der Endlichkeit. Gott hat sie nicht": Martin Heidegger, "Davoser Disputation zwischen Ernst Cassirer und Martin Heidegger" in *Kant und das Problem der Metaphysik,* 4th enl. ed. (Frankfurt am Main: Vittorio Klostermann, 1973), 252.30–31 = Martin Heidegger, *Kant and the Problem of Metaphysics,* 4th enl. ed., trans. Richard Taft (Bloomington: Indiana University Press, 1990), 175.35–36.

69. "Der Entzug aber ist des Da-seins . . . der Entzug . . . als die Schenkung": GA 65, §168, 293.9, 16–17; "das Sichentziehende" as "höchste Schenkung": ibid., §129, 246.17–19.

70. "Wir können das mit dem Namen 'das Ereignis' Gennante nicht mehr am Leitfaden der geläufigen Wortbedeutung vorstellen; denn sie versteht 'Ereignis' im Sinne von Vorkommnis und Geschehnis—nicht aus dem Eignen als dem lichtend verwahrenden Reichen und Schicken": *Zur Sache des Denkens,* 21.24–29 = *On Time and Being,* 20.29–33.

71. "Dieser [d.h., der Kehre] eignet keine besondere Art von Geschehen": "Vorwort," xxi.17–18.

72. "Das 'Geschehen' der Kehre, wonach Sie fragen, 'ist' das Seyn als solches": "Vorwort," xxi.16–17. The question that was put to Heidegger is recorded at ibid., xvii.9–11.

73. On the equivalence of *Seyn* and *Ereignis* cf. "Das Seyn aber ist zugleich hier begriffen als *Er-eignis*. Beides gehört zusammen: die Rückgründung in das Da-sein und die Wahrheit des Seyns als Ereignis": GA 65, §195, 318.21–23.

74. "Vorwort," xxi.17.

75. Compare being-unto-death as "Die eigenste, unbezügliche und unüberholbare Möglichkeit": GA 2, 333.32, with "Die Einzigkeit des Todes im Da-sein des Menschen gehört in die ursprünglichste Bestimmung des Da-seins, nämlich von Seyn selbst ereignet zu werden": GA 65, §161, 283.10–12.

76. For προϋποκείμενον, see Damascius, *De Principiis* in *Traité des premiers principes*, ed. Leendert Gerrit Westerink, trans. Joseph Combès, 3 vols. (Paris: Les Belles Lettres, 1986–1991), 3:153.2; or in Damascii Successoris, *Dubitationes et solutiones de primis principiis, in Platonis Parmenidem*, ed. Carolus Aemelius Ruelle (Paris, 1889; reprinted, Amsterdam: Adolf M. Hakkert, 1966), 2 vols., here 1:312.21.

77. See "geworfener"/"er-eignet": GA 65, §122, 239.5; "geworfen"/"er-eignet": ibid., §182, 304.8; and "geworfene"/"zugehörig der Er-eignung": ibid., §134, 252.24.

78. GA 2, 431.13; GA 65, §204, 327.6–7.

79. GA 65, §198, 322.7–8. Compare "Übernahme der Zugehörigkeit in die Wahrheit des Seins, Einsprung in das Da": ibid., §197, 320.16–17.

80. "Die Er-eignung, das Geworfenwerden": GA 65, §13, 34.9.

81. "Die im Ereignis wesende Kehre ist der verborgene Grund aller anderen . . . Kehren, Zirkel und Kreise": GA 65, §255, 407.8–11. Compare "Die gemeine Daseinsauslegung droht mit der Gefahr des Relativismus. Aber die Angst vor dem Relativismus ist die Angst vor dem Dasein." Martin Heidegger, *The Concept of Time* (with German and English texts), trans. William McNeill (Oxford: Blackwell, 1992), 20.15–17 = 20E.14–16.

82. Pindar, Pythian Odes, II, 72, in *The Works of Pindar*, ed. Lewis Richard Farnell (London: Macmillan, 1932), *The Text*, 3:56; and GA 2, 194.3.

83. "Statt des boden- und endlosen Geredes über die 'Kehre' [the scare quotes show that this refers to 'die Wendung im Denken'] wäre es ratsamer und fruchtbar, sich erst einmal auf den genannten Sachverhalt einzulassen": "Vorwort," xix.9–12. Such engagement is ultimately a matter of *Entschlossenheit*, or resolution: "es gilt eine Verwandlung des Menschseins selbst," ibid., xxi.9–10, citing the 1937–38 course, GA 45, 214.18 = Martin Heidegger, *Basic Questions of Philosophy: Selected "Problems" of "Logic,"* trans.

Robert Rojcewicz and André Schuwer (Bloomington: Indiana University Press, 1994), 181.7–8.

84. "Was der Spruch des Parmenides ausspricht, ist eine Bestimmung des Wesens des Menschen aus dem Wesen des Seins selbst": GA 40, 152.30–32 (cf. 149.15–16); "weil das Überwältigende als ein solches, um waltend zu erscheinen, die Stätte der Offenheit für es *braucht*": ibid., 171.32–34; "Wenn jedoch zum Sein als φύσις das Erscheinen gehört, muß der Mensch als Seiender diesem Erscheinen zugehören": ibid., 148.15–16 (cf. 148.8–10). See "So gehört der Mensch notwendig zu-, und hat seinen Ort in der Offenheit (und gegenwärtig in der Vergessenheit) des Seins. Das Sein aber braucht, um sich zu öffnen, den Menschen als das Da seiner Offenbarkeit": GA 15, 370.16–19 (= *Vier Seminare*, 108.16–19); re "gebraucht" as "utilisé," see ibid., 370.11 (= *Vier Seminare*, 108.11).

85. Compare "Zu ihr [= φύσις] *gehört* Vernehmung, ihr [d.h. der φύσις] Walten ist Mitwalten von Vernehmung": GA 40, 147.33–34.

86. "Das Sichverbergen ist das innerste Wesen der Bewegung des Erscheinens": GA 15, 343.24–25 (= *Vier Seminare*, 81.24–25).

87. "Mit dem Ereignis wird nicht mehr griechisch gedacht": GA 15, 366.31–32 (= *Vier Seminare*, 104.31–32).

88. Richardson, *Heidegger*, 247.11.

89. "Vorwort," xvii.19.

90. "Aber diese Wendung erfolgt nicht auf grund einer Änderung des Standpunktes oder gar der Preisgabe der Fragestellung in 'Sein und Zeit' ": "Vorwort," xvii.26–28. See also "Dadurch wird jedoch die Fragestellung in 'Sein und Zeit' keineswegs preisgegeben": ibid., xix.28–29. In "Humanismusbrief" Heidegger had made the same claim, not about *die Wendung* but about *die Kehre:* "Diese Kehre ist nicht eine Änderung des Standpunktes [footnote: d.h. der Seinsfrage] von 'Sein und Zeit'. . .": GA 9, 328.7–8 = *Pathmarks*, 250.7–8.

91. Compare *er-gänzt, Ergänzen, Ergänzung:* "Vorwort," xix.34–36.

92. "Vorwort," xvii.29–31 ("p. 39" refers to SZ, 39.39 = GA 2, 53.22). Compare "Damit wird nicht gesagt, 'Sein und Zeit' sei für mich selbst etwas Vergangenes geworden; ich bin auch heute noch nicht 'weitergekommen,' dies schon deshalb, weil ich immer deutlicher weiß, daß ich nicht 'weiter' kommen darf; aber vielleicht bin ich dem in 'Sein und Zeit' Versuchten um einiges näher gekommen": *Schellings Abhandlung* 229.13–18 = *Schelling's Treatise*, 189.6–9.

93. "Der Entwurf . . . nur Antwort auf den Zuruf": GA 65, §21, 56.12–13; "[der Entwurf als die] Einrückung in das Offene, dergestalt, daß der Werfer des Entwurfs als geworfener sich erfährt, d.h. er-eignet durch das Seyn": ibid., §122, 239.4–5; "die Entwurfung als *geworfene* und das will sagen zugehörig der Er-eignung durch das Seyn

selbst": ibid., §134, 252.23–25; "Im Verstehen als geworfenem Entwurf liegt notwendig gemäß dem Ursprung des Daseins die Kehre; der Werfer des Entwurfs ist ein geworfener, aber erst im Wurf und durch ihn": ibid., §138, 259.30–32; "Ent-wurf . . . als geworfener": ibid., §172, 295.123; "Der Werfer selbst, das Da-sein, ist geworfen, ereignet durch das Seyn": ibid., §182, 304.7–9; cf. ibid., §258, 422.29–31; "Ausgesetztheit als offene Stelle": GA 2, 216, note a; "Da-sein als geworfenem des (Wurfs)": ibid., 244, note a.

94. Richardson, *Heidegger,* xxvi.17.

95. GA 2, 51.9, and note a, which equates this with *Ereignis.*

96. "Die entscheidende Frage (*Sein und Zeit,* 1927) nach dem Sinn, d.h. (S.u.Z. S. 151) nach dem Entwurfbereich, d.h. nach der Offenheit, d.h. nach der Wahrheit des Seins": GA 9, 210.31–32 = *Pathmarks,* 154.12–14. Compare GA 65, §16, 43.25–26.

97. "Leistung der Subjektivität": GA 9, 327.25–26 = *Pathmarks,* 249.31–32. Compare GA 65, §180, 303.22.

98. Homelessness: GA 40, 160.10 ff., 176.2–4, 178.19. Neediness: ibid., 171.32, 176.30, 177.13–14, 178.15, 178.31–32, 181. 23–25, 183.2.

99. "Der fragliche Abschnitt wurde zurückgehalten, weil das Denken im zureichenden Sagen [gloss in note b: Sichzeigenlassen] dieser Kehre versagte [etc.]": GA 9, 328.1–3 = *Pathmarks,* 250.1–3.

Chapter 3. Being as Appearing

1. Friedrich Nietzsche, *Twilight of the Idols,* trans. R. Polt (Indianapolis: Hackett Publishing, 1997), " 'Reason' in Philosophy," §4.

2. For example, Heidegger's "On the Essence and Concept of Φύσις in Aristotle's *Physics* B, 1," trans. T. Sheehan, in *Pathmarks,* ed. W. McNeill (Cambridge: Cambridge University Press, 1998). Thomas Sheehan has explored Heidegger's vocabulary of movement and its Greek roots extensively, for example, in his entries on Heidegger in the Routledge *Encyclopedia of Philosophy* (1998) and the *Companion for Philosophers,* ed. R. Arrington (Oxford: Blackwell, 1998).

3. For a clear and succinct exposition of these points, see Thomas Sheehan, "Nihilism: Heidegger/Jünger/Aristotle," in *Phenomenology: Japanese and American Perspectives,* ed. B.C. Hopkins (Dordrecht: Kluwer Academic Publishers, 1998): 273–316, especially 288–89.

4. See the essays in this volume by Susan Schoenbohm and Charles E. Scott.

5. The term "Dasein," as I understand it, refers to the fact that there is a (finite) understanding of Being. On the assumption that humans are the only beings with an understanding of Being, Dasein appears in, or at least arises only where there are, humans. Having an understanding of Being (i.e., being the opening in which beings can show up) is humanity's most essential trait: as Heidegger says, "Humanity is the Here that is

open in itself. Beings stand within this Here and are set to work in it. We therefore say: the Being of humanity is . . . '*Being-here*' ['Dasein']" (*Introduction to Metaphysics,* 156). But even though Dasein occurs only where there are humans, it would be wrong to suppose that Dasein is simply a synonym for "human." Humans (as we know them, at least) are individuals, have subjectivity, band together into collectives, have bodies, are male or female, eat, reproduce, and so on; Dasein has none of these traits. Even to speak of our capacity for *selfhood* "does not mean that humanity [insofar as it is Dasein] is primarily an 'I' and an individual . . . any more than it is a We and a community" (ibid., 110).

6. Martin Heidegger, *Zur Seinsfrage* (Frankfurt am Main: Klostermann, 1956), 28, 27; translated as *The Question of Being* by J. T. Wilde and W. Kluback (New Haven: Twayne Publishers, 1958), 77, 75. Both are cited in Sheehan, "Nihilism," 293.

7. Ferdinand de Saussure, *Course in General Linguistics,* trans. W. Baskin (New York: McGraw-Hill, 1983); Ludwig Wittgenstein, *Philosophical Investigations,* trans. G. E. M. Anscombe (New York: Macmillan, 1958).

8. Ludwig Wittgenstein, *On Certainty,* trans. G. E. M. Anscombe and G. H. von Wright (New York: Harper & Row, 1972), 21.

9. Martin Heidegger, "The Origin of the Work of Art," in *Poetry, Language, Thought,* trans. A. Hofstadter (New York: Harper & Row, 1971), 42; hereafter cited as OWA.

10. Harold Bloom, *Shakespeare: The Invention of the Human* (New York: Riverhead Books, 1998).

11. Hans-Georg Gadamer, *Truth and Method,* trans. J. Weinsheimer and D. G. Marshall (New York: Crossroad, 1989).

12. GA 65, 68.

13. Given this view of the dual nature of humans, Heidegger's Dasein seems to be a prime example of what Foucault called the "empirio-transcendental doublet" of modernity: humans as *both* the source of the clearing in which entities can show up *and* one entity among others within that clearing. See Michel Foucault, *The Order of Things: An Archaeology of the Human Sciences* (New York: Vintage, 1973). Whether this dual nature of Dasein entails the extreme sort of instability Foucault sees as characteristic of the modern concept of "man" is yet to be decided.

14. Sheehan, "Nihilism," 288–89 and passim.

15. See Heidegger's "On the Essence and Concept of Φύσις in Aristotle's *Physics B,* 1," esp. 215–17. On page 217 of this essay Heidegger clarifies the concept of "end" as follows: " 'End' is not the result of stopping the movement, but is the beginning of movedness as the ingathering and storing up of movement."

16. Martin Heidegger, *Plato's "Sophist,"* trans. R. Rojcewicz and A. Schuwer (Bloomington: University of Indiana Press, 1997), 158.

17. The adage is found in the citation from Pindar in *Introduction to Metaphysics*, 77, and in the shortened, Nietzschean form in SZ, 146.

18. Friedrich Nietzsche, *The Gay Science*, trans. R. Polt, in *Existentialism: Basic Writings*, ed. C. Guignon and D. Pereboom (Indianapolis: Hackett Publishing, 1995), §290.

19. Paul Ricoeur has worked out the implications of Heidegger's conception of Dasein for narrative in *Time and Narrative*, trans. K. Blamey and D. Pellauer (Chicago: University of Chicago Press, 1984–1988) and in *Oneself as Another*, trans. K. Blamey (Chicago: University of Chicago Press, 1992). Alasdair MacIntyre develops the conception of human life as a narrative in *After Virtue* (Notre Dame: University of Notre Dame Press, 1981). See also my "Narrative Explanation in Psychotherapy," in *American Behavioral Scientist* 41 (January 1998): 558–577.

20. Charles Guignon, "Truth as Disclosure: Art, Language, History," in *Heidegger and Praxis*, ed. T. J. Nenon, 1989 Spindel Conference, *Southern Journal of Philosophy* Supplement 29 (1990): 105–120.

21. As is well known, the word *Ereignis*, the ordinary German word for "event," signifies considerably more than event in the writings of the later Heidegger: it is designed to capture all the richness of a notion of "event of appropriation." Nevertheless, the details of this crucial concept are not relevant in this context.

22. Martin Heidegger, *What Is a Thing?*, trans. W. B. Barton Jr. and V. Deutsch (Chicago: Henry Regnery, 1969), 26.

23. Ernst Tugendhat, *Der Wahrheitsbegriff bei Husserl und Heidegger* (Berlin: de Gruyter, 1967); see also Tugendhat's "Heidegger's Idea of Truth" in *The Heidegger Controversy: A Critical Reader*, ed. R. Wolin (Cambridge: MIT Press, 1993): 245–263.

24. See, e.g., *Being and Time*, §44; "The Essence of Truth," in *Basic Writings*, ed. D. F. Krell (New York: Harper & Row, 1977); "The Origin of the Work of Art," especially pp. 53–54, as well as the passages in *Introduction to Metaphysics*.

25. See Bernard A. Williams, *Descartes: The Project of Pure Enquiry* (Atlantic Highlands, N.J.: Humanities Press, 1978).

Chapter 4. The Question of Nothing

I thank Gregory Fried, Charles Guignon, and Thomas Sheehan for their generous comments on this chapter.

1. Martin Heidegger, "What Is Metaphysics?" in *Pathmarks*, ed. William McNeill (Cambridge: Cambridge University Press, 1998), 96.

2. See, e.g., GA 65, 111–12, 183, 293, 425–26. Briefly, Heidegger's point is that as an *abstraction* from beings, the concept of beingness takes beings for granted and presupposes a Platonic metaphysics of universals.

3. See, e.g., GA 65, 76–77. I thank Thomas Sheehan for pointing out the importance of this distinction for this essay.

4. For the rendering of *Seyn* as "be-ing," see Martin Heidegger, *Contributions to Philosophy (From Enowning)*, trans. Parvis Emad and Kenneth Maly (Bloomington: Indiana University Press, 1999), xxii–xxiii. I gratefully adopt Emad and Maly's solution but capitalize "Be-ing" in order to fit our translation of *Sein* as "Being" in *Introduction to Metaphysics.* The translations from the *Contributions* in this essay are my own.

5. In 1969 Heidegger says, "the fundamental thought of my thinking is precisely that Being, or the manifestation of Being, *needs* human beings and that, vice versa, human beings are only human beings if they are standing in the manifestation of Being": "Martin Heidegger in Conversation," in *Martin Heidegger and National Socialism: Questions and Answers,* ed. G. Neske and E. Kettering (New York: Paragon House, 1990), 82.

6. *Das Nichts* is a vexing term to translate. Heidegger uses it, instead of the ordinary negative pronoun *nichts,* when he wants to indicate that he is considering some issue that is relevant to the problems of Be-ing or the Being of beings, in various ways that we explore below. (He also sometimes capitalizes *Nichts* but does not use the definite article, as in his formulations of the "why-question.") "Nothingness," the most idiomatic English rendition of *das Nichts,* inappropriately suggests an abstraction or an essence. "The nothing" and "no-thing" are awkward. The capitalized "Nothing" might suggest some supernatural force. Still, in our judgment, "Nothing" is the least bad solution. I will adopt the same convention for referring to other thinkers' philosophically significant conceptions of Nothing, even when they differ from Heidegger's. I use the expression "the Nothing" at the beginning of sentences.

7. To cite a few examples, Sartre combined Heidegger's language with Hegel's to develop his own description of freedom and consciousness in terms of Nothing. Those who saw Heidegger as a pessimistic thinker took his references to Nothing as evidence of nihilism. Analytic philosophers scoffed: what greater logical error can there be than to suppose that "nothing" refers to something? More recently, postmodernists have embraced Heidegger's critique of the "metaphysics of presence" and explored Nothing as absence, ungroundedness, or otherness.

8. The meaning of the term "finitude" should not, of course, be taken as self-evident. (At one point, Heidegger warns us that the expression "finitude of Being" is simply an anti-idealistic figure of speech: GA 65, 268; cf. GA 66, 87–88.) In other words, "finitude" must be interpreted in its specifically Heideggerian context. For another reading of Heidegger in terms of "finitude," see Jean Grondin, *Sources of Hermeneutics* (Albany: State University of New York Press, 1995), 61–81.

9. For a meticulous survey of negation and Nothing in Western philosophy, see G.

Kahl-Furthmann, *Das Problem des Nicht: Kritisch-Historische und Systematische Untersuchungen*, 2nd ed., Monographien zur philosophischen Forschung, vol. 56 (Meisenheim am Glan: Anton Hain, 1968). This valuable work, first published in 1934, is at a loss when it comes to explicating Heidegger (307–312).

10. Parmenides, fr. 2. My references to the pre-Socratics will follow the standard Diels-Kranz fragment numbers. On the difficulties of interpreting this fragment, see Leonardo Tarán, *Parmenides* (Princeton: Princeton University Press, 1965), 33–40, and Ernst Tugendhat, " 'Das Sein und das Nichts,' " in *Durchblicke: Martin Heidegger zum 80. Geburtstag* (Frankfurt am Main: Vittorio Klostermann, 1970), 135–146.

11. The phrase "Being is" (*estin gar einai,* fr. 6)—a solecism in Heideggerian terms—suggests that Parmenides did not recognize the "ontological difference" between Being and that which is. This ambiguity infects Greek thought as a whole, according to *Introduction to Metaphysics* (23–24). On the ontological difference, see, e.g., Heidegger, *The Basic Problems of Phenomenology,* trans. Albert Hofstadter (Bloomington: Indiana University Press, 1982), 17, 319. For Heidegger's further interpretations of Parmenides, see GA 54; *What Is Called Thinking?,* trans. J. Glenn Gray (New York: Harper & Row, 1968), pt. 2, lectures 5–11; "Moira (Parmenides VIII, 34–41)," in *Early Greek Thinking,* trans. David Krell and Frank Capuzzi (New York: Harper & Row, 1975).

12. Sometimes Parmenides speaks of "nonbeing," in the ambiguous sense (*mē eon,* fr. 2, 8; *ouk eon,* fr. 8); at other times, he speaks of "the things that are not" (*mē eonta,* fr. 7), "(the) nothing" (*mēden,* fr. 6; *to mēden,* fr. 8), "not-Being" (*mē einai,* fr. 2) or "is not" (*ouk esti,* fr. 8).

13. "For to think and to be is the same" (fr. 3). "It is the same to think and the thought that it is; for without being, in what has been said, you will not find thinking" (fr. 8, ll. 34–36).

14. See Patricia Curd, *The Legacy of Parmenides: Eleatic Monism and Later Presocratic Thought* (Princeton: Princeton University Press, 1998).

15. Heidegger's interpretation of the *Sophist* in a lecture course of 1925 (GA 19) is one of his most important and detailed readings of ancient philosophy; on nonbeing as otherness, see esp. 548–573. For his account of a related passage in the *Theaetetus,* see GA 34, 271–277.

16. This is the theme that started Heidegger on his philosophical path when he read Brentano's *On the Manifold Meaning of Being According to Aristotle:* see "My Way to Phenomenology," in *On Time and Being,* trans. Joan Stambaugh (New York: Harper & Row, 1972), 74.

17. *Met.* N 2, 1089a 26–28. On falsehood and nonbeing, see also *Met.* Δ 29.

18. On being as both actuality *and* potentiality, see *Met.* Δ 7, 1017b 1–9. See also Aristotle's arguments against the Megarians, who reject potentiality altogether: *Met.* Θ 3. Heidegger's comments on this text can be found in his *Aristotle's Metaphysics Θ 1–3,*

trans. Walter Brogan and Peter Warnek (Bloomington: Indiana University Press, 1995), chap. 3. (For Descartes, in contrast, "potential being . . . strictly speaking is nothing": Third Meditation, AT 47, in *Selected Philosophical Writings,* trans. John Cottingham et al. [Cambridge: Cambridge University Press, 1988], 95.)

19. See, e.g., Thomas Aquinas, *Summa Theologica,* pt. 1, 17, 4. Cf. Aristotle's concept of *steresis,* e.g., *Met.* Γ 2.

20. In his *Liber de Nichilo* (1510), Charles de Bovelles makes the intriguing proposal that it is strictly impossible for God to do away with Nothing by replacing it entirely with being. The being that would result would be infinite, for it would actualize all possibilities—and thus would constitute an impermissible rival to God Himself: *Le livre du néant,* trans. Pierre Magnard (Paris: Vrin, 1983), 88. In short, "Just as God cannot be emptied by beings, Nothing cannot be filled by beings" (90). On Bovelles's interesting essay and its influence on a lively discussion of Nothing in seventeenth-century Italy, see Stanislas Breton, *La pensée du rien* (Kampen: Kok Pharos, 1992), chaps. 1 and 2. In Breton's judgment, "without having to reify the *nichil,* [Bovelles] was able to give it the sense and importance of a function that is as indispensable to thought as the zero is in mathematics" (33).

21. Thomas Aquinas, *De Veritate,* 3, 4, 6; *Summa Theologica,* pt. 1, 48, 2–3.

22. See Pseudo-Dionysius Areopagite, *The Divine Names and Mystical Theology,* trans. John D. Jones (Milwaukee: Marquette University Press, 1980). This thought is repeated by commentators on Dionysius (including Aquinas) as well as by Scotus Erigena and Nicholas of Cusa. For a discussion and references, see Jean-Luc Marion, "Nothing and Nothing Else," in *The Ancients and the Moderns,* ed. Reginald Lillly (Bloomington: Indiana University Press, 1996), 189, 194–195; Kahl-Furthmann, *Das Problem des Nicht,* 352–357. For a contemporary revival of this motif, see Jean-Luc Marion, *God Without Being,* trans. Thomas A. Carlson (Chicago: University of Chicago Press, 1995).

23. Meister Eckhart, *On Detachment,* in *Selected Treatises and Sermons,* trans. J. M. Clark and J. V. Skinner (London: Faber & Faber, 1958), 167 (translation modified); quoted in John D. Caputo, *The Mystical Element in Heidegger's Thought,* rev. ed. (New York: Fordham University Press, 1986), 15. The Eckhartian ideal of "releasement" *(Gelassenheit)* is adopted by Heidegger in his later thought; Caputo explores this connection in depth. Other figures in the German mystical tradition, such as Angelus Silesius and Jacob Böhme, express similar thoughts on Nothing.

24. Descartes, *Selected Philosophical Writings,* 99 (Fourth Meditation, AT 54).

25. Blaise Pascal, *Pensées,* trans. A. J. Krailsheimer (Harmondsworth: Penguin, 1966), 90 (translation modified).

26. "For he who says that he apprehends a figure, thereby means to indicate simply this, that he apprehends a determinate thing and the manner of its determination. This

determination therefore does not pertain to the thing in regard to its being; on the contrary, it is its non-being. So since figure is nothing but determination, and determination is negation, figure can be nothing other than negation": Spinoza, *The Letters*, trans. Samuel Shirley (Indianapolis: Hackett, 1995), 260 (Epistle 50).

27. The four meanings are (1) "the object of a concept to which no assignable intuition whatsoever corresponds . . . *(ens rationis)*"; (2) "the absence of an object, such as shadow, cold *(nihil privativum)*"; (3) "the mere form of intuition, without substance . . . pure space and pure time *(ens imaginarium)*"; (4) "the object of a concept which contradicts itself . . . *(nihil negativum)*." Immanuel Kant, *Critique of Pure Reason*, trans. Norman Kemp Smith (New York: St. Martin's Press, 1965), 295 (A290–291/B347–348). Further references to this text will be parenthetical. For Heidegger's comment on this passage, see *Kant and the Problem of Metaphysics*, 4th ed., trans. Richard Taft (Bloomington: Indiana University Press, 1990), 98–99.

28. Hölderlin, for example, speaks in *Hyperion* (1797) of "that Nothing which rules over us, who are thoroughly aware that we are born for Nothing, believe in a Nothing, work ourselves to the bone for a Nothing, until we gradually dissolve into Nothing": quoted by Michael Hamburger in Friedrich Hölderlin, *Poems and Fragments*, trans. Michael Hamburger, 3rd ed. (London: Anvil Press, 1994), xxi.

29. On negation and dialectic, see, e.g., *Hegel's Science of Logic*, trans. A. V. Miller (New York: Humanities Press, 1969), 54–57. Heidegger focuses on negativity in his "confrontation" with Hegel of 1938–1939 (GA 68, 1–61).

30. Sheer Being, lacking all specification, is tantamount to Nothing. Thus, "*Pure Being* and pure *Nothing* are . . . the same": Hegel, *Science of Logic*, 82 (translation modified). Parmenides' position is consequently a "simple and one-sided abstraction": *Science of Logic*, 83. Cf. Hegel, *Encyclopedia Logic*, §87. For Heidegger's comments on this saying, see "What Is Metaphysics?" in *Pathmarks*, 94–95, and GA 68, 19–21. See also P. Christopher Smith, "Heidegger, Hegel and the Problem of das Nichts," *International Philosophical Quarterly* 7 (1968): 379–405. (Schopenhauer, like Hegel, prefers determinate negation: "the concept of *nothing* is essentially relative, and always refers to a definite something that it negates": *The World as Will and Representation*, trans. E. F. J. Payne [New York: Dover, 1966], 1:409.)

31. G. W. F. Hegel, *Phenomenology of Spirit*, trans. A. V. Miller (Oxford: Oxford University Press, 1977), 117, ¶194.

32. Søren Kierkegaard, *The Concept of Dread*, trans. Walter Lowrie, 2nd ed. (Princeton: Princeton University Press, 1957), 38–39 (translation modified). Heidegger echoes this passage at SZ, 187.

33. Jacobi leveled a charge of nihilism at Fichte in 1799 and apparently invented the word. See Wolfgang Janke, *Fichte: Sein und Reflexion—Grundlagen der kritischen Vernunft* (Berlin: Walter de Gruyter, 1970), 30–36.

34. Friedrich Nietzsche, *The Will to Power*, ed. Walter Kaufmann, trans. Walter Kaufmann and R. J. Hollingdale (New York: Random House, 1967), 9. For Heidegger's interpretation, see his *Nietzsche*, vol. 4, *Nihilism*, trans. Frank A. Cappuzzi, ed. David Farrell Krell (San Francisco: Harper & Row, 1982).

35. Friedrich Nietzsche, *Twilight of the Idols*, trans. Richard Polt (Indianapolis: Hackett, 1997), 21 (" 'Reason' in Philosophy," §6, translation modified).

36. Ibid., 19 (" 'Reason' in Philosophy," §4). In *Introduction to Metaphysics,* Heidegger takes this statement as the culmination of a tradition that has forgotten its own roots and as a challenge to rediscover the lost meaning of Being (27–28, 66).

37. A classic instance of this approach is Rudolf Carnap, "The Elimination of Metaphysics Through Logical Analysis of Language" (1932), in *Logical Positivism* , ed. A. J. Ayer (New York: Free Press, 1959). We consider Carnap's attack on Heidegger below.

38. On linguistics and the question of Being, see Gregory Fried's contribution to this volume; on Heidegger's critique of logic, see the chapter by Daniel Dahlstrom. For an interesting critique of attempts to analyze Nothing by means of formal logic, see Stanley Rosen, *The Limits of Analysis* (New York: Basic Books, 1980), 129–142. An earlier version of Rosen's argument can be found in his "Thinking About Nothing" in *Heidegger and Modern Philosophy,* ed. Michael Murray (New Haven: Yale University Press, 1978), 116–137.

39. Reinhard May, *Heidegger's Hidden Sources: East Asian Influences on His Work,* trans. Graham Parkes (London: Routledge, 1996), chap. 3; Graham Parkes, "Rising Sun Over Black Forest," in May, *Heidegger's Hidden Sources,* 87–92.

40. Martin Heidegger, "A Dialogue on Language Between a Japanese and an Inquirer," in *On the Way to Language,* trans. P. D. Hertz and J. Stambaugh (New York: Harper & Row, 1971), 19.

41. There is, however, some conflict within Hindu tradition about the status of nonbeing. "In the beginning this world was merely non-being": *Chandogya Upanishad* 3.19.1, in *The Thirteen Principal Upanishads,* trans. R. E. Hume, 2nd ed. (Delhi: Oxford University Press, 1985), 214. But "How from Non-being could Being be produced? On the contrary . . . in the beginning this world was just Being, one only, without a second": *Chandogya Upanishad* 6.2.2, in ibid., 241.

42. For brief explanations, see Stephan Schuhmacher and Gert Woerner, eds., *The Encyclopedia of Eastern Philosophy and Religion* (Boston: Shambhala, 1994), s.vv. "Nāgārguna," "Shūnyatā." For a detailed study, see Donald S. Lopez Jr., *Elaborations on Emptiness: Uses of the Heart Sūtra* (Princeton: Princeton University Press, 1996).

43. Remarkably, *wu* originally refers to a forest clearing—Heidegger's *Lichtung.* See May, *Heidegger's Hidden Sources,* 32–33.

44. Here we can find resonances with Heidegger's *Gelassenheit.* In fact, around the time that he developed this notion, in the mid-1940s, he also collaborated on a transla-

tion of the *Tao Te Ching* with a Chinese scholar: see Paul Shih-yi Hsiao, "Heidegger and Our Translation of the *Tao Te Ching*," in *Heidegger and Asian Thought,* ed. Graham Parkes (Honolulu: University of Hawaii Press, 1987), 93–101.

45. Leibniz's principle can be seen as a variant of the ancient axiom that something cannot come from nothing, and one can argue that the principle of sufficient reason was already implicitly assumed by the earliest Greek philosophers. For instance, Anaximander argues that the earth is at rest because it is exactly in the center of the cosmos. Since there is no reason for it to move in one direction rather than another, it *cannot* move (Anaximander, testimonium 26). On the principle of reason, see Heidegger, "On the Essence of Ground," in *Pathmarks,* 97–135, and *The Principle of Reason,* trans. Reginald Lilly (Bloomington: Indiana University Press, 1991).

46. G. W. Leibniz, "Principles of Nature and Grace, Based on Reason," in *Philosophical Essays,* ed. and trans. Roger Ariew and Daniel Garber (Indianapolis: Hackett, 1989), 210.

47. F. W. J. Schelling, *Schellings Werke,* ed. Manfred Schröter, 4:588 (Munich: C. H. Beck, 1927) (= Schelling, *Werke* [Stuttgart: Cotta, 1856–1861], 8:212). For a helpful introduction to Schelling's late thought, see Dale E. Snow, *Schelling and the End of Idealism* (Albany: State University of New York Press, 1996), chap. 7; see 204–205 for the possibility that Schelling understood the problem of Being and Nothing in terms of *Angst.*

48. *Schellings Werke,* 4:610 (= 8:234); 4:611 (= 8:235).

49. William James, *Some Problems of Philosophy* (Cambridge: Harvard University Press, 1979), chap. 3 (26–30). James begins by quoting Schopenhauer (*The World as Will and Representation,* app. 17) and tries to maintain the radical mystery of the question.

50. Anna-Teresa Tymieniecka, *Why Is There Something Rather Than Nothing? Prolegomena to the Phenomenology of Cosmic Creation* (Assen: Van Gorcum, 1966). Tymieniecka quickly dismisses the problem of Nothing (10) and proceeds to develop a phenomenological anthropology and an account of phenomenological constitution, which she assimilates speculatively to the "constitutive system of the real universe" (159).

51. See esp. Robert Nozick, *Philosophical Explanations* (Cambridge: Harvard University Press, Belknap Press, 1981), 115–164; Nicholas Rescher, *The Riddle of Existence: An Essay in Idealistic Metaphysics* (Lanham, Md.: University Press of America, 1984). Both Nozick (115, 123) and Rescher (4) refer to Heidegger in passing, but both take for granted many of the metaphysical concepts and oppositions whose genealogy Heidegger questions in *Introduction to Metaphysics.*

52. Bergson considers the question in *Creative Evolution,* only to dissolve it: the expression "nothing" has no meaning when it is detached from the sphere of what exists.

Bergson thus accepts Plato's analysis of nonbeing as signifying a difference between beings, rather than a complete absence of being. See *Creative Evolution,* trans. Arthur Mitchell (New York: Modern Library, 1944), 296–324.

53. "I wonder at the existence of the world. And I am then inclined to use such phrases as 'how extraordinary that anything should exist' or 'how extraordinary that the world should exist' ": Ludwig Wittgenstein, "A Lecture on Ethics" (1929), in *Philosophical Occasions, 1912–1951* (Indianapolis: Hackett, 1993), 41. Wittgenstein approaches this experience as a problem about the limits of language, giving a linguistic twist to a broadly Kantian position. Around the same time he composed this lecture, Wittgenstein remarked: "I can readily think what Heidegger means by Being and Dread. Man has the impulse to run up against the limits of language. Think, for example, of the astonishment that anything exists. This astonishment cannot be expressed in the form of a question, and there is also no answer to it. . . . Yet the tendency represented by the running-up against points to something": "On Heidegger on Being and Dread," in Murray, *Heidegger and Modern Philosophy,* 80–81.

54. Max Scheler, "The Nature of Philosophy and the Moral Preconditions of Philosophical Knowledge" (1917), in *On the Eternal in Man,* trans. Bernard Noble (Hamden, Conn.: Archon Books, 1972), 98. For Heidegger's tribute to Scheler, see *The Metaphysical Foundations of Logic,* trans. Michael Heim (Bloomington: Indiana University Press, 1984), 50–52.

55. Martin A. Bucher and David N. Spergel, "How Did the Universe Begin?" *Scientific American* 280, 1 (Jan. 1999): 68.

56. After considering a few of these contexts, Jean-Luc Marion judges Heidegger's confrontation with Nothing a failure. According to Marion, Heidegger unsuccessfully attempts to reduce Nothing to Being ("Nothing and Nothing Else," 185–188). See also Marion, *Reduction and Givenness: Investigations of Husserl, Heidegger, and Phenomenology,* trans. Thomas A. Carlson (Evanston: Northwestern University Press, 1998), chap. 6. Stanley Rosen reaches a similar conclusion (*The Limits of Analysis,* 143–148). In my view, such conclusions are premature but also understandable, because Heidegger's use of "Nothing" is so fluid and ambiguous. Three extended studies of the theme stay close to Heidegger's own language and offer more sympathetic interpretations: Priscilla N. Cohn, *Heidegger: Su filosofía a través de la nada* (Madrid: Ediciones Guadarrama, 1975); Richard Regvald, *Heidegger et le problème du néant* (Dordrecht: Martinus Nijhoff, 1987); and Fuchun Peng, *Das Nichten des Nichts: Zur Kernfrage des Denkwegs Martin Heideggers* (Frankfurt am Main: Peter Lang, 1998). Cohn focuses on *Being and Time* and "What Is Metaphysics?"; she explains Heidegger clearly and successfully addresses early critics such as Carnap and Sartre. Regvald considers a wider variety of texts and convincingly interprets "Nothing" in terms of the transcendence of Dasein and the withdrawal of Being (184–185). Peng provides a different but equally appropriate per-

spective on nihilation, interpreting it in terms of "the refusal [*Verweigerung*] of the world" in Heidegger's early work, "the expropriation [*Enteignung*] of history" in the 1930s, and "the silence [*Verschweigung*] of language" in the postwar period (17–18). Finally, on nihilism and Nothing, see also David Farrell Krell's valuable "Analysis" in Heidegger, *Nietzsche*, vol. 4, *Nihilism*, 253–294.

57. Throughout my account of *Being and Time* I have changed Macquarrie and Robinson's "the 'nothing'" to "Nothing." Otherwise I follow their translation.

58. Heidegger, "What Is Metaphysics?" 84 (translation modified).

59. The relation between Nothing and negation is already raised as a problem in some earlier texts: SZ, 285–286; GA 19, 571.

60. Heidegger, "What Is Metaphysics?" 88; 90 (translation modified); 91 (translation modified). Similar statements are found in *Kant and the Problem of Metaphysics*, 162, 177.

61. Carnap, "The Elimination of Metaphysics," 71.

62. Heidegger, "What Is Metaphysics?" 108 (translation modified).

63. Heidegger's critics frequently fail to confront this fundamental Heideggerian claim. For instance, while disagreeing with Carnap's exclusive reliance on symbolic logic, Tugendhat holds that "essentially, his criticism hits the mark quite correctly": "'Das Sein und das Nichts,'" 151. Like Carnap, Tugendhat simply cannot imagine that the canons of *propositional discourse* are not the final arbiters of this question: the question of negation is exclusively a question of "the *form* of speaking" (156). Similarly, Kahl-Furthmann rejects Heidegger's position and asserts that negation precedes Nothing, on the grounds that "no positing [*setzende*] function other than the function of thinking is given to human beings, unless, like willing, it is based on the function of thinking; thus, objects that are not given by reality [such as Nothing] must be posited exclusively by thinking": *Das Problem des Nicht*, 520. Here Kahl-Furthmann understands thinking as forming propositional judgments.

64. These texts have been published, respectively, as GA 65, GA 66, and GA 69. See also GA 68, esp. 45–49.

65. For an example of a postwar reflection on nihilism and Nothing, see "On the Question of Being" (1955), in *Pathmarks*. For further references to this theme in the 1930s and later, see Joan Stambaugh, *The Finitude of Being* (Albany: State University of New York Press, 1992).

66. Martin Heidegger, *Vier Seminare* (Frankfurt am Main: Vittorio Klostermann, 1977), 101. Compare, e.g., GA 66, 294. In his later writings, Heidegger often interprets even the "nothing" in the why-question as referring to Being. The why-question then asks why we remain on the level of beings instead of considering Being: GA 66, 377; "Introduction to 'What Is Metaphysics?'" in *Pathmarks*, 290; "On the Question of Being," in *Pathmarks*, 317–318; *Vier Seminare*, 100.

67. On nihilation as belonging to Being, see also "Letter on 'Humanism,'" in *Pathmarks*, 272–273. Are Marion and Rosen correct to say that Heidegger *reduces* Nothing to Being (see note 56 above)? The answer depends, of course, on what one means by "Nothing" and "Being." We have seen that Heidegger uses "Nothing" in a variety of senses and does not always identify it with Being. Heidegger certainly does tend to view all phenomena in *relation* to Being, however, and perhaps this is inappropriate in some cases. Still, it does not seem unreasonable to gather the main discussions of Nothing in both Eastern and Western traditions under the general rubric of the problem of Being: we have seen that traditional reflections on Nothing have formed part of attempts to understand the Being of beings (including both ourselves and other entities) and have also at least implicitly raised the problem of how we are open to the Being of beings (see the end of section 1 of this chapter). When he "equates" Being and Nothing, or says that nihilation belongs to Being, Heidegger is claiming that the coming-to-pass of the significance of beings lacks a final ground and is pervaded by temporal finitude. This is surely such a fundamental claim that it can be related in legitimate and fruitful ways to all the traditional senses of "Nothing." Whether the claim is *true* is a question that I cannot address within the space of this essay.

68. For further discussion of the originary leap, see Charles E. Scott's contribution to this volume.

69. In "What Is Metaphysics?" (87) the list of fundamental moods includes love. On love, see Dieter Thomä's contribution to this volume and Giorgio Agamben, "The Passion of Facticity: Heidegger and the Problem of Love," in Lilly, *The Ancients and the Moderns*, 211–229.

70. Scheler, "The Nature of Philosophy," 101.

71. On celebration as a recognition that beings are, rather than are not, see GA 52, 64.

72. On these moods as corresponding to "the first inception" and "the other inception," see GA 65, 46.

73. In fact, the passage is so obscure that one may well suspect a slip of the pen. Heidegger claims that in the case of an entity, comparisons "increase its determinability," yet leave it "multiply undefined" (60). This claim looks inconsistent in itself, and furthermore fits poorly with the claim that Being's incomparability makes it *most* determinate.

74. In 1941 Heidegger was to structure a brief lecture course (GA 51) around several such paradoxes.

75. On the historical uniqueness of *Seyn*, see, e.g., GA 65, 460.

76. "Where struggle ceases, beings indeed do not disappear, but world turns away" (48). See also SZ, 222 on unconcealment as a struggle. For an extended study of this theme, see Gregory Fried, *Heidegger's Polemos* (New Haven: Yale University Press, 2000).

77. This is not Heidegger's own understanding of becoming: the interpretation of temporality in terms of the "no longer" and "not yet" is beholden to the metaphysics of presence (157). Still, this passage echoes his view of the finitude of temporality.

78. For such an account, see Clare Pearson Geiman's "Heidegger's *Antigones,*" in this volume.

79. *Liddell and Scott's Greek-English Lexicon* provides no support for Heidegger's reading of the *ouden* in line 360, even though *ouden* does have meanings beyond functioning as a simple negative pronoun: *ouden einai* can mean "to amount to nothing" in the sense of being useless or a nobody. Liddell and Scott also list *oudenia,* "nothingness" in the sense of worthlessness (e.g., Plato, *Theaetetus* 176c). I am not aware of any use of *ouden* to mean annihilation or death.

80. For death as testimony to the strangeness and negativity of Being, see GA 65, §§160–163 and §202. When Heidegger revisits this Sophoclean ode in 1942 (GA 53), he stresses the relation between Being and Nothing: see Geiman, "Heidegger's *Antigones.*"

81. We saw that Aristotle calls potentiality a type of nonbeing, yet affirms that it *is;* similarly, Kant calls the noumena a type of nothing, yet affirms that they *are.* Do all metaphysical systems end up needing what they exclude?

Chapter 5. The Scattered *Logos*

I am especially grateful to Troy Catterson, Judd Webb, and the editors of the present volume, Gregory Fried and Richard Polt, for their insightful and thorough criticisms of earlier drafts of the present paper.

1. Aristotle, *Metaphysics* 1003a21 f.

2. Martin Heidegger, *Einführung in die Metaphysik,* fourth edition (Tübingen: Niemeyer, 1976), 15 (hereafter EiM). By way of anticipation of themes discussed below, it bears recalling that some apparent violations of the laws of noncontradiction and excluded middle are based upon ambiguities or vagueness, e.g., "it is raining and it is not raining in Paris."

3. The term "sense" *(Sinn)* is not equivalent to the term "meaning" *(Bedeutung);* Heidegger, like the mature Husserl, distinguishes the two (though their distinctions do not coincide). For the purposes of this paper, I adopt the Husserlian rubric of restricting meaning to the sense of linguistic or symbolic items. In other words, inquiring into the meaning of "being" supposes a sense of being.

4. Compare EiM, 15,19, 32, 33, 153 (or EiM 13, 34, 56: "the fundamental question of metaphysics," though he also calls it "the guiding question," see EiM, 30). As an indication that Heidegger's thinking about metaphysics is, if not in flux, at least in search of terminology during the mid-1930s, it bears noting that "the prior question" in the *Introduction to Metaphysics* of 1935 is akin to what Heidegger in the *Beiträge* (1936–

1938) dubs the "basic question" and sets in contrast to what, again in the *Beiträge,* is construed as the "leading question" *(Leitfrage: ti to on).* The later terminology is reflected in Heidegger's insertion on page 15 of the 1953 edition of EiM: "Die Grundfrage der Vorlesung ist anderer Art als die Leitfrage der Metaphysik." Compare *Beiträge zur Philosophie (Vom Ereignis),* GA 65, 6f., 73–77, 179f.

5. Compare EiM 21 f., 24f.; also 30, where the *Vorfrage* is said to be "contained" in the *Leitfrage;* 32, where the *Vorfrage* is deemed "the glowing hearth in the questioning of the *Grundfrage*"; 33, 156; see also *Besinnung,* GA 66, 362. See, too, Max Scheler, *Die Stellung des Menschen im Kosmos,* 7th ed. (Bern: Francke, 1966), 87–93.

6. Martin Heidegger, *Vorträge und Aufsätze* (Pfullingen: Neske, 1985), 71–74 (hereafter VA); GA 9, 408; *Identität und Differenz,* 7th ed. (Pfullingen: Neske, 1982), 65; *Der Satz vom Grund,* 5th ed. (Pfullingen: Neske, 1978), 158 (hereafter SG). Heidegger later speaks of the *Verwindung* and *Überwindung,* the turning (twisting) from and overturning of metaphysics; cf. *Holzwege* (Frankfurt am Main: Klostermann, 1950), 92; GA 65, 171 f.; GA 66, 400; also Gianni Vattimo, *The End of Modernity* , trans. Jon R. Snyder (Baltimore: Johns Hopkins University Press, 1991), 172f.; Reiner Schürmann, *Heidegger on Being and Acting: From Principles to Anarchy* (Bloomington: Indiana University Press, 1990), 327 n. 14. On the difference between *Wiederholung* and *Andenken,* paralleling the difference between the Aristotelian orientation of the *logos* in *Sein und Zeit* and the pre-Socratic orientation after the *Kehre,* see Werner Marx, *Heidegger und die Tradition* (Stuttgart: Kohlhammer, 1961), 121–27; Schürmann, 344 n. 77, 314f. n. 46.

7. EiM, 91. "Thinking," though central to the EiM and Heidegger's later works, is avoided in SZ; on this point see Winfried Franzen, *Von der Existenzialontologie zur Seinsgeschichte* (Meisenheim am Glan: Hain, 1975), 216. The importance accorded the theme of thinking, after *Sein und Zeit,* coincides with Heidegger's most celebrated *Kehre,* a coincidence aptly overstated by Schürmann: "However, to say 'thinking' instead of Dasein amounts to dismissing all reference, even remote, to subjectivity, to existence, to me who is thinking," Schürmann, 373 n. 120.

8. Compare *Heraklit,* GA 55, 230f., 236; W. V. O. Quine, *Methods of Logic,* 4th ed. (Cambridge: Harvard University Press, 1982), 4: "The chief importance of logic lies in implication"; ibid., 46: "In a word, *implication is validity of the conditional.*"

9. GA 55, 236, 253; also ibid., 254, 257f., 275f., 284. It should be apparent that this logical prejudice cuts a wide swath, encompassing alleged antimetaphysicians (e.g., Russell the logical atomist, Carnap the formal semanticist, and even or perhaps especially Quine the pragmatist) as well as avowed metaphysicians (e.g., Aristotle, Aquinas, Scheler), in short, all who insist on or simply declare the preferability of some overriding commitment to the canons of formal logic in the determination of what Heidegger naively terms "thinking and being." An alliance of a sort could, on the other hand, be

fashioned between Heidegger and Wittgenstein; cf. *Philosophical Investigations,* trans. G. E. M. Anscombe (New York: Macmillan, 1953), §97, p. 44: "Thinking is surrounded by a halo.—Its essence, logic, presents an order, in fact the a priori order of the world: that is, the order of *possibilities,* which must be common to both world and thought. We are under the illusion that what is peculiar, profound, essential in our investigation, resides in its trying to grasp . . . the order existing between the concepts of proposition, word, proof, truth, experience, and so on. . . . Whereas, of course, if the words 'language,' 'experience,' 'world,' have a use, it must be as humble a one as that of the words 'table,' 'lamp,' 'door.'" Ibid., §107, p. 46: "For the crystalline purity of logic was, of course, not a *result of investigation* [nicht *ergeben*]; it was a requirement [or better: a demand *(Forderung)*]." Compare Ludwig Wittgenstein, *Philosophische Untersuchungen,* in *Werkausgabe* I (Frankfurt am Main: Suhrkamp, 1984), 294, 297 (hereafter *Werkausgabe* I).

10. The contention, in other words, is that logic neither is committed to nor presupposes (implies) any particular conception of the content of thought (beings, being, or truth). Alternatively: Heidegger commits the metaphysical mistake of assuming that logic is grounded in a conception of being. Compare Walter Bröcker, "Heidegger und die Logik," in *Heidegger,* ed. Otto Pöggeler (Cologne: Kiepenheuer & Witsch, 1970), 298–304. Heidegger's claim, however, is that metaphysics is grounded in logic (and, hence, oblivious to being) and not that logic is grounded in metaphysics; see n. 67 below. For some typical affirmations of logic's neutrality, predating Heidegger's lectures, see B. Russell, *Mysticism and Logic* (Garden City, N.J.: Doubleday, 1957), 70 f.; B. Russell, *Our Knowledge of the External World* (London: George Allen & Unwin, 1969), 19; R. Carnap, *Der logische Aufbau der Welt* (Hamburg: Meiner, 1961), 5 f.

11. This statement might be dubbed "the bivalence thesis." The first parentheses in the statement are not meant to suggest that an identity or even a strong equivalence obtains among the items listed. Instead, the list is merely given to indicate that a version of the logical prejudice can be formulated under a variety of different descriptions of "truth-bearers." On the connection of bivalence with realistic and objectivistic semantics and with the weaker principle (dubbed "valence") that "every unambiguous statement must be determinately either true or not true," see Michael Dummett, *The Seas of Language* (Oxford: Clarendon, 1997), 235, 467. For the purposes of this paper, in keeping with the classical logic that Heidegger has in his sights, I treat the principle of bivalence and the law of excluded middle as roughly equivalent, though this equivalence is disputed; see Dummett, 237, 267, and Susan Haack, *Deviant Logic* (Cambridge: Cambridge University Press, 1974), 64–68. The remark about tautologies is not universally accepted; for endorsements of it, see Ludwig Wittgenstein, *Tractatus Logico-philosophicus,* trans. D. F. Pears and B. F. McGuiness (London: Routledge &

Kegan Paul, 1961), p. 68 f. (*Werkausgabe* I, 43), 4.461 ff., and R. Carnap, *Introduction to Symbolic Logic and Its Applications* (New York: Dover, 1958), 15.

12. This challenge paraphrases that advanced by Ernst Tugendhat in *Der Wahrheitsbegriff bei Husserl und Heidegger* (Berlin: de Gruyter, 1967), 331–337. For a more recent defense of bivalence, cf. W. V. O. Quine, *Pursuit of Truth*, rev. ed. (Cambridge: Harvard University Press, 1992), 90–93; for considerations of the limits of the principle in connection with theories of meaning, see Dummett, *Seas of Language*, 62–84; Haack, 66 f.

13. GA 55, 269.

14. EiM, 88, 89, 148 f., 156; even the desire for the "irrational" and the "alogical" stands under this relation (EiM, 111); cf. GA 55, 236, 251–258; GA 65, 198: "Das Denken: der Leitfaden der Leitfrage der abendländischen Philosophie"; ibid., 196 for reference to the section "Being and Thinking" in EiM.

15. EiM, 91. While Heidegger in EiM (143 f.) finds corroboration for this claim in Kant's remark about the *apparent* completeness of logic since Aristotle (*Critique of Pure Reason*, B viii), he later interprets the remark as an indication of Kant's awareness that *appearances* are deceiving in this case; cf. GA 55, 231.

16. But see Heidegger's second published article, "Neue Forschungen über Logik" (1912), in which works of Frege, Russell, Whitehead, and Meinong—among others—are reviewed; *Frühe Schriften*, GA 1, 17–43. Heidegger's *Auseinandersetzung* with *Logistik* (symbolic logic) is a life-long affair, though his repeated reference to it in terms of computation and technique suggests an appreciation for what the logicians would call "logic in the narrower sense" and a disregard for their treatments of it in a broad sense; cf. Martin Heidegger, *Sein und Zeit* (Tübingen: Niemeyer, 1972), 159 (hereafter SZ); *Frage nach dem Ding* 122 (GA 12); *Unterwegs zur Sprache*, 6th ed. (Pfullingen: Neske, 1979), 125; *Nietzsche*, 4th ed. (Pfullingen: Neske, 1961), 2:487; VA, 75 f., 234; *Was heißt Denken?* 3rd ed. (Tübingen: Niemeyer, 1971), 10, 102, 145 (hereafter WhD); SG 163. For a review of this confrontation, see Albert Borgmann, "Heidegger and Symbolic Logic," in *Heidegger and the Quest for Truth*, ed. Manfred S. Frings (Chicago: Quadrangle, 1968), 139–162. Borgmann rightly observes that "Heidegger does not clearly distinguish between the calculus and its interpretation" (147). On the distinction between narrow and broad senses of "logic," see W. V. O. Quine, *Mathematical Logic*, rev. ed. (New York: Harper & Row, 1951), 3.

17. Nevertheless, for his historical view of logic's continuity Heidegger has an ally in Quine. "Traditional formal logic," Quine maintains, is "the direct progenitor of mathematical logic. . . . They both have, vaguely speaking, the same subject matter." Quine, *Mathematical Logic*, 1.

18. Compare Husserl, *Formale und transzendentale Logik*, ed. Paul Janssen (The

Hague: Martinus Nijhoff, 1974), 53: "1. Kapitel. Die formale Logik als apophantische Analytik." For "schemata" and "schematic form" see Quine, *Mathematical Logic*, 5; *Methods of Logic*, 4th ed. (Cambridge: Harvard University Press, 1982), 33, 53, 114, 147, 172. Reference to Quine in this connection is anachronistic inasmuch as Heidegger likely has in mind a conception of logic centered, not on forms of sentences, but on the theoretical structure of the world, as Frege and Russell (at times) conceived it, or a "theory of theories," as Husserl puts it. Nevertheless, there is reason, as noted below, to think that Heidegger would regard his criticisms as applicable to Quine's allegedly weaker, i.e., ontologically relative and pragmatic conception of logic. One of the major difficulties besetting any attempt to assess Heidegger's pronouncements on logic circa 1935 is determining their relevance with respect to developments in logical theory at that time. For example, a faint echo of some of his criticisms can be detected in Carnap's project, following Tarski, of supplementing syntactic theory with semantic theory (despite the fact that Heidegger—again showing more affinities with Wittgenstein— would have objected to Carnap's attempted formalization of semantics); see R. Carnap, *Introduction to Semantics* (Cambridge: Harvard University Press, 1968), x–xii.

19. EiM, 92; cf. ibid.: "Meditation *(Besinnung)* on the essence of thinking is consequently a truly unique sort of meditation when it is undertaken as a meditation on *logos*, thereby becoming logic." Compare EiM, 90 f.

20. This conception and its history are elaborated in the next section; see EiM, 19: "It could be the other way around, that the whole logic that we know and that we treat like a gift from heaven is grounded in a very definite answer to the question about beings, and that consequently any thinking that simply follows the laws of thought of established logic is intrinsically incapable of even beginning to understand the question about beings, much less of actually unfolding it and leading it toward an answer." See also GA 55, 232.

21. Dummett, *Seas of Language*, 241. Does the fact that Heidegger directs his attack on thinking that holds fast to this classical logic mean that his criticisms do not apply or cannot be extended to the nonclassical logic of the sort emerging from Heyting's intuitionistic semantic theory for mathematical statements or to the antirealist views trumpeted by Dummett himself? Insofar as the aim of these developments continues to be largely theoretical and to turn on distinctions between affirmations and declarations (or justifications), they would continue to be subject to Heidegger's basic criticisms. The very fact that they challenge a classical version of the logical prejudice, however, suggests, at least at some level, a proximity to Heidegger's way of thinking about being and truth. See his reference to intuitionism in mathematics in SZ, 9. On the distinction between affirmations and declarations as well as the corresponding distinction between truth-conditional and justificationist meaning-theories, see Dummett, 466 and 474 f.

22. Dummett, *Seas of Language*, 235, 237.

23. Donald Davidson, *Inquiries into Truth and Interpretation* (Oxford: Clarendon, 1991), 24; cf. Wittgenstein, *Tractatus Logico-philosophicus*, 41 (*Werkausgabe* I, 28): "4.024 To understand a proposition means to know what is the case if it is true"; Gottlob Frege, *Schriften zur Logik und Sprachphilosophie*, ed. G. Gabriel (Hamburg: Meiner, 1971), 88: "Wenn ein Satz überhaupt eine Bedeutung hat, dann ist diese entweder das Wahre oder das Falsche"; Carnap, *Introduction to Symbolic Logic*, 15: "knowledge of the truth-conditions of a sentence is identical with an understanding of its meaning."

24. Wittgenstein, *Tractatus Logico-philosophicus*, 50 f. (*Werkausgabe* I, 33 f.): "4.121 Propositions *show* the logical form of reality" and "4.1212 What *can* be shown, *cannot* be said." See, too, Frege, *Schriften zur Logik*, 23: "Was wahr sei, halte ich für nicht erklärbar." Appeals to a metalanguage merely defer the issue, for what legitimates the rules of the metalanguage cannot be said in that language—or at least not if they are rules of its own truth or referentiality; see, too, Dummett, *Seas of Language*, 472 ff.

25. In the *Introduction to Metaphysics* Heidegger mentions the principle of non-contradiction more frequently than the law of excluded middle (see EiM, 18, 19, 142, 143); since, however, he iterates that his target is "traditional logic," which has remained ever the same (EiM, 19, 91, 144), it bears recalling that the principles are equivalent in traditional logic. See DeMorgan's laws: -(p-p) $\leftrightarrow$ (p v -p), in Quine, *Methods of Logic*, 14. n. 2.

26. Wittgenstein, *Tractatus Logico-philosophicus*, : "4.12. Propositions can represent the whole of reality, but they cannot represent what they must have in common with reality in order to be able to represent it—logical form. In order to be able to represent logical form, we should have to be able to station ourselves with propositions somewhere outside logic, that is to say outside the world."

27. As Davidson (*Inquiries into Truth*, 24) reminds his readers, his theory of meaning, modeled on Tarski's semantic conception of truth, makes no use of meanings.

28. There is, of course, more structure and, in that sense, more content accorded to the subject matter in the case of existential quantification, as is evident from the logical equivalence of existential quantification to a disjunction of propositions assigning predicates to names of objects within a given universe.

29. In other words, variables bound by existential quantifiers within a given theory indicate what it countenances as existing; see W. V. O. Quine, *Ontological Relativity and Other Essays* (New York and London: Columbia University Press, 1969), 91–95; quotation is on 92.

30. Heidegger sometimes refers to his own work as a "propaedeutic logic," thus, as an expansion and not a contraction of logic; reasons for this extension of logic to what by some accounts seems alogical can be found in Emil Lask, *Die Logik der Philosophie und die Kategorienlehre* (Tübingen: Mohr, 1911).

31. See Quine, *Pursuit of Truth*, 78 f.; Carnap, *Introduction to Symbolic Logic*, 101:

"One who constructs a syntactical system usually has in mind from the outset some interpretation of this system...While this intended interpretation can receive no explicit indication in the syntactical rules—since these rules must be strictly formal—the author's intention respecting interpretation naturally affects his choice of the formation and transformation rules of the syntactical system. E.g. he chooses primitive signs in such a way that certain concepts (perhaps those of some given unsystematized theory) can be expressed."

32. Heidegger's assault on the collusion of metaphysics with the logical prejudice bears a striking resemblance to Wittgenstein's critique of the "subliming" of logic; cf. *Werkausgabe* I, 291–294, 306 f.

33. In a sense, Heidegger's dispute with the logical tradition as the perpetration of a certain severance of thinking and being can be reconstructed as an attack on the restriction of thinking about the sense of being to the constraints of logic as so-called "correct" thinking; in other, more contemporary terms, he is contesting the hegemony of a semantic conception of meaning, based upon bivalent truth-conditions or, in effect, a semantics driven by syntactical concerns.

34. Quine, *Ontological Relativity,* 97. There are, in fact, two distinct ways in which logic may be said to prejudice thinking about being: by insisting that logic has nothing to do with metaphysics and by assuming a limited or unjustified sense of what it means to be. I am grateful to Troy Catterson for reminding me of the importance of this distinction.

35. See nn. 19 and 20 above.

36. See Martin Heidegger, *Logik: Die Frage nach der Wahrheit,* GA 21, 12–18.

37. But see EiM, 93: "It is important to prune the outgrowths of contemporary intellectualism."

38. See EiM, 92–94; John Dewey, *Experience and Nature* (Chicago: Open Court, 1994), 21 f.

39. EiM, 93 f.; on the notion of *Andenken,* cf. n. 6 above.

40. The expression "metaphysical oblivion" is meant to capture Heidegger's thesis that Western metaphysics, precisely by advancing a theoretical science of being, has "forgotten" being. So stated, the thesis comes across as little more than another example of one thinker claiming to have a more adequate view of things than did his predecessors. This dimension is unmistakably present in Heidegger's elaboration of this thesis, but there is also a novel wrinkle to that elaboration that presents difficulties all its own. For Heidegger insists that such "forgottenness of being" *(Seinsvergessenheit),* far from being regarded simply as an oversight on the part of a finite mind, must itself be understood as part of the history of being.

41. The unity—(a)—supposed by this differentiation—more precisely, an equivalence of *"logos"* and *"phusis,"* the original term for "being"—is present in the pre-Socratic

fragments of Heraclitus (and Parmenides). For the differentiation itself—(b)—Heidegger turns to Parmenides' writings, and for the identification of thinking with this differentiation—(c)—in effect, the cementing of the logical prejudice, he looks to the end of the Greek beginning, namely, to Plato and Aristotle. In modernity, finally, Heidegger locates the construal of being as subordinate to thinking—(d)—the completion of the logical prejudice. In order to keep this chapter to a reasonable length, this last stage is not elaborated here. It should be noted that this account of the origin of the logical prejudice expands decisively on the story told in SZ, where, instead of the pre-Socratic *logos,* Aristotle's elucidation of the apophantic structure of the *logos* provides the point of departure for considerations of it as an utterance, a synthesis, and a truth-or-falsehood; see SZ, 32–34, 226.

42. EiM, 95; Heidegger claims that Greek mathematicians used the term in this way; he also cites the *Odyssey,* XXIV, 106 and Aristotle's *Physics,* Theta, 1, 252a13; see also SZ, 33; VA, 201; WhD, 121; GA 55, 266–270, 282. For a useful discussion of Heidegger's reading, in contrast to traditional interpretations, see Klaus Held, "Der *Logos*-Gedanke des Heraklit," in *Durchblicke,* ed. Vittorio Klostermann (Frankfurt am Main: Klostermann, 1970), 162–206. In the present volume, in addition to providing a useful review of linguistic and analytic attitudes toward the question of "being" and "truth," Gregory Fried makes a valuable comparison of Heidegger's and Charles Kahn's studies of the uses of the verb "to be" and its cognates.

43. Compare Karl Reinhardt, *Parmenides und die Geschichte der griechischen Philosophie* (Bonn: F. Cohen, 1916), 217 ff.; SZ, 223; GA 9, 140. Heidegger also praises Reinhardt's interpretations of Sophocles (EiM, 82) and Heraclitus (VA, 267 f.); H. Boeder, "Der frühgriechische Wortgebrauch von *Logos* und *Aletheia,*" *Archiv für Begriffsgeschichte* IV (1958): 82–112. The turn to the Heraclitean *logos* begins in SZ; see SZ, 219 f.

44. From the talk in some fragments (notably fr. 1, 50, and 73) of "hearing the *logos,*" one might infer, Heidegger concedes, that it is a kind of word or discourse. Nevertheless, Heidegger insists that it is meant in a prelinguistic way since, as Heraclitus puts it quite clearly in fr. 1, people do not grasp the *logos,* despite its constant presence, before or after they have heard or listened and, indeed, even if they attempt to put it into words or action. In fr. 50, moreover, Heraclitus discriminates between listening to him and listening to the *logos,* a discrimination that Heidegger takes as saying: "You should not cling to words, but instead apprehend the *logos*" (EiM, 99). Heidegger thus distinguishes the *logos* from words and talk, and two sorts of hearing, respectively. See also GA 55, 215, 239 f., 259, 270–272, 276.

45. EiM, 47 f.; VA, 210–214; cf. Marx, *Heidegger und die Tradition,* 158.

46. According to Heidegger, just as the Heraclitean *logos* is traditionally misconstrued as sheer impermanence and restlessness, so, too, the Parmenidean *logos* is typ-

ically misinterpeted as signalling the collapse of being and thinking or objectivity and subjectivity and, hence, as an anticipation of modern forms of idealism.

47. For a valuable interpretation of the same passages from *Antigone,* see David Roochnik, *Of Art and Wisdom: Plato's Understanding of Techne* (University Park: Pennsylvania State University, 1996), 57–63.

48. EiM, 129; cf. GA 55, 258: "Rückgang durch den *logos* als Aussage zum vormetaphysischen *Logos.*" Here and elsewhere Heidegger capitalizes *"Logos"* to signify the originary gathering in contrast to the human *"logos."*

49. Where, Heidegger asks, could the word *"legein"* have acquired the meaning of "revealing" (unconcealing) if not on the basis of its essential relation to *logos* in the sense of *phusis?* Whereas *phusis* as unconcealment is the holding sway or the prevailing that arises and shows itself, *legein* produces the unconcealed as such, beings in their unconcealment; cf. EiM, 130.

50. EiM, 129. In a passage as remarkable as it is difficult to interpret (EiM, 135 f.) Heidegger asserts that those who exercise violence (viz., humans) must shrink back from the use of violence and yet cannot avoid it. At such moments, he maintains, it must occur that surmounting the overwhelming is most secure and complete if the hiddenness of being (*Logos* as the gatheredness of the conflicting) is preserved and thus, in a certain way, every possibility of appearing is withheld—upholding the mystery of being rather than attempting to overcome it by forcing it out into the open (as if it were some yet-unnoticed strand of DNA). Such an undertaking means surrendering one's essence, in effect, exiting being and never entering into Dasein, something that appears to be the most immoderate *(vermessen)* thing a human being can do, though it is in truth, Heidegger declares, the highest recognition (apparently of and by being). By not beinghere, that is to say, by doing violence to itself, Dasein breaks the supreme power or violence of being (inasmuch as Dasein in every act of violence must shatter against being). "Not-being-here is the ultimate victory over being. Dasein is the constant urgency of defeat and of the renewed resurgence of the act of violence against being, in such a way that the almighty sway of being violates Dasein (in the literal sense), makes Dasein into the site of its appearing, envelops and pervades Dasein in its sway, and thereby holds it within being" (EiM, 136). Here there is apparently a place for being human that falls short of fatally falsifying being by futilely attempting to treat it as an entity or something that appears; but this very act is, like all human acts, one of violence—only now an act of violence against itself and thereby against being. For a cognate discussion, see GA 65, 170 f.

51. EiM, 129. This determination of the essence of being-human, the inception of Western philosophy, is not a matter of picking out only the properties that set humans off from other living beings. Rather, what determines being-human is a relation to beings as such and as a whole. EiM, 130: "Being-human, as the urgency *(Not)* of appre-

hending and gathering, is the urging *(Nötigung)* into the freedom of taking over *techne,* the knowing setting-to-work of being. Thus there is history."

52. EiM, 130: "Das Menschen*wesen* zeigt sich hier als der Bezug, der dem Menschen erst das Sein eröffnet."

53. EiM, 131. For an insightful account of how *logos ("montrer")* passes into language *("designer"),* see Jean Beaufret, "Du Logos au Langage," in *Dialogue avec Heidegger* (Paris: Les éditions de minuit, 1974), 68–87; in regard to the point just raised, see especially 78 f.

54. This account provides a specification of the second sense of *logos* (the human *logos*) or, alternatively, a third sense of *logos* (in addition to the *logos* of being and that of being-human). In this connection, see Roochnik, *Of Art and Wisdom,* 65 f.

55. EiM, 131 f.; cf. Beaufret "Du Logos au Langage," 87.

56. EiM, 20; WhD, 87; Heidegger, *Vier Seminare* (Frankfurt am Main: Klostermann, 1977), 70: "More originarily than 'speaking,' *logos* means 'letting presence.'" The opposition between what is said and what is unsaid, what is gathered by being named and what is not, is a special case of the *Logos* as the original gatheredness of things, once again, something unheard by most people; cf. Schürmann, *Heidegger on Being and Acting,* 175.

57. EiM, 131. It might be useful to consider a few namings that seem to have performed the function described by Heidegger here: "the unconscious," "exchange value," *distensio, to ti en einai, aletheia.*

58. A great deal more would need to be added to forestall the easy charge of idealism here; for a cognate criticism of the sweep of Heidegger's interpretation see Marx, *Heidegger und die Tradition,* 201.

59. EiM, 132. In this account of the essence of language, as Heidegger plays "poetic language," "everyday talk," and "palaver" against each other, he is once more revising basic themes of SZ, in this case two themes, each a variation on the existential (that is to say, a way of being that is distinctive of Dasein) characterized as discourse, namely, fallenness in the sense of palaver, as the discourse of inauthentic existence, and conscience as the discourse of authentic existence. There is a further revision worthy of mention here: in SZ *Sprache* is construed as derivative of *Rede,* whereas in EiM *Rede*'s foundational character is not distinguished from *Sprache.* This shift seems to parallel the move away from a transcendental-phenomenological characterization of Dasein to its *seynsgeschichtliche Gründung.*

60. EiM, 134; cf. GA 55, 223 f.; SZ, 165.

61. Heidegger elaborates this transformation in terms of the roles assigned to *idea,* the Greek term for "what is seen," and *eidos,* the Greek term for the "appearance" of what is seen, in relation to being as *phusis;* cf. EiM, 138, 144.

62. EiM, 139. In an important sense, this interpretation of being as *idea* follows

from the experience of being as *phusis,* the emerging and appearing prevailing, the emerging appearing *(aufgehendes Scheinen).* From this vantage point, it might seem that Plato and Aristotle were merely conceiving the inception of Greek thought in a more developed and acute way. Yet insofar as *idea* is construed as "the sole and definitive interpretation of being," this follow-up *(Folge)* is a downfall *(Abfall),* Heidegger insists; for now being *(phusis),* instead of being construed as "the emergent prevailing" *(das aufgehende Walten),* is now construed in terms of *idea,* merely a determination of what stands there "insofar and only insofar as it stands opposite a seeing" (EiM, 139). For helping me understand Heidegger's conception of the relation between *phusis* and *idea,* I am grateful to Gregory Fried and Richard Polt.

63. EiM, 123: "Das Sein, die *phusis,* ist als Walten ursprüngliche Gesammeltheit: *logos,* ist fügender Fug."

64. EiM, 141. This explanation of the logical prejudice is thus the same as the one given in SZ; see SZ, 168 f.

65. EiM, 142: "Anfänglich *ist* der Logos als Sammlung das Geschehen der Unverborgenheit, in diese gegründet und ihr dienstbar. Jetzt wird der Logos als Aussage umgekehrt der Ort der Wahrheit im Sinne der Richtigkeit." See also ibid., 146 f.; SZ, 32 f., 219, 225.

66. EiM, 147. Heidegger asks us to read this account of the transformation of unconcealment to undistortedness to correctness together with the transformation of both *phusis* to *idea* and the *logos* as gathering to *logos* as assertion; "on the basis of all of them" the interpretation of being as presence works itself out and becomes definitive.

67. EiM, 143; in the wake of this transformation of the sense of *logos,* the principle of contradiction becomes the basis for countenancing anything at all. Claiming that the old conflict over whether the principle is ontological or logical is accordingly anachronistic, Heidegger observes: "The principle of contradiction has instead 'ontological' meaning because it is a basic law of the *logos,* a 'logical' proposition." A more adequate teatment of the transformations of *logos* into logic would have to examine this observation critically.

68. Heidegger is walking with seven-league (indeed, Hegelian) boots through the history of Western philosophy. This totalizing gesture, apart from its chutzpah, is possible only through an invocation of a series of parallel family resemblant expressions, ranging from *ratio* (reason, *Vernunft*) and *intellectus* (understanding, *Verstand*) to judgment (assertion, proposition) and calculation as the site of truth; see EiM, 136, 142, 148 f.

69. Martin Heidegger, *Nietzsche,* 4th ed. (Pfullingen: Neske, 1961), 1:28: "den schwersten Gedanken der Philosophie denken, heißt, das Sein als Zeit denken."

70. So, too, in the terms set by SZ, linguistic phenomena can be understood as an object of science (present-at-hand), a tool (ready-to-hand), or as an existential (the disclosive discourse of being-here).

71. EiM, 111; see SZ, 22: "Diese Aufgabe verstehen wir als die *am Leitfaden der Seinsfrage* sich vollziehende *Destruktion* des überlieferten Bestandes der antiken Ontologie auf die ursprünglichen Erfahrungen, in denen die ersten und fortan leitenden Bestimmungen des Seins gewonnen wurden."

72. See nn. 18 and 21 above. For an account with a slightly different accent on Heidegger's attempt to juggle truth as disclosure and the demands of bivalence, see the concluding section of Charles Guignon's excellent chapter in the present volume.

73. On this point, see Borgmann, "Heidegger and Symbolic Logic," 146 f.

74. See Ernest Nagel and James R. Newman, *Gödel's Proof* (London: Routledge & Kegan Paul, 1959), 96 f.

75. G. W. F. Hegel, *Wissenschaft der Logik* (Hamburg: Meiner, 1969), 2:58: "Alle Dinge sind an sich selbst widersprechend, und zwar in dem Sinne, daß dieser Satz gegen die übrigen vielmehr die Wahrheit und das Wesen der Dinge ausdrücke." Of course, one might argue that Hegel is simply more forthright than Heidegger in this respect. As Troy Catterson rightly reminds me, the vagueness of a presentation at crucial junctures may account for our inability to detect inconsistencies in it. (For Heidegger's comment on "the sublation of the principle of contradiction in Hegel's dialectic," see EiM, 143.)

Chapter 6. The Name on the Edge of Language

1. From a letter quoted by H. G. Gadamer in *Philosophische Lehrjahre: Eine Rückschau* (Frankfurt: Klostermann, 1977), 217; cf. (in a different translation) Gadamer, *Philosophical Apprenticeships* (Cambridge: MIT Press, 1985), 50. Gadamer does not let us know when he received this letter, but he refers to it as being written "then," i.e., shortly after Heidegger's return to Freiburg in 1928.

2. Compare GA 29/30, 223–228 = *The Fundamental Concepts of Metaphysics: World, Finitude, Solitude,* trans. William McNeill and Nicholas Walker (Bloomington: Indiana University Press, 1995), 149–152; *Die Selbstbehauptung der deutschen Universität. Das Rektorat 1933/34* (Frankfurt: Klostermann, 1983), 14 = "The Self-Assertion of the German University," trans. William S. Lewis, in *The Heidegger Controversy: A Critical Reader,* ed. Richard Wolin (Cambridge: MIT Press, 1993), 33–34; GA 38, 127–130; "Der Ursprung des Kunstwerks," in *Holzwege* (Frankfurt: Klostermann, 1950), 51–55 = "The Origin of the Work of Art," trans. Albert Hofstadter, in Heidegger, *Basic Writings,* ed. David Farrell Krell, 2nd ed. (San Francisco: HarperSanFrancisco, 1993), 187–192; *Nietzsche* (Pfullingen: Neske, 1961), 1:161 = *Nietzsche,* vol. 1, *The Will to Power as Art,* trans. David Farrell Krell (San Francisco: Harper & Row, 1979), 136–137; GA 65, 57. It would be illuminating to compare my approach to Thomas Sheehan's interpretation of the "turning" (see his essay in this collection). In my view, Sheehan is right in stressing the point that the "turning" is an organizing prin-

ciple rather than an intellectual development. This becomes evident from the fact that the "turning" is already implied in the would-be completion of *Being and Time*. Accordingly, Heidegger's philosophical development could be understood as a possibly slightly revised execution of a layout designed at the outset. But in my opinion, the changes in Heidegger's thinking are not mere adjustments; hence, instead of being the clue to its pretended consistency, the "turning" is the title of an unwritten play. For the problem of consistency see D. Thomä, " 'Sein und Zeit' im Rückblick: Heideggers Selbstkritik," in *Heidegger—"Sein und Zeit": Klassiker auslegen*, ed. Thomas Rentsch (Berlin: Akademie, 2001); as an overall interpretation of Heidegger's philosophical development see D. Thomä, *Die Zeit des Selbst und die Zeit danach: Zur Kritik der Textgeschichte Martin Heideggers 1910–1976* (Frankfurt: Suhrkamp, 1990). In this book I give a fuller account of the revisions and digressions I mention here in the text all too briefly; see 496 ff.; 581 ff.; 708 ff.; 644 ff., 771; with regard to the turning, see 459 ff.

3. Compare GA 66, 411.

4. Compare GA 26, 201 = *The Metaphysical Foundations of Logic*, trans. Michael Heim (Bloomington: Indiana University Press, 1984), 158.

5. For the theory of the two turnings see C. F. Gethmann, *Verstehen und Auslegung: Das Methodenproblem in der Philosophie Martin Heideggers* (Bonn: Bouvier, 1974), 281; Jean Grondin, *Le tournant dans la pensée de Martin Heidegger* (Paris: Presses Universitaires de France, 1987), 94–99.

6. SZ, 161, 87–88, 84 *(Bedeutungsganzes, Verweisungszusammenhang, Bewandtnisganzheit)*. Here and in the following, citations give the page numbers from the German edition, but I use Joan Stambaugh's translation: *Being and Time* (Albany: SUNY Press, 1996). The original pagination is to be found in the margins of this edition, too.

7. SZ, 83 *(Dienlichkeit, Verwendbarkeit)*.

8. Compare M. Okrent, *Heidegger's Pragmatism* (Ithaca: Cornell University Press, 1988); R. Rorty, "Heidegger, Contingency, and Pragmatism," in *Essays on Heidegger and Others: Philosophical Papers* (Cambridge: Cambridge University Press, 1991), 2:27–49; R. Brandom, "Heidegger's Categories in *Being and Time*," in *Heidegger: A Critical Reader*, ed. H. L. Dreyfus and H. Hall (Oxford: Blackwell, 1992), 45–64.

9. GA 20, 285; here and in the following, I quote from the translation by Theodore Kisiel: *History of the Concept of Time: Prolegomena* (Bloomington: Indiana University Press, 1985; it also gives the original pagination). "So ist alles Zeichennehmen, Zeichengebrauch, Zeichenstiftung nur eine bestimmte Ausformung des spezifischen Besorgens der Umwelt, sofern sie verfügbar sein soll."

10. SZ, 175 ("Das Dasein ist zunächst und zumeist *bei* der besorgten 'Welt.' "). Italics in this quotation (and all the following) are Heidegger's.

11. SZ, 144: "Das Dasein ist als wesenhaft befindliches je schon in bestimmte Möglichkeiten hineingeraten, als Seinkönnen, das es *ist*, hat es solche vorbeigehen

lassen, es begibt sich ständig der Möglichkeiten seines Seins, ergreift sie und vergreift sich."

12. SZ, 126: "Das Dasein steht als alltägliches Miteinandersein in der *Botmäßigkeit der Anderen*. Nicht es selbst ist, die Anderen haben ihm das Sein abgenommen."

13. Compare Cristina Lafont, *Sprache und Welterschließung: Zur linguistischen Wende der Hermeneutik Heideggers* (Frankfurt am Main: Suhrkamp, 1994) (with critical remarks on, among others, Charles Taylor and a discussion of the controversy between realism and contextualism).

14. SZ, 84: "Die Bewandtnisganzheit selbst aber geht letztlich auf ein Wozu zurück, bei dem es *keine* Bewandtnis mehr hat, was selbst nicht Seiendes ist in der Seinsart des Zuhandenen innerhalb einer Welt, sondern Seiendes, dessen Sein als In-der-Welt-sein bestimmt ist, zu dessen Seinsverfassung Weltlichkeit selbst gehört."

15. SZ, 236 *(zugänglich)*.

16. Compare R. Marten, *Heidegger lesen* (Munich: Fink, 1991), 34–35. I am well aware of the fact that distinguished Heidegger scholars argue against this contention by referring, e.g., to SZ, 298: cf. Charles B. Guignon, "Heidegger's 'Authenticity' Revisited," *Review of Metaphysics* 38 (1984): 321–339. The controversy dealing with the relation between authenticity and everydayness is as yet undecided. The salient point seems to be the question whether Heidegger is able to provide a plausible understanding of what authentic "presence" may be—the presence authentic Dasein is supposed to come back to. (In my opinion, this understanding is missing.)

17. GA 20, 439–440: "Die Welt ist im Sterben in dieser Weise des In-der-Welt-seins das, worauf das Dasein nicht mehr angewiesen ist; Welt ist nur noch das pure Worin des Gerade-noch-seins. . . . Das Sein verlegt sich jetzt gerade eigentlich erst in das 'Ich bin.' Erst im Sterben kann ich gewissermaßen absolut sagen 'ich bin.' " I give Kisiel's translation, slightly revised.

18. E. Martineau, "La modernité de *Sein und Zeit*," *Revue philosophique de Louvain* 78 (1980): 22–70, 51.

19. SZ, 126: "Herrschaft der Anderen."

20. GA 26, 257–258 (= *The Metaphysical Foundations of Logic*, 199): "Herr[en] der Macht, die wir selbst sind."

21. This audacious statement is to be found in his correspondence both with Elisabeth Blochmann and with Hannah Arendt (I am inclined to say: writing that twice, luring two women with the same line, is a bit too much). Compare Martin Heidegger and Elisabeth Blochmann, *Briefwechsel 1918–1969*, ed. J. Storck (Marbach: Deutsche Schillergesellschaft, 1989), 23; Hannah Arendt and Martin Heidegger, *Briefe 1925– 1975 und andere Zeugnisse*, ed. U. Ludz (Frankfurt: Klostermann, 1998), 31 (for the possible sources of this phrase, which is borrowed from Augustine, see Ludz's comments on Heidegger's letter in this edition). I know of only one passage in Heidegger's work

where that connection becomes explicit; it is to be found in "What Is Metaphysics?" and reads as follows: "Die tiefe Langeweile . . . offenbart das Seiende im Ganzen. Eine andere Möglichkeit solcher Offenbarung birgt die Freude an der Gegenwart des Daseins—nicht der bloßen Person—eines geliebten Menschen." *Wegmarken* (Frankfurt: Klostermann, 1967), 8; Heidegger, "What Is Metaphysics?" in *Pathmarks*, ed. W. McNeill (Cambridge: Cambridge University Press, 1998), 87. This passage is, to say the least, enigmatic; it lacks any systematic backup and appears as a gem clandestinely dedicated to one person (in all likelihood): Hannah Arendt.

It may be said that the conception of authentic "concern" *(Fürsorge)* as developed in §26 of *Being and Time* can serve as a social complement of indexical language, since it is supposed to save the independence of another Dasein. But the sociality established by the logic of this kind of concern consists in independent persons individually dedicated to their own self-assertion, hence it reconfirms the reservations about sociality known from Heidegger's critique of "falling prey." Following Heidegger, this authentic concern is a helpful additional gift rather than a necessary condition for authenticity. I would say that the very language of authenticity is intrinsically addressed to others.

22. Martin Heidegger, *Unterwegs zur Sprache* (Pfullingen: Neske, 1959), translated as *On the Way to Language* by Peter D. Hertz (New York: Harper and Row, 1971), 162/60. Here and in the following, the first page number refers to the German edition, the second to the translation.

23. Ibid., 163/61 ("Ist der Name, ist das Wort ein Zeichen?" "Alles liegt daran, wie wir das denken, was die Worte 'Zeichen' und 'Namen' besagen"), 163–164/61 ("'Namen' im Sinne einer bloßen Bezeichnung"), 164/62 ("Demnach müssen wir betonen: Kein Ding ist, wo das Wort, d.h. der Name fehlt. Das Wort verschafft dem Ding erst das Sein"); cf. 170/66, 193–194/88.

24. Ibid., 171/68.

25. Heidegger, *Wegmarken*, 164 = "Letter on 'Humanism,'" in *Pathmarks*, 254.

26. Heidegger, *Unterwegs zur Sprache*, 254/123.

27. Compare the essays "Das Ding" and "Bauen Wohnen Denken" in Martin Heidegger, *Vorträge und Aufsätze* (Pfullingen: Neske, 1954) = "The Thing" and "Building Dwelling Thinking" in *Poetry, Language, Thought*, trans. A. Hofstadter (New York: Harper & Row, 1971).

28. Compare *Vorträge und Aufsätze*, 171. For his critique and reorientation of ethics, cf. *Wegmarken*, 183, 187f. = "Letter on 'Humanism,'" in *Pathmarks*, 268, 271–272.

29. SZ, 169: "Boden des Beredeten."

30. "Processes" *(Vorgänge)* are mentioned in a quite disparaging depiction of the traditional understanding of language (66).

31. Compare *Wegmarken*, GA 9, 29–32 = "Comments on Karl Jaspers's *Psychology of Worldviews*," in *Pathmarks*, 25–28. (Although I elsewhere follow the pagination of the

first edition of *Wegmarken,* I refer to the GA here, since this review is to be found there only.)

32. Martin Heidgger, *Die Frage nach dem Ding* (Tübingen: Niemeyer, 1962), 19 = *What Is a Thing?,* trans. W. B. Barton Jr. and Vera Deutsch (Chicago: Henry Regnery, 1967), 25; *Holzwege,* 60–61 = "The Origin of the Work of Art," in *Basic Writings,* 198–199.

33. In terms of systematic cohesion and formal unity, the *Introduction to Metaphysics* is not to be regarded as one of Heidegger's strongest texts. There are passages of striking conclusiveness, and unexplainable shortcomings. The tone of the book is uneven, changing among bold appeals, philological details, simple mistakes, and succinct arguments. Let me give some examples of the less flattering aspects of this book. For a rather bold appeal, see, for instance, the reference to "rank" and "depth" (35); for an utterly misleading argument see the passage where Heidegger illustrates the opposition between "Being" and "not-Being" with the question whether "the window over there . . . *is* closed or *is not*" (59); alas, in this case, the negation "not" does not refer to "being" at all but to "closed." (The phrase "the window is not closed" can be transformed into "the window is open" without damaging its meaning, and by that, all of a sudden, the "not-Being" to which Heidegger alludes disappears: the negation does not apply to Being here.) I take this unevenness of the *Introduction to Metaphysics* as a symptom of Heidegger's general difficulties in this particular period of his development as they are described in the first part of my essay (see n. 2).

34. Compare *Zur Sache des Denkens* (Tübingen: Niemeyer, 1969), 42–3 = "Summary of a Seminar on the Lecture 'Time and Being'," in *On Time and Being,* trans. Joan Stambaugh (New York: Harper & Row, 1972), 39–40.

35. Compare R. Schürmann, "Situating René Char: Hölderlin, Heidegger, Char, and the 'There Is,'" in *Martin Heidegger and the Question of Literature,* ed. William V. Spanos (Bloomington: Indiana University Press, 1979), 173–194. I have some doubts whether Schürmann's reading of Apollinaire is accurate. Almost every single line of his poem "Il y a" begins with this same "Il y a," and Schürmann states that this figure stands for a "celebration of what is purely present." Yet the sober mood in Apollinaire's poem, written in 1915 and referring to a mixture of more or less agreeable experiences ("Il y a les prisonniers qui passent la mine inquiète"), does not fit the idea of celebration. It is, rather, an almost cool presentation arousing a couple of fragmented experiences, where memories of a beloved woman stand side by side with events linked to the war. It is the image of an inventory that is induced by Apollinaire's poem; cf. G. Apollinaire, *Oeuvres poétiques,* ed. Marcel Adéma and Michel Décaudin (Paris: Gallimard [Pléiade], 1965), 280–281.

36. Compare Walter Benjamin, *Gesammelte Schriften,* ed. Tiedemann and Schweppenhäuser, vol. 2 (Frankfurt: Suhrkamp, 1977), 150–153, 209, 362–365. The simi-

liarity between Benjamin and Heidegger is especially striking with regard to the "saving" power of naming, though their respective readings of the linguistic context to which something or somebody belongs are radically different. Benjamin is alluding to transitory correspondences and similarities, whereas Heidegger is longing for what may be called a new order.

37. Compare R. Antelme, *The Human Race* (Marlboro, Vt.: Marlboro Press, 1993 = *L'Espèce humaine,* 1947; reprint, Paris: Gallimard, 1957). For the first type of naming, see 21: "When my name is called . . . I reply 'Present.' . . . And so for one brief instant I had been directly designated here, I and no other had been addressed, I had been specially solicited—I, myself, irreplaceable! And there I was." For the second type of naming, see 45: "A railroad car that is railroad car, a horse, that's horse, the clouds coming in from the west—all the things that the SS cannot contest are royal things. . . . Everything speaks, we hear everything, everything possesses some power"; 193–194: "A language was taking shape that wasn't one of belches and foulness anymore, nor one of dogs yapping around the bucket of seconds. And this language was creating a distance between the men and the muddy, yellow dirt, rendering them distinct from it and no longer buried within it, rendering them masters of it and able also to tear themselves away from the grinding emptiness of their stomachs. In the depths of the mine, in their bent bodies and disfigured faces, the world was opening up." Sarah Kofman provides us with a link between Antelme and Heidegger by proposing a Heideggerian reading of Antelme's experience with language. Kofman makes the observation that his text is marked by the recurrent word *on,* that is, by the triumph of the anonymous "they" (Heidegger's *das Man*), abolishing the "singularity" and "identity" of the "Me" and the "proper name": S. Kofman, *Paroles suffoquées* (Paris: Galilée, 1986), 53. Yet I think her description is not totally accurate. It is not coincidental that Antelme speaks of the prisoner's experience of "irreplaceability" when called out by the guards *(Human Race,* 21). This term is of course well known from the analysis of the authentic self's anticipating its death in *Being and Time,* but it may be used in a totally different context (and without any conscious reference to Heidegger) here. Instead of simply opposing "Me" and "They," I suggest that we distinguish between different, more and less appealing or bearable uses of the "Me" or the name.

38. *Wegmarken,* 191 = "Letter on 'Humanism,' " in *Pathmarks,* 274.

39. Jean-Jacques Rousseau, *Emile, or On Education,* ed. A. Bloom (New York: Basic Books, 1979), 41–42.

40. Jean-Jacques Rousseau, *Les rêveries d'un promeneur solitaire,* in *Oeuvres complètes,* ed. Bernard Gagnebin and Marcel Raymond (Paris: Gallimard [Pléiade], 1959), 1:1047. The most impressive offspring of Rousseau's notion of existence is to be found in Romantic poetry, for instance, in Wordsworth and Coleridge. For Coleridge's reflection on the "IT IS . . . without reference . . . to this or that particular mode or form of

existence" (and its vicinity to Heidegger) see G. Steiner, *Heidegger* (London: Harvester Press, 1978), 149. For Wordsworth see L. Trilling, *Sincerity and Authenticity* (New York: Harcourt Brace Jovanovich, 1980), 85: "It is impossible to exaggerate the force that the word 'be' has for Wordsworth. . . . When he undertakes to argue his sister-in-law into a correct appreciation of 'Resolution and Independence,' he says, 'What is brought forward? "A lonely place, a Pond, by which an old man *was*, far from all house or home"—not stood, not sat, but "was"—the figure represented in the most naked simplicity possible.' " Heidegger ignores Rousseau and, with him, the long-lasting genealogy of the idea of the "it is." Rousseau is Heidegger's stepfather not only because he is ignored by him but because his idea of the "sentiment of existence" can be understood as an alternative to the latter's conception. (See D. Thomä, *Erzähle dich selbst: Lebensgeschichte als philosophisches Problem* [Munich: C. H. Beck, 1998], chap. 4.3.)

Chapter 7. What's in a Word?

1. "Letter on Humanism," in Martin Heidegger, *Pathmarks,* ed. William McNeill (Cambridge: Cambridge University Press, 1998), 254, translation modified. The reader should consult the essays by Daniel Dahlstrom and Dieter Thomä in this anthology for further discussion of the place of language in Heidegger's work.

2. For argument's sake we can take Heidegger at his word, but this assertion would require more rigorous examination in a fuller philosophical history of linguistics. For some recent treatments of the history of grammar, see Even Hovdhaugen, *Foundations of Western Linguistics* (Oslo: Universitetsforlaget, 1982) and *History of Linguistics. Volume II: Classical and Medieval Linguistics,* ed. Giulio Lepschy (London and New York: Longman, 1994).

3. For a discussion of the difficulty of distinguishing noun and verb, see Emile Benveniste, *Problems in General Linguistics,* trans. Mary Elizabeth Meek (Coral Gables: University of Miami Press, 1971), 131 ff. (hereafter cited as PGL).

4. We cannot examine in detail the fascinating resonances with Heidegger's question of Being in Sanskrit, but it suffices to indicate verse 17.23 of the *Bhagavad-Gita: Om tat sat* ("OM—that—it is"). The Sanskrit *sat,* for one thing, is based on the same Indo-European root *es* as the cognate forms *ist,* is, *esti* (German, English, Greek). See R. C. Zaehner, trans., *The Bhagavad-Gita* (Oxford: Oxford University Press, 1973), 379–383.

5. See the entries for *bheu, es,* and *wes* in Calvert Watkins, ed., *The American Heritage Dictionary of Indo-European Roots* (Boston: Houghton Mifflin, 1985). The English form *are* is based on the root *er,* which Watkins gives as having the sense of "to move, to set in motion," which brings it close to the root meaning of *bheu* for Heidegger: to arise, to come to appearance, to unfold.

6. I am indebted here to Michael Zimmerman's discussion of "decline" in this anthology.

7. Roughly translated: "War is the father of all and the king of all, and on the one hand shows forth the gods and on the other humans, on the one hand makes the slaves, on the other, the free." For a discussion of this theme, see Gregory Fried, *Heidegger's Polemos: From Being to Politics* (New Haven: Yale University Press, 2000).

8. The reader might want to begin with Charles Kahn, "The Greek Verb 'To Be' and the Concept of Being," *Foundations of Language* 2 (1966): 245–265, "Linguistic Relativism and the Greek Project of Ontology," in *The Question of Being: East-West Perspectives,* ed. Mervyn Sprung (University Park: Pennsylvania State University Press, 1978), and "Retrospect on the Verb 'To Be' and the Concept of Being," in *The Logic of Being: Historical Studies,* ed. Simo Knuutila and Jaakko Hintikka (Dordrecht: D. Reidel Publishing, 1986). There is also his book-length study *The Verb 'Be' in Ancient Greek,* vol. 6 of *The Verb 'Be' and Its Synonyms: Philosophical and Grammatical Studies,* ed. John W. M. Verhaar (Dordrecht: D. Reidel Publishing, 1973).

9. Kahn, "Retrospect," 1.

10. Kahn, "Linguistic Relativism."

11. Benjamin Lee Whorf, *Language, Thought, and Reality,* ed. John B. Carroll (Cambridge: MIT Press, 1956), 221; see also 214. For a clear and succinct history of linguistic relativism, see Julia M. Penn, *Linguistic Relativity Versus Innate Ideas: The Origins of the Sapir-Whorf Hypothesis in German Thought* (The Hague: Mouton, 1972). Penn focuses on the well-known distinction between two forms of linguistic relativism: the weak form asserts that language *influences* the domain of thought; the strong form asserts that language utterly *determines* this domain. As she demonstrates, linguistic relativists often shift ambiguously between the weak and the strong thesis. For our purposes, the strong thesis will be addressed, but we should bear in mind that even in its weaker version, linguistic relativism calls into question the "universality" of philosophical questions generated by reflection on forms of the verb "to be" in the Indo-European tradition. For a recent review of the issue of relativism and language, especially with regard to the Sapir-Whorf hypothesis that language conditions thought, see *Rethinking Linguistic Relativity,* ed. John J. Gumperz and Stephen C. Levinson (Cambridge: Cambridge University Press, 1996).

12. Cited in Kahn, *The Verb 'Be' in Ancient Greek,* 2.

13. J. S. Mill, *A System of Logic,* bk. 1, chap. 4, sec. 1.

14. Kahn, *The Verb 'Be' in Ancient Greek,* 4.

15. Ludwig Wittgenstein, *Philosophical Investigations,* trans. G. E. M. Anscombe (New York: Macmillan Publishing, 1968), 8.

16. See, e.g., W. V. O. Quine, "On What There Is," in *From a Logical Point of View* (Cambridge: Harvard University Press, 1980); "Existence and Quantification," in *Ontological Relativity and Other Essays* (New York: Columbia University Press, 1969); *Word and Object* (Cambridge: MIT Press, 1960), chap. 5.

17. Rudolf Carnap, "The Overcoming of Metaphysics Through Logical Analysis of Language," in *Heidegger and Modern Philosophy,* ed. Michael Murray (New Haven: Yale University Press, 1978).

18. See John Van Buren, *The Young Heidegger: Rumor of the Hidden King* (Bloomington: Indiana University Press, 1994), 55–56.

19. Kahn, *The Verb 'Be' in Ancient Greek,* 331 f.

20. Kahn, "Linguistic Relativism," 35.

21. Ibid., 36.

22. Ibid., 40.

23. Ibid., 40–41.

24. Ibid., 41.

25. Kahn, "Greek Verb," 245.

26. Kahn, "Linguistic Relativism," 32.

27. For Heidegger's rejection of the title "existentialist," see his "Letter on Humanism," 28. A particularly egregious oversight on Heidegger's part is one we can understand perhaps because it allows him to exclude utterly the great texts of the Jews as equals to the Greeks in the "destiny" of the history of Being in the "West": he never once raises the question of the meaning of Being in the Hebrew Bible. How could Heidegger in good faith ignore the words of a God who *names* himself "I am that I am" (*Ehyeh asher ehyeh,* Exod. 3:14, also rendered, following Rashi, "I will be what I will be")? The complexities of interpreting this name as a play on forms of the Hebrew for *to be,* from the same root *hayah* as the divine name YHWH, are profound, and it comes as a shock that no serious Heideggerian attempt has been made, to my knowledge, to integrate *this* understanding of Being into the history of the West (and not only of the West).

29. For a brief overview of the history of linguistics, with bibliography, see R. H. Robins's appendix to *Linguistics: The Cambridge Survey,* vol. 1: *Linguistic Theory: Foundations,* ed. Frederick M. Newmeyer (Cambridge: Cambridge University Press, 1988).

Chapter 8. Heidegger's Interpretation of *Phusis*

1. What my essay will need to postpone is an examination of the ways in which Heidegger elaborates his interpretation of *phusis* on the basis of other texts in the history of philosophy. It would be an interesting enterprise to compare his interpretation of *phusis* in the present text with, for example, his treatment of *phusis* in his work on Aristotle, specifically in his lecture course on Aristotle's *Metaphysics* Θ (GA 33, translated as *Aristotle's Metaphysics* Θ *1–3,* by Walter Brogan and Peter Warnek [Bloomington: Indiana University Press, 1995]) as well as his essay on Aristotle's *Physics* B1 in *Pathmarks,* ed. William McNeill (Cambridge: Cambridge University Press, 1998). There are all kinds of ways in which Heidegger's discussion in this text also prefigures areas of his interest

that appear in his later works. Notice, for example, how his work with Anaximander, Parmenides, and Heraclitus in the essays in *Holzwege* and *Vorträge und Aufsätze* (translated by David Farrell Krell and Frank Capuzzi as *Early Greek Thinking* [New York: Harper and Row, 1975]) is prepared by his discussion of these figures in the *Introduction to Metaphysics*.

2. *Webster's New Collegiate Dictionary*, 9th ed., s.v. "nature."

3. Peter Angeles, *Dictionary of Philosophy* (New York: Harper and Row, 1981), s.v. "nature." Aristotle himself defines "nature" in Book Delta of his *Metaphysics* along the lines of Angeles's dictionary but with several significant additions. Aristotle's definition concludes as follows: "From what has been said, nature [*phusis*] spoken of in the primary and main sense is the substance [*ousia*] of things which have a principle of motion in themselves qua what they are; for the matter is called 'a nature' by the fact that it is receptive of nature in the primary and main sense, and generations and growth are called so by the fact that they are motions from the point of view of nature in that sense. And the principle of motion in things existing by nature is also this nature somehow present in those objects, either potentially or actually": Aristotle, *Metaphysics,* trans. H. Apostle (Grinnell, Iowa: Peripatetic Press, 1979), 78. According to most accounts one of the most difficult features of Aristotle's thought is his interpretation of *ousia,* which is implied here in his definition of *phusis.* Aristotle's account of *ousia* involves a complex analysis of the many ways and contexts in which *ousia* and its cognates *on* and *einai,* not to mention the Greek word for becoming *(gignesthai),* are used in Greek thought and literature. Insofar as this complexity of *ousia* also riddles Aristotle's conception of *phusis,* we can at the very least see that the meaning of *phusis* resists superficial definitions and accounts.

4. Unlike Fried and Polt in their extremely fine translation of *Introduction to Metaphysics,* I am deliberately not capitalizing the word "being" in this essay. This is because, first, even though the German word for being, *Sein,* is capitalized in German, capitalizing this word seems forced in an English context. More important, however, I believe that it is critical to preserve where possible the verbal meaning of the word *Sein,* which it clearly has in German. Its capitalization in English tends, in my mind, not only to render the word's meaning more as a substantive than a verb, but also to effect a resemblance to the English habit of capitalizing proper names, particularly of transcendental entities such as God. I want clearly to disassociate Heidegger's thinking of *Sein* from such resemblances, since on my reading, Heidegger clearly does not mean by *Sein* anything like a transcendent being.

5. In which case, *phusis* means something over against its counterphenomenon, which *phusis* then is thought *not* to be.

6. As in many other of Heidegger's texts, the meaning of the word "same" here is not that of homogeneity. Rather it means something like "related in differentiation" or "dif-

ferentiating in relation." See Heidegger's discussion in this text of *to auto* in his interpretation of Parmenides (106 ff.).

7. The point in the text at which Heidegger explicitly formulates his meaning in this way is also part of an insertion (14–15) that Heidegger adds in 1953. I note this because the remark is couched within Heidegger's caution that his introduction to metaphysics is "intentionally presented in a cursory and thus basically ambiguous way." By this he means, as I noted above, that it is still unclear whether metaphysics is a consideration primarily of beings or a matter of a question concerning being as distinct from beings.

8. What I hear in the German phrase as a whole is something like a dynamic, emerging pulsion of emerging interrelationships among emerging things. The "sway" of *phusis* is the way in which the coming into being of things determines each thing to be in relation to all the others, so that each has sway or influence over the other. I do not believe that Heidegger means to suggest by *Walten* that there is some one "previous" thing with greater power than other things that gives rise to and has sway over and beyond the mutually determinative sway of things with each other.

9. A case could be made, I think, that Heidegger's eventual thinking of being, for example, in his *Beiträge zur Philosophie,* in contrast to his interpretation of the way in which the ancient Greeks thought of being, includes this radical eventfulness, and that it is this dimension of being, especially, that traditional metaphysics' preoccupation with beings forgets.

10. I italicize the "that which" here and in what follows to signify the "not yet anything and yet not nothing" character of the referent of the "that which" out of which originary determination first occurs.

11. What remains unquestioned in this phenomenological description, however, is the eventfulness of the conscious subject's coming to be determined as subject in the process. Heidegger's thinking of *phusis,* in contrast, does not assume the preexistence of a subject but is able to think of the emergence of thinking as included in the originary eventfulness of *phusis.* I concur with Charles Scott's claim in his essay in this volume that the very occurrence of things (including human, conscious subjects) is physical.

12. In what sense does the word "overwhelming" in "overwhelming sway" *(überwaltigendes Walten)* characterize *phusis* in this context? Insofar as *phusis* includes both (or all) sides of a struggle, each side, in struggling against the others, struggles with and against itself at the same time. And insofar as the "whole" of *phusis* always exceeds the bounds of any of its aspects, any aspect will inevitably have to give in to that which it is not, that against which it takes a stand. In both these senses, *phusis* overwhelms the beings that arise in and out of it.

13. The question of how we are to think of that to which this naming power belongs reinvokes many of the complexities that we have been attempting to think through

with respect to the meaning of *phusis*. Since the power of naming is an originary power that brings something first to be, it "calls itself" for the first time. But this again puts in radical question the very *status* of whatever the naming power is thought to belong to. If we push this point, we might say that the power to name belongs to nothing, since before the originary naming, there "is" no thing. If we think of this power as belonging to anyone or anything, we need to remember that that to which we assign the power, that to which we think the power belongs, is not originary but subsequent, secondary, "after" that which is originarily named. Thus the meaning of the word "creators" here is also very problematic; it is not to these creators that originary naming can first belong, since the determination "creators" must be secondary to that originary, physical determination of no thing that makes itself into a something.

14. Heidegger translates the Heraclitean word *logos* as "gathering," in a sense that I discuss below.

15. I am not going to examine the fourth of the pairs of opposites that Heidegger discusses, being in opposition to "the ought," because the references to *phusis* in this section relate to what he has discussed in the other sections with no new content.

16. On the basis of an etymological connection between *logos* and the German word *lesen,* Heidegger articulates the wider and more originary meaning as "gathering," "the relation *(Verhältnis)* of one thing to another," but "at the same time, the one…contrasted with the other" (95). Heidegger maintains that this meaning of *logos* as gathering provides, on one hand, a kind of unitary basis that the other, presumably later interpretations of the word (such as its meaning according to traditional logic, or its meaning as *ratio,* or as thinking in the sense of rationality, intellection, or understanding) all have in common. On the other hand, interpreting *logos* as gathering provides a basis for following the latter development of the narrower meanings of the word in which being and *logos* "can and even must be disjoined" (95).

17. In German, the verb *vernehmen* means "to perceive, become aware of; hear, learn, understand."

18. I feel obliged to note how puzzling Heidegger's use of the superlative *deinotaton* is to me when the Sophoclean text plainly uses the comparative form of the word. Even after working through his interpretation of the "doubling" of the strangeness *(deinon)* which, according to the ode, is the manner of being human, I fail to see the grounds for Heidegger's employment of the superlative in his reading. In any case, the motives for his importation of the superlative warrant more careful examination.

19. I find Heidegger's emphasis on violence, on conflict as opposition, tearing, capturing, subjugating, and surmounting, to be overdone. His interpretation of the ode develops the theme of violence in terms of the uncanniness of "the uncanniest," which I also find problematic. (See n. 18 above.) This emphasis ignores the senses in which hu-

man being and other physical things *can* relate to each other in ways other than dominating or being dominated. Heidegger says, for example, that human being "deals with and conserves the familiar" (by which I take him to mean things that are "really" uncanny, only rendered familiar by our subjugation of them) "*only* in order to break out of it, and to let what overwhelms it break in" (125, emphasis added). This seems not just overstated to me but indicative of a kind of obsession with breakage, with violence. I would argue that, in order to be strange, the strange does not always *have* to be violent, nor do humans always *have* to be violent in relation to it. We can, for example, be careful and refrain from breaking things, particularly if there is no need to do so. We can protect things, even those that seem strange to us and are not able to be subjugated by us. Despite his pointing in the next section of the text to the way in which human being remains disposed by an toward *phusis,* he does not, as far as I can tell, ease off in this text from the tone of and obsession with violence that he manifests here. An awareness of the possibilities of reciprocal cooperation with things, I would argue, changes, if not the strangeness of conflictual relations between humans and things, then at least the way this conflict may itself be related to and experienced. Heidegger seems to speak of such reciprocality only in terms of the inevitability of death of dasein—dasein also must inevitably undergo shattering. Perhaps during this period of his writing, Heidegger's obsession with his historical circumstance rendered him *unable to think* in terms of the possibility of cooperation rather than in terms of dominating or being dominated. Perhaps both the focus of his attention and his primary philosophical inspiration here were decisive for him. In this regard, it might be interesting to look at the ways in which Heidegger appears *unquestioningly* to follow this purportedly ancient Greek sense of conflict with things as violent, and of nature as needing to be dominated, which is very different from, for example, a Taoist understanding of things.

When asked what I would say to the question, "Is there a 'proper' way of relating to 'nature'?" or, "How are we to relate 'properly' to nature, to *phusis?*" I might reply with a reminder that by thinking of power and vulnerability not just in terms of dominating and being dominated but also in terms of the importance of the possibilities of cooperating, we can experience power in ways that are still strange but not necessarily threatening.

20. I have translated *scheinen* in this sentence as "appear" instead of "seem." *Phusis* does not only come to "seem" in a work, it comes to *appear* there.

21. The German word *Notwendigkeit,* translated in the English text as *necessity,* cognate with *Not* (urge, urgency, need) carries, in German, also the sense of turning *(wenden).* This word, then, carries a meaning something like "turning urgency" or even "over-turning urgency"—perhaps urgency arising, falling, going under, arising again only to fall again.

Chapter 9. Heidegger's *Antigones*

1. Most readers of the 1942 interpretation miss the radicality of the revision that takes place here because they read the references to poetry in light of the concept of poetry developed in the 1934 reading of Hölderlin and consonant with the artwork as it comes to light in "The Origin of the Work of Art." Thus, for instance, the otherwise informative account of Michael Zimmerman (*Heidegger's Confrontation with Modernity: Technology, Politics, Art* [Bloomington: Indiana University Press, 1990]), who briefly discusses the changes in the accounts and the movement from violent confrontation to acceptance of a *Geschick* (see pp. 118–121) but goes on to develop an account of the development of *technē* in Heidegger's thought that ends in an authentic *technē* and *poiēsis* and does not note the move beyond this that the second reading articulates (see 222–247). Kathleen Wright addresses the difference in the two readings in two articles ("Heidegger's Hölderlin and the Mo(u)rning of History," *Philosophy Today* 37 [winter 1993]: 423–435, and "Heidegger on Hegel's *Antigone:* The Memory of Gender and the Forgetfulness of the Ethical Difference," forthcoming), the second of which specifically notes the shift from *technē* to poetry, but it is not the intention of her articles to analyze the meaning of this shift, and because she reads it as embedded in a sexual difference, she dismisses the later reading as not substantially revising or rejecting the earlier one. Miguel de Beistegui, in his *Heidegger and the Political: Dystopias* (London: Routledge, 1998), gives a careful and detailed account of the differences in the two readings but similarly misses the move to a radical distinction between poetry and *technē;* as a result, he concludes that the displacement of the political accomplished in the second reading is not also a displacement of violence but instead a move to a more originary level of reading that casts the violent inauthenticity of technical mastery against the equally "strifely" authenticity of poetic knowing (143). Alexander Schwan, in *Politische Philosophie im Denken Heideggers* (Opladen: Westdeutscher Verlag, exp. edition 1989), 247–252, presents a detailed account of some of the differences but reads the whole as a "feigned" distancing from politics and does not recognize that the second reading of the ode develops a new concept of human historical dwelling that is meant not only to step out of metaphysics and politics but also to counter and transform these in this move.

2. Aristotle, *Nicomachean Ethics*, 1140a25–1140b30.

3. For the importance of the Aristotelean distinction between *technē* and *phronēsis*, see Jacques Taminiaux, *Heidegger and the Project of Fundamental Ontology*, trans. and ed. Michael Gendre (Albany: SUNY Press, 1991), 111–137. Robert Bernasconi, in "The Fate of the Distinction between Praxis and Poiēsis," *Heidegger Studies* 2 (1986): 110–139, gives a careful and insightful account of the way in which Heidegger's later concept of "dwelling" preserves a sense of *praxis* not reducible to *poiēsis* and *technē*,

though this dwelling is no longer thought in terms of an opposition between *poiēsis* and *praxis,* given that that opposition itself is seen as metaphysical.

4. *Platon: Sophistes,* GA 19, 49.

5. For Heidegger's understanding of conscience, see SZ, 270–300 = *Being and Time,* trans. John Macquarrie and Edward Robinson (New York: Harper and Row, 1962), 315–348.

6. For a detailed account of the development of the productionist model in Heidegger's thought, see Zimmerman, *Heidegger's Confrontation with Modernity.*

7. I discuss this in detail in "From the Metaphysics of Production to Questioning Empowering: Heidegger's Critical Interpretation of the Platonic and Aristotelean Accounts of the Good," *Heidegger Studies* 11: *The New Onset of the Thinking of Being* (1995): 95–121.

8. This move is already suggested, though not fully developed, in 1933 by Heidegger's use of *technē* in the Rectoral Address. See de Beistegui, *Heidegger and the Political,* 47–54.

9. All citations will be taken from Martin Heidegger, *Introduction to Metaphysics,* trans. Gregory Fried and Richard Polt (New Haven: Yale University Press, 2000), hereafter IM. Where the translation is modified, I relied on GA 40.

10. "Global technology" is one way of expressing what Heidegger also refers to variously as the forgetfulness of Being, the flight of the gods, and nihilism; all these phrases highlight different aspects of the same situation and experience.

11. Although Heidegger refers to the original "poetic grounding," "poetry" here means as much as linguistic *technē,* or the setting of truth into work in language, as he makes clear when he elaborates on it as something that "sets beings into limits and form, projects something new (not yet present)" (IM, 110); this is fundamentally different from his use of the phrase in 1942 and beyond.

12. Heidegger indicates that *Fug* first means *"Fuge"* and *"Gefüge."* Although he does not directly bring out the musical sense of *Fuge* as "fugue," this should not be overlooked as a background connotation. A fugue is a temporally given arrangement or ordering of a (potentially inexhaustible) manifold of variations on a theme, whose unity (like Heidegger's interpretation of the unity of the manifold meanings of Being in Aristotle) is analogical.

13. Martin Heidegger, "The Origin of the Work of Art," in *Poetry, Language, Thought,* trans. Albert Hofstadter (New York: Harper & Row, 1971). See especially 49–57 ("The Work and Truth").

14. Though the usual translation is "uncanny," I have preferred "unsettling" because it seems more explicitly to indicate the movement out of the *heimisch* as it is developed in the 1942 reading of the ode in the lecture course on *The Ister.*

15. This is not to suggest that the Greek does not bear his interpretation but merely that his translation definitively stresses the aporetic character of death and leaves no room for a reading that downplays this in the face of the scope of the rest of human achievement (a reading that traditional translations leave open).

16. See Friedrich Nietzsche, *Thus Spoke Zarathustra: A Book for All and None,* trans. Walter Kaufmann (New York: Penguin Books, 1985), esp. 9–25. Nietzsche develops an elaborate word play on *untergehen* and *Untergang,* "setting, decline, or destruction," and *übergehen* and *Übermensch,* "crossing over" and "overman," to express the idea that the human being who affirms will to power must embrace his own destruction because the expression of power always demands that the given actuality be sacrificed for the sake of creating something beyond itself.

17. See Jacques Taminiaux's discussion of the differences between the 1935 and 1936 versions of the lecture and their respective relation to *Introduction to Metaphysics* in Taminiaux, *Heidegger and the Project of Fundamental Ontology,* 213–226, and again in *Poetics, Speculation, and Judgement: The Shadow of the Work of Art from Kant to Phenomenology* (Albany: SUNY Press, 1993, 153–169). There are three versions of the lecture, the first draft (available in *Heidegger Studies* 5 [1989]: 5–22), the second draft of the 1935 lecture, available only in a privately circulated copy, and the final published version, revised between the 1935 and 1936 lectures. Taminiaux bases most of his argument on the private copy of the second draft. He sums up the difference between this version and the final version by saying, "from the outset, the difference in tone between the two is striking. The demand for a decision, the appeal to the will, the call to the German people, in short the previous tone of proclamation and Promethean style have all but faded away in the 1936 text." He then highlights this difference by calling attention to a passage in the later version that rejects the use of force as appropriate in coming to understand the thingly character of the thing (*Heidegger and the Project of Fundamental Ontology,* 225).

18. Heidegger, "Origin of the Work of Art," 87.

19. GA 53. See also *Hölderlin's Hymn "The Ister,"* trans. William McNeill and Julia Davis (Bloomington: Indiana University Press, 1996). The extent of this revision can be partly indicated by the change in his interpretation of the relation between Hölderlin and Nietzsche. In his 1934 lecture course on Hölderlin (GA 39, see esp. 166, 191, 294), Heidegger identifies Hölderlin's concept of the poet explicitly with Nietzsche's *Übermensch* and Hölderlin's understanding of "the essence of historical Dasein" with Nietzsche's conception of the Dionysian and Apollonian, giving Hölderlin credit only for having penetrated more deeply. When he returns to Hölderlin in the 1941–42 lecture course (GA 52), he attacks this comparison and argues instead that "Nietzsche's distinction and role in his metaphysics of will to power is not Greek, but is rooted in modern metaphysics. Hölderlin's distinction on the contrary we must learn to under-

stand as the precursor of the overcoming of all metaphysics" (GA 52, 143). He sums this up by commenting: " 'Nietzsche and Hölderlin'—an abyss separates both. Abyssally differently both determine the nearest and most distant future of the Germans and of the West" (GA 52, 78). This suggests that an "abyss" has likewise been crossed in the move from the earlier work on Hölderlin and poetry to the later.

20. Although Heidegger's *Beiträge zur Philosophie,* which is begun in 1936 and broken off in 1938, initially develops the concept of *Ereignis,* Heidegger continues to work out this concept in other writings between 1938 and 1942.

21. Martin Heidegger, "Time and Being" (1962), in *On Time and Being,* trans. Joan Stambaugh (New York: Harper and Row, 1972), 23. The essay "Building Dwelling Thinking" arguably reworks the concept of the "site" found in IM and in "The Origin of the Work of Art." In the later (1951) essay, Heidegger rejects the world-revealing role of the temple as work, indicating that architecture too must be understood with respect to the place-character of human dwelling, so that "the erecting of buildings would not be suitably defined *even if* we were to think of it in the sense of the original Greek *technē* as *solely* a letting-appear, which brings something made, as present, among the things that are already present" ("Building Dwelling Thinking," in *Poetry, Language, Thought,* 159). Significantly, the earlier example of the temple (an image of religious founding) is replaced with the less presumptuous image of a bridge (the image of the transition that poetic thinking enacts).

22. See GA 53, especially the third section, 153–206.

23. This phrase is from the 1951 lecture ". . . Poetically Man Dwells," in *Poetry, Language, Thought,* 222. Heidegger announces Hölderlin as the poet who founds a new essence of poetry and of history in both GA 39 and in GA 53, though he interprets the meaning of this founding differently. See n. 19 above.

24. A phrase from Hölderlin's poem "In lovely blueness." In his original (1934) interpretation of the Rhine hymn, Heidegger reads Oedipus as the model for authentic human Dasein and interprets this "eye too many" positively, as "a vision for the origin" (GA 39, 267). In the 1942 reading he rejects Oedipus, stressing both the sense of violation and the way in which the Rhine indicates a way of Being that abandons and turns away from the place of origin. In the 1951 ". . . Poetically Man Dwells" he revises his early reading even more explicitly, saying, "Hölderlin says (lines 75–76), 'King Oedipus has perhaps one eye too many.' Thus it might be that our unpoetic dwelling, its incapacity to take the measure, derives from a curious excess of frantic measuring and calculating" (*Poetry, Language, Thought,* 228).

25. See esp. GA 52, 63 and 178, where he stresses this difference.

26. Heidegger develops this concept in the "Memorial Address" in *Discourse on Thinking,* trans. John M. Anderson and E. Hans Freund (New York: Harper and Row, 1966), 43–57.

27. See Graham Parkes, ed., *Heidegger and Asian Thought* (Honolulu: University of Hawaii Press, 1967).

28. The political import of Heidegger's conception of "action" as "letting be" and as poetic dwelling is widely rejected, often in a way that simply begs the essential questions. For instance, Stephen White, in *Political Theory and Postmodernism* (Cambridge: Cambridge University Press, 1991), 31–54, argues that *Gelassenheit* is an "empty category" that is inherently unable to address itself to the problem of intersubjective action because, in the absence of normative standards of legitimacy, such action cannot be conceived except as coercion. But in this he assumes that *Gelassenheit* cannot "act" because it cannot "will," and he does not engage Heidegger's argument that it has its own nonnormative measure of legitimacy. Zimmerman (*Heidegger's Confrontation with Modernity,* 256–257) makes a similar move when he dismisses the claim that "it is precisely the disclosure of the lack of metaphysical foundations that opens up the possibility for freedom" by rhetorically asking, "How can we define 'freedom' in terms other than those associated with the 'selfhood' traditionally linked with the capacity for freely chosen action?" This is precisely the question, but he fails to elaborate on his grounds for rejecting the very possibility.

29. See especially GA 52, 64–103.

30. As Leslie Paul Thiele suggests in *Timely Meditations: Martin Heidegger and Postmodern Politics* (Princeton: Princeton University Press, 1995), 206, "waiting for a god is an attendance upon the reawakening of our capacity for fundamental questioning, nothing more or less."

31. I owe thanks to Gregory Fried for some very helpful suggestions about the phrasing of these closing remarks.

Chapter 10. The Ontological Decline of the West

My thanks to Gregory Fried and Richard Polt for their many suggestions, which improved this essay. Thanks also to David Pettigrew, who offered helpful criticisms of this essay when it was presented at the Heidegger Conference at DePaul University on April 23, 1999. Parenthesized numbers refer to the pagination of the Niemeyer edition of *Einführung in die Metaphysik.* I refer to this text as "*EM.*"

1. See Michael E. Zimmerman, *Heidegger's Confrontation with Modernity* (Bloomington: Indiana University Press, 1990).

2. The literature on Heidegger's Nazi involvement is voluminous. An important statement by Heidegger himself, "The Rectorate 1933/34: Facts and Thoughts," is translated in Günther Neske and Emil Kettering, ed., *Martin Heidegger and National Socialism* (New York: Paragon House, 1990). Secondary literature includes Tom Rockmore and Joseph Margolis, eds., *The Heidegger Case* (Philadelphia: Temple University Press, 1992); Richard Wolin, ed., *The Heidegger Controversy* (New York: Columbia Uni-

versity Press, 1991); Zimmerman, *Heidegger's Confrontation with Modernity;* James F. Ward, *Heidegger's Political Thinking* (Amherst: University of Massachusetts Press, 1995); Julian Young, *Heidegger, Philosophy, Nazism* (New York: Cambridge University Press, 1997). See also Hugo Ott, *Martin Heidegger: A Political Life,* trans. Allan Blenden (New York: Basic Books, 1993), and Rüdiger Safranski, *Martin Heidegger: Between Good and Evil,* trans. Ewald Osers (Cambridge: Harvard University Press, 1998).

3. In *Reconstructing America: The Symbol of America in Modern Thought* (New Haven: Yale University Press, 1997), James W. Ceaser describes how many conservative Europeans—including Heidegger—scorned America as a degenerate society, ruled by technocrats and motivated by money lust. See Richard Wolin's review "The Anti-American Revolution," in *The New Republic,* August 17 and 24, 1998, 35–41.

4. Had he chosen to do so, the postwar Heidegger could have said that this passage helps explain the demonic character of the Holocaust, in which Jews and other peoples were treated like industrial wastes. But in so saying, he would have been expected to address other aspects of the Holocaust, including its specifically German dimensions. This, unfortunately, he never did. See Alan Milchman and Alan Rosenberg, eds., *Heidegger and the Holocaust* (Atlantic Highlands, N.J.: Humanities Press, 1994).

5. It is not clear whether Heidegger meant to use the mirror metaphor as a way of describing Dasein's capacity for understanding Being. If he did so intend, however, the mirror metaphor may be inconsistent with his critique of representationalism. Discussion of this complex topic must await another opportunity.

6. For Heidegger's discussion of the superficiality of the "symptoms" of decay, see *The Fundamental Concepts of Metaphysics,* trans. William McNeill and Nicholas Walker (Bloomington: Indiana University Press, 1995), 162–163.

7. See Michael E. Zimmerman, *Eclipse of the Self: The Development of Heidegger's Concept of Authenticity* (Athens: Ohio University Press, 1981).

8. See *Von Wesen der Wahrheit,* GA 34. On this topic, see Michael E. Zimmerman, "Ontical Craving vs. Ontological Desire," in *From Phenomenology to Thought, Errancy, and Desire,* ed. Babette Babich (Dordrecht: Kluwer Academic Publishers, 1995), 503–525.

9. On the moods of boredom and horror, see Heidegger, *The Fundamental Concepts of Metaphysics,* 142–144, 160–162; GA 34, 195–197, 207; GA 45, 197.

10. GA 39, 141.

11. See Kathleen Wright, "Heidegger's Hölderlin and The Mo(u)rning of History," *Philosophy Today* 37 (winter 1993): 423–435. See John D. Caputo, *Demythologizing Heidegger* (Bloomington: Indiana University Press, 1993), for a good account of Heidegger's attitude of manly hardness in the 1930s.

12. Arthur Herman, *The Idea of Decline in Western History* (New York: Free Press, 1997). I am indebted to this important and informative book.

13. Cited in ibid., 84.

14. Cited in ibid., 69.

15. On the "blond beast," see Friedrich Nietzsche, *The Genealogy of Morals,* trans. Walter Kaufmann (New York: Modern Library, 1968), first essay, sec. 11, 476. Kaufmann's footnote to this disturbing term warns that Nietzsche himself did not envision that right-wing ideologues would eventually use his image of the "blond beast" in connection with their anti-Semitic ideology.

16. See Zimmerman, *Heidegger's Confrontation with Modernity.*

17. Herman, *Idea of Decline,* 238. Oswald Spengler, *The Decline of the West,* 2 vols., trans. Charles Francis Atkinson (New York: Alfred A. Knopf, 1947).

18. Michael Pauen, *Pessimismus: Geschichtsphilosophie, Metaphysik und Moderne von Nietzsche bis Spengler* (Berlin: Akademie Verlag, 1997), 181.

19. Herman, *Idea of Decline,* 234.

20. Ibid.

21. Pauen, *Pessimismus,* 183.

22. John Farrenkopf, "The Transformation of Spengler's Philosophy of World History," *Journal of the History of Ideas* 52:3 (July–September, 1991), 463–485; quotation is from 477.

23. Jeffrey Andrew Barash, *Martin Heidegger and the Problem of Historical Meaning* (Dordrecht: Martinus Nijhoff, 1988), 151. To this excellent book I am greatly indebted.

24. Pauen, *Pessimismus,* 191.

25. Farrenkopf, "Transformation," 479.

26. Barash, *Problem of Historical Meaning,* 55.

27. See ibid., 163 n. 52.

28. Quoted in John Farrenkopf, "Hegel, Spengler, and the Enigma of World History," *Clio* 19:4 (summer 1990), 331–344; citation is from 336. On Spengler's performative contradiction, see 337.

29. Herman, *Idea of Decline,* 239.

30. Spengler, *Decline of the West,* 1:5.

31. Herman, *Idea of Decline,* 239.

32. Ibid.

33. Ibid., 240.

34. Spengler, cited by Herman, *Idea of Decline,* 240.

35. Spengler, *Decline of the West,* 2:504–505.

36. Ibid., 506.

37. Ibid., 2:507; Herman, *Idea of Decline,* 240.

38. Herman, *Idea of Decline,* 245.

39. Ibid., 246.

40. Pauen, *Pessimismus,* 182.

41. As cited in Herman, *Idea of Decline,* 249.

42. For examples of Heidegger on Spengler, see GA 63, 39, 55–57; GA 59, 16 ff.; GA 61, 26–75; GA 29/30, 105–107; GA 66, 27–28. Concerning Spengler's influence on Heidegger, see Zimmerman, *Heidegger's Confrontation with Modernity,* 17, 26–31.

43. See Barash, *Problem of Historical Meaning,* 147.

44. Heidegger, *Holzwege* (Frankfurt am Main: Vittorio Klostermann, 1972), 301; *Nietzsche,* I (Günther Neske: Pfullingen, 1961), 360.

45. See Pauen, *Pessimismus,* 188.

46. Heidegger, "The Origin of the Work of Art," in *Poetry, Language, Thought,* trans. Albert Hofstadter (New York: Harper & Row, 1971), 42.

47. On the notion of language as the "house of Being," see Martin Heidegger, "Letter on 'Humanism,' " trans. Frank A. Capuzzi, in *Pathmarks,* ed. William McNeill (New York: Cambridge University Press, 1998), 239.

48. Herman, *Idea of Decline,* 241.

49. Barash, *Problem of Historical Meaning,* 157.

50. Ibid.

51. On the eschatology of Being, see John D. Caputo, *Radical Hermeneutics* (Bloomington: Indiana University Press, 1987), 153–186; Christopher Fynsk, *Heidegger: Thought and Historicity* (Ithaca: Cornell University Press, 1986); and Reiner Schürmann, *Heidegger on Being and Acting: From Principles to Anarchy* (Bloomington: Indiana University Press, 1987).

52. Barash, *Problem of Historical Meaning,* 157.

53. GA 61, 74.

54. Ibid.

55. Barash, *Problem of Historical Meaning,* 158–159.

56. GA 63, 56.

57. Barash, *Problem of Historical Meaning,* 158–159.

58. GA 61, 73–74.

59. Ibid., 74.

60. Barash, *Problem of Historical Meaning,* 220, 253–254.

61. Ken Wilber, *Sex, Ecology, Spirituality* (Boston: Shambhala, 1995); Wilber, *A Brief History of Everything* (Boston: Shambhala, 1996).

62. Barash, *Problem of Historical Meaning,* 250.

63. Ken Wilber, *The Marriage of Sense and Soul: Integrating Science and Religion* (New York: Random House, 1998), 103.

64. On this point, see Caputo, *Demythologizing Heidegger.*

65. In *Demythologizing Heidegger,* 97, Caputo cites *Der Satz vom Grund* (Pfullingen: Günther Neske, 1957) as abandoning the search for origin.

66. See Wilber, *Sex, Ecology, Spirituality;* Brian Swimme and Thomas Berry, *The Universe Story* (HarperSanFrancisco, 1992); Paul Davies, *The Mind of God* (New York: Touchstone, 1992).

67. For a brilliant defense of Hegel against his postmodern detractors, see Cyril O'Regan, *The Heterodox Hegel* (Albany: SUNY Press, 1993).

Chapter 11. "Conflict Is the Father of All Things"

I owe thanks to Andrew Norris, Piotr Hoffman, Hubert Dreyfus, and the editors of this volume for critical comments and questions about an earlier version of this paper.

1. Karl Löwith, "Last Meeting with Heidegger," in *Mein Leben in Deutschland vor und nach 1933,* trans. Richard Wolin, in Günther Neske and Emil Kettering, *Martin Heidegger and National Socialism* (New York: Paragon House, 1990), hereafter NK, 158.

2. Heidegger, "The Rectorate 1933/34: Facts and Thoughts," in NK, 17, 19.

3. Martin Heidegger and Karl Jaspers, *Briefwechsel 1920–1963,* ed. Walter Biemel and Hans Saner (Frankfurt: Vittorio Klostermann, 1990), 157. The letter was Heidegger's first communication with Jaspers since 1933.

4. Even many years later, in the *Spiegel* interview, Heidegger would say that "today, and today more resolutely than ever, I would repeat the speech on the 'Self-Assertion of the German University' " (NK, 46). And what was true for him in 1969 must surely have held in 1935.

5. Heidegger, "The Self-Assertion of the German University," in NK, 6, hereafter referred to as RA.

6. Heidegger, *Nietzsche,* trans. David Farrell Krell, (New York: Harper & Row, 1979), 1:166.

7. Ibid.

8. Heidegger speaks of a *Walten* of *physis*—rendered here as "sway." It proves unfortunately impossible in English to maintain the association between *Walten, unbewältigt* (not surmounted), *überwältigend* (overhelming), and *Welt* (world) on which Heidegger draws in this passage, as well as his later reliance on the association of *Walten* and *Gewalt* (force).

9. The term *polis* meant originally not a place of habitation (as city=*civitas* does) but a place of defensive fortification. The connotation is still alive in the term "acropolis."

10. The German word *Gewalt* has no equivalent in English. *Staatsgewalt* is the power of the state, *rohe Gewalt* is crude force, and a *Gewalttat* is an act of violence. Heidegger's formulations mobilize the whole spectrum of meanings of this term. In order to preserve some of these distinctions, I render *Gewalt* as "force," *Gewalttätigkeit* as "violence," and their derivatives accordingly.

11. Martin Heidegger, "The Origin of the Work of Art," in *Poetry, Language, Thought,* trans. Albert Hofstadter (New York: Harper & Row, 1971), 61 f., hereafter referred to as WA.

12. I remain deeply skeptical of Lacoue-Labarthe's characterization of National Socialism as a "national aestheticism" and of his claim that "racism—and anti-semitism in particular—is primarily, fundamentally, an aestheticism." Philippe Lacoue-Labarthe, *Heidegger, Art and Politics* (Oxford: Basil Blackwell, 1990), 69.

13. Friedrich Nietzsche, "The Greek State," in *The Complete Works of Friedrich Nietzsche,* ed. Oscar Levy, vol. 2, *Early Greek Philosophy & Other Essays,* trans. M. A. Mügge (New York: Russell & Russell, 1964), 11, 13, hereafter GS.

14. Carl Schmitt, *The Concept of the Political,* trans. George Schwab (Chicago: University of Chicago Press, 1996), 25 f., hereafter CP.

15. For the German text and an English translation see *Telos* 72 (summer 1987): 132.

16. The whole episode is described at length in Hugo Ott's *Martin Heidegger: A Political Life,* trans. A. Blunden (New York: Basic Books, 1993).

17. Paul Noack, *Carl Schmitt: Eine Biographie* (Frankfurt: Propyläen, 1993), 179 f. Heidegger had also been offered a position at Berlin at the same time that he turned down after some hesitation. It is possible that Schmitt may have known of this offer and that he may have sent Heidegger his brochure in order to make contact with his prospective colleague.

18. CP, 58. In support of his thesis Schmitt draws on Helmuth Plessner's *Macht und menschliche Natur* (Berlin: Juncker & Dünnhaupt, 1931). See also Heiner Bielefeldt, *Kampf und Entscheidung: Politischer Existentialismus bei Carl Schmitt, Hellmuth Plessner und Karl Jaspers* (Würzburg: Königshausen & Neumann, 1994).

19. Carl Schmitt, *Political Theology,* trans. George Schwab (Cambridge: MIT Press, 1988), 46.

20. Carl Schmitt, "The Age of Neutralizations and Depoliticizations," trans. Matthias Konzett and John P. McCormick, *Telos* 96 (1993): 136, hereafter AND.

21. The lecture was appended to the edition of *The Concept of the Political* with which Heidegger was familiar according to his letter to Schmitt. The lecture was not included in the English translation of that work.

22. Bruno Bauch, "Das Volk als Natur- und Sinngebilde," *Völkische Kultur* 2 (1934): 122. Cited from Hans Sluga, *Heidegger's Crisis* (Cambridge: Harvard University Press, 1993), chap. 9, where the philosophical and political dispute between Heidegger and the Nazi value-theorists is discussed.

23. Karl Löwith, "The Occasional Decisionism of Carl Schmitt," in Löwith, *Martin Heidegger and European Nihilism,* ed. R. Wolin, trans. Gary Steiner (New York: Colum-

bia University Press, 1995), 144, hereafter ODS. Löwith had published the article originally in 1935 under the pseudonym "H. Fiala" in the *Internationale Zeitschrift für The-
orie des Rechts.*

24. Carl Schmitt, *Gesetz und Urteil: Eine Untersuchung zum Problem der Rechtspraxis,*
2nd ed. (Munich: C. H. Beck, 1969), v.

25. GA 53, 98.

Chapter 12. Heidegger's Philosophical Geopolitics

1. Citations from *Introduction to Metaphysics* (IM) follow the pagination of the
Niemeyer editions. I have sometimes revised the Fried and Polt translation.

2. Jacques Derrida, *Of Spirit: Heidegger and the Question,* trans. G. Bennington and
R. Brown (Chicago: University of Chicago Press, 1989), 70.

3. Richard Wolin, *The Politics of Being: The Political Thought of Martin Heidegger*
(New York: Columbia University Press, 1990), 105.

4. Derrida, *Of Spirit,* 45–46. Heidegger will go one step further in shifting geopolitics from geographical location and spiritual position to the ontological site of concrete
Da-sein in its particular place in the history of be-ing, which, following the clues of ancient Greek tragedy, he will call the πόλις. By this transposition, this history of the West
from ancient Greek Da-sein to modern German Da-sein itself becomes a geopolitics, a
term that Heidegger never uses but that suggests itself through his use of its common-
places, images, and quasi-geographical oppositions such as East and West, Greek and
German. Geopolitics is a discipline that came into full flourish in World War I, which
was commonly understood as a clash of contending worldviews. Broadly defined, geopolitics is a study of the international politics and power relations that develop from the
geographical juxtaposition of indigenous peoples, each with its unique character shaped
by its domestic environment, beginning with the natural landscape (e.g., Schlageter's
Schwarzwald) with its natural resources and viable occupations (e.g., agrarian vs. mari-
time), and extending to the tradition that each locale cultivates, its customs, folklore,
popular mythos, art, all embodied in a common language. In order to express these two
elements of folk environment, Heidegger will develop two poietic-ontological concepts:
the ways and mores of a folk's inhabitation joined in a unifying style named ἦθος
(= *Brauch:* "tradition, custom, usage"), environmentally "the habit of a habitat"; and
bodenständig(keit) ("indigenous, autochthonous, native": IM, 30), rootedness in a native land or homeland and attachment to that *Vaterland.* National Socialist geopolitics
was based on both blood and soil *(Blut und Boden)* to justify its demands for adequate
"living space" and its policy of displacing non-Germanic populations from their lands,
and worse. See my conclusion for more on ontological geopolitics, especially on the
wholesale deracination of its ethnic pluralism through the leveling incurred by cos-
mopolitan universalism and by technological globalization.

5. "Beings and their be-ing [*Sein*]," i. e., their dynamic ordering, which imparts context and direction to beings, gives them sense, which Heidegger in BT identifies with time, *Temporalität*. The translation of *Sein* as "Being" has become a conceptual hypostatization obfuscating the temporal action that the highly verbal German language naturally conveys. The relational hyphen not only dynamizes be-*ing* into a current event (It's happen*ing!*) and a power *(Es zeitigt sich!)* but also suggests that It is fundamentally the action of relational structuring, of organizing and contextualizing (It's worlding!), and in that articulated context identifying (It's appropriating, It's properizing!) and differentiating *(Es gegnet!)* beings (cf. below on λόγος as discriminating gathering), thereby allotting them position (It's taking place!), rank (It's regioning!), and a historical "reason" (λόγος) to be. The be-ing of Da-sein, itself already an ever-developing nexus of I-myself-here-and-now-with-others-amidst-things-in the world permeated in every domain by the urgency of a tendential care-to-be, have-to-be, potential-to-be, is in particular a temporally charged historical context tense with the immediacy of transition. When Heidegger asks, "What be-ing do we name in the sentence, 'we *are*'?" (IM, 53), he is not referring to a static and permanent group identity but first to the critical transitional nexus of German Da-sein in 1935, extending back to its roots as a "metaphysical folk," and then forward to its fate in a developing commonwealth of nations by way of the present decision over its historical "geopolitical" mission.

6. *Entborgenheit,* a Heideggerian neologism substituting for the more customary *Unverborgenheit* (unconcealment), first appears in the 1930 talk marking Heidegger's *Kehre,* "Vom Wesen der Wahrheit," to which he refers in this bracketed addendum. But Heidegger also misleadingly refers to the 1927 text of *Sein und Zeit,* in which *Entborgenheit* does not yet appear.

7. Martin Heidegger, *Die Selbstbehauptung der deutschen Universität; Das Rektorat 1933/34,* ed. Hermann Heidegger (Frankfurt: Klostermann, 1983), 14 = *Martin Heidegger and National Socialism: Questions and Answers,* ed. Günther Neske and Emil Kettering, trans. Lisa Harries (New York: Paragon House, 1990), 9, translation modified.

8. In 1934–1935, Heidegger served on the committee for philosophy of law within the Academy for German Law; in November 1935, he became a member of the scholarly committee for the historical-critical edition of Nietzsche's works. See M. Heinz and T. Kisiel, "Heideggers Beziehungen zum Nietzsche-Archiv im Dritten Reich," in *Annäherungen an Martin Heidegger: Festschrift für Hugo Ott zum 65. Geburtstag,* ed. H. Schäfer (Frankfurt: Campus, 1996), 103–136.

9. In the winter semester of 1934–35, Heidegger held a seminar jointly with his colleague in the philosophy of law, Erik Wolf, called "Hegel und der Staat," in which a few remarks on the current political situation occur. It is recorded in the notebooks of S. Bröse and W. Hallwachs, who also took notes in the course of the summer semester 1935, as we shall see.

10. Actually, the last line was "Heil Hitler!" Article in the Freiburg student newspaper on November 3, 1933, cited in full in Guido Schneeberger, *Nachlese zu Heidegger: Dokumente zu seinem Leben und Denken* (Bern 1962), 135 f.

11. GA 53, 100 = *Hölderlin's Hymn "The Ister,"* trans. William McNeill and Julia Davis (Bloomington: Indiana University Press, 1996), 81. The Sophoclean chorus is again taken up for extensive interpretation in similar terms in the following semester's course (WS 1942–1943), titled *Parmenides;* cf. GA 54: 132–143/89–96. The most detailed assessment of this series of "political" renditions of the Sophoclean chorus, performed by Heidegger from 1935 to 1943, is to be found in Miguel de Beistegui, *Heidegger and the Political: Dystopias* (London: Routledge, 1998), chap. 5, "Before Politics." See also the article in this volume by Clare Pearson Geiman, "Heidegger's *Antigones.*"

12. GA 39, 214. The reference here is to Hölderlin as "poet of the Germans" who articulates the "saga" of the history of his people with an eye to its "farthest future" in its primal language (214–217, 220). The brief cross-reference to Sophocles' *Antigone* (216) as an act of institution of the archaic be-ing of Greek Dasein suggests that the *seynsgeschichtliche* conception is equiprimordially the "poietic" conception of the political as it spans ("sends") from Greek to German Dasein.

13. Otto Pöggeler, "Heidegger's Political Self-Understanding," trans. Steven Galt Crowell, in *The Heidegger Controversy: A Critical Reader,* ed. Richard Wolin (Cambridge: MIT Press, 1993), 200–244, esp. 217 f.

14. GA 38. A leaner transcript of this course made by Luise Grosse has been published in a Spanish bilingual edition by Víctor Farías, *Lógica: Lecciones de M. Heidegger (semestre verano 1934) en el legado de Helene Weiss* (Barcelona: Anthropos, 1991).

15. Jürgen Habermas, "Zur Veröffentlichung von Vorlesungen aus dem Jahre 1935," in *Philosophisch-politische Profile* (Frankfurt: Suhrkamp, 1971), 67–75, here 75; = "On the Publication of Lectures of 1935," trans. W. S. Lewis, in Wolin, *Heidegger Controversy,* 190–197, here 197. There is an earlier English translation by Dale Ponikvar in *Graduate Faculty Philosophy Journal* 6:2 (fall 1977): 155–164.

16. "Das Ge-Stell," in GA 79, 24–45, here 27. This passage is not to be found in previous editions of this talk, and so in extant English translations of it.

17. Christian E. Lewalter, "Wie liest man 1953 Sätze von 1935? Zu einem politischen Streit um Heideggers Metaphysik," *Die Zeit*, 13 August 1953, 6.

18. GA 40. The editor's postscript (231–234) cites in full not only this letter of September 15, 1953, but also Heidegger's letter of March 18, 1968, to S. Zemach in Jerusalem.

19. " 'Nur noch ein Gott kann uns retten': *Spiegel*-Gespräch mit Martin Heidegger am 23. September 1966," *Der Spiegel* 33 (May 31, 1976), 193–219, here 204, 206 =

Neske and Kettering, *Martin Heidegger and National Socialism*, 41–66, here 54. There are also invaluable English translations of this important interview, one of Heidegger's more public *Denkwege*, by Maria P. Alter and John D. Caputo in *Philosophy Today* 20:4 (winter 1976): 267–284, and by William J. Richardson, S.J., in *Heidegger: The Man and the Thinker*, ed. Thomas Sheehan (Chicago: Precedent, 1981), 45–67. But the translation in Neske and Kettering is based on "Heidegger's own copy" and contains clarifying sentences that are not in the magazine rendition. The interview was in part prompted by a prior magazine article on Heidegger by the editors, "Mitternacht einer Weltnacht," *Der Spiegel* 7 (February 1966): 110–113, which provides the basis for many of the questions posed by the editors to Heidegger. Unfortunately, they never asked about Heidegger's attitude toward Hitler himself, developing from admiration to disgust, in distinction from his party functionaries (the "Rosenberg nonsense"), who began to attack Heidegger publicly after he resigned as rector.

20. The most detailed account comes from Hartmut Buchner, "Fragmentarisches," in *Erinnerung an Martin Heidegger*, ed. Günther Neske (Pfullingen: Neske, 1977), 47–51, esp. 49. The other two student assistants were Rainer Marten and Heribert Boeder.

21. Dominique Janicaud, *The Shadow of That Thought: Heidegger and the Question of Politics*, trans. Michael Gendre (Evanston: Northwestern University Press, 1996), 55, citing from chap. 4, "The Purloined Letter," devoted entirely to the offensive sentence of 1935 and 1953. Another translation of this chapter is to be found in Tom Rockmore and Joseph Margolis, eds., *The Heidegger Case: On Philosophy and Politics* (Philadelphia: Temple University Press, 1992), 348–363, here 353.

Some sense of how well his student auditors understood Heidegger's words in this double-hour on June 27, 1935, that concluded the course (IM, 144 lines 23–157, end of book) is manifested in the two extant student notebooks that are accessible in the Heidegger Archive in Marbach (Deutsches Literaturarchiv). We begin with the text of IM, 152, as it is recorded in Fritz Heidegger's typed transcript of p. 78 of the original handwritten manuscript. (At the end of ms. p. 73 of this transcription, we find a penciled note in Heidegger's hand, "74 ff. Meßkirch." This is a reference to the original ms. pp. 74–81, i.e., the concluding double-hour of the course, which the GA's editor now reports as "missing from the archive" [GA 40: 231, 234].)

From Fritz Heidegger's *Abschrift*, which is in fact a true and accurate transcript (aside from a few random errors in deciphering his brother's handwriting) of the original manuscript from which Heidegger read his course (= IM, 152, lines 5–13):

"Vermutlich sind es inzwischen tausend geworden; das alles nennt sich Philosophie. [Und wenn man jetzt noch jene komische Wissenschaft der Aporetik auf die Wertlehre anwendet, wird alles noch komischer und überschlägt sich in den Unsinn.] Aber wohlgemerkt, das gilt heute als streng wissenschaftliche Philosophie. Was nun vollends heute als Philosophie des Nationalsozialismus herumgeboten wird, aber mit der inneren Wahrheit und Größe des N. S. nicht das Geringste zu tun hat, das macht seiner Fischzüge in diesen trüben Gewässern der 'Werte' und der 'Ganzheiten'.

"Wie hartnäckig. . . ."

("Probably by now there are a thousand. All this calls itself philosophy. [And if one now applies that strange science of aporetics to the doctrine of values, everything becomes still stranger and quickly turns into nonsense.] But mark it well, today this counts as rigorously scientific philosophy. In particular, what is peddled about nowadays as the philosophy of National Socialism, but which has not the least to do with the inner truth and greatness of National Socialism, is fishing in these troubled waters of 'values' and 'totalities.'

"Yet we can see how stubbornly. . . .")

The sentence in brackets was clearly not read in the course, as we can see from the student notebooks, and was omitted from the published edition (GA 40, 234).

From Sigmund Bröse's notes of 27 June:

"Aber nur die Buchstaben haben gewechselt, es bleiben Halbheiten.

"Was heute als Philosophie des National-Sozialismus herausgeboten wird, macht seine Fischzüge im Trüben der Werte und Ganzheiten, und hat nichts zu tun mit der großen Idee des Nationalsozialismus.

"Nietzsche bleibt noch ganz in der Verstrickung und in der Wirrnis der Wertvorstellungen. . . ."

("But only the letters have changed; these remain half measures.

"In particular, what is peddled about nowadays as the philosophy of National Socialism is fishing in the troubled waters of values and totalities, and has nothing to do with the great idea of National Socialism.

"Nietzsche remains entirely entangled in the confusion of the representation of values. . . .")

From Wilhelm Hallwachs's notes on 27 June (272):

"Bei Literaturverzeichnis zählt 661 Schriften über Wertbegriff auf; alles nennt sich Philosophie. Was nun vollends heute unter der Flagge des National Sozialismus (sehr gegen den wahren Geist dieser Bewegung) herumgeboten wird, der macht seinen Fischzug in den trüben Gewässern von Werten und Ganzheiten. Wie hartnäckig der Wertgedanke sich festgesetzt hat. . . ."

("The bibliography lists 661 works on the concept of value; all this calls itself philosophy. In particular, what is peddled about now under the flag of National Socialism (very much against the true spirit of this movement) is fishing in the troubled waters of values and totalities. How stubbornly the thought of values entrenched itself. . . .")

22. This is a quick summary of "The Age of the World Picture," the talk first delivered in Freiburg on June 9, 1938, which constitutes Heidegger's public philosophical

response to the Four Year Plan and which some regard as his first unequivocal critique of National Socialism. Martin Heidegger, "Die Zeit des Weltbildes," in *Holzwege* (Frankfurt: Klostermann, 1951), 69–104 = *The Question Concerning Technology and Other Essays,* trans. William Lovitt (San Francisco: Harper Colophon, 1977), 115–154.

23. The following collation of scattered "technical" passages in SS 1937 is drawn from Martin Heidegger, *Nietzsche I* (Pfullingen: Neske, 1961) = *Nietzsche,* trans. David Farrell Krell, vol. 2, *The Eternal Recurrence of the Same* (San Francisco: HarperCollins, 1991). Remarks on the technologizing of science and scholarship continue into WS 1937–1938 in the course titled *Basic Questions of Philosophy:* see GA 45: 3f./5f., 53–55/49f., 110–113/96–99, 141–143/123f., 179/154.

24. Martin Heidegger, "Die Bedrohung der Wissenschaft: Arbeitskreis von Dozenten der naturwissenschaftlichen und medizinischen Fakultät (November 1937)—(Auszüge)," in *Zur philosophischen Aktualität Heideggers,* ed. D. Papenfuss and O. Pöggeler, vol. 1, *Philosophie und Politik* (Frankfurt: Klostermann, 1991), 5–27. Page references here are first to the delivered talk itself (5–11) and then to an accompanying set of loose "notes on the working circle" that was held *privatissime* since the fall of 1936, which the editor (Hartmut Tietjen) has titled "Philosophie, Wissenschaft und Weltanschauung" (14–27). A middle section titled "Besinnung auf die Wissenschaft" (11–14) is not cited in the above.

25. Martin Heidegger, "Überwindung der Metaphysik," in *Vorträge und Aufsätze* (Pfullingen: Neske, 1954), 71–99, esp. 94, 96 = *The End of Philosophy,* trans. Joan Stambaugh (New York: Harper & Row, 1973), 84–110, esp. 105, 107; reproduced in Wolin, *Heidegger Controversy,* "Overcoming Metaphysics (1936–1946)," 67–90, esp. 85, 87; references are to no. XXVI of this collection of notes, a note that was written no earlier than late 1942. Heidegger's last reference to Hitler as statesman, tinged with a mild critique, occurs in the Schelling course of SS 1936: "It is in fact evident that the two men who have initiated countermovements [to nihilism] in Europe for the political formation of their nation as well as their people, that both Mussolini and Hitler are essentially determined by Nietzsche, again in different ways, and this without the authentic metaphysical domain of Nietzschean thought having an immediate impact in the process" (GA 42, 40f.).

26. "The gigantic is rather that through which the quantitative becomes a special quality and thus an exceptional kind of greatness. Every historical age is not only great in a different way when compared to others; it also has, in each instance, its own concept of greatness" ("The Age of the World Picture," 88/135). On the development of the concept of the greatness of Dasein (in each case ours) at this time, also see the following: GA 29/30 (WS 1929–1930), 244/163; GA 45 (WS 1937–1938), 55/49, 82/74, 125f./109f., 199/161. Silvio Vietta is still a year or two too early in declaring that the "greatness" of NS in the 1935 sentence "no longer has a positive connotation"

because of its equation with the quantitatively gigantic, say, mass rallies: Silvio Vietta, *Heideggers Kritik am Nationalsozialismus und an der Technik* (Tübingen: Niemeyer, 1989), 31.

27. GA 29/30 = *The Fundamental Concepts of Metaphysics: World, Finitude, Solitude,* trans. William McNeill and Nicholas Walker (Bloomington: Indiana University Press, 1995).

28. Fruitful philosophical interchanges with Scheler shortly before his death in 1928 prompted Heidegger to become involved in the process of preparing Scheler's literary remains for publication. Thus, Heidegger became intimately acquainted with the opus of his older phenomenological colleague, who throughout his career did not hesitate to cross over into political commentary, from his war books of 1914–1918 to this 1927 address at the military college in Berlin. Scheler's numerous essays on the "spirit of capitalism" are no doubt a proximate source of Heidegger's remark that capitalism and socialism are "metaphysically the same." For a useful synopsis, see Manfred S. Frings, *The Mind of Max Scheler* (Milwaukee: Marquette University Press, 1997), 167–180. For allusions to this double economic-political front threatening the German democracy of 1927, situated at the heart of the "tensions between London and Moscow," with "dictatorial tendencies from right and left," see "Der Mensch im Weltalter des Ausgleichs," in Max Scheler, *Späte Schriften,* vol. 9 of the *Gesammelte Werke,* ed. Manfred S. Frings (Bern: Francke, 1976), 145–170, esp. 145, 152, 165f. "The most gruesome vision for Scheler was a Europe being squeezed to death between America and Russia": Otto Pöggeler, "Scheler und die heutigen anthropologischen Ansätze zur Metaphysik," in *Schritte zu einer hermeneutischen Philosophie* (Freiburg: Alber, 1994), 203–226, esp. 220. In part because of the changes in the political situation of the thirties, but perhaps also because Scheler was part Jewish, Heidegger never acknowledges Scheler as one of his "journalistic" sources after 1929.

29. See Wolin, *Heidegger Controversy,* 119–139, for a translation of "Total Mobilization." The penultimate section (no. 8) speaks of the enfranchised masses being "tossed around like a ball by the 'right' and 'left.' . . . The identity of these two sides is now becoming more and more apparent in all lands; even the dream of freedom is disappearing as in a pincers's iron grasp" (138). Jünger's literary elegance is in this instance no match for Heidegger's clear phenomenological prose in making the European "squeeze" more dramatic and tense.

30. Friedrich Naumann, *Mitteleuropa* (Berlin: Georg Reiner, 1915) = *Central Europe,* intro. W. J. Ashley, trans. C. M. Meredith (London: P. S. King, 1916).

31. On Americanism and the Americans, see GA 34 (WS 1931–1932), 209; "Die Zeit des Weltbildes" (1938), 103/153; GA 66 (1939), 39; GA 52 (WS 1941–1942), 10, 35, 133f.; GA 53 (SS 1942), 68/54f., 80/65f., 86/70; "Wozu Dichter?" (1946), in

Holzwege, 268 f.; "Letter on Humanism" (1947), in *Basic Writings,* 220; "Zürcher Seminar" (1951), GA 15, 437. The abuse intensifies with America's entry into the war and ebbs when Heidegger meets native Americans fluent in German and in his philosophy, such as Glenn Gray.

32. GA 65. On the *Volk,* see 24 f., 28, 30, 40, 42 f., 48–54, 61, 97–99, 117, 219, 319, 398 f., 414, 496, 507. On the various facets of *Technik,* see 107–9, 119–166, 277 f., 392, 408 f. (giganticism versus greatness), 441–443 (ditto), 493–495. On the political, see 19, 41 (as total), 99, 140–142, 155 f., 309, 422, 507.

33. Theodore Kisiel, "Situating Rhetorical Politics in Heidegger's Protopractical Ontology (1923–25: The French Occupy the Ruhr)," *International Journal of Philosophical Studies* 8:2 (summer 2000): 185–208. See also Kisiel, "In the Middle of Heidegger's Three Concepts of the Political," in *Heidegger and Practical Philosophy,* ed. François Raffoul and David Pettigrew (forthcoming).

34. On polemic contention and struggle, see Gregory Fried, *Heidegger's Polemos: From Being to Politics* (New Haven: Yale University Press, 2000).

35. See note 4 above. The development of these two central notions of Heidegger's philosophical geopolitics needs to be traced in his intertext, especially in view of their perverse usage by National Socialist propaganda. *Bodenständigkeit* (autochthony, nativity, indigeneity) surfaces in SS 1924 in the context of Aristotle's *Rhetoric* (I, 5, 1360 b20) and first refers to rootedness in a native language. In SS 1925, it refers to the phenomenological sense of demonstration as "back to native ground": GA 20, 104/76, 119/87, 423/307. Compare also GA 34, 210; GA 39, 181; IM, 30; GA 54, 223/150. With postwar rebuilding and the theme of "poetic dwelling," Heidegger looks for a new posttechnological autochthony that might recall the old one "in a different gestalt," and "a new ground . . . to strike new roots" (*Gelassenheit,* 26/55, 28/56 f.).

Chapter 13. At the Crossroads of Freedom

1. GA 65, 185, 205.

2. See GA 20, 20–21 = *History of the Concept of Time,* trans. Theodore Kisiel (Bloomington: Indiana University Press, 1985), 17–18. See also Charles M. Bambach, *Heidegger, Dilthey, and the Crisis of Historicism* (Ithaca: Cornell University Press, 1995), 112, 117, and Ingo Farin, "Heidegger's Critique of Value Philosophy," *Journal of the British Society for Phenomenology* 29:3 (Oct. 1998): 268–280.

3. GA 2, 107–108 = *Being and Time,* trans. John Macquarrie and Edward Robinson (New York: Harper and Row, 1962), 111–112. Heidegger remarks: "In interpreting, we do not, so to speak, throw a 'signification' over some naked thing which is present-at-hand, we do not stick a value on it; but when something within-the-world is encountered as such, the thing in question already has an involvement which is disclosed in

our understanding of the world, and this involvement is one which gets laid out by the interpretation" (200–201/190–191).

4. Martin Heidegger, "Brief über den 'Humanismus,'" in GA 9, 350 = "Letter on 'Humanism,'" trans. Frank A. Capuzzi, in *Pathmarks,* ed. William McNeill (Cambridge: Cambridge University Press, 1998), 265. In this same paragraph, Heidegger points out that to assign value to something is really to deprive it of worth, insofar as "what is valued is admitted only as an object for human estimation" (GA 9, 350/265).

5. For Heidegger's plan to destroy the history of ontology—beginning with an analysis of Kant's conception of time—see GA 2, 52/63–64.

6. Max Weber, "The Meaning of 'Value-freedom' in the Sociological and Economic Sciences," in *The Methodology of the Social Sciences,* ed. Edward Shils and Henry Finch (Glencoe, Ill.: Free Press, 1949), 2, 11, 12. I am grateful to Jay Ciaffa for providing me with this reference. Also see G. Ritzen, *Sociological Theory* (New York: Alfred A. Knopf, 1983), 131. In his essay on Karl Jaspers, Heidegger points to the unquestioned link between Weber's sociological analysis and the promotion of values in world views. See Martin Heidegger, "Anmerkungen zu Karl Jaspers 'Psychologie der Weltanschauungen,'" in *Wegmarken,* GA 9, 33 = "Comments on Karl Jaspers's *Psychology of Worldviews*" (1919–1921), trans. John van Buren, in *Pathmarks,* 35.

7. Martin Heidegger, *Vom Wesen des Grundes,* in GA 9, 172 = *On the Essence of Ground,* trans. Terrence Malick (with William McNeill), in *Pathmarks,* 133–134.

8. GA 26, 206–208 = *The Metaphysical Foundations of Logic,* trans. Michael Heim (Bloomington: Indiana University Press, 1984), 162.

9. GA 26, 199/157.

10. GA 31, 292. See Frank Schalow, *The Renewal of the Heidegger-Kant Dialogue: Action, Thought, and Responsibility* (Albany, NY: SUNY Press, 1992), 383–397.

11. Heidegger remarks: "The basic structure of respect and its significance for the Kantian interpretation of morality has been overlooked in phenomenology, in consequence of which Scheler's criticism of the Kantian ethics in *Formalism in Ethics and Material Ethics of Value* missed the point completely." *Die Grundprobleme der Phänomenologie,* GA 24, 193 = *The Basic Problems of Phenomenology,* trans. Albert Hofstadter (Bloomington: Indiana University Press, 1982), 136.

12. GA 2, 388–389/339. For a different viewpoint, see Manfred S. Frings, "The Background of Max Scheler's 1927 Reading of *Being and Time,*" *Philosophy Today* 34:2 (summer 1990): 110.

13. GA 20, 441/319.

14. GA 31, 296.

15. GA 41, 74–76 = *What Is a Thing?,* trans. W. B. Barton and Vera Deutsch (Chicago: Gateway, 1969), 75–77.

16. GA 3, 240 = *Kant and the Problem of Metaphysics,* trans. Richard Taft, 5th ed. (Bloomington: Indiana University Press, 1997), 169.

17. Friedrich Nietzsche, *The Will to Power,* ed. Walter Kaufmann, trans. Walter Kaufmann and R. J. Hollingdale (New York: Random House, 1967), 9.

18. Martin Heidegger, "The Word of Nietzsche: 'God Is Dead,'" in *The Question Concerning Technology and Other Essays,* trans. William Lovitt (New York: Harper & Row, 1977), 61.

19. Heidegger, "The Question Concerning Technology," in *Question Concerning Technology,* 19–25.

20. GA 43, 167 = *Nietzsche I: The Will to Power as Art,* trans. David Farrell Krell (New York: Harper & Row, 1979), 136.

21. See Hans Jonas, "Heidegger's Resoluteness and Resolve," in *Martin Heidegger and National Socialism,* ed. Gunther Neske and Emil Kettering (New York: Paragon Press, 1990), 202, and Richard Wolin, *The Politics of Being* (Ithaca: Cornell University Press, 1990), 33–37.

22. Charles E. Scott, *The Question of Ethics* (Bloomington: Indiana University Press, 1990), 7–15.

23. GA 31, 135.

24. Martin Heidegger, "Überwindung der Metaphysik," in *Vorträge und Aufsätze* (Pfullingen: Günther Neske, 1954), 97 = "Overcoming Metaphysics," in *The End of Philosophy,* trans. Joan Stambaugh (New York: Harper & Row, 1973), 109. For an insightful view of Heidegger's strengths and weaknesses as an ecological thinker, see Michael E. Zimmerman, *Contesting Earth's Future* (Berkeley: University of California Press, 1994), 4, 7.

25. Michel Haar, *Heidegger and the Essence of Man,* trans. William McNeill (Albany: SUNY Press, 1993), 141.

26. E. Levinas, *Philosophical Essays,* trans. Alphonso Lingis (The Hague: Martinus Nijhoff, 1989), 52–53.

27. GA 42, 262–263 = *Schelling's Treatise on the Essence of Human Freedom,* trans. Joan Stambaugh (Athens: Ohio University Press, 1985), 150–151.

28. In the *History of the Concept of Time,* Heidegger writes: "It is assumed that a subject is encapsulated within itself and now has the task of empathizing with another subject. This way of formulating the question is absurd, since there never is such a subject in the sense it is assumed here. If the constitution of what is Dasein is instead regarded without presuppositions as in being and being-with in the presuppositionless immediacy of everydayness, it then becomes clear that the problem of empathy is just as absurd as the question of the reality of the external world" (GA 20, 334/243). Two years later Heidegger remarks: "'Empathy' does not first constitute Being-with; only on the

basis of Being-with does 'empathy' become possible" (GA 2, 167/162). On Heidegger and empathy, see Lawrence Hatab, *Ethics and Finitude: Heideggerian Contributions to Moral Philosophy* (Lanham, Md.: Rowman & Littlefield, 2000), chap. 6.

29. GA 9, 354–360/233–239.

30. GA 31, 292. For a discussion of the issue of "freedom of speech" as it applies to Heidegger's thought, see Frank Schalow, *Language and Deed: Rediscovering Politics through Heidegger's Encounter with German Idealism* (Amsterdam and Atlanta: Editions Rodopi, 1998), 194–204. For a discussion of the role that dialogue plays for the participation of the other, see Richard Polt's analysis of Heidegger's lectures on Plato's *Sophist*, "Heidegger's Topical Hermeneutics: The *Sophist* Lectures," *Journal of the British Society for Phenomenology* 27:1 (January 1996): 53–76.

31. GA 65, 15.

ABOUT THE CONTRIBUTORS

DANIEL DAHLSTROM (Boston University) is the author of *Das logische Vorurteil: Untersuchungen zur Wahrheitstheorie des frühen Heidegger*. He has also written on figures such as Hegel, Husserl, Kant, Moses Mendelssohn, and Schiller.

GREGORY FRIED (Boston University) is the author of *Heidegger's Polemos: From Being to Politics* and the co-translator, with Richard Polt, of *Introduction to Metaphysics*.

CLARE PEARSON GEIMAN is currently preparing a book on Heidegger and Hölderlin. Her research has appeared in *Heidegger Studies*.

CHARLES B. GUIGNON (University of Vermont) is the author of *Heidegger and the Problem of Knowledge*, co-author of *Re-Envisioning Psychology: Moral Dimensions of Theory and Practice*, and editor of *The Cambridge Companion to Heidegger*. His interests include hermeneutics and the philosophy of psychotherapy.

THEODORE KISIEL is Presidential Research Professor at Northern Illinois University. He is the author of *The Genesis of Heidegger's "Being and Time"* and co-editor of *Reading Heidegger from the Start*. He has translated Heidegger's lecture course of summer 1925, *History of the Concept of Time*, and published numerous articles on Heidegger's development from the vantage of his still-unpublished archival manuscripts.

RICHARD POLT (Xavier University, Cincinnati) is the author of *Heidegger: An Introduction* and the co-translator, with Gregory Fried, of *Introduction to Metaphysics*. He is completing a book titled *The Emergency of Being: On Heidegger's "Contributions to Philosophy."*

FRANK SCHALOW (University of New Orleans) is the author of *The Renewal of the Heidegger-Kant Dialogue: Action, Thought, and Responsibility; Imagination and Existence: Heidegger's Retrieval of the Kantian Ethic;* and *Language and Deed: Rediscovering Politics Through Heidegger's Encounter with German Idealism.* He is the co-author of *Traces of Understanding: A Profile of Heidegger's and Ricoeur's Hermeneutics.*

SUSAN SCHOENBOHM is senior lecturer in philosophy and women's studies at Pennsylvania State University. Her publications include articles on Heidegger, Nietzsche, Merleau-Ponty, and Aristotle; she is also interested in Confucius and Lao Tzu. She is currently completing two manuscripts, one on physicality and perception and another that reexamines issues of "virtue" from a contemporary feminist viewpoint.

CHARLES E. SCOTT is Edwin Erle Sparks Professor of Philosophy at Pennsylvania State University. His books include *The Language of Difference; The Question of Ethics: Nietzsche, Foucault, Heidegger; On the Advantages and Disadvantages of Ethics and Politics;* and *The Time of Memory.*

THOMAS SHEEHAN (Stanford University) is the author of *Karl Rahner: The Philosophical Foundations,* of *The First Coming: How the Kingdom of God Became Christianity,* and of numerous essays on Heidegger, as well as being the editor of *Heidegger: The Man and the Thinker* and (with Richard Palmer) *Edmund Husserl: Phenomenological and Transcendental Phenomenology and the Confrontation with Heidegger.*

HANS SLUGA (University of California, Berkeley) is the author of *Heidegger's Crisis: Philosophy and Politics in Nazi Germany* and *Gottlob Frege.* He has edited the multivolume *Philosophy of Frege* and co-edited *The Cambridge Companion to Wittgenstein.* He is currently finishing a book on political philosophy.

DIETER THOMÄ (University of St. Gallen, Switzerland) is the author of *Die Zeit des Selbst und die Zeit danach: Zur Kritik der Textgeschichte Martin Heideggers 1910–1976; Erzähle dich selbst; Eltern;* and *Unter Amerikanern.* He is currently editing a handbook on Heidegger's thought.

MICHAEL E. ZIMMERMAN (Tulane University) is the author of *Eclipse of the Self: The Development of Heidegger's Concept of Authenticity; Heidegger's Confrontation with Modernity: Technology, Politics, and Art;* and *Contesting Earth's Future: Radical Ecology and Postmodernity.* He is the editor of *The Thought of Martin Heidegger.*

INDEX

absence. *See* Being

abyss: 59, 72, 76; *see also* ground

alētheia: and accessibility of beings, 6; as disclosure, 154, 163; truth as, 39, 52; *see also* truth

America, 251, 326–327*n31*

Americanism, 245–247, 262

analytic philosophy: on Being, 136–138, 1 42; on Nothing, 64; *see also* logic

Anaximander, 282*n 45*

Angst (anxiety), 63, 68

animal. *See* Dasein; *zōon logon echōn*

Antelme, R., 117, 120, 302*n37*

Antigone, 79, 92–93, 157, 161–182 *passim,* 210–211, 236–238

anxiety. *See Angst*

appearance and appearing: as Being, 30–31, 34–56 *passim,* 154, 210; Being and thinking united with, 29–31; as *phainesthai,* 6, 38–39, 51; and seeming, 78; and Why-question, 20

apprehension (*noein*): and *phusis,* 156–157; as violence, 92–93

appropriation. See *Ereignis*

Aquinas, T., 265*n11*

Arendt, H., 222

Aristotle: on Being, 137, 265n11; and categories, 61, 135; and Heidegger, 11;

and history of Being, 35–36; on language, 128; on nature, 306n3; and Nothing, 61–62; on phronēsis, praxis, and technē, 162–163; and psuchē, 8; and telos, 46; see also metaphysics; ousia; substance

art and artwork: creators and preservers of, 44; and phusis, 41–44; as event, 41; Greek temple as, 41–43, 198, 313n21; *see also* creators; polemos; politics; work

as-structure, 39

assertion : see logic

attunement, 25–26

Auseinandersetzung, 262

Austin, J. L., 119

authenticity: and everyday ness, 107–110; and fallenness, 254; and finitude, 68–69; and history, 201; and homelessness, 168–170, 17 6; and owning one's life, 48, 187; and self-assertion, 300n21

Barash, J., 195, 199, 200

Bauch, B., 221

Be-ing. *See* Seyn under Being

Beaufret, J., 8

becoming, 39, 78–79, 146, 153, 286n77

hilation, 70, 81; the negative as positive, 59–60; and Nietzsche, 64–65; and nihilism, 60, 79, 81; paradoxical, 74; and Plato, 61; as pseudo-problem, 64; and Schelling, 66; and seeming, 78; and sophists, 61; and temporality, 69; as translation for das Nichts, 277n6; and Why-question, 73–74, 76; *See also* Angst; Being; Eastern thought; finitude; Parmenides; phusis

objectivity, 29, 32–33
Oedipus, 313n24
Olympic games, 244
ontological difference, 94, 173–174, 278n11
ontology, 74; *See also* event ontology
opening, openness: and art, 43; and Dasein, 5, 8, 10–12, 231, 253; and Ereignis, 10–12; and freedom, 258, 261; and thrownness, 13, 258
opinion. *See* doxa
"The Origin of the Work of Art," 41–51 passim, 168, 172, 197–198, 212–213
Other, 260–262
Ought, the, 220, 224
ousia, 36, 97; *See also* substance

Parmenides: on becoming, 153; on Being and nonbeing, 60–61, 65, 78–79, 139, 153; on the Logos, 92–96; and seeming, 78, 153–154; *See also* thinking
Pascal, B., 62
perspective, 54–56; *See also* relativism
pessimism, 194, 201, 203–204
phenomenology, 6, 95
philosophy: as culture-forming, 199; and grammar, 128; neither poetry nor science, 75; as "perennial philosophy," 234; and politics, 186, 206, 233; as revolutionary, 234–235; transformative thinking, 24; as useless, 234–235; *See also* analytic philosophy; poetry

phronēsis, 162–164, 232
phusis: and abiding, 150–151; and appearing, 38–39, 154; and art, 41–44; and Being, 147, 149–50, 156–157; and beings, 27, 145, 147, 150; and creation, 152; and Dasein, 40, 46, 159; as emergence, 7, 145–149, 154; its etymology, 131; as history, 48–51; and idea, 96, 296n62; in Introduction to Metaphysics, 143–160; and language, 26–27, 148; as logos, 156; as movement, 46; as "nature," 143–146, 167; and noein, 156–157; and Nothing, 149–150; as phainesthai (shining-forth), 38–39, 51; and Plato, 96; not a presence or a being, 27; as process, 146, 148; as sway (Walten), 27–29, 38, 147, 150–151, 307n8, 318n8; and telos, 46; unites Being, appearing, and thinking, 29, 33; wider and narrower meaning of, 146–147; *See also* art; Being; death; givenness; Greeks; logos; polemos; power; standing
Pindar, 48
Plato: and history of Being, 35–36, 139; and idea and eidos, 96; and the idea of the Good, 254–257; on language, 115, 128; and nihilism, 257; and Nothing, 61; and philosopher-kings, 206; and recollection, 201; and Sophists, 61; *See also* metaphysics; phusis
poetic thinking, 179–182
poetry, 75–76, 94–95, 152, 165–166, 175, 179; *See also* poetic thinking
polemos: and artwork, 42; and Being, 40, 53; as creative, 133; and history, 51; and human existence, 47; and language, 40; lets gods and humans appear, 40, 209–210, 216; as logos, 92, 133, 156; and phusis, 39–40, 151; and rank, 209, 224; and revolution, 187–188; and violence, 157–158, 211; *See also* Heraclitus; politics